Central Counterparties

For other titles in the Wiley Finance Series
please see www.wiley.com/finance

Central Counterparties

Mandatory Clearing and Bilateral Margin Requirements for OTC Derivatives

Jon Gregory

This edition first published 2014

Registered office
John Wiley & Sons Ltd, The Atrium, Southern Gate, Chichester, West Sussex PO19 8SQ, United Kingdom

For details of our global editorial offices, for customer services and for information about how to apply for permission to reuse the copyright material in this book, please see our website at www.wiley.com.

A catalogue record for this book is available from the Library of Congress

A catalogue record for this book is available from the British Library.

ISBN 978-1-118-89151-3 (hardback) ISBN 978-1-118-89157-5 (ebk)
ISBN 978-1-118-89158-2 (ebk) ISBN 978-1-118-89156-8 (obk)

Cover design: Kathy Davis/Wiley
Cover image: © Mark Evans/Getty Images

Set in 10/12pt Times by Sparks – www.sparkspublishing.com
Printed in Great Britain by CPI Group (UK) Ltd, Croydon, CR0 4YY

For Mum and Dad

Contents

Acknowledgements

Less than a year has passed since I decided that it might be useful to compliment my existing text on counterparty credit risk with a book covering central clearing and bilateral margining rules applied to over-the-counter (OTC) derivatives. Given the implementation of mandatory clearing and margining rules is progressing rapidly, I do hope that this book will be of increasing relevance to anyone with an interest in financial markets, and OTC derivatives in particular.

It should be mentioned upfront that the focus of this book is very much on the future role of central counterparties (CCPs) in OTC derivative markets and not as much their (rather different) historical role in exchange-traded markets. I will often make this fact clear by the use of the terms such as 'OTC CCP'. The reader should have in mind that, whilst much of the theory, discussion and analysis is relevant to all aspects of central clearing, the OTC angle has been the major driver for this work and is therefore the main focus.

As with my other book covering counterparty credit risk and credit value adjustment, this is a challenging topic to write about since the area is changing rapidly, with new regulation and market innovations appearing frequently. The reader may find it useful to visit my personal website at **www.cvacentral.com** for corrections and updates to the book. In particular, I plan to keep a list of errata and updated URLs there (since the links are commonly changed). There will also be some spreadsheets included that may be useful. You can also contact me via this website – I would be pleased to hear from readers with any comments on the book, which I will certainly seek to incorporate into the next edition.

Whilst this is the first book on mandatory clearing and bilateral margining requirements for OTC derivatives, I would like to mention two other useful and complementary books on the subject. Norman (2011) provides a very in-depth historical background of the development of central counterparties whilst Murphy (2013) compares the traditional bilateral derivatives market with the future market under mandatory central clearing and other new regulation brought about by the global financial crisis.

I am extremely grateful to Craig Pirrong for many interesting discussions on this subject and for his excellent research in this area (which I strongly recommend to any reader). I am also grateful to Craig, together with Alistair Milne, for providing very useful feedback on the first version of the text. Additionally, I would like to thank my colleagues at Solum Financial Partners in London for interesting discussions around many topics related to counterparty risk, margining and central clearing.

I am grateful to Werner Coetzee, Sam Hartley and Jennie Kitchin at Wiley for assisting with this project and to Tom Fryer and the team at Sparks Publishing for the efficiency in the copy editing process to facilitate a timely publishing schedule. Thanks to Rebecca Newenham and Jane Knight at Get Ahead VA for help around administration and proofreading. Any remaining errors are my responsibility.

Finally, special thanks to my wife Ginnie and children George and Christy for their continuing support, encouragement and humour.

Jon Gregory
April 2014

Part I

Background

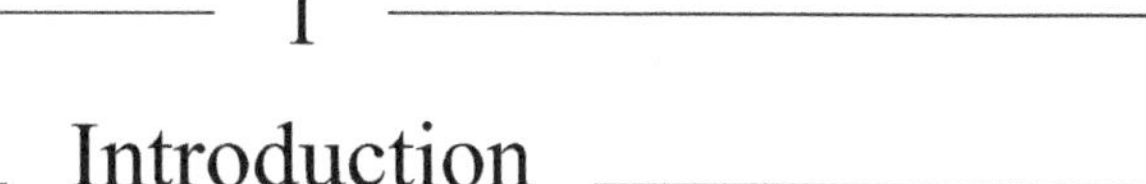

1 Introduction

> *What we know about the global financial crisis is that we don't know very much.*
>
> Paul Samuelson (1915–2009)

1.1 THE CRISIS

In 2007, a US housing crisis led to a credit crisis, which caused the failures of large financial institutions and a severe economic downturn. The aftermath of the 'global financial crisis' (GFC) is still being felt across the general economy, and has led to significant changes in the functioning of financial markets and the way in which financial institutions are regulated. The GFC highlighted the importance of controlling risk in over-the-counter (OTC) derivatives to maintain global financial stability. Whilst OTC derivatives did not cause the GFC, they likely contributed to amplifying various problems and provided channels for systemic risk to propagate.

A derivative trade is a contractual relationship that may be in force from a few days to several decades. During the lifetime of the contract, the two counterparties have claims against each other such as in the form of cashflows that evolve as a function of underlying assets and market conditions. Derivatives transactions create counterparty credit risk (counterparty risk) due to the risk of insolvency of one party. This counterparty risk in turn creates systemic risk due to derivatives trading volume being dominated by a relatively small number of large derivatives counterparties ('dealers') that are then key nodes of the financial system. Counterparty risk refers to the possibility that a counterparty may not meet its contractual requirements under the contract when they become due. Counterparty risk is managed over time through clearing: this can be performed bilaterally, where each counterparty manages the risk of the other, or centrally through a central counterparty (CCP). Historically, bilateral clearing is far more dominant for OTC derivatives.

During the GFC, authorities had to make key decisions over large failing financial institutions such as Bear Stearns, Lehman Brothers, the Royal Bank of Scotland and AIG. These decisions were made with a very opaque view of the situation the firms were in and the potential knock-on impact of any choices made. One of the reasons for the opacity was the large volume of bilateral OTC derivatives contracts on the balance sheets of such large financial institutions. Bilateral OTC derivatives are essentially private contracts that may be illiquid and have non-standard or exotic features. A key concern over the global OTC derivatives market has always been systemic risk, which in this context refers to financial system instability exacerbated by the distress of financial institutions. In the context of the GFC, systemic risk arose due to the failure of large financial institutions and the resulting domino effects.

Bilateral OTC derivatives were clearly in the eye of the financial storm from 2007 onwards, and the creditworthiness of financial institutions and counterparty risks between them clearly contributed to the ongoing crisis. The large web of OTC derivatives positions between banks and other financial institutions suddenly became a major issue as the creditworthiness of such institutions worsened. For example, American International Group (AIG) exploited its strong credit rating to sell protection via credit default swaps (CDS). When AIG could not post additional collateral (referred to hereafter as 'margin') and was required to provide funds to counterparties in the face of deteriorating reference obligations in the CDS, the US government bailed them out. Politicians and regulators were concerned that default of AIG would ripple through the counterparty chains and create a systemic crisis. This led to the view that counterparty risk and the interconnectedness of large financial institutions was a channel of contagion that could amplify and transmit financial shocks.

One particular problem in relation to counterparty risk in OTC derivatives is the close out process. When a party to a contract defaults, their counterparties typically need to terminate and replace the underlying trades. In the aftermath of a large default, the OTC derivative replacement process can be associated with market illiquidity and large volatility of prices during a scramble to replace trades. Such problems were clearly illustrated in the Lehman bankruptcy and are a key reason behind some financial institutions being 'too big to fail'.

In contrast to OTC derivatives, the derivatives market that was cleared via central counterparties (CCPs) or 'clearinghouses' was much more stable during the GFC. CCPs such as LCH.Clearnet coped well with the Lehman bankruptcy when virtually every other element of the OTC derivative market was creaking or failing. One of the reasons for this is that, unlike most market participants, they had actually envisaged and prepared for such a situation. Hence, whilst CCPs still experienced problems (such as identifying the positions of Lehman's clients), they were able, with help from their members, to transfer or close out a large volume of Lehman derivatives positions without major issues. Indeed, within a week of Lehman's bankruptcy most of their outstanding OTC-cleared positions had been hedged, and within another week most of their client accounts had been transferred. Centrally cleared OTC derivatives were seemingly much safer than their bilateral equivalents.

1.2 THE MOVE TOWARDS CENTRAL CLEARING

In the aftermath of the GFC, policymakers (not surprisingly) embarked on regulatory changes that seemed largely aimed at moving risk away from global banks, and the dangerous bilateral OTC derivatives market. This seemed to be driven generally by the view that the size, opacity and interconnectedness of the market were too significant. One aspect of these policy changes were greater bank capital requirements for OTC derivatives, hardly surprising given the seemingly high leverages and accordingly low capital bases of stricken banks. Another aspect was in relation to mandatory central clearing for certain products, with CCPs seemingly emerging as a panacea for financial markets' stability. For example:

> How do we establish good regulatory structure without destroying the incentive to innovate, without destroying the marketplace? We agree that we need to improve our regulations and to ensure that markets, firms, and financial products are subject to proper regulation and oversight. For example, credit default swaps – financial products that ensure against potential losses – should be processed through centralized clearinghouses.
>
> George Bush, 15 November 2008.

As a part of financial reform, important legislative changes with respect to the OTC derivatives market were introduced. In September 2009, G20 leaders agreed that all standardised OTC derivatives would, in the future, need to be cleared through CCPs. This was done with the belief that a CCP can reduce systemic risk, operational risks, market manipulation and fraud, and contribute to overall market stability. It is interesting to note that the original push towards central clearing seemed to be much lighter. The G20 meeting in 2008 defined a regulatory goal to be:

> Strengthening the resilience and transparency of credit derivatives markets and reducing their systemic risks, including by improving the infrastructure of over-the-counter markets
>
> G20 declaration, Washington, November 2008

Less than a year later, the clearing mandate was clear and the focus on credit derivatives had expanded greatly to cover potentially all OTC derivatives:

> All standardized OTC derivative contracts should be traded on exchanges or electronic trading platforms, where appropriate, and cleared through central counterparties by end-2012 at the latest. OTC derivative contracts should be reported to trade repositories. Non-centrally cleared contracts should be subject to higher capital requirements. We ask the FSB [Financial Stability Board] and its relevant members to assess regularly implementation and whether it is sufficient to improve transparency in the derivatives markets, mitigate systemic risk, and protect against market abuse.
>
> G20 declaration, Pittsburg, September 2009

The Dodd–Frank Wall Street Reform and Consumer Protection Act enacted in July 2010, and the European Market Infrastructure Regulation (EMIR) proposed in September 2010 were legislative responses to this call for a new regulation of OTC derivatives markets. Key parts of both Dodd–Frank and EMIR were formal legislative proposals that all standardised OTC derivatives should be cleared through CCPs.

In the period since the G20 agreement on mandatory clearing, the scale and complexity of the task has gradually emerged. The requirement to clear a large fraction of OTC derivatives that are more complex and illiquid than existing cleared products is far from trivial. Furthermore, the number and variety of OTC derivative users represents a massive challenge for CCPs, who will have to develop the capability to clear new OTC derivatives and develop their offerings in the area of client clearing (where CCP 'clearing members' clear trades on behalf of clients). The case of client clearing gives rise to many important questions such as where the risk lies in the CCP–clearing member–client chain. Additional problems arise around the possible fragmentation of regulatory regimes globally, leading to potential arbitrages. Questions have also been raised regarding the systemic and operational risks represented by a large 'OTC CCP'. CCPs may also need to develop linkages with each other to be 'interoperable', leading to the question of the increased risk that may arise out of such connections.

1.3 WHAT IS A CCP?

Clearing is a process that occurs after the execution of a trade in which a CCP may step in between counterparties to guarantee performance. The main function of a CCP is, therefore, to interpose itself directly or indirectly between counterparties to assume their rights and obligations by acting as buyer to every seller and vice versa. This means that the original counterparty to a trade no longer represents a direct risk, as the CCP to all intents and purposes becomes the new counterparty. CCPs essentially reallocate default losses via a variety of methods including netting, margining and loss mutualisation. Obviously, the intention is that the overall process will reduce counterparty and systemic risks.

CCPs are not a new idea and have been a part of the derivatives landscape for well over a century in connection with exchanges. An exchange is an organised market where buyers and sellers can interact to trade. Central clearing developed to control the counterparty risk in exchange-traded products, and limit the risk that the insolvency of a member of the exchange may have. CCPs for exchange-traded derivatives are arguably a good example of market forces privately managing financial risk effectively. The two clearing structures, bilateral and central, share many common elements such as netting and margining but also have fundamental differences. The fact that neither has become dominant suggests that they may each have their own strengths and weaknesses that are more or less emphasised in different markets.

CCPs provide a number of benefits. One is that they allow netting of all trades executed through them. In a bilateral market, an institution being long a contract with counterparty A and short the same contract with counterparty B has counterparty risk. However, if both contracts are centrally cleared then the netted position has no risk. CCPs also manage margin requirements from their members to reduce the risk associated with the movement in the value of their underlying portfolios. CCPs also allow loss mutualisation; one counterparty's losses are dispersed throughout the market rather than being transmitted directly to a small number of counterparties with potential adverse consequences. Moreover, CCPs can facilitate orderly close out by auctioning off the defaulter's contractual obligations with netting reducing the total positions that need to be replaced, which reduces price impact. A well-managed centralised auction mechanism can be liquid, and result in smaller price disruptions than uncoordinated replacement of bilateral positions during periods of pronounced uncertainty. CCPs can also facilitate the orderly transfer of client positions from financially troubled intermediaries. The margins and other financial resources they hold protects against losses arising from this auction process.

The general role and mechanics of a CCP are:

- A CCP sets certain standards for its clearing members.
- The CCP takes responsibility for closing out all the positions of a defaulting clearing member.
- To support the above, the CCP maintains financial resources to cover losses in the event of a clearing member default:
  - Variation margin to closely track market movements.
  - Initial margin to cover worst-case liquidation or close out costs above the variation margin.
  - A default fund to mutualise losses in the event of a severe default.

- The CCP also has a documented plan for the very extreme situation when all their financial resources (initial margin[1] and the default fund) are depleted. For example:
  - o Additional calls to the default fund.
  - o Variation margin gains haircutting.
  - o Selective tear-up of positions.

It is important to note that many 'end users' of OTC derivatives (e.g. pension funds) will access CCPs through a clearing member and will not become members themselves. This will be due to the membership, operational and liquidity requirements related to being a clearing member. Some end users will also be exempt from the clearing obligation and will therefore be able to choose whether to clear via a CCP or not.

1.4 INITIAL MARGINS

A key method to mitigate counterparty credit risk is the provision of margin based on a contractual agreement. Margin serves as an effective insurance against counterparty risk if exchanged in a timely manner in a legally enforceable way. Bilateral margin arrangements tend to be relatively customised, may not require the posting of full margin, and typically allow margin to be posted in relatively illiquid assets. They also tend to allow 'rehypothecation' or reuse of margin. Whilst such flexibility is useful in promoting liquidity, it can be dangerous when counterparties default and the margin held is insufficient, declining in value or not legally enforceable.

Centrally cleared markets tend to have tighter margin requirements compared to bilateral ones, for example by only allowing cash or liquid bonds to be posted. The most important difference, though, is in relation to initial margin. The majority of bilateral arrangements provide only for the exchange of variation margin (covering fluctuations in the value of the underlying contracts). Centrally cleared markets also require initial margin (covering the potential cost of replacing the underlying contracts in case the original counterparty defaults). For example, a CCP member whose positions have a value of minus 10 units may have to post 15 units to the CCP, 10 of which is variation margin and an extra 5 is the initial margin. Initial margin is taken by CCPs to provide the first defence against potential losses in the event that one of their members defaults. As such, initial margin has the potential to reduce counterparty risk as defaulting parties essentially pay for their default via the initial margin held by the CCP. Although it reduces counterparty risk, initial margin is expensive as it represents parties posting more in margin than they owe. Furthermore, the expense of initial margin is increased by the fact that it cannot typically be rehypothecated or reused.

Since central clearing applies only to 'standardised' OTC derivatives, there is a potential issue that market participants could simply argue that a given contract was 'non-standard' to circumvent the clearing mandate and avoid the requirement to post initial margin. To avoid this problem, policymakers have decided to impose initial margin requirements for non-cleared OTC derivatives. This means that the extra protective margin will be present whether a trade is centrally cleared or not.

The push towards higher margin requirements is not surprising. A key problem of the GFC was that many OTC derivatives counterparties (for example, sovereigns, central banks

[1] Note that only the defaulter's initial margin can be used.

and high credit quality financial counterparties) typically did not post margin at all. Financial counterparties such as large OTC derivatives dealers usually did post margin to each other, but historically such agreements have been under- rather than over-margined. Another problem is that margin in OTC markets can be made up of assets with significant market, credit and liquidity risks. This creates the risk that when margin is required in an insolvency scenario, its price has declined or it is difficult to liquidate quickly except at 'fire sale' prices.

An obvious drawback of margin is the underlying cost. This may be seen through a decline in liquidity, as more margin has to be posted within the financial system. This may be particularly acute for counterparties who struggle to meet margin requirements due to not having enough liquid assets to post. In turn, this may lead to financial engineering techniques to generate more high-quality margin and even regulatory arbitrage where market participants attempt to find ways to circumvent the various rules. Obviously, these effects are not desirable.

1.5 POSSIBLE DRAWBACKS

Despite the obvious advantages, mandatory central clearing of OTC derivatives is not without criticism. CCPs have failed in the past and have therefore been shown to be potentially dangerous. For instance, the difficulties faced by CCPs in the stock market crash of 1987 posed a serious threat to the entire financial system. For the past century and longer, clearing has been limited to listed derivatives traded on exchanges. Bilateral OTC markets have been extremely successful and their growth has been greater than that of exchange-traded products over the last two decades. Whilst LCH.Clearnet has been clearing certain OTC derivatives (notably interest rate swaps) since 1999, the majority of OTC products have not moved to central clearing by means of natural forces. At the end of 2010, whilst a large proportion of all outstanding OTC interest rate products (mainly swaps) were centrally cleared, less than 10% of credit default swaps (CDS) and almost no OTC foreign exchange or equity derivatives were cleared through CCPs.

The trouble with clearing OTC derivatives is that they are more illiquid, long-dated and complex compared to their exchange-traded relatives. Hence they may prove a challenge for traditional CCP risk management methods, especially with cross-border activity being so important. To some, the role of CCPs in making financial markets safer seems to be more of a hope than an expectation. What is indisputable is that centralised clearing will have significant structural and behavioural effects on the management and allocation of risk in financial markets, causing a profound change in market structure and trading practices. The financial system is extremely complex, and the potential changes in behaviour will be far-reaching, dynamic and impossible to predict with any precision.

A first obvious and almost paradoxical problem with mandatory clearing is that CCPs clearing OTC products will likely become 'systemically important', creating a potential moral hazard if it is clear that government financial support will be forthcoming in the event of a CCP risk management failure. After all, bailing out a CCP is ultimately no better than bailing out any other financial institution. CCPs do not magically make counterparty risk vanish, and forcing derivatives through CCPs could create sizable financial risks via concentrating counterparty risk within a single systemic point in the system. As CCPs clear more complex, less liquid and longer-term instruments, their potential risks will likely increase.

A second concern is the costs and instabilities that CCPs (and bilateral margin requirements) will introduce through requiring a significant amount of liquid margin to be posted by members and their clients, with various estimates putting this increase in the region of trillions of US dollars. There is a question over the economic impact of such margin, which may start via financial institutions being less profitable but will eventually have an impact on economic growth in general. A more subtle problem is that margining can transmit systemic disturbances as changes in requirements can induce destabilising trading. This can occur, for example, when firms that must meet large margin calls respond by selling assets and reducing positions in ways that exacerbate the price changes that caused the margin calls. Moreover, initial margins generally increase in volatile markets, which could have the effect of catalysing rather than resolving financial distress via a damaging system-wide liquidity drain.

A third potential problem is related to the loss mutualisation that CCPs use whereby any losses in excess of a member's own financial resources (mainly initial margin) are generally mutualised across all the surviving members. The impact of such a mechanism is to homogenise the underlying credit risk such that all CCP members are more or less equal. The most creditworthy market participants may see less advantage of their stronger credit quality with CCP clearing. As with any form of insurance, adverse selection is a problem and can make risk sharing costly. Adverse selection occurs when the insured know more about risks than the insurer. In a clearing context, to the extent where firms that trade OTC derivatives know more about the risks of particular cleared products than the CCP, these firms will tend to over-trade the product for which the CCP underestimates risk, and under-trade the products for which the CCP overestimates risk. CCPs could encourage excessive risk taking compared to bilateral trading since an institution knows that their potential losses are mutualised among other members. Many firms trading derivatives (e.g. large banks and hedge funds) specialise precisely in understanding risks and pricing, and hence are likely to have better information than CCPs especially for more complex derivatives.

1.6 CLEARING IN CONTEXT

It is worthwhile emphasising that this book is focused on the role of CCPs in OTC derivative markets and not their more traditional role in securities markets. The central clearing of securities trades (although it may be carried out by the same CCPs) is very different from that of OTC derivatives. The primary role of central clearing in securities trades is to standardise and simplify operational processes. In OTC derivative markets, central clearing is more focused on the reduction of counterparty risk.

Some other high-level points are important to mention at this stage. First, when assessed in terms of a given characteristic, CCPs will probably give rise to both positive and negative aspects. For example, CCPs reduce systemic risk (e.g. mitigating the impact of clearing member failure) but also increase it (e.g. by increasing margin requirements during a period of stress). Hence, CCPs transform risk but do not definitely reduce it overall. CCPs may also be beneficial for certain products and markets and less so for others, depending on the characteristics of the product or market in question.

CCPs perform a number of functions such as netting, margining, transparency, loss mutualisation and default management. Another important point to note is that some of these functions can be achieved via other mechanisms. For example, trade compression can facilitate greater netting benefits, bilateral markets can (and do) have margining mechanisms, and trade repositories can provide greater transparency.

The ability of CCPs to prevent future financial crises is not completely clear. What is clear is that the analysis of the impact of CCPs leads to many unanswered questions and a balance of advantages and disadvantages. On the one hand, policymakers seem to believe that mandatory central clearing of OTC derivatives will make financial markets safer, but on the other hand some of the criticism has gone so far as to say that this is completely wrong.

The aim of this book is not to define whether CCPs are good or not. Indeed, there is no question that CCPs can be beneficial as one of a choice of potential risk-mitigating mechanisms. However, the mandatory clearing requirement means that OTC CCPs will develop and grow rapidly over the coming years. This, together with the bilateral margin requirements, will create a significant underlying cost. Hence there is a need to provide a detailed analysis of the theory and practice of central clearing of OTC derivatives together with a balanced analysis of the pros and cons of mandatory clearing and margin requirements for OTC derivatives.

2
Exchanges, OTC Derivatives, DPCs and SPVs

A too-big-to-fail firm is one whose size, complexity, interconnectedness, and critical functions are such that, should the firm go unexpectedly into liquidation, the rest of the financial system and the economy would face severe adverse consequences.

Ben Bernanke (1953–)

2.1 EXCHANGES

2.1.1 What is an exchange?

In derivative markets, many contracts are exchange-traded. An exchange is a central financial centre where parties can trade standardised contracts such as futures and options at a specified price. An exchange promotes market efficiency and enhances liquidity by centralising trading in a single place. The process by which a financial contract becomes exchange-traded can be thought of as a long journey where a critical trading volume, standardisation and liquidity must first develop.

Exchanges have been used to trade financial products for many years. The origins of central counterparties (CCPs) date back to futures exchanges, which can be traced back to the 19th century (and even further). A future is an agreement by two parties to buy or sell a specified quantity of an asset at some time in the future at a price agreed upon today. Futures were developed to allow merchants or companies to fix prices for certain assets, and therefore be able to hedge their exposure to price movements. An exchange was essentially a market where standardised contracts such as futures could be traded. Originally, exchanges were simply trading forums without any settlement or counterparty risk management functions. Transactions were still done on a bilateral basis and trading through the exchange simply provided a certification through the counterparty being a member of the exchange. Members not fulfilling their requirements were deemed in default and were fined or expelled from the exchange.

An exchange performs a number of functions:

- *Product standardisation:* An exchange designs contracts that can be traded where most of the terms (e.g. maturity dates, minimum price quotation increments, deliverable grade of the underlying, delivery location and mechanism) are standardised.
- *Trading venue:* Exchanges provide either a physical or an electronic trading facility for the underlying products they list, which provides a central venue for trading and hedging. Access to an exchange is limited to approved firms and individuals who must abide by the

rules of the exchange. This centralised trading venue provides an opportunity for price discovery.[1]

- *Reporting services:* Exchanges provide various reporting services of transaction prices to trading participants, data vendors and subscribers. This creates a greater transparency of prices.

2.1.2 The need for clearing

In addition to their functions as described above, exchanges have also provided methods for improving 'clearing' and therefore mitigating counterparty risk. Clearing is the term that describes the reconciling and resolving of contracts between counterparties, and takes place between trade execution and trade settlement (when all legal obligations have been made). A buyer or seller suffering a large loss on a contract may be unable or unwilling to settle the underlying position and two methods have developed for reducing this risk, namely margining and netting.

Margining involves exchange members receiving and paying cash or other assets against gains and losses in their positions (variation margin) and providing extra coverage against losses in case they default (initial margin). Exchange rules developed to specify and enforce the mechanics of margin exchange.

Netting involves the offsetting of contracts, which is useful to reduce the exposure of counterparties and the underlying network to which they are exposed. It therefore reduces the costs of maintaining open positions such as via the margins needing to be posted. Historically, netting can be seen in all of the three forms of clearing that have developed, namely direct clearing, ring clearing and complete clearing, which are described next.

2.1.3 Direct clearing

Direct clearing refers to a bilateral reconciliation of commitments between the original two counterparties (which is obviously the standard clearing mechanism if no other is specified). Here, the specified terms of a transaction may be performed directly, e.g. one counterparty may deliver the underlying contractual amount of an asset to the other in exchange for the pre-specified payment in cash. Alternatively, if the counterparties have offsetting trades then they can reduce obligations as illustrated in Figure 2.1. Here, counterparties A and B have offsetting positions with each other in the same contracts: A has an agreement to buy 100 contracts from B at a price of $105 at a later date, whilst B has the exact reverse position with A but at a lower price of $102. Clearly, standardisation of terms facilitates such offset by making contracts fungible. Rather than A and B physically exchanging 100 contracts worth of the underlying and making associated payments of $10,500 and $10,200 to one another they can use 'payment of difference'. Payment of difference, rather than delivery, became common in futures markets to reduce problems associated with creditworthiness. In Figure 2.1, this would involve counterparty A paying counterparty B the difference in the value of the contracts of $300. This could occur at the settlement date of the contract or at any time before. In the OTC derivatives market, this form of direct clearing is now generally called netting.

[1] This is the process of determining the price of an asset in a marketplace through the interactions of buyers and sellers.

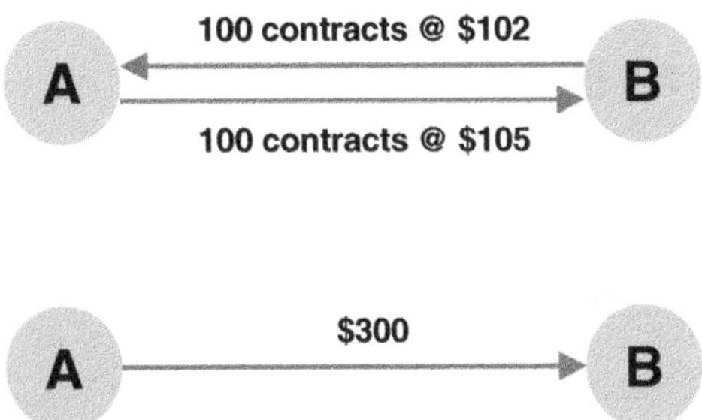

Figure 2.1 Illustration of direct clearing.

Obviously, in direct clearing original counterparties still have exposure to one another, albeit potentially reduced by methods such as payment of differences. Although exchanges facilitate such approaches by, for example, defining standard contractual terms, they have limited additional roles to play in such a structure, potentially just as mediators in any ensuing dispute.

2.1.4 Clearing rings

The fungibility created by standardisation means that direct clearing can be extended to more than two counterparties. Historically, the development of 'clearing rings' was a means of utilising standardisation to ease aspects such as closing out positions and enhancing liquidity. For instance, prior to the adoption of 'complete clearing' at the Chicago Board of Trade, groups of three or more market participants would 'ring out' offsetting positions. Clearing rings were relatively informal means of reducing exposure via a ring of three or more members. To achieve the benefits of 'ringing', participants in the ring had to be willing to accept substitutes for their original counterparties. Rings were voluntary but once joining a ring, exchange rules bound participants to the ensuing settlements. Some members would choose not to join a ring whereas others might participate in multiple rings. In a clearing ring, groups of exchange members agree to accept each other's contracts and allow counterparties to be interchanged. This can be useful for reducing bilateral exposure as illustrated in Figure 2.2. Irrespective of the nature of the other positions, the positions between C and D, and D and B can allow a 'ringing out' where D is removed from the ring and two obligations are replaced with a single one from C to B.

Clearing rings clearly reduce counterparty risk. They also simplify the dependencies of a member's open positions and allow them to close out contracts more easily, increasing liquidity. Clearly, all members of the ring must agree a price for settling contracts, which may be facilitated by the exchange. Historically, exchanges (and courts) have generally upheld the contractual features of ringing. For example, if (via a ring) a counterparty had their original counterparty replaced via another that subsequently defaulted, then they could not challenge the clearing ring reassignment that led to this.

It is important to note that not all counterparties in the example shown in Figure 2.2 benefit from the clearing ring illustrated (although of course there may be other clearing simplifications not shown that may benefit them). Whilst D clearly benefits from being able to offset readily the transactions with C and B, A is indifferent to the formation of the ring since

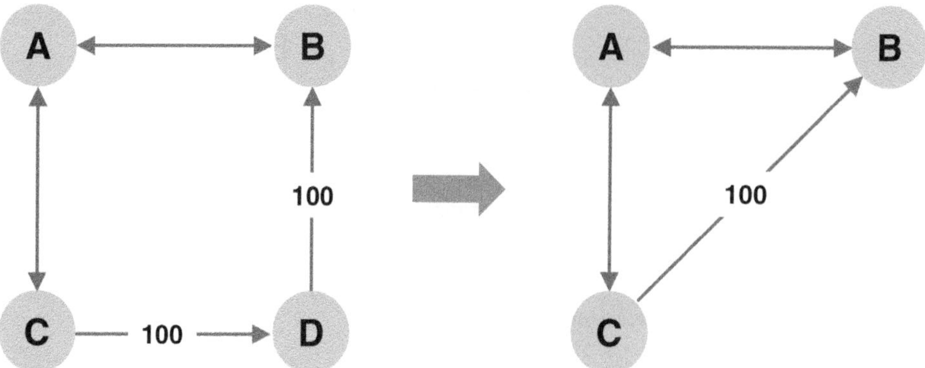

Figure 2.2 Illustration of a clearing ring. The equivalent obligations between C and D and between D and B are replaced with a single obligation between C and B.

its positions are not changed. Furthermore, the positions of B and C have changed only in terms of the replacement counterparty they have been given. Clearly, if this counterparty is considered to have stronger (weaker) credit quality then they view the ring as a benefit (detriment). A ring, whilst offering a collective benefit, is unlikely to be seen as beneficial by all participants. A member at the 'end of a ring' with only a long or short position and therefore standing not to benefit has no benefit to ring out. Historically, such aspects have played out with members refusing to participate in rings because, for example, they preferred larger exposures to certain counterparties rather than smaller exposures to other counterparties.

In the current OTC derivative market, compression (section 5.2.3) offers a similar mechanism to the historical role of clearing rings.

2.1.5 Complete clearing

Clearing rings reduce but do not completely eliminate the counterparty-specific nature of contracts and the resulting risk in the event of counterparty failure. Members are still exposed to the failure of their counterparties. Furthermore, like dominoes, contract failures can create a cascading effect and lead a string of seemingly unrelated counterparties to fail. A good historical example of this is the 1902 bankruptcy of George Phillips, which affected hundreds of clearing members of the Chicago Board of Trade representing almost half of the total membership. To remedy such problems, the final stage in the development of clearing is complete clearing where a CCP or 'clearinghouse' becomes counterparty to all transactions.

When trading a derivative, the counterparties agree to fulfil specific obligations to each other. By interposing itself between two counterparties,[2] which are clearing members, a CCP assumes all such contractual rights and responsibilities as illustrated in Figure 2.3. This facilitates the offsetting of transactions as in clearing rings but also reduces counterparty risk further, as a member no longer needs to be concerned about the credit quality of its counterparty. Indeed, the counterparty to all intents and purposes is the CCP.

[2] Sometimes CCPs do not interpose themselves but rather guarantee the performance of the trade. This has historically been the case in US markets compared to Europe. Nevertheless, the end result is similar.

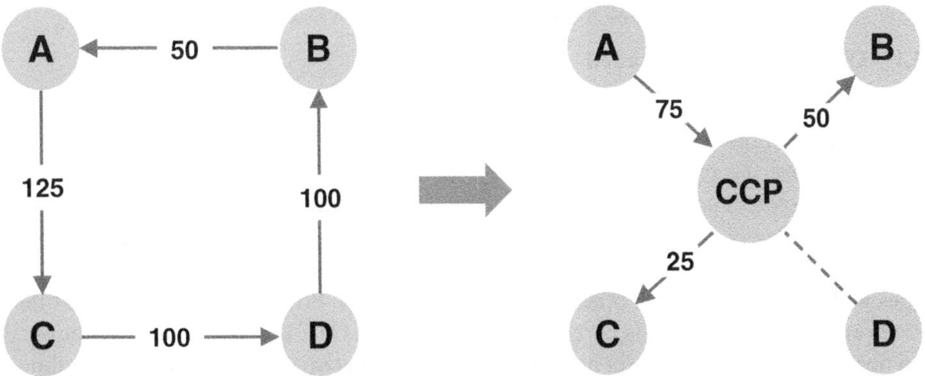

Figure 2.3 Illustration of complete clearing. The CCP assumes all contractual responsibilities as counterparty to all contracts.

Complete clearing originated in Europe and was adopted in the US by the end of the 19th century (although full novation of contracts did not occur until the early 20th century). Following the development of central clearing, as new futures exchanges were established, central counterparty clearing was often the chosen structure from the start.

Faced with counterparty risk, CCPs adopted rules to limit their exposures. In addition to the offset that this clearing structure facilitated, they used already developed margining rules to protect themselves from the risk of insolvency of one of their members. Margin generally evolved to be dynamic using daily mark-to-market valuation to define *variation margin* relating to daily payment of profits and losses, as well as *initial margin* to cover the potential close out cost of positions that a CCP could experience when a member defaulted. Additional to margin requirements, CCPs developed a loss sharing model. All clearing members had to make share purchases, which entitled them to use the exchange. In the event of a clearing member failure, the clearing members were at risk of losing their equity investment (but not more). This equity is the basis of what CCPs define as default funds today.

Adoption of central clearing has not been completely without resistance: the Chicago Board of Trade (CBOT) did not have a CCP function for around 30 years until 1925 (and then partly as a result of government pressure). One of the last futures exchanges to adopt a CCP was the London Metal Exchange in 1986 (again with regulatory pressure being a key factor). An obvious and often cited reason for these resistances is the fact that clearing homogenises counterparty risk and therefore would lead to strong credit quality members of the exchange suffering under central clearing compared to the weaker members. The reluctance to adopt clearing voluntarily certainly raises the possibility that the costs of clearing exceed the benefits, at least in some markets.

Nevertheless, all exchange-traded contracts are currently subject to central clearing. The CCP function may either be operated by the exchange or provided to the exchange as a service by an independent company. All derivatives exchanges have adopted some form of a CCP and central counterparty clearing was therefore the standard practice for derivatives markets clearing until the arrival of the OTC derivatives market in the last quarter of the 20th century.

2.2 OTC DERIVATIVES

2.2.1 OTC vs. exchange-traded

Exchange-traded derivatives are standardised contracts (e.g. futures and options) and are actively traded in the secondary markets. It is easy to buy a contract and sell the equivalent contract to close the position, which can be done via one or more derivative exchanges. Prices are transparent and accessible to a wide range of market participants.

OTC markets work very differently compared to exchange-traded ones, as outlined in Table 2.1. OTC derivatives are traditionally privately negotiated and traded directly between two parties without an exchange or other intermediary involved. Prices are not firm commitments to trade and price negotiation is purely a bilateral process. OTC derivatives have traditionally been negotiated between a dealer and end user or between two dealers. OTC markets did not historically include trade reporting, which is difficult because trades can occur in private, without activity being visible on any exchange. Documentation is also bilaterally negotiated between the two parties, although certain standards have been developed. In bilateral OTC markets, each party takes counterparty risk to the other and must manage it themselves.

The most important factor influencing the popularity of OTC products is the ability to tailor contracts more precisely to client needs, for example by offering a particular maturity date. Exchange-traded products by their nature do not offer customisation. Key players in the OTC market are banks and other highly sophisticated parties, such as hedge funds. Inter-dealer brokers also play a role in intermediating OTC derivatives transactions. Prior to 2007, whilst the OTC market was the largest market for derivatives, it was largely unregulated.

It is important not to confuse customised with exotic OTC derivatives. For example, a customer wanting to hedge their production or use of an underlying asset at specific dates may do so through a customised OTC derivative. Such a hedge may not be available on an exchange, where the underlying contracts will only allow certain standard contractual terms (e.g. maturity dates) to be used. A customised OTC derivative may be considered more useful for risk management than an exchange-traded derivative, which would give rise to additional 'basis risk' (in this example, the mismatch of maturity dates). It has been reported that the majority of the largest companies in the world use derivatives in order to manage their financial risks.[3] Due to the idiosyncratic hedging needs of such companies, OTC derivatives are commonly used instead of their exchange-traded equivalents.

Customised OTC derivatives are not without their disadvantages, of course. A customer wanting to unwind a transaction must do it with the original counterparty, who may quote

Table 2.1 Comparison between exchange-traded and OTC derivatives.

	Exchange-traded	Over-the-counter (OTC)
Terms of contract	• Standardised (maturity, size, strike, etc.)	• Flexible and negotiable
Maturity	• Standard maturities, typically at most a few months	• Negotiable and non-standard • Often many years
Liquidity	• Very good	• Limited and sometimes very poor for non-standard or complex products
Credit risk	• Guaranteed by CCP	• Bilateral

[3] Over 94% of the World's Largest Companies Use Derivatives to Help Manage Their Risks, According to ISDA Survey", ISDA Press Release, 23 April 2009, http://www.isda.org/press/press042309der.pdf.

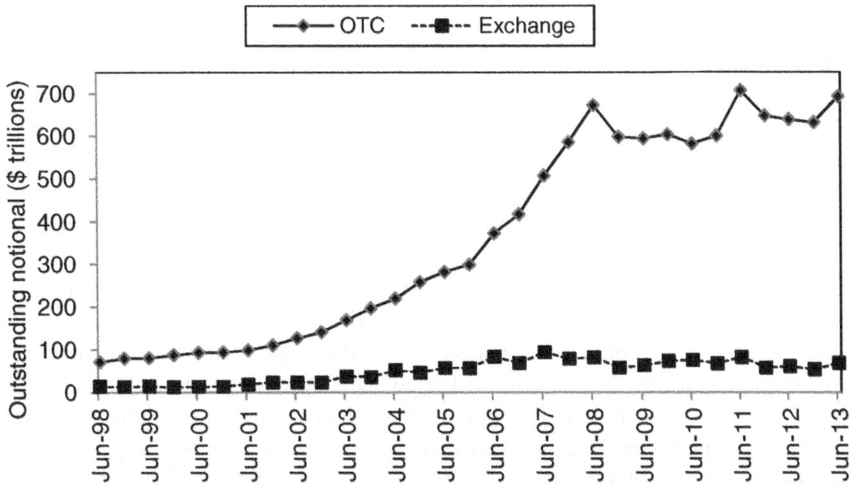

Figure 2.4 Total outstanding notional of OTC and exchange-traded derivatives transactions. The figures cover interest rate, foreign exchange, equity, commodity and credit derivative contracts. Note that notional amounts outstanding are not directly comparable to those for exchange-traded derivatives, which refer to open interest or net positions whereas the amounts outstanding for OTC markets refer to gross positions, i.e. without netting. Centrally cleared trades also increase the total notional outstanding due to a double counting effect since clearing involves book two separate transactions. Source: BIS.

unfavourable terms due to their privileged position. Even assigning or novating the transaction to another counterparty typically cannot be done without the permission of the original counterparty. This lack of fungibility in OTC transactions can also be problematic. This aside, there is nothing wrong with customising derivatives to the precise needs of clients as long as this is the sole intention. However, this is not the only use of OTC derivatives: some are contracted for regulatory arbitrage or even (arguably) misleading a client. Such products are clearly not socially useful and generally fall into the (relatively small) category of exotic OTC derivatives which in turn generate much of the criticism of OTC derivatives in general.

OTC derivatives markets remained relatively small until the 1980s, in part due to regulation, and also due to the benefits in terms of liquidity and counterparty risk control for exchange-traded derivatives. However, from that point on, advances in financial engineering and technology together with favourable regulation led to the rapid growth of OTC derivatives as illustrated in Figure 2.4. The strong expansion of OTC derivatives against exchange-traded derivatives is also partly due to exotic contracts and new markets such as credit derivatives (the credit default swap market increased by a factor of 10 between the end of 2003 and end of 2008). OTC derivatives have in recent years dominated their exchange-traded equivalents in notional value[4] by something close to an order to magnitude.

Another important aspect of OTC derivatives is their concentration with respect to a relatively small number of commercial banks, often referred to as 'dealers'. For example, in the US, four large commercial banks represent 90% of the total OTC derivative notional amounts.[5]

[4] Not by number of transactions, as OTC derivatives trades tend to be much larger.

[5] Officer of the Comptroller of the Currency, 'OCC's Quarterly Report on Bank Trading and Derivatives Activities First Quarter 2013', Table 3, http://www.occ.gov/topics/capital-markets/financial-markets/trading/derivatives/dq113.pdf.

2.2.2 Market development

The total notional amount of all derivatives outstanding was $761 trillion in mid-2013. The curtailed growth towards the end of the history in Figure 2.4 can be clearly attributed to the global financial crisis (GFC), where firms have reduced balance sheets and re-allocated capital, and clients have been less interested in derivatives, particularly as structured products. However, the reduction in recent years is also partially due to compression exercises that seek to reduce counterparty risk by removing offsetting and redundant positions (discussed in more detail in the next chapter).

OTC derivatives include the following five broad classes of derivative securities: interest rate derivatives, foreign exchange derivatives, equity derivatives, commodity derivatives and credit derivatives. The split of OTC derivatives by product type is shown in Figure 2.5. Interest rate products contribute the majority of the outstanding notional, with foreign exchange and credit default swaps seemingly less important. However, this gives a somewhat misleading view of the importance of counterparty risk in other asset classes, especially foreign exchange and credit default swaps. Whilst most foreign exchange products are short-dated, the long-dated nature and exchange of notional in cross-currency swaps means they carry a lot of counterparty risk. Credit default swaps not only have a large volatility component but also constitute significant 'wrong-way risk'. Therefore, whilst interest rate products make up a significant proportion of the counterparty risk in the market, one must not underestimate the other important (and sometimes more subtle) contributions from other products.

A key aspect of derivatives products is that their exposure is substantially smaller than that of an equivalent loan or bond. Consider an interest rate swap as an example: this contract involves the exchange of floating against fixed coupons and has no principal risk because only cashflows are exchanged. Furthermore, even the coupons are not fully at risk because, at coupon dates, only the difference in fixed and floating coupons or *net* payment will be

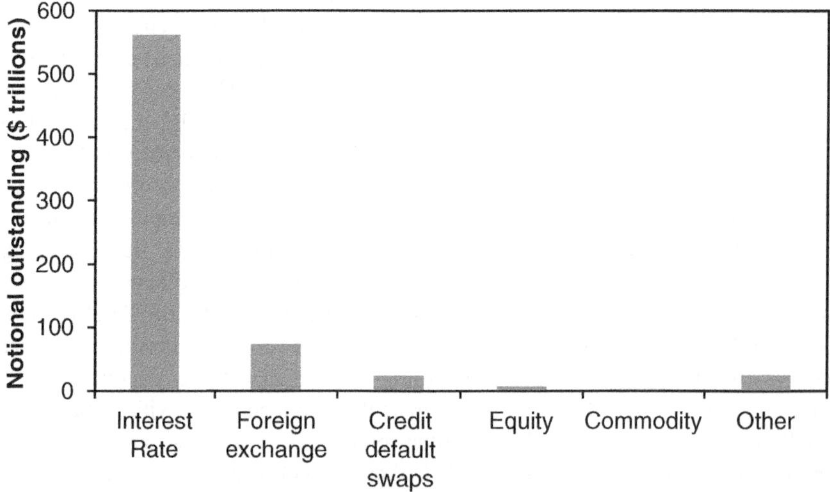

Figure 2.5 Split of OTC derivative gross outstanding notional by product type as of June 2013. Note that centrally cleared products are double counted since a single trade is novated into two trades in a CCP. This is particularly relevant for interest rate products, for which a large outstanding notional is already centrally cleared. Source: BIS.

Table 2.2 Comparison of the total notional outstanding and the market value of OTC derivatives (in $ trillions) for different asset classes as of June 2013. Source: BIS.

	Gross notional outstanding	Gross market value*	Ratio
Interest rate	561.3	15.2	2.7%
Foreign exchange	73.1	2.4	3.3%
Credit default swaps	24.3	0.7	3.0%
Equity	6.8	0.7	10.2%
Commodity	2.4	0.4	15.7%

* This is calculated as the sum of the absolute value of gross positive and gross negative market values, corrected for double counting.

exchanged. If a counterparty fails to perform then an institution will have no obligation to continue to make coupon payments. Instead, the swap will be unwound based on (for example) independent quotations as to its current market value. If the swap has a negative value for an institution then they may stand to lose nothing if their counterparty defaults.[6] For this reason, when we compare the actual total market of derivatives against their total notional amount outstanding, we see a massive reduction as illustrated in Table 2.2. For example, the total market value of interest rate contracts is only 2.7% of the total notional outstanding.

Derivatives contracts have, in many cases, become more standardised over the years through industry initiatives. This standardisation has come about as a result of a natural lifecycle where a product moves gradually from non-standard and complex to becoming more standard and potentially less exotic. Nevertheless, OTC derivative markets remain decentralised and more heterogeneous, and are consequently less transparent than their exchange-traded equivalents. This leads to potentially challenging counterparty risk problems. OTC derivatives markets have historically managed this counterparty risk through the use of netting agreements, margin requirements, periodic cash resettlement, and other forms of bilateral credit mitigation.

2.2.3 OTC derivatives and clearing

An OTC derivatives contract obliges its counterparties to make certain payments over the life of the contract (or until an early termination of the contract). 'Clearing' is the process by which payment obligations between two or more firms are computed (and often netted), and 'settlement' is the process by which those obligations are effected. The means by which payments on OTC derivatives are cleared and settled affect how the credit risk borne by counterparties in the transaction is managed. A key feature of many OTC derivatives is that they are not settled for a long time since they generally have long maturities. This is in contrast to exchange-traded products, which often settle in days or, at the most, months. Clearing is therefore more important and difficult for OTC derivatives.

OTC and exchange-traded derivatives generally have two distinct mechanisms for clearing and settlement: bilateral for OTC derivatives and central for exchange-traded structures. Risk-management practices, such as margining, are dealt with bilaterally by the counterparties to each OTC contract, whereas for exchange-traded derivatives the risk management functions are typically carried out by the associated CCP. However, an OTC derivative does

[6] Assuming the swap can be replaced without any additional cost.

not have to become exchange-traded to benefit from central clearing. CCPs have for many years operated as separate entities to control counterparty risk by mutualising it amongst the CCP members. Prior to any clearing mandate, almost half the (OTC) interest-rate swap market was centrally cleared by LCH.Clearnet's SwapClear service (although almost all other OTC derivatives were still bilaterally traded).

An important aspect for CCPs is the heterogeneity of the OTC market, since clearing requires a degree of homogeneity between its members. Historically, the large OTC derivatives players have had much stronger credit quality than the other participants. However, some small players such as sovereigns and insurance companies have had very strong (triple-A) credit quality, and have used this to obtain favourable terms such as one-way margin agreements.

Banks have historically dealt with counterparty risk in a variety of ways. For instance, a bank may not require a counterparty to post any margin at the initiation of a transaction as long as the amount it owes remains below a pre-established credit limit. Counterparty risk is now commonly priced into transactions via credit value adjustment (CVA), as discussed in more detail in Chapter 7. Before we discuss central clearing in more detail in the next chapter, it is useful to first review some of the other counterparty risk reduction methods used in the OTC market prior to 2007.

2.3 COUNTERPARTY RISK MITIGATION IN OTC MARKETS

2.3.1 Systemic risk

A major concern with respect to OTC derivatives is systemic risk. A major systemic risk episode would likely involve an initial spark followed by a proceeding chain reaction, potentially leading to some sort of explosion in financial markets. Thus, in order to control systemic risk, one can either minimise the chance of the initial spark, attempt to ensure that the chain reaction does not occur, or simply plan that the explosion is controlled and the resulting damage limited.

Historically, most OTC risk mitigants focused on reducing the possibility of the initial spark mentioned above. Reducing the default risk of large, important market participants is an obvious route. Capital requirements, regulation and prudential supervision can contribute to this but there is a balance between reduction of default risk and encouraging financial firms to grow and prosper.

OTC derivatives markets have netting, margining and other methods to minimise counterparty and systemic risk. However, such aspects create more complexity and may catalyse growth to a level that would never have otherwise been possible. Hence it can be argued that initiatives to stifle a chain reaction may achieve precisely the opposite and create the catalyst (such as many large exposures supported by a complex web of margining) to cause the explosion.

The OTC derivative market also developed other mechanisms for potentially controlling the inherent counterparty and systemic risks they create. Examples of these mechanisms are SPVs, DPCs, monolines and CDPCs, which are discussed next. Although these methods have been largely deemed irrelevant in today's market, they share some common features with CCPs and a historical overview of their development is therefore useful.

However, without the correct management and regulation, ultimately even seemingly strong financial institutions can collapse. The ultimate solution to systemic risk may therefore be simply to have the means in place to manage periodic failures in a controlled manner, which is one role of a CCP. If there is a default of a key market participant, then the CCP will guarantee all the contracts that this counterparty has executed through them as a clearing member. This will mitigate concerns faced by institutions and prevent any extreme actions by those institutions that could worsen the crisis. Any unexpected losses[7] caused by the failure of one or more counterparties would be shared amongst all members of the CCP (just as insurance losses are essentially shared by all policyholders) rather than being concentrated within a smaller number of institutions that may be heavily exposed to the failing counterparty. This 'loss mutualisation' is a key component as it mitigates systemic risk and prevents a domino effect.

2.3.2 Special purpose vehicles

A Special Purpose Vehicle (SPV) or Special Purpose Entity (SPE) is a legal entity (e.g. a company or limited partnership) created typically to isolate a firm from financial risk. SPVs have been used in the OTC derivatives market to protect from counterparty risk. A company will transfer assets to the SPV for management or use the SPV to finance a large project without putting the entire firm or a counterparty at risk. Jurisdictions may require that an SPV is not owned by the entity on whose behalf it is being set up.

SPVs aim essentially to change bankruptcy rules so that, if a derivative counterparty is insolvent, a client can still receive their full investment prior to any other claims being paid out. SPVs are most commonly used in structured notes, where they use this mechanism to guarantee the counterparty risk on the principal of the note to a very high level (triple-A typically), better than that of the issuer. The creditworthiness of the SPV is assessed by rating agencies who look in detail at the mechanics and legal specifics before granting a rating.

SPVs aim to shift priorities so that in a bankruptcy, certain parties can receive a favourable treatment. Clearly, such a favourable treatment can only be achieved by imposing a less favourable environment on other parties. More generally, such a mechanism may then reduce risk in one area but increase it in another. CCPs also create a similar shift in priorities, which may move, rather than reduce, systemic risk.

An SPV transforms counterparty risk into legal risk. The obvious legal risk is that of *consolidation*, which is the power of a bankruptcy court to combine the SPV assets with those of the originator. The basis of consolidation is that the SPV is essentially the same as the originator and means that the isolation of the SPV becomes irrelevant. Consolidation may depend on many aspects such as jurisdictions. US courts have a history of consolidation rulings, whereas UK courts have been less keen to do so, except in extreme cases such as fraud.

Another lesson is that legal documentation often evolves through experience, and the enforceability of the legal structure of SPVs was not tested for many years. When it was tested in the case of Lehman Brothers, there were problems (although this depended on jurisdiction). Lehman essentially used SPVs to shield investors in complex transactions such as Collateralised Debt Obligations (CDOs) from Lehman's own counterparty risk (in retrospect a great idea). The key provision in the documents is referred to as the 'flip' provision, which essentially meant that if Lehman were bankrupt then the investors would be first in line as creditors. However, the US Bankruptcy Court ruled the flip clauses were unenforceable, putting them at loggerheads with the UK courts, which ruled that the flip clauses were enforceable. Just to add to the jurisdiction-specific question of whether a flip clause and therefore an

[7] Meaning those above a certain level that will be discussed later.

SPV was a sound legal structure, many cases have been settled out of court.[8] Risk mitigation that relies on very sound legal foundations may fail dramatically if any of these foundations prove to be unstable. This is also a potential lesson for CCPs, who must be certain of their legal authorities in a situation such as a default of one of their members.

2.3.3 Derivatives product companies

Long before the GFC of 2007 onwards, whilst no major derivatives dealer had failed, the bilaterally cleared dealer-dominated OTC market was perceived as being inherently more vulnerable to counterparty risk than the exchange-traded market. The derivatives product company (or corporation) evolved as a means for OTC derivative markets to mitigate counterparty risk (e.g. see Kroszner 1999). DPCs are generally triple-A rated entities set up by one or more banks as a bankruptcy-remote subsidiary of a major dealer, which, unlike an SPV, is separately capitalised to obtain a triple-A credit rating.[9] The DPC structure provides external counterparties with a degree of protection against counterparty risk by protecting against the failure of the DPC parent. A DPC therefore provided some of the benefits of the exchange-based system while preserving the flexibility and decentralisation of the OTC market. Examples of some of the first DPCs include Merrill Lynch Derivative Products, Salomon Swapco, Morgan Stanley Derivative Products and Lehman Brothers Financial Products.

The ability of a sponsor to create their own 'mini derivatives exchange' via a DPC was partially a result of improvements in risk management models and the development of credit rating agencies. DPCs maintained a triple-A rating by a combination of capital, margin and activity restrictions. Each DPC had its own quantitative risk assessment model to quantify their current credit risk. This was benchmarked against that required for a triple-A rating. Most DPCs use a dynamic capital allocation to keep within the triple-A credit risk requirements. The triple-A rating of a DPC typically depends on:

- *Minimising market risk:* In terms of market risk, DPCs can attempt to be close to market-neutral via trading offsetting contracts. Ideally, they would be on both sides of every trade as these 'mirror trades' lead to an overall matched book. Normally the mirror trade exists with the DPC parent.
- *Support from a parent:* The DPC is supported by a parent with the DPC being bankruptcy-remote (like an SPV) with respect to the parent to achieve a better rating. If the parent were to default, then the DPC would either pass to another well-capitalised institution or be terminated, with trades settled at mid-market.
- *Credit risk management and operational guidelines (limits, margin terms, etc.):* Restrictions are also imposed on (external) counterparty credit quality and activities (position limits, margin, etc.). The management of counterparty risk is achieved by having daily mark-to-market and margin posting.

Whilst being of very good credit quality, DPCs also aimed to give further security by defining an orderly workout process. A DPC defined what events would trigger its own failure (rating

[8] For example, see 'Lehman opts to settle over Dante flip-clause transactions' http://www.risk.net/risk-magazine/news/1899105/lehman-opts-settle-dante-flip-clause-transactions.

[9] Most DPCs derived their credit quality structurally via capital, but some simply did so more trivially from the sponsors' rating.

downgrade of parent, for example) and how the resulting workout process would work. The resulting 'pre-packaged bankruptcy' was therefore supposedly simpler (as well as less likely) than the standard bankruptcy of an OTC derivative counterparty. Broadly speaking, two bankruptcy approaches existed, namely a continuation and termination structure. In either case, a manager was responsible for managing and hedging existing positions (continuation structure) or terminating transactions (termination structure).

There was nothing apparently wrong with the DPC idea, which worked well since its creation in the early 1990s. DPCs were created in the early stages of the OTC derivative market to facilitate trading of long-dated derivatives by counterparties having less than triple-A credit quality. However, was such a triple-A entity of a double-A or worse bank really a better counterparty than the bank itself? In the early years, DPCs experienced steady growth in notional volumes, with business peaking in the mid-to-late 1990s. However, the increased use of margin in the market, and the existence of alternative triple-A entities led to a lessening demand for DPCs.

The GFC essentially killed the already declining world of DPCs. After their parent's decline and rescue, the Bear Stearns DPCs were wound down by J.P. Morgan, with clients compensated for novating trades. The voluntary filing for Chapter 11 bankruptcy protection by two Lehman Brothers DPCs, a strategic effort to protect the DPCs' assets, seems to link a DPC's fate inextricably with that of its parent. Not surprisingly, the perceived lack of autonomy of DPCs has led to a reaction from rating agencies, who have withdrawn ratings.[10]

Whilst DPCs have not been responsible for any catastrophic events, they have become largely irrelevant. As in the case of SPVs, it is clear that the DPC concept is a flawed one. The perceived triple-A ratings of DPCs had little credibility as the counterparty being faced was really the DPC parent, generally with a worse credit rating. Therefore, DPCs again illustrate that a conversion of counterparty risk into other financial risks (in this case not only legal risk as in the case of SPVs but also market and operational risks) may be ineffective.

2.3.4 Monolines and CDPCs

As described above, the creation of DPCs was largely driven by the need for high-quality counterparties when trading OTC derivatives. However, this need was taken to another level by the birth and exponential growth of the credit derivatives market from around 1998 onwards. The first credit derivative product was the single name credit default swap (CDS). The CDS represents an unusual challenge since its mark-to-market is driven by credit spread changes whilst its payoff is linked solely to one or more credit events (e.g. default). The so-called wrong-way risk in CDS (for example, when buying protection on a bank from another bank) meant that the credit quality of the counterparty became even more important than it would be for other OTC derivatives. Beyond single name credit default swaps, senior tranches of structured finance CDOs had even more wrong-way risk and created an even stronger need for a 'default remote entity'.

Monoline insurance companies (and similar companies such as AIG)[11] were financial guarantee companies with strong credit ratings that they utilised to provide 'credit wraps'

[10] For example, see 'Fitch withdraws Citi Swapco's ratings' http://www.businesswire.com/news/home/20110610005841/en/Fitch-Withdraws-Citi-Swapcos-Ratings.

[11] For the purposes of this analysis, we will categorise monoline insurers and AIG as the same type of entity, which, based on their activities in the credit derivatives market, is fair.

which are financial guarantees. Monolines began providing credit wraps for other areas but then entered the single name CDS and structured finance arena to achieve diversification and better returns. Credit derivative product companies (CDPCs) were an extension of the DPC concept discussed in the last section that had business models similar to those of monolines.

In order to achieve good ratings (e.g. triple-A), monolines/CDPCs had capital requirements driven by the possible losses on the structures they provide protection on. Capital requirements were also dynamically related to the portfolio of assets they wrapped, which is similar to the workings of the DPC structure. Monolines and CDPCs typically did not have to post margin (at least in normal times) against a decline in the mark-to-market value of their contracts (due to their excellent credit rating).

From November 2007 onwards, a number of monolines (for example, XL Financial Assurance Ltd, AMBAC Insurance Corporation and MBIA Insurance Corporation) essentially failed. In 2008, AIG was bailed out by the US government to the tune of approximately US$182 billion (the reason why AIG was bailed out and the monoline insurers were not was the size of AIG's exposures[12] and the timing of their problems close to the Lehman Brothers bankruptcy). These failures were due to a subtle combination of rating downgrades, required margin postings and mark-to-market losses leading to a downwards spiral. Many banks found themselves heavily exposed to monolines due to the massive increase in the value of the protection they had purchased. For example, as of June 2008, UBS was estimated to have US$6.4 billion at risk to monoline insurers whilst the equivalent figures for Citigroup and Merrill Lynch were US$4.8 billion and US$3 billion respectively.[13]

CDPCs, like monolines, were highly leveraged and typically did not post margin. They fared somewhat better during the GFC but only for timing reasons. Many CDPCs were not fully operational until after the beginning of the GFC in July 2007. They therefore missed at least the first 'wave' of losses suffered by any party selling credit protection (especially super senior)[14]. Nevertheless, the fact that the CDPC business model is close to that of monolines has not been ignored. For example, in October 2008, Fitch Ratings withdrew ratings on the five CDPCs that it rated.[15]

2.3.5 Lessons for central clearing

The aforementioned concepts of SPVs, DPCs, monolines and CDPCs have all been shown to lead to certain issues. Indeed, it could be argued that as risk mitigation methods they all have fatal flaws, which explains why there is little evidence of them in today's OTC derivative market. It is important to ask to what extent such flaws may also exist within an OTC CCP, which does share certain characteristics of these structures.

Regarding SPVs and DPCs, two obvious questions emerge. The first is whether shifting priorities from one party to another really helps the system as a whole. CCPs will effectively give priority to OTC derivative counterparties and in doing so may reduce the risk in this market. However, this will make other parties (e.g. bondholders) worse off and may therefore

[12] Whilst the monolines together had approximately the same amount of credit derivatives exposure as AIG, their failures were at least partially spaced out.

[13] See 'Banks face $10bn monolines charges', Financial Times, 10 June 2008, http://www.ft.com/cms/s/0/8051c0c4-3715-11dd-bc1c-0000779fd2ac.html#axzz2qH4m4ZLD.

[14] The widening in super senior spreads was on a relative basis much greater than credit spreads in general during late 2007.

[15] See, for example, 'Fitch withdraws CDPC ratings', Business Wire, 2008.

increase risks in other markets (see sections 5.1.6 and 6.4.1 for further detail). Second, a critical reliance on a precise sound legal framework creates exposure to any flaws in such a framework. This is especially important, as in a large bankruptcy there will likely be parties who stand to make significant gains by challenging the priority of payments (as in the aforementioned SPV flip clause cases). Furthermore, the cross-border activities of CCPs also expose them to bankruptcy regimes and regulatory frameworks in multiple regions.

CCPs also share some similarities with monolines and CDPCs as strong credit quality entities set up to take and manage counterparty risk. However, two very important differences must be emphasised. First, CCPs have a 'matched book' and do not take any residual market risk (except when members default). This is a critical difference since monolines and CDPCs had very large, mostly one-way, exposure to credit markets. Second, a related point is that CCPs require variation and initial margin in all situations whereas monolines and CDPCs would essentially post only variation margin and would often only do this in extreme situations (e.g. in the event of their ratings being downgraded). Many monolines and CDPCs posted no margin at all at the inception of trades. Nevertheless, CCPs are similar to these entities in essentially insuring against systemic risk. However, the term 'systemic risk insurance' is a misnomer, as systemic risk cannot be diversified.

Although CCPs structurally do not suffer from the flaws that caused the failure of monoline insurers or bailout of AIG, there are clearly lessons to be learnt with respect to the centralisation of counterparty risk in a single large and potentially too-big-to-fail entity. One specific example is the destabilising relationship created by increases in margin requirements. Monolines and AIG failed due to a significant increase in margin requirements during a crisis period. CCPs could conceivably create the same dynamic with respect to variation and initial margins, which will be discussed later.

Furthermore, it is possibly unhelpful that some commentators have argued that CCPs would have helped prevent the GFC, for example in relation to AIG. It is true that central clearing would have prevented AIG from building up the enormous exposures that it did. However, AIG's trades would not have been eligible for clearing as they were too non-standard and exotic. Additionally, when virtually all financial institutions, credit ratings agencies, regulators and politicians believed that AIG had excellent credit quality and would be unlikely to fail, it is a huge leap of faith to suggest that a CCP would have had a vastly superior insight or intellectual ability to see otherwise.

2.3.6 Clearing in OTC derivatives markets

From the late 1990s, several major CCPs began to provide clearing and settlement services for OTC derivatives and other non-exchange-traded products. This was to help market participants reduce counterparty risk and benefit from the fungibility that central clearing creates. These OTC transactions are still negotiated privately and off-exchange but are then novated into a CCP on a post-trade basis.

In 1999, LCH.Clearnet set up two OTC CCPs to clear and settle repurchase agreements (RepoClear) and plain vanilla interest rate swaps (SwapClear). Commercial interest in OTC-cleared derivatives grew substantially in the energy derivatives market following the bankruptcy of Enron in late 2001. InterContinentalExchange (ICE) responded to this demand by offering cleared OTC energy derivatives solutions beginning in 2002. ICE now offers OTC clearing for credit default swaps (CDSs) also.

Although CCP clearing and settlement of OTC derivatives did develop in the years prior to the GFC, this has been confined to certain products and markets. This suggests that there are both positives and negatives associated with using CCPs and, in some market situations, the positives may not outweigh the negatives. As mentioned in the last chapter, the distinction between securities and OTC clearing is important, with the latter being far less straightforward. For this reason, the major focus of this book is OTC CCPs.

2.4 SUMMARY

Most CCPs were originally created by the members of futures exchanges to manage default risk more efficiently and were not designed specifically for OTC derivatives. It is useful to understand the historical development of central clearing and compare it to other forms of counterparty risk mitigation used in derivatives markets such as SPVs, DPCs and monolines. This can provide a good basis for understanding some of the consequences that central clearing will have in the future and some of the associated risks that may be created.

The next chapter will explain the operation of a CCP in more detail.

3

Basic Principles of Central Clearing

[CCPs] emerged gradually and slowly as a result of experience and experimentation.

Randall Kroszner (1962–)

3.1 WHAT IS CLEARING?

Broadly speaking, clearing represents the period between execution and settlement of a transaction, as illustrated in Figure 3.1. At trade execution, parties agree to legal obligations in relation to buying or selling certain underlying securities or exchanging cashflows in reference to underlying market variables. Settlement refers to the completion of all such legal obligations and can occur when all payments have been successfully made or alternatively when the contract is closed out (e.g. offset against another position). Clearing refers to the process between execution and settlement, which in the case of classically cleared products is often a few days (e.g. a spot equity transaction) or at most a few months (e.g. futures or options contracts). For OTC derivatives, the time horizon for the clearing process is more commonly years and often even decades. This is one reason why OTC clearing has such importance in the future as more OTC products become subject to central clearing.

Broadly speaking, clearing can be either bilateral or central. In the former case, the two parties entering a trade take responsibility (potentially with the help of third parties) for the processes during clearing. In the latter case, this responsibility is taken over by a third party such as a central counterparty (CCP).

3.2 FUNCTIONS OF A CCP

It is important to emphasise that in the central clearing of non-OTC trades (e.g. securities transactions), the primary role of the CCP is to standardise and simplify operational processes. In contrast, OTC CCPs have a much more significant role to play in terms of counterparty risk

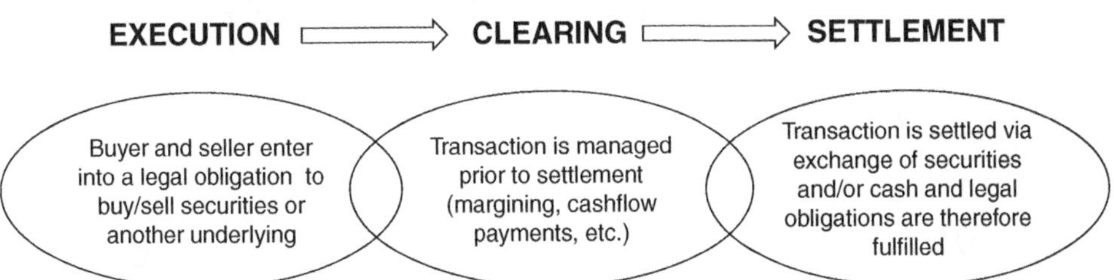

Figure 3.1 Illustration of the role of clearing in financial transactions.

mitigation due the longer maturities and relative illiquidity of OTC derivatives. As this book is concerned with OTC clearing, much of the discussion below will be focused in this direction.

3.2.1 Financial markets topology

A CCP represents a set of rules and operational arrangements that are designed to allocate, manage and reduce counterparty risk in a bilateral market. A CCP changes the topology of financial markets by inter-disposing itself between buyers and sellers as illustrated in Figure 3.2. In this context, it is useful to consider the six entities denoted by D, representing large global banks often known as 'dealers'. Two obvious advantages appear to stem from this simplistic view. First, a CCP can reduce the *interconnectedness* within financial markets, which may lessen the impact of an insolvency of a participant. Second, the CCP being at the heart of trading can provide more *transparency* on the positions of the members. An obvious problem here is that a CCP represents the centre of a 'hub and spoke' system and consequently its failure would be a catastrophic event.

OTC CCPs will change dramatically the topology of the global financial system. The above analysis is clearly rather simplistic and although the general points made are correct, the true CCP landscape is much more complex than represented above.

3.2.2 Novation

A key concept in central clearing is that of contract novation, which is the legal process whereby the CCP is positioned between buyers and sellers. Novation is the replacement of one contract with one or more other contracts. Novation means that the CCP essentially steps in between parties to a transaction and therefore acts as an insurer of counterparty risk in both directions. The viability of novation depends on the legal enforceability of the new contracts and the certainty that the original parties are not legally obligated to each other once the novation is completed. Assuming this viability, novation means that the contract between the original parties ceases to exist and they therefore do not have counterparty risk to one another.

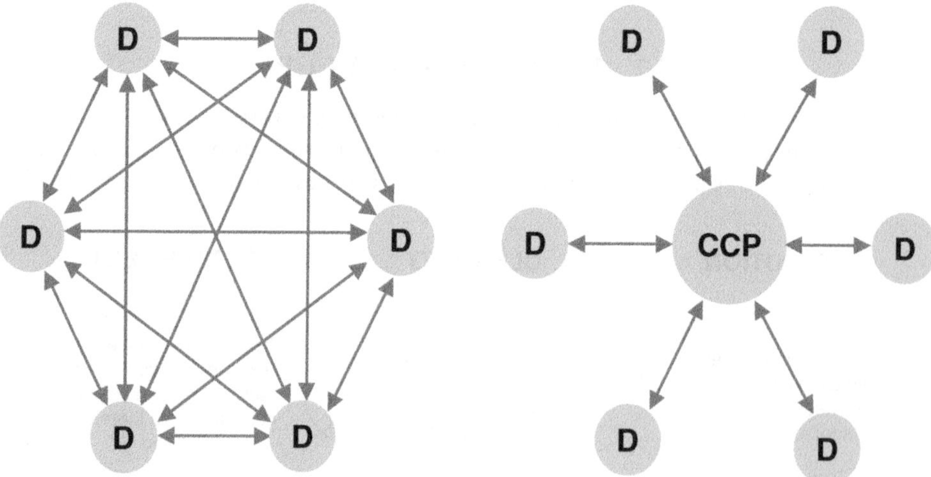

Figure 3.2 Illustration of bilateral markets (left) compared to centrally cleared markets (right).

Because it stands between market buyers and sellers, the CCP has a 'matched book' and bears no net market risk, which remains with the original party to each trade. The CCP, on the other hand, does take the counterparty risk, which is centralised in the CCP structure. Put another way, the CCP has 'conditional market risk' since in the event of a member default, it will no longer have a matched book. In order to return to a matched book, a CCP will have various methods, such as holding an auction of the defaulting member's positions. CCPs also mitigate counterparty risk by demanding financial resources from their members that are intended to cover the potential losses in the event that one or more of them default.

3.2.3 Multilateral offset

A major problem with bilateral clearing is the proliferation of overlapping and potentially redundant contracts, which increases counterparty risk and adds to the interconnectedness of the financial system. Redundant contracts have generally arisen historically because counterparties may enter into offsetting trades, rather than terminating the original one. For dealers, this redundancy may be even more problematic as they may hedge contracts with similar, but not identical, ones.

The first advantage of central clearing is multilateral offset.[1] This offset can be in relation to various aspects such as cashflows or margin requirements, which will be discussed in more detail in Chapters 5 and 6 respectively. In simple terms, multilateral offset is as illustrated in Figure 3.3. In the bilateral market, the three participants have liabilities marked by the directions of the arrows. The total liabilities to be paid are 180. In this market, A is exposed to C by an amount of 90. If C fails then there is the risk that A may fail also, creating a domino effect. Under central clearing, all assets and liabilities are taken over by the CCP and can offset one another. This means that total risks are reduced: not only is the liability of C offset to 60 but also the insolvency of C can no longer cause a knock-on effect to A since the CCP has intermediated the position between the two.

Whilst the above representation is generally correct, it ignores some key effects. These are the impact of multiple CCPs (section 12.1.4), the impact of non-cleared trades (section 5.2.6) and even the impact on non-derivatives positions (section 5.1.6). As noted, these aspects will be addressed later.

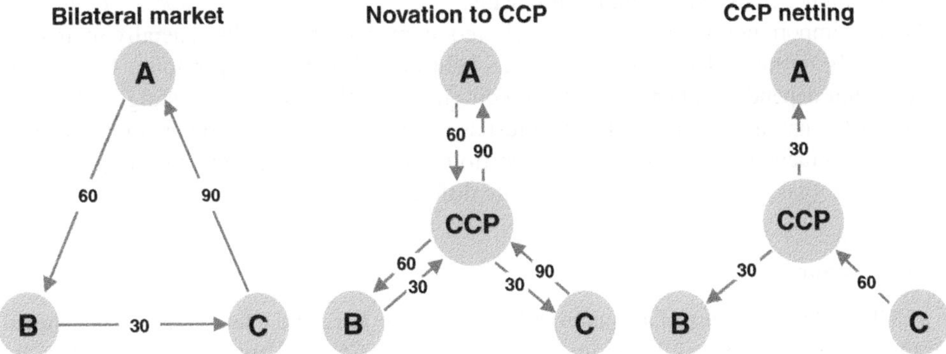

Figure 3.3 Illustration of multilateral offsetting afforded by central clearing.

[1] Although there are other bilateral methods that can achieve this such as trade compression, discussed in Chapter 5.

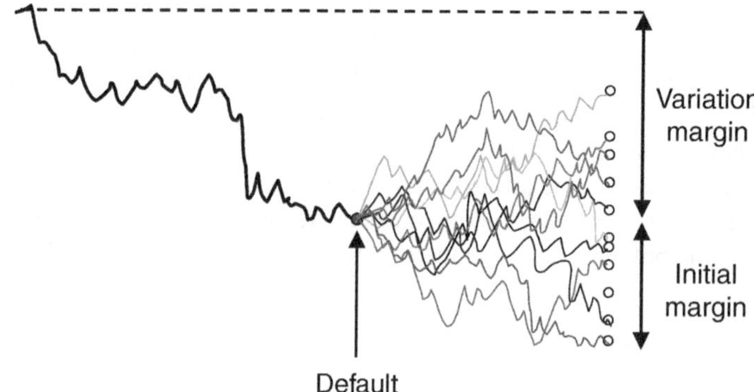

Figure 3.4 Illustration of the role of initial and variation margins. Variation margin tracks the value prior to default and initial margin provides a cushion against potential losses after default (e.g. close out costs).

3.2.4 Margining

Given that CCPs sit at the heart of large financial markets, it is critical that they have effective risk control and adequate financial resources. The most obvious and important method for this is via the margins that CCPs charge to cover the market risk of the trades they clear. Margin comes in two forms as illustrated in Figure 3.4. Variation margin covers the net change in market value of the member's positions. Initial margin is an additional amount, which is charged at trade inception, and is designed to cover the worst-case close out costs (due to the need to find replacement transactions) in the event a member defaults.

Margin requirements by CCPs are in general much stricter than in bilateral derivative markets. In particular, variation margin has to be transferred on a daily or even intra-daily basis, and must usually be in cash. Initial margin requirements may also change frequently with market conditions and must be provided in cash or liquid assets (e.g. treasury bonds). The combination of initial margins and increased required liquidity of margin, neither of which has historically been a part of bilateral markets, means that clearing potentially imposes significantly higher costs via margin requirements.

Another important point to note on margin requirements is that CCPs generally set margin levels solely on the risks of the transactions held in each member's portfolio. Initial margin does not depend significantly on the credit quality of the institution posting it: the most creditworthy institution may need to post just as much initial margin as others more likely to default. Two members clearing the same portfolio may have the same margin requirements even if their total balance sheet risks are quite different.

3.2.5 Auctions

In a CCP world, the failure of a counterparty, even one as large and interconnected as Lehman Brothers, is supposedly less dramatic. This is because the CCP absorbs the 'domino effect' by acting as a central shock absorber. In the event of default of one of its members, a CCP will aim to terminate swiftly all financial relations with that counterparty without suffering any losses. From the point of view of surviving members, the CCP guarantees the performance of their trades. This will normally be achieved not by closing out trades at their market value but rather by replacement of the defaulted counterparty with one of the other clearing members for each trade. This is typically achieved via the CCP auctioning the defaulted members' positions amongst the other members.

Assuming they wish to continue doing business with the CCP, members may have strong incentives to participate in an auction in order to collectively achieve a favourable workout of a default without adverse consequences such as making losses through default funds or other mechanisms (Chapter 10). This means that the CCP may achieve much better prices for essentially unwinding/novating trades than a party attempting to do this in a bilaterally cleared market. However, if a CCP auction fails then the consequences are potentially severe as other much more aggressive methods of loss allocation may follow.

3.2.6 Loss mutualisation

The ideal way for CCP members to contribute financial resources is in a 'defaulter pays' approach. This would mean that any clearing member would contribute all the necessary funds to pay for their own potential future default. This is impractical though, because it would require very high financial contributions from each member, which would be too costly. For this reason, the purpose of financial contributions from a given member is to cover losses to a high level of confidence in a scenario where they would default. This leaves a small chance of losses not following the 'defaulter pays' approach and thus being borne by the other clearing members.

Another basic principle of central clearing is that of loss mutualisation, where losses above the resources contributed by the defaulter are shared between CCP members. The most obvious way in which this occurs is that CCP members all contribute into a CCP 'default fund' which is typically used after the defaulter's own resources to cover losses. Since all members pay into this default fund, they all contribute to absorbing an extreme default loss.

Note that in a CCP, the default losses that a member incurs are not directly related to the transactions that this member executes with the defaulting member. Indeed, a member can suffer default losses even if it never traded with the defaulted counterparty, has no net position with the CCP, or has a net position with the CCP in the same direction as the defaulter (although there are other potential methods of loss allocation that may favour a member in this situation as discussed in Chapter 10).

Loss mutualisation is a form of insurance. It is well known that such risk pooling can have positive benefits such as allowing more participants to enter a market. It is equally well known, however, that such mechanisms are also subject to a variety of incentive and informational problems, most notably moral hazard and adverse selection.

3.3 BASIC QUESTIONS

3.3.1 What can be cleared?

Quite a large proportion of the OTC derivatives market will be centrally cleared in the coming years (and indeed quite a large amount is already cleared).[2] This is practical since some

[2] See section 12.1.2 for more detailed analysis.

clearable products (e.g. interest rate swaps) make up such a large proportion of the total outstanding notional. Although clearing is being extended to cover new products, this is a slow process since a product needs to have a number of features before it is clearable.

For a transaction to be centrally cleared, the following conditions are generally important:

- *Standardisation:* Legal and economic terms must be standard since clearing involves contractual responsibility for cashflows.
- *Complexity:* Only vanilla (or non-exotic) transactions can be cleared as they need to be relatively easily and robustly valued on a timely basis to support variation margin calculation.
- *Liquidity:* Liquidity of a product is important so that risk assessments can be made to determine how much initial margin and default fund contribution should be charged. In addition, illiquid products may be difficult to replace in an auction in the event of the default of a clearing member. Finally, if a product is not widely traded then it may not be worthwhile for a CCP to invest in developing the underlying clearing capability because they do not stand to clear enough trades to make the venture profitable.

For an actively traded instrument, there is a large volume of transactions and positions that can be robustly valued or 'marked to market' in a timely fashion. Moreover, extensive historical data is readily available to calibrate risk models, and the liquidity of the market will permit relatively straightforward close out in case of the default of a market participant. For such instruments, central clearing is straightforward. Things are different for instruments that are more complex and/or traded in less liquid markets, meaning that current market price information is harder to come by. Indeed, it may be necessary to use quite complex models in order to value these transactions. Such valuations are relatively subjective, leading to much more uncertainty in evaluating their risks and closing them out in default where the underlying market may be very illiquid.

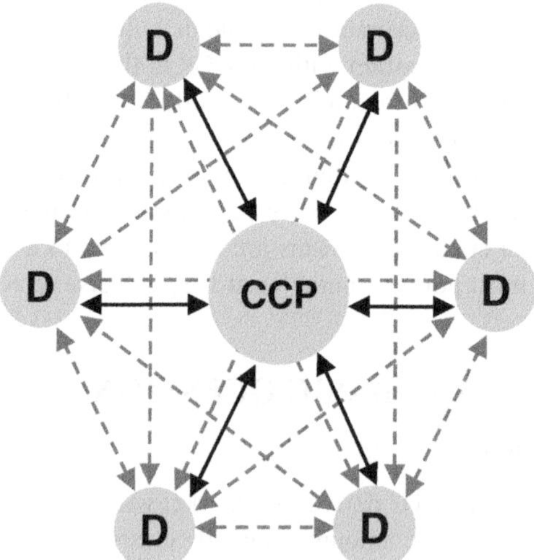

Figure 3.5 Illustration of a centrally cleared market with bilateral transactions still existing between members (D). Solid lines represent CCP cleared trades and dotted lines bilateral ones.

At the current time, there are OTC derivatives that have been centrally cleared for some time (e.g. interest rate swaps), those that have been recently cleared (e.g. index credit default swaps), those that are on the way to being centrally cleared (e.g. interest rate swaptions, inflation swaps and single-name credit default swaps). Finally, there are of course products that are a long way away and indeed may never be centrally cleared (e.g. Asian options, Bermudan swaptions and interest rate swaps involving illiquid currencies).

Since it is likely that a material proportion of OTC derivatives will not be centrally cleared, it is relevant to re-draw the simplistic diagram showing the potential bilateral connections that exist for non-cleared trades (Figure 3.5).

3.3.2 Who can clear?

Only clearing members can transact directly with a CCP. Becoming a clearing member involves meeting a number of requirements and will not be possible for all parties. Generally, these requirements fall into the following categories:

- *Admission criteria:* CCPs have various admission requirements such as credit rating strength (e.g. triple-B minimum) and requirements that members have a sufficiently large capital base (e.g. US$50 million).
- *Financial commitment:* Members must contribute to the CCP's default fund. Whilst such contributions will be partly in line with the trading activity, there may be a minimum commitment and it is likely that only institutions intending to execute a certain volume of trades will consider this default fund contribution worthwhile.
- *Operational:* Being a member of a CCP has a number of operational requirements associated to it. One is the frequent posting of liquid margin and others are the requirement to participate in 'fire drills' which simulate the default of a member, and auctions in the event a member does indeed default.

The impact of the above is that large global banks and some other very large financial institutions are likely to be clearing members whereas smaller banks, buy side and other financial firms, and other non-financial end users are unlikely to be direct clearing members. Large global banks will fulfill their role as prime brokers by being members of multiple CCPs globally so as to offer a full choice of clearing services to their clients. Large regional banks may be members of only a local CCP so as to support domestic clearing services for their clients.

Institutions that are not CCP members, so-called non-clearing members ('clients'), can clear through a clearing member. This can work in two ways: so-called principal-to-principal or agency methods (section 11.1.2 and 11.1.3 respectively). The general rule, though, is that the client effectively has a direct bilateral relationship with their clearing member and not the CCP. Clients will generally still have to post margin, but will not be required to contribute to the CCP default fund. Clearing members will charge their clients (explicitly and implicitly) for the clearing service that they provide, which will include elements such as the subsidisation of the default fund. The position of clearing members to their clients is still bilateral and so would normally be unchanged. However, it is likely that clearing members will partially 'mirror' CCP requirements in their bilateral client relationships, for example in relation to margin posting.

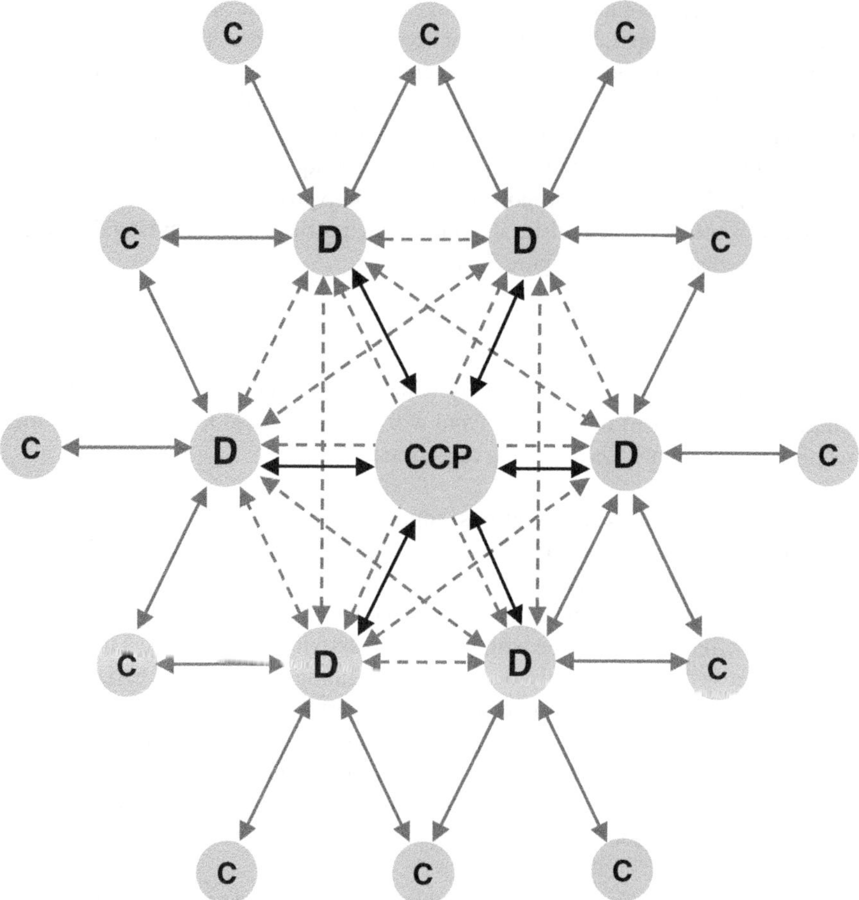

Figure 3.6 Illustration of a centrally cleared market, including the position of non-clearing members (C) who clear through clearing members (D).

Updating the CCP landscape to include non-clearing members leads to the illustration shown in Figure 3.6. It is important to note that non-clearing members (C) will likely have relationships with more than one clearing member.

Many questions arise regarding the risks that clients face in this clearing structure. What is key in this respect is the way in which margin posted by the client is passed through to the clearing member, and/or the CCP, and how it is segregated. Depending on this, it is possible for the client to have risk to the CCP, their clearing member, or their clearing member together with other clients of their clearing member. Another closely related question is one of 'portability', which refers to a client being able to transfer ('port') their positions to another clearing member (for example in the event of default by their original clearing member). These issues are covered in more depth in Chapter 11.

It is often stated that CCPs will reduce the interconnections between institutions, especially those that are systemically important. However, as seen in Figure 3.6, CCPs will rather change the connections – potentially in a favourable way, of course.

3.3.3 How many OTC CCPs will there be?

A large number of CCPs will maximise competition but could lead to a race to the bottom in terms of cost, leading to a much more risky CCP landscape. Having a small number of CCPs is beneficial in terms of offsetting benefits and economies of scale. Whilst a single global CCP is clearly optimal for a number of reasons, it seems likely that the total number of CCPs will be relatively large. This is due to bifurcation on two levels:

- *Regional.* Major geographical regions view it as important to have their own 'local' CCPs, either to clear trades denominated in their own currency or all trades executed for financial institutions in that region. Indeed, regulators in some regions require that financial institutions under their supervision clear using their own regional CCP.
- *Product.* CCPs clearing OTC derivatives have tended to act as vertical structures and specialise in certain product types (e.g. interest rate swaps or credit default swaps) and thus there is no complete solution of one CCP that can offer coverage of every clearable product.

An illustration of the impact of multiple CCPs is shown in Figure 3.7. A key feature is that clearing members of one CCP may well be members of another also. Additionally, there may be a need for *interoperability* between CCPs. Interoperability may be important to circumvent regulatory requirements such as two regulators requiring trades to be cleared through regional CCPs. It may also improve the efficiency of clearing by recognising offsetting positions between CCPs, leading, for example, to lower margin requirements. However, interoperability will increase interconnectedness in financial markets, potentially increasing systemic risk.

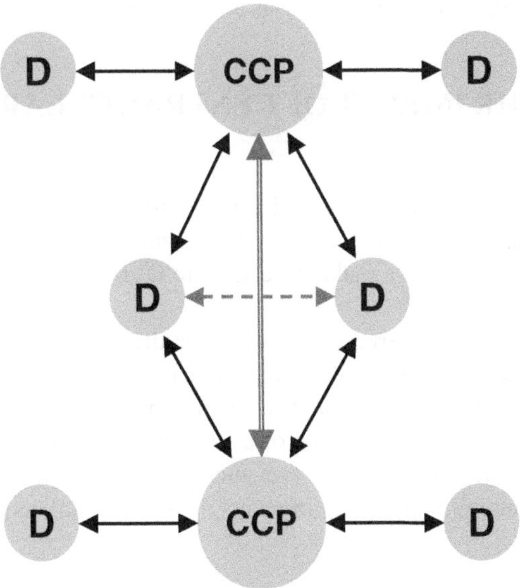

Figure 3.7 Illustration of a centrally cleared market with two CCPs. The dotted line represents bilateral trades. Interoperability between the CCPs is also shown.

3.3.4 Utilities or profit-making organisations?

Clearing trades obviously has an associated cost. CCPs cover this cost by charging fees per trade and by deriving interest from margins they hold. As fundamental market infrastructures and nodes of the financial system, CCPs clearly need to be resilient, especially during major financial disturbances. This may imply that a utility CCP driven by long-term stability and not short-term profits may be a preferable business model. However, it could also be argued that CCPs will need to have the best personnel and systems to be able to develop the advanced risk management and operational capabilities. Moreover, competition between CCPs will benefit users and provide choice. Expertise and competition implies that CCPs should be profit-making organisations. Clearly, this introduces a risk of a possible race to the bottom with respect to certain practices (e.g. margin calculations) that could increase the risk posed by CCPs.

3.3.5 Can CCPs fail?

The failure of a large and complex CCP, such as one clearing many OTC derivatives, would represent an event potentially worse than the failure of financial institutions such as Lehman Brothers. Furthermore, a bailout of a CCP could be a more complex and sizable task than even bailouts of banks and financial institutions such as Bear Stearns and AIG. CCPs must therefore maintain financial resources, such as initial margins and default funds, to absorb losses in all but extreme situations. In such extreme situations, CCPs need to have loss allocation methods (Chapter 10) that aim to absorb losses beyond their financial resources in a manner that does not create or exasperate systemic market disturbances. Of course, it is still a possibility that a CCP's financial resources may be breached, and they are unable to recover via some loss allocation process. In such a situation, the provision of liquidity support from a central bank must be considered. Regulators seem to accept that systemically important CCPs would need such support although only as a last resort.[3]

3.4 THE IMPACT OF CENTRAL CLEARING

3.4.1 General points

Although later chapters will make a more in-depth analysis of the strengths and weaknesses of central clearing, it is useful to discuss some of the general advantages and disadvantages of OTC CCPs now. Important points to make in relation to OTC central clearing are:

- A CCP is not a panacea for the perceived problems in the OTC derivatives market.
- A CCP does not make counterparty risk disappear. What it does is centralise it and convert it into different forms of financial risk such as operational and liquidity.
- As with most things, for every advantage of a CCP, there are related disadvantages. For example, CCPs can *reduce* systemic risk (via auctions for example) but can also *increase* it (for example by changing margin requirements in volatile markets).

[3] For example, see 'BoE's Carney: liquidity support for CCPs is a "last-resort" option', Risk, November 2013, http://www.risk.net/risk-magazine/news/2309908/boes-carney-liquidity-support-for-ccps-is-a-last-resort-option.

- CCPs provide a variety of functions, most of which can already be achieved by bilateral markets via other mechanisms. CCPs may or may not execute redundant functions more efficiently and CCP-specific functionality offers advantages and disadvantages.
- Central clearing may be beneficial overall for some markets but not others.
- There are likely to be unintended consequences of the expanded use of CCPs, which are hard to predict a priori.
- Like any financial institution, CCPs can fail, and indeed there are historical CCP insolvencies from which to learn (Chapter 14).

3.4.2 Comparing OTC and centrally cleared markets

Table 3.1 compares OTC markets with CCP and exchange-based ones. In CCP markets, whilst trades are still executed bilaterally, there are many differences that are required by central clearing, such as the need for standardisation, margining practices and the use of mutualised default funds to cover losses. Exchange-traded markets are similar to CCP ones except that in the former case the trade is executed on the exchange rather than beginning life as a bilateral trade.

3.4.3 Advantages of CCPs

CCPs offer many advantages and potentially offer a more transparent, safer market where contracts are more fungible and liquidity is enhanced. The following is a summary of the advantages of a CCP:

- *Transparency:* A CCP is in a unique position to understand the positions of market participants. This may disperse panic that might otherwise be present in bilateral markets due to a lack of knowledge of the exposure faced by institutions. If a member has a particularly extreme exposure, the CCP is in a position to act on this and limit trading (for example by charging larger margins).
- *Offsetting:* As mentioned above, contracts transacted between different counterparties but traded through a CCP can be offset. This increases the flexibility to enter new transactions and terminate existing ones, and reduces costs.

Table 3.1 Comparing OTC derivatives markets with CCP and exchange-traded markets.

	OTC	CCP	Exchange
Trading	Bilateral	Bilateral	Centralised
Counterparty	Original	CCP	
Products	All	Must be standard, vanilla, liquid, etc.	
Participants	All	Clearing members are usually large dealers Other margin posting entities can clear through clearing members	
Margining	Bilateral, bespoke arrangements dependent on credit quality and open to disputes	Full margining, including initial margin enforced by CCP	
Loss buffers	Regulatory capital and margin (where provided)	Initial margins, default funds and CCP own capital	

- *Loss mutualisation:* Even when a default creates losses that exceed the financial commitments from the defaulter, these losses are distributed throughout the CCP members, reducing their impact on any one member. Thus a counterparty's losses are dispersed partially throughout the market, making their impact less dramatic and reducing the possibility of systemic problems.
- *Legal and operational efficiency:* The margining, netting and settlement functions undertaken by a CCP potentially increase operational efficiency and reduce costs. CCPs may also reduce legal risks in providing a centralisation of rules and mechanisms.
- *Liquidity:* A CCP may improve market liquidity through the ability of market participants to trade easily and benefit from multilateral netting. Market entry may be enhanced through the ability to trade anonymously and through the mitigation of counterparty risk. Daily margining may lead to a more transparent valuation of products.
- *Default management:* A well-managed central auction may result in smaller price disruptions than the uncoordinated replacement of positions during a crisis period associated with default of a clearing member.

3.4.4 Disadvantages of CCPs

A CCP, by its very nature, represents a membership organisation, which therefore results in the pooling of member resources to some degree. This means that any losses due to the default of a CCP member may to some extent be shared amongst the surviving members, and this lies at the heart of some potential problems. The following is a summary of the disadvantages of a CCP:

- *Moral hazard:* This is a well-known problem in the insurance industry. Moral hazard has the effect of disincentivising good counterparty risk management practice by CCP members (since all the risk is passed to the CCP). Institutions have little incentive to monitor each other's credit quality and act appropriately because a third party is taking most of the risk.
- *Adverse selection:* CCPs are also vulnerable to adverse selection, which occurs if members trading OTC derivatives know more about the risks than the CCP themselves. In such a situation, firms may selectively pass these more risky products to CCPs that under-price the risks. Obviously, firms such as large banks specialise in OTC derivatives and may have superior information and knowledge on pricing and risk than a CCP.
- *Bifurcations:* The requirement to clear standard products may create unfortunate bifurcations between cleared and non-cleared trades. This can result in highly volatile cashflows for customers, and mismatches (of margin requirements) for seemingly hedged positions.
- *Procyclicality:* Procyclicality refers to a positive dependence with the state of the economy. CCPs may create procyclicality effects by, for example, increasing margins (or haircuts) in volatile markets or crisis periods. The greater frequency and liquidity of margin requirements under a CCP (compared with less uniform and more flexible margin practices in bilateral OTC markets) could also aggravate procyclicality.

3.4.5 Impact of central clearing

Some of the impacts of central clearing are difficult to assess since they may represent both advantages and disadvantages depending on the products and markets in question. There are also aspects in which CCPs may be considered to increase and decrease various financial risks. For example, it is often stated that CCPs will reduce systemic risk. They can clearly do this by providing greater transparency, offsetting positions and dealing with a large default in an effective way. However, they also have the potential to increase systemic risk, for example by increasing margins in turbulent markets. Overall, in accordance with a sort of conservation of risk principal, CCPs will not so much reduce counterparty risk but rather distribute it and convert it into different forms such as liquidity, operational and legal risks. CCPs also concentrate these risks in a single place and therefore magnify the systemic risk linked to their own potential failure.

OTC derivative clearing is fundamentally different from the clearing of other financial transactions (such as spot market securities or forward contracts). Unlike these contracts, which are completed in a few days, OTC derivative contracts (for example, swaps), remain outstanding for potentially years or even decades before being settled. It is not completely obvious that CCPs are as effective in risk mitigation for these longer-dated, more complex and illiquid products. In addition, central clearing for non-standard and/or exotic OTC derivatives may not be feasible. OTC markets have proved over the years that they are a good source of financial innovation and can continue to offer cost-effective and well-tailored risk reduction products. They are also likely to remain important in the future at providing incentives for innovation. There is a risk that mandatory central clearing has a negative impact on the positive role that OTC derivatives play.

A final point to note is that even if CCPs make OTC derivatives safer, this does not necessarily translate into more stable financial markets in general. The mechanisms used by a CCP, such as netting and margining, protect OTC derivative counterparties at the expense of other creditors. Furthermore, a CCP's beneficial position in being able to define their own rules and having preferential treatment with respect to aspects such as bankruptcy laws comes at a detriment to other parties. These distributive effects of central clearing are often overlooked. It is also important to note that financial markets have a tendency to adjust rapidly, especially in response to a significant regulatory mandate. It might be argued that CCPs can make OTC derivative markets safer. However, even if this is true then it cannot be extrapolated to imply that they will definitely enhance financial market stability in general.

4

The Global Financial Crisis and the Clearing of OTC Derivatives

I view derivatives as time bombs, both for the parties that deal in them and the economic system.
Warren Buffett (1930–) (quote from 2002)

4.1 THE GLOBAL FINANCIAL CRISIS

4.1.1 Build-up

The causes of the global financial crisis (GFC) were complex and related to a mixture of macroeconomic events, government policies, the relaxation of lending standards by financial institutions and the failure of regulation. However, many attach the most significant amount of blame to the very existence of over-the-counter (OTC) derivatives.

In 2008, the global derivatives market reached a total notional of over seven hundred trillion US dollars (Figure 2.4). Around nine tenths of this amount was over-the-counter (OTC), dwarfing exchange-traded products. In hindsight, this has been viewed as creating a dangerous mix of complexity, leverage and interconnectedness. This is perhaps epitomised by the rapid growth of credit derivatives during the period leading up to the GFC.

Another problem was that banks trading the majority of these OTC derivatives were very large as a result of a period of mergers and takeovers. Examples include Citigroup (Citicorp, Travellers Group, Smith Barney, Salomon Brothers), J.P. Morgan Chase & Co. (Chase Manhattan, Bank One), and Royal Bank of Scotland (ABN AMRO). Furthermore, other large financial firms, notably American International Group (AIG), had effectively become very exposed to the OTC derivatives market. This market was large, complex, opaque and only lightly regulated.

4.1.2 Impact of the GFC

Over the course of the GFC, governments had no easy way of dealing with financial institutions whose failure could trigger the collapse of other firms through the OTC derivatives market. Central banks such as the Federal Reserve and Bank of England were forced to manage the systemic risk posed by such institutions on an ad hoc and trial and error basis. To prevent cascading defaults, viewed as possibly leading to a breakdown of the entire financial system, governments facilitated the sale of some large financial institutions (e.g. Bear Stearns, HBOS), and injected capital into many others (e.g. Bank of America, Royal Bank of Scotland, AIG). Whilst such actions were undesirable, the aftermath of the bankruptcy of Lehman Brothers provided ample evidence as to the potential impact of not rescuing stricken large financial firms.

The problems governments faced were not just that large financial institutions were 'too big to fail' but also that they were 'too interconnected to fail'. This interconnectedness was largely blamed on the OTC derivatives market. Regulators therefore believed that the GFC events demonstrated the obvious need to develop a clear regulatory framework to efficiently manage the systemic risk posed by this market and its participants.

4.1.3 CCPs in the GFC

It is important to note that even before the GFC, some OTC derivatives were being centrally cleared (most notably interest rate swaps). Despite OTC derivatives being at the centre of the financial chaos during the GFC, one area of this market did seem to be functioning well. Even the Lehman Brothers bankruptcy did not cause huge problems for central counterparties (CCPs) such as LCH.Clearnet (US$9 trillion notional Lehman portfolio) and Depository Trust and Clearing Corporation (DTCC) (US$500 million notional Lehman portfolio). CCPs acted quickly (within hours) to suspend insolvent Lehman entities from trading and therefore prevented the build-up of more risk. On the other hand, solvent Lehman entities were also identified and continued trading. The CCPs also swiftly facilitated the transfer of solvent client accounts to other clearing members. In general, the response by CCPs provided stability and safety to Lehman counterparties and clients in cleared markets. In the CCP world, this prevented knock-on systemic effects due to the bankruptcy of a major OTC derivatives player.

Most of the products dealt with by CCPs in the aftermath of the Lehman bankruptcy were the more traditionally central cleared ones. However, there was also a significant notional amount of OTC derivatives, which were dealt with relatively easily.

4.1.4 LCH.Clearnet and SwapClear

The best and most commonly cited example of the benefits of CCPs for OTC derivatives is LCH.Clearnet's London-based SwapClear service, which provided interest-rate swap central clearing for 20 large banks including Lehman. The total SwapClear portfolio exceeded US$100 trillion notional across 14 currencies,[1] and represented close to half the global interest rate swap market at the time. LCH.Clearnet had previously experienced defaults, such as Drexel Burnham Lambert (1990) and Barings (1995), however, the Lehman failure became the biggest default in CCP history.

At SwapClear, Lehman Brothers Special Financing Inc. (LBSF) was a big player, with a US$9 trillion OTC portfolio comprising tens of thousands of trades, which was much larger than the exchange-traded portfolios of Lehman. On 15 September 2008, LBSF did not transfer margin payments and was therefore declared in default within hours. The goal now was for LCH.Clearnet to close out the large OTC portfolio (66,390 trades) as quickly as possible without creating large losses or knock-on effects. To help achieve this, LCH.Clearnet had a substantial amount (around US$2 billion) of initial margin from Lehman that was held precisely for such a situation.

The events at LCH.Clearnet 's SwapClear clearing service in the aftermath of the Lehman default were:

[1] LCH.Clearnet annual report 2007.

- As required by CCP rules, clearing members were obliged (on a rotational basis) to offer representatives to assist LCH in dealing with the defaulted member. LCH.Clearnet formed a default management group with senior traders from a total of six banks in order to assist in the close out process.
- In the first couple of days, hedges were applied to neutralise the macro-level market risk in Lehman's portfolio. The risk positions were reviewed daily and further hedges were executed in response to the changing portfolio and underlying market conditions.
- The majority of Lehman client positions were transferred to other solvent clearing members within the first week.
- Auctions were arranged to sell Lehman portfolios (together with their macro-hedges) to the remaining SwapClear members. Under the CCPs rules, members had to be involved in the auction. These auctions were arranged in each of the five relevant currencies between Wednesday 24 September and Friday 3 October. All auctions were deemed successful.

The events were hailed as a success by LCH.Clearnet[2] and required only around a third of the initial margin, with the rest being returned to the Lehman administrators.

It should be noted that the Lehman close out was not without its problems. In some cases, a client's margins were returned to the administrator and frozen for many months (this was partly related to poor record keeping by Lehman and partly due to UK law, which did not have requirements over customer segregation that existed in the US). Indeed, even getting access to Lehman's offices was not immediately possible (Norman 2011).

4.1.5 Lehman and other CCPs

Despite the general success of LCH's SwapClear with respect to the bankruptcy of Lehman, there were some negative implications involving other CCPs. The Chicago Mercantile Exchange (CME) cleared a combination of interest rate, equity, agriculture, energy and FX positions for Lehman and had to rely on gains from three of these asset classes to offset losses on the two others (Pirrong 2013). Furthermore, there are suggestions that the three winning bidders in the CME auction for Lehman positions made a combined profit of US$1.2 billion on taking over the portfolios (see later discussion in section 10.2.1).

Also regarding the Lehman bankruptcy, in December 2008, Hong Kong Exchanges and Clearing Ltd (HKEx) disclosed a loss of HK$157 million in relation to the portfolio of Lehman Brothers Securities Asia (LBSA) being closed out by the Hong Kong Securities Clearing Company (HKSCC). As a result of this, HKSCC needed to draw on resources including their HK$394 million default fund and call for additional default fund contributions from their most active members. In contrast to the SwapClear story, this should be viewed as a partial failure since clearing members suffered losses via their default fund contributions.

It is important to consider how much hindsight bias may be associated with the CCP handling of the Lehman bankruptcy. Could a CCP cope with a Lehman-like default in a situation where many more OTC derivatives (such as the credit derivatives that played a significant role in their downfall) had been cleared? One thing is indisputable: centrally cleared OTC derivatives markets functioned much better than bilateral ones during the GFC. However, due to the type and quantity of OTC products cleared, this is perhaps not completely surprising.

[2] LCH.Clearnet Press Release, '$9 trillion Lehman OTC interest rate swap default successfully resolved', http://www.lchclearnet.com/images/2008-10-08%20swapclear%20default_tcm6-46506.pdf.

4.1.6 Responses

Prior to events of the GFC there was no obvious push by regulators for CCPs. However, from the rescue of Bear Stearns onwards, calls for central clearing started to emerge from regulators globally. In the US, market participants and regulators agreed an agenda[3] for bringing about further improvements in the OTC derivatives market infrastructure, one of the points being 'developing a central counterparty for credit default swaps that, with a robust risk-management regime can help reduce systemic risk'. A statement from the European Commission[4] described a CCP for credit default swaps as a 'pressing need'. The Lehman events of September 2008 gave further weight to such viewpoints. The rationale behind the clearing requirement seemed to be that systemic risk in the GFC was exacerbated by counterparty risk concerns that could be mitigated by CCPs.

CCPs were being seen as a kind of OTC derivatives market 'shock absorber' in the event of the default of one or more market participants, as they would allow such an event to be managed with the least disruption. A key problem in such situations was the need to replace large numbers of defaulted positions within a short time in an illiquid market. Such a requirement can clearly lead to large price moves together with increased volatilities and dependencies. In turn, the price shocks arising from the rush to replace defaulted trades can impose substantial losses that can threaten the solvency of other market participants. CCPs widely became seen as the solution to such problems by providing greater transparency and reducing risk via their margining practices. CCPs could establish and enforce the 'rules' for the OTC derivatives market.

In 2009, the G20 leaders agreed in Pittsburg (G20 2009) to require:

- All standardised OTC derivatives should be traded on exchanges or electronic platforms.
- Central clearing of standardised OTC derivatives.
- Reporting of OTC derivatives to trade repositories.
- Higher capital requirements for non-centrally-cleared OTC derivatives.

Whilst much of the initial discussion and research on risks associated with OTC derivatives was focused on credit derivatives (via credit default swaps), the clearing mandate had now been broadened to cover the whole OTC derivatives market. This was perhaps not surprising[5] since credit derivatives made up less than one tenth of the overall notional OTC derivatives market.

One could ask why, if clearing was such a panacea for OTC derivatives, it had not been particularly well developed prior to the GFC (except the case of the interest rate swap market and SwapClear). An obvious reason is that public policy intervention on clearing is required on the basis that private incentives for clearing are weak. Another is, of course, that CCPs will not definitely make OTC derivatives markets safer.

[3] Federal Reserve Bank of New York (9 June 2008), 'Statement regarding June 9 meeting on over-the-counter derivatives', http://www.newyorkfed.org/newsevents/news/markets/2008/ma080609.html.

[4] European Commission (17 October 2008), 'Statement of Commissioner McGreevy on reviewing derivatives markets before the end of the year'.

[5] Although other theories have been forwarded, for example see http://latimesblogs.latimes.com/money_co/2010/03/chris-dodds-wife-and-her-strange-entanglement-with-derivatives-trading-.html.

4.1.7 Objections

Not surprisingly, given that regulation will catalyse substantial OTC CCP growth, there has been criticism of the regulatory requirement to clear standardised OTC derivatives. The arguments generally fall into two groups. The first is related to the potentially prohibitive costs of central clearing, whilst the second questions whether CCPs will actually make financial markets any safer in the long term. We consider these issues separately below.

There are a number of assessments of the cost impact of central clearing. One early estimate (Singh and Aitken 2009b and Singh 2010) was that moving risk to CCPs will require posting sizable extra margin of up to US$2 trillion (although the figure may vary depending on the assumptions made). More direct effects have been postulated by, for example, a survey[6] in 2010 which found that three quarters of respondents believed that margin requirements would have a significant impact on their hedging activities. This survey also estimated that 'a 3% OTC derivative margin requirement might be expected to eliminate approximately 100,000 to 120,000 jobs economy wide'.

The view that clearing would be expensive is seemingly disputed by certain studies. For example, Heller and Vause (2012) report that 'Initial margin requirements of CCPs that cleared all of G14 dealers' IRS or CDS positions would only amount to a small proportion of the dealers' unencumbered assets.' However, even if dealers do not find clearing costs significant then other market participants such as pension funds may.

Counterparty risk in OTC derivatives markets is generally under-margined due to certain counterparties posting no or only partial margin against their positions, and quite commonly using illiquid assets for margins. These counterparties are most often the so-called 'end users' of OTC derivatives such as corporates, asset managers, pension funds, hedge funds, multilateral development banks and governments. A key argument often made is that they are often hedging (as opposed to speculating) and therefore are not embarking on behaviour that is overall detrimental to financial markets. Furthermore, if derivatives contracts become more standardised then they are potentially less useful for hedging (for example, not qualifying for hedge accounting). Such arguments imply that end users should be exempt from certain rules intended for institutions more central to the functioning of OTC derivative markets.

Specific comments from end users of OTC derivatives include the Foreign Currency Risk Manager for 3M Company stating that '…robust margin requirements would create substantial incremental liquidity and administrative burdens for commercial users, resulting in higher financing and operational costs. Capital currently deployed in growth opportunities would need to be maintained in a clearinghouse. This could result in slower job creation, lower capital expenditures, less R&D and/or higher costs to consumers'.[7] Other corporate end users (e.g. Caterpillar and Boeing in US, Luftansa and EADS in Europe) warned that mandatory clearing would make their commercial hedging programmes impractical due to intolerable pricing which was unreasonable since such hedging did not pose systemic risk.

In January 2010, the European Association of Corporate Treasurers[8] submitted an Open Letter to the Commissioners of the European Union stating that: 'We are deeply concerned

[6] Keybridge Research, 'An analysis of the business roundtable's survey on over-the-counter derivatives', 14 April 2010, http://businessroundtable.org/uploads/studies-reports/downloads/An_Analysis_of_the_Business_Roundtables_Survey_on_Over-the-Counter_Derivatives.pdf.

[7] Murphy, Timothy, 2009, Testimony to the House Financial Services Subcommittee on Capital Markets, Insurance, and Government-Sponsored Enterprises, Hearing on the Effective Regulation of the Over-the-Counter Derivatives Markets, Statement for the Record, 9 June.

[8] European Association of Corporate Treasurers, 'Ensuring efficient, safe and sound derivatives markets', 6 January 2010, http://www.dact.nl/upload/file/EACTlettertoEUregOTC.pdf.

by some of the proposed reforms to the OTC derivatives market currently being considered, in that they will disadvantage many end users who rely on OTC derivatives to hedge underlying commercial exposures.'

The end user complaints, such as those quoted above, have led to certain exemptions, which are discussed in more detail below.

Regarding the question of whether CCPs will actually make financial markets safer, it is important to note that futures and other exchange-traded derivatives are generally short-term (weeks to months) and they tend to be highly liquid. On the contrary, OTC derivatives tend to be more long-dated (up to decades) and relatively illiquid. This means that an OTC CCP will have to take much longer-dated and illiquid credit exposure to its members. In general, it is this large difference that it cited as an obvious problem for CCPs clearing OTC derivatives (as opposed to traditional CCPs), particularly significant points being:

- Most major OTC CCPs members are likely to be large systemically important banks and any default will therefore be highly significant.
- In stressed conditions, closing out a large OTC derivatives portfolio could take a long time and suffer from poor market conditions and illiquidity.
- Initial margin and default fund contributions for OTC derivatives are much more difficult to define due to the greater complexity and illiquidity of the underlying products.

A very commonly cited paper on OTC central clearing by Duffie and Zhu (2011) shows that having multiple CCPs for a single asset class (as according to the landscape for CCP clearing of CDS in the US and Europe for example) reduces netting efficiency, and therefore may increase exposure in the event of default (see section 5.2.6). The possibility of having bifurcated 'split netting sets' between clearable and non-clearable trades leads also to this possibility, especially since many more complex OTC products are often hedged with less exotic and potentially clearable products. Since multilateral netting at a CCP was often cited as reducing systemic risk, then presumably this splitting of netting sets by CCPs might also increase systemic risk. Reducing netting benefits would also lead to higher initial margin requirements.

The criticisms highlighted above are not changing the general direction on OTC clearing, although they are leading to exemptions and may have contributed to a general slowdown of the clearing mandate timescales. A more detailed discussion of these and other possible weaknesses of central clearing for OTC derivatives can be found in Chapter 14.

4.2 REGULATORY CHANGES

Over the years, OTC derivatives have given institutional investors, corporates, sovereigns and supranationals a flexible tool for hedging a large range of risks and the market has grown to be very large. Critics have accused the OTC derivatives market of triggering and amplifying the GFC, and accordingly, regulators have proposed a number of initiatives aimed at making it safer. Chief among such initiatives are the Dodd–Frank Act in the US and the European Market Infrastructures Regulation (EMIR) in European Union (EU). The two are similar in the way they treat OTC derivatives, particularly in terms of aspects such as reducing systemic risk and improving transparency. Both the EU and US regimes aim to impose clearing and reporting on a broadly defined class of OTC derivatives (with differences for some asset classes) and give regulators the ultimate decision on when the clearing obligation applies.

Table 4.1 Comparison of clearing and related requirements in the US and Europe.

	US	**Europe**
Clearing requirements	Dodd–Frank	EMIR
Margin requirements	BCBS/IOSCO	Basel III/IOSCO
Capital requirements (for bilateral and CCP trades)	Basel III	

The key areas of legislation are clearing requirements, margin requirements and capital requirements. Table 4.1 characterises the relevant regulation in the US and Europe with respect to these aspects. Note that similar reforms are being put in place in other G20 countries and will likely be similar, although the US and Europe are not surprisingly ahead of other regions[9] where OTC derivatives markets are less significant.

4.2.1 Basel III

A requirement of the G20 Pittsburg commitments was that 'non-centrally cleared contracts should be subject to higher capital requirements'.

The Basel II capital rules in force at the time of the GFC were seen as dramatically undercapitalising banks and promoting dangerous behaviour such as regulatory arbitrage prior to the GFC. Defining the increased capital requirements is the job of the Basel Committee on Banking Supervision (BCBS), which did this as part of 'Basel III'.[10] Basel III proposed rules to dramatically increase capital by a combination of re-parameterisation of existing methods and addition of new requirements. Counterparty risk is a key focus for Basel III, with the view that the failure to adequately capture OTC derivatives exposure was a key factor in amplifying the GFC. In particular, the BCBS noted that only around one third of the counterparty risk was capitalised prior to the crisis. The remaining two thirds would be captured by a new credit value adjustment (CVA) capital charge to cover the mark-to-market of the counterparty risk of a bank. This would capture the potential losses when credit spreads widened, even in the absence of any actual defaults. Notably, the only exemption (under Basel III at least)[11] from the CVA capital charge for OTC derivatives trades was for those cleared with a central counterparty.

Other small changes to Basel III rules would increase counterparty risk capital requirements also, for example the so-called 'margin period of risk' used by advanced banks for computing capital requirements on margined transactions was increased in certain situations, basically reducing the benefit from a bilateral margin agreement. The overall total effect of Basel III is to increase a bank's capital requirements for counterparty risk by a significant factor, which clearly incentivises a push towards central clearing. This push is potentially made more relevant by the nature of the CVA capital charge, which penalises higher rated counterparties in particular,[12] and by the changes to the rules for margined counterparties.

[9] See, for example, Holes expected in South Africa's draft clearing rules, *Risk*, 14 March 2014, http://www.risk.net/risk-magazine/news/2334173/holes-expected-in-south-africa-s-draft-clearing-rules.

[10] Basel Committee on Banking Supervision, 'Basel III: A global regulatory framework for more resilient banks and banking systems – revised version June 2011', http://www.bis.org/publ/bcbs189.htm.

[11] In the EU, trades with sovereign and non-financial counterparties have been exempted under CRD IV, the implementation of Basel III. However, it seems likely that some local regulators may at least partially reverse this decision by requiring more capital to be held.

[12] Since the CVA capital charge is based on credit spread volatility and not default probability, the relative effect of a stronger rating is not as beneficial.

High-quality, margined counterparties are most likely to be other financial institutions, which are clearly the aim of the clearing mandate (compared to end users for example).

Regarding CCP exposures themselves, previously, derivatives contracts with a CCP were given a zero exposure under the so-called Basel II framework (2004), whereas a moderate risk weight of 2% is proposed under Basel III to reflect the fact that CCPs are not completely risk-free. However, default fund contributions to CCPs are recognised as being more risky and requiring a risk-sensitive charge. CCP capital charges will be discussed in more detail in section 10.4. The capital charges also depend on whether or not the CCP in question is qualifying or not. Qualifying CCPs (QCCPs) are recognised by local regulators as conforming to global principles and accordingly give rise to a lower capital charge than non-qualifying CCPs.

4.2.2 Dodd–Frank

On 21 July 2010, President Obama signed into law a major overhaul of US financial regulations known as the Dodd–Frank Act.[13] It was extremely tough towards banks and OTC derivatives and reflected resentment against Wall Street at a time of poor economic conditions for the people on 'Main Street', who had essentially been behind the bailouts of the previous three years.

OTC derivatives are the subject of a significant proportion of the 848 pages of Dodd–Frank. Title VII of Dodd–Frank requires that so-called swaps (although this is a general term that can apply to other OTC derivatives also) must be cleared. The CCP used for clearing must be regulated by the Commodity Futures Trading Commission (CFTC) or the Securities and Exchange Commission (SEC). Additionally, the trade must be executed electronically on an exchange or swap execution facility (SEF) and reported to a trade repository. Standardised OTC derivatives are not defined: this is left to the CFTC and SEC to decide as jointly responsible regulators. Of course, a product is not required to be centrally cleared until covered by at least one eligible CCP. Under Dodd–Frank, there is a potential exemption for commercial non-financial end users entering into certain hedging transactions. This applies to situations where one of the parties is a non-financial firm using the swap to hedge or reduce risk, provided that the firm notifies the CFTC or SEC and explains how it meets its financial obligations arising from the non-cleared swap.

The Dodd–Frank Act requires clients domiciled in the United States to clear through entities registered with the CFTC as FCMs (Futures Commission Merchants). Regulated FCMs can clear proprietary business, US domiciled client business and also non-US domiciled client business.

The CFTC released its first Mandatory Clearing Determination in November 2012, requiring mandatory clearing for certain interest rate swaps (fixed to floating, basis swaps, forward rate agreements, overnight index swaps) and credit default swaps (US CDX North American corporate indices and European iTraxx corporate indices). The implementation of the CFTC's clearing determination is progressing in three phases according to counterparty type (for example, major market participants are in Phase 1 and some pension funds are in Phase 3).

4.2.3 EMIR

The European equivalent of Dodd–Frank is the European Market Infrastructure Regulation (EMIR 2012). This requires that eligible OTC derivatives between covered counterparties are

[13] http://www.sec.gov/about/laws/wallstreetreform-cpa.pdf.

cleared through a CCP registered in Europe. It seems that eligibility would follow 'bottom-up', where CCPs may offer to clear certain products, and 'top-down', where regulators may decide which contracts should be cleared on the basis of systemic risk, liquidity and other material aspects. It would not be possible to avoid clearing by not being a clearing member, as such an institution would simply have to clear as a client of a clearing member.

The current guidelines require mandatory clearing between mid-2014 and mid-2015. As with Dodd–Frank, EMIR provides exemptions for non-financial end user transactions hedging risks directly related to their commercial activity. Specifically, the regulation applies only to transactions between financial counterparties, certain non-EU entities and non-financial counterparties whose positions (excluding certain hedges)[14] exceed a specified clearing threshold. Furthermore, pension funds have a specific exemption until 2015 (a 3-year exemption was granted in August 2012), which pension funds are pushing for an extension to.

4.2.4 Differences between the US and Europe

Dodd–Frank and EMIR are broadly similar in requiring clearing of all standardised OTC derivatives between most large users. Differences are important to characterise, not least because they raise the spectre of 'transatlantic arbitrage'. Under EMIR, the scope of clearing is slightly more relaxed for end users, with non-financial counterparties only obliged to clear if their positions exceed a specified clearing threshold (with certain hedges excluded from contributing to this threshold). In the US, the clearing obligation is absolute except for narrow exemptions for non-financial entities entering into certain hedging transactions. It could be questioned as to how easy it may be to identify hedging transactions (see section 13.2.3).

Another contentious area in Europe has been pension funds, which may use derivatives to hedge interest rate, inflation and longevity risks. Under EMIR, most pension funds will be allowed a three-year exemption[15] from the central clearing requirements. This is intended to avoid dramatic shifts that could force major changes in asset allocation and gives CCPs more time to develop models for the main pension scheme products, namely interest rate and particularly inflation derivatives. Note that pension funds are not exempt from the margin requirements discussed in section 4.2.5.

Table 4.2 compares the US and European requirements according to Dodd–Frank and EMIR respectively.

Table 4.2 Comparison of clearing requirements in the US and Europe.

	US	Europe
Dealers/banks	Yes	Yes
Other financials	Yes	Yes (pensions funds 3-year exemption)
Non-financials	Can obtain exemption for transactions hedging commercial risk	Only above certain thresholds (to which certain hedges don't contribute)

[14] Contracts 'entered into to cover the risks arising from an objectively measurable commercial activity' are not included when assessing whether the 'clearing threshold' has been breached.

[15] Pension funds which are 'institutions for occupational retirement provision' are exempt from central clearing requirements for at least the first three years from the date of entry into force of the new regulation, for OTC derivative contracts which are 'objectively measurable as reducing investment risks directly relating to the financial solvency of pension scheme arrangements'.

Other differences that will exist between the US and Europe relate to client clearing. In Europe, client clearing follows a 'principal-to-principal' model where the CCP has a bilateral relationship with each clearing member, who in turn has a bilateral relationship with clients for whom they clear. In contrast, the US model is an extension of the way that US futures markets have traditionally operated, where a Futures Commission Merchant (FCM) acts as an agent to introduce a client to the CCP and guarantees the client's margin and other obligations to the CCP. This is discussed in more detail in Chapter 11.

Related to clearing, the US regime requires the execution of OTC derivatives subject to the clearing obligation on a Swap Execution Facility (SEF) and requires real time post-trade transparency. In the EU, these issues are being addressed separately as part of the legislative proposals as part of the Markets in Financial Instruments Directive (MiFID).

Both the Dodd–Frank Act and the proposed EU regulation seek to allow cross-border clearing by permitting the recognition or exemption of non-domestic CCPs. Under both sets of regulation, 'backloading' (transactions entered into before the regulations are in effect) is optional. However, 'frontloading' where a trade is deemed clearable during its lifetime may be a problem (see section 4.2.6). Finally, both the EU and US regimes envisage that there will be mandatory margin rules for non-standard OTC derivatives that are not centrally clearable. These rules are discussed next.

4.2.5 Bilateral margin requirements

Following the previous 2009 agreements described in section 4.1.6, in November 2011 in Cannes the G20 leaders agreed to add a mandate for margin requirements for non-centrally cleared derivatives, stating:

> We call on the Basel Committee on Banking Supervision (BCBS), the International Organization for Securities Commission (IOSCO) together with other relevant organizations to develop for consultation standards on margining for non-centrally cleared OTC derivatives by June 2012, and on the FSB [Financial Stability Board] to continue to report on progress towards meeting our commitments on OTC derivatives.

The BCBS and IOSCO accordingly produced a consultative paper (BCBS-IOSCO 2012) on the subject of bilateral margin requirements.

The Working Group on Margin Requirements (WGMR) was formed in October 2011 to develop the framework for margins. The WGMR is run jointly by the IOSCO, the BCBS, the Committee on Payment and Settlement Systems (CPSS) and the Committee on the Global Financial System (CGFS).

Margin requirements will apply to both variation and initial margins. Since variation margin is quite common already in the OTC derivatives market (with the obvious exception of end users), these requirements can be seen as tightening practices. Initial margins, which are uncommon in bilateral OTC derivative markets, will create a more significant impact. An obvious interpretation of margin rules is to align bilateral practices more closely with those at CCPs. This will obviously reduce any incentive that might exist to make products non-standard so as to avoid the clearing mandate.

Initial margins are intended, like higher capital charges and central clearing, to reduce systemic risk and seem to have been introduced due to the fact that a large fraction of OTC derivatives will not be centrally cleared. It could be questioned as to why initial margins are required for non-clearable OTC derivatives that would be more heavily capitalised under Basel III. BCBS-IOSCO explain the reasons for initial margin over capital as being:

- Initial margin follows a 'defaulter pays' approach rather than a 'survivor pays' one and therefore does not consume the financial resources of surviving entities.
- Initial margin is more 'targeted' to a specific portfolio and is furthermore adjusted over time to reflect changes in the risk of that portfolio in market conditions.

Initial margins, in terms of amount and liquidity, will be broadly in line with those required by CCPs and therefore they can be seen to promote central clearing and narrow the gap between the treatment of clearable and non-clearable OTC derivatives.

The finalising of initial margin requirements (BCBS-IOSCO 2013b) are discussed in more detail in Chapter 11, but the key requirements are outlined below:

- Variation margin should be taken to reflect current exposure with no threshold (a threshold as described in section 6.3.3 represents an amount below which margin is not exchanged).
- Initial margin should be taken against the potential increase in exposure in the future, and should be calculated to cover a confidence level of (at least) 99%.
- A time horizon for close out of 10 days should be assumed where relevant.
- Margin must be accessible when needed, i.e. it must be segregated (this is presumed to apply to only initial margin although this is not yet clarified at the time of writing).
- Margin must be liquid: not just in normal market conditions but also in volatile periods, to the extent that it can be sold rapidly and predictably even in a time of financial stress.

All financial and systemically important non-financial entities must exchange margins for new contracts after the regulation comes into force (not existing contracts). The regulation is being phased in from 1 December 2015 (although this may be dependent on local regulators).

A key issue with initial margin requirements is segregation. Without any specific segregation (such as custodial or segregation agreement), a party having posted initial margin would essentially only be treated as an unsecured creditor in the event of default of the margin receiver. Since non-segregated initial margin leads to counterparty risk (in case the receiver defaults), then initial margin segregation is a key aspect (see section 6.2.3).

Like the requirements for clearing, there are objections over initial margin requirements (discussed in more detail in Chapter 13). These are based on the fact that posting initial margin, which has to be segregated, will be extremely costly and that margin rules may not reduce systemic risk due to the likelihood that they may increase sharply in crisis periods (procyclicality). One recent suggestion by dealers to reduce the burden of bilateral initial margin requirements is margin sharing. In such an arrangement, the two counterparties would post an amount to a custodian that covers the default of either of them. For example, if two counterparties were required to post initial margins to each other of 60 and 50 then they would post the maximum amount of 60 to the custodial account thereby saving almost half of the required total margin. If one party defaults then the surviving party would have access to the full amount in the custody account. Such an idea is not supported by the WGMR standards and so it remains to be seen if regulators allow this proposal.

4.2.6 Exemptions

To determine whether a given transaction must be cleared or subject to margin requirements then the following questions must be asked:

- Are both parties subject to mandatory clearing or margin requirements?
- Is the transaction itself subject to mandatory clearing or bilateral margining requirements?

If the answer to both the above questions is 'yes', then the transaction is subject to mandatory clearing or bilateral margining requirements. The above questions relate to a number of exemptions that are broadly similar across both clearing/margining requirements, and can relate to either the counterparties or transactions involved. The counterparty-related exemptions apply generally to end users undertaking hedging activities. However, the precise definitions are slightly different:

- *Clearing exemptions under US regulation (Dodd–Frank):* Exemptions for non-financial entities entering into transactions in order to hedge their commercial risk (such entities must notify the CFTC as to how they generally meet the financial obligations associated with non-cleared OTC derivatives).
- *Clearing exemptions under EU regulation (EMIR):* Non-financial counterparties are only obliged to clear if their positions exceed a specified clearing threshold (with certain hedges excluded from contributing to this threshold).
- *Bilateral margin exemptions (global guidelines via the Basel Committee and International Organization of Securities Commissions).* Covered entities are financial firms and systemically important non-financial entities. There is a threshold below which initial margins need not be posted (section 6.5.3).

A significant transaction-related exemption is that of certain FX products. Market participants lobbied hard to argue that FX represents a special case since contracts are generally short-dated, and existing market practice such as CLS (continuous linked settlement) reduces risk significantly already (see discussion in section 5.1.2 for a description of CLS functionality). The US Treasury has exempted FX swaps and forwards from the mandatory clearing requirements of Dodd–Frank. Physically settled FX forwards and swaps are also exempted from the BCBS-IOSCO initial (but not variation) margin requirements. This includes the FX exchange component of cross-currency swaps (i.e. a cross-currency swap will have an initial margin corresponding to only the interest rate swap component).

Despite the clearing exemption, some non-deliverable forwards (cash-settled FX forwards) have been cleared on a voluntary basis. However, physically settled FX products are creating problems due to regulatory requirements for gross settlement due to the inherent settlement risks which creates a significant liquidity cost.

There is continuing debate regarding the FX exemptions. For example, Duffie (2011) argues that, whilst many contracts are short-dated, some FX trades have significant counterparty risk due to the exchange of notional together with aspects such as the relatively high FX volatilities, fat tails and sovereign risk.

It is also important to note that the clearing and initial margin rules apply only to trades done after the regulation requiring these changes. Market participants can therefore decide voluntarily whether or not to 'backload' older trades to CCPs or post initial margins against them. One potential issue, however, arises with respect to 'frontloading' of CCP trades. Once a CCP has been authorised to do business in a given region then regulators will decide if product offerings from that CCP will lead to mandatory clearing of these products. However, trades executed in the time period between CCP authorisation and this decision would need to be cleared if their remaining maturity is above a threshold. This means that a bilateral transaction may later become subject to mandatory clearing, which introduces confusion as the costs of bilateral and cleared transactions are different. This will give market participants a difficult decision as, when pricing and executing the trades, they would be uncertain as to whether or not they would be hit by a clearing mandate in the future. Dealers are hoping the maturity threshold for frontloading will be sufficiently large to minimise the effect of frontloading.[16]

4.3 REGULATION OF CCPS

4.3.1 Problems with mandates

The problem with regulating financial products is that innovation is generally one step ahead of regulation, and regulation tends to solve the problem of the last crisis and not the next. This is not a criticism of regulation but simply a comment that it is impossible to consider all possible financial product innovations and potentially unintended consequences related to new regulation.

Given the clearing mandate, the regulation of CCPs themselves obviously then becomes a key issue. CCPs clearly need to be financially secure, especially in the context of taking ever more risk to relatively complex OTC derivatives. There also needs to be harmonisation across regions to avoid regulatory arbitrage by trading in jurisdictions with weakened requirements.

4.3.2 Oversight

It is worth emphasising that CCPs have generally performed well during the GFC. Nevertheless, the increased reliance on OTC CCPs in the future exposes the need for closer regulatory oversight, with international coordination. CCPs clearly need to have extremely sound infrastructure and risk management practices, especially as they become more critical failure points in the future. Some of the aspects that need to be considered with respect to the safety of a CCP, its members and their clients are:

- CCP ownership, governance, record keeping, disclosure, regulatory reporting, etc.
- CCP membership standards (designed to ensure creditworthiness of members but not to disincentivise competition).
- Standards for calculation of financial resources (initial margin, default funds) including identification of stress scenarios.
- Definitions of acceptable margin and haircuts that should be applied to non-cash margin.
- Procedure for default management.
- International recognition of a CCP.
- Local regulator recognition and supervision of CCPs in their region and potential recognition of CCPs outside the region.
- Rules on client clearing (portability and segregation).

[16] Emir frontloading: crunch talks due this week, *Risk*, 31 March 2014, http://www.risk.net/risk-magazine/news/2337146/crunch-talks-on-emir-frontloading-due-this-week.

- Rules of interoperability (linkages) between CCPs.
- Access to central bank liquidity.

Given the global nature of OTC derivatives markets and the fact that CCPs will operate internationally, there is a need for close cross-border coordination of regulation to avoid regulatory arbitrage and mitigate systemic risk. Operational procedures should be carefully implemented and, in particular, margining rules should be monitored extremely carefully.

The oversight of CCPs falls to the CPSS and the Technical Committee of the IOSCO. In 2004, following a consultative period, CPSS-IOSCO published a set of recommendations (CPSS-IOSCO 2004) for the practices of CCPs which covered aspects such as membership requirements, margin requirements, default procedures, operational risk and legal risk. Such recommendations, like those from the Basel Committee, are intended to represent international standards but are not legally binding.

Regulation of CCPs will fall on local regulators in the relevant region. For example, in the US, a CCP could be regulated by the CFTC or SEC depending on its legal status.

Following the GFC and the requirements for mandatory central clearing of standardised OTC derivatives, there was clearly a need to focus more on the practices of CCPs themselves. The aforementioned CPSS-IOSCO recommendations have been updated accordingly (CPSS-IOSCO 2012) as a set of 'new and more demanding' guidelines for 'financial markets infrastructures (FMIs)'. FMI is a term used to cover systemically important payment systems, central securities depositories, securities settlement systems, and trade repositories, as well as central counterparties. These principles are aimed to ensure that the global financial market is more robust and thus better placed to withstand financial shocks.

Some of the key points contained within the CPSS-IOSCO principles are summarised below:

- Type of margin:
  - Margins held should have low credit, liquidity and market risks.
  - Haircuts should be regularly tested and should account for stressed market conditions.
  - Holding concentrated assets as margins should be avoided.
- Variation margin calculation:
  - CCPs should have the capacity to mark-to-market and call for variation margin on a daily basis. They should also have the capability to make intra-daily margin calls.
  - Margins calculated should be sensitive to the risks of each product, portfolio and market.
  - Margin calculations should rely on timely data and have sound valuation models for when pricing data is not available.
- Initial margin calculation:
  - Initial margin should be calculated to cover the potential future exposure between the last margin collection and close out of the portfolio at a confidence level of at least 99%.
  - CCPs should be conservative in estimating the dependencies that determine offsets for different products accounting for correlations and also for estimating the time to close out portfolios.
  - Performance of initial margin models should be assessed via backtesting.
- Default funds:
  - A CCP that is involved in complex activities or is systemically important should maintain additional financial resources to cover a wide range of potential stress scenarios, including the default of the two largest participants.

  - A CCP should determine the amount and regularly test the sufficiency of its total financial resources available in the event of a default or multiple defaults in extreme but plausible market conditions through rigorous stress testing.
  - A CCP should consider the effect of a wide range of relevant stress scenarios in terms of both defaulters' positions and possible price changes in liquidation periods.
- Segregation and portability:
  - A CCP must have transparent segregation and portability arrangements to protect client's positions and their margin.
  - A CCP should be able to readily identify customers of participants and keep their margin in separate accounts where relevant.
  - A CCP should disclose policies and procedures on segregation and whether accounts are omnibus (comingled) or individually segregated.

4.3.3 CCPs and liquidity support

In addition to the important individual areas of CCP operation, a subtle but critical question which is unresolved, is what sort of liquidity support CCPs should have at their disposal to be used in the case of extreme liquidity problems. First, it is probably important to distinguish between two forms of liquidity support:

- *Intraday funding:* A CCP could need intraday funding to ensure certain payments (e.g. variation margin) could be made, which may be relevant in case of a late payment by a clearing member.
- *Liquidity backstop:* Access to backstop liquidity in the event of a financial crisis.

The first point above is not especially controversial. Given the vast amount of cashflows and margin payments that will be processed in a single day, CCPs are clearly exposed to problems (see later discussion in section 14.2.5), although features such as automated payment systems should reduce this. Intraday funding could be provided by banks as opposed to central banks although the latter would provide greater certainty. Indeed, some European CCPs (for example, LCH.Clearnet SA and Eurex Clearing AG) are licensed as banks, and consequently have access to central bank liquidity. Some other European central banks offer intradaily liquidity to financial institutions including CCPs. CCPs may also wish to deposit margin with central banks.

The more contentious issue is the liquidity support available to a CCP in a crisis, which would likely need to come from the relevant central bank. On the one hand, more and more CCPs are likely to become systemically important through their increasing exposure to the OTC derivatives market, and therefore support from a central bank may be a requirement. On the other hand, the potentially fine line between central bank liquidity support and bailout can lead to moral hazards, and the obvious accusation that it is no better to have to bail out a CCP than a bank.

The failure of a CCP is likely to arise from an insolvency of one or more of its clearing members, and especially concerning OTC derivatives, such a member is likely to be a large global bank. Indeed, the defaults of banks are likely to be strongly correlated. In turn, the underlying market conditions may be extremely volatile. Hence, CCP failure could potentially represent a financial meltdown accompanied by conditions more extreme even than the bankruptcy of Lehman Brothers.

As commercial providers of liquidity may not be available in the market conditions that would likely surround a failing CCP, a question arises over the role of a central bank. There seems to be a general agreement on CCPs needing central bank support in an emergency. Disagreements by regulators globally seem to be centred more on how explicit such support should be, and whether there should be deliberate ambiguity over the scale and terms of public sector assistance. To give some closer insight into regulatory views, a paper by the International Monetary Fund (IMF 2010) on making CCPs safer states 'At a minimum, CCPs should have access to liquidity backup commitments from banks and other financial institutions that are preferably not CMs [clearing members], in order to cover temporary shortfalls in payments from otherwise solvent CMs, and as an additional source of support to fulfil contract performance.' and also '....those deemed to be systemically important should have access to emergency central bank liquidity'.

In the US, Dodd–Frank explicitly rules out CCP access to Federal Reserve liquidity facilities. This could in theory be overridden (so-called 'exigent circumstances' in clause 16 of the Federal Reserve Act) although this would have a significant political barrier. However, the Dodd–Frank Act allows a Financial Market Utility (FMU) to be designated as 'systemically important' if its failure could create or increase the risk of significant liquidity or credit problems spreading among financial institutions or markets and consequently threaten the stability of the financial system. The following FMUs are currently listed as systemically important under the Dodd–Frank Act:[17]

- The Clearing House Payments Company L.L.C. on the basis of its role as operator of the Clearing House Interbank Payments System.
- CLS Bank International.
- Chicago Mercantile Exchange, Inc.
- The Depository Trust Company.
- Fixed Income Clearing Corporation.
- ICE Clear Credit LLC.
- National Securities Clearing Corporation.
- The Options Clearing Corporation.

The designation of a CCP as a 'systemically important' FMU may exacerbate moral hazard problems. This can occur either by market participants considering their complex CCP activities as safe, thanks to seemingly explicit support for CCPs, or CCPs themselves believing that they can rely on the same level of support that the US banking sector benefited from in 2008 and 2009. A CCP remaining liquid in the event of the failure of one or more participants is clearly critical, but it needs to be defined carefully if, when and to what extent CCPs should have access to central bank credit facilities.

[17] http://www.treasury.gov/initiatives/fsoc/designations/pages/default.aspx.

Part II

Counterparty Risk, Netting and Margin

5
Netting

I'm more concerned about the return of my money than with the return on my money.
Will Rogers (1879–1935)

5.1 BILATERAL NETTING

5.1.1 Origins of netting

Derivatives markets are fast-moving, with participants regularly changing their positions and where a large number of transactions may partially offset (hedge) one another. If a derivatives counterparty defaults, then it is possible that a given institution may have hundreds or even thousands of separate derivatives transactions with that counterparty. For OTC transactions that are not exchange-traded or centrally cleared, this is potentially a major issue.

The need for netting is illustrated in Figure 5.1. Suppose parties A and B trade bilaterally and have two transactions with one another, each with its own set of cashflows. Without netting, this situation is potentially over-complex for two reasons:

- *Cashflows:* Parties A and B are exchanging cashflows or assets on a periodic basis in relation to Trade 1 and Trade 2. However, where cashflows occur on the same day, this requires exchange of *gross* amounts, giving rise to settlement risk. It would be preferable to amalgamate payments and exchange only a *net* amount (see discussion on settlement risk in section 7.1.3).
- *Close out:* In the event that either party A or B defaults, the surviving party may suffer from being responsible for one transaction that has moved against them but not be paid for the other transaction that may be in their favour. Furthermore, they may have to close out two transactions even if one offsets some or all of the other.

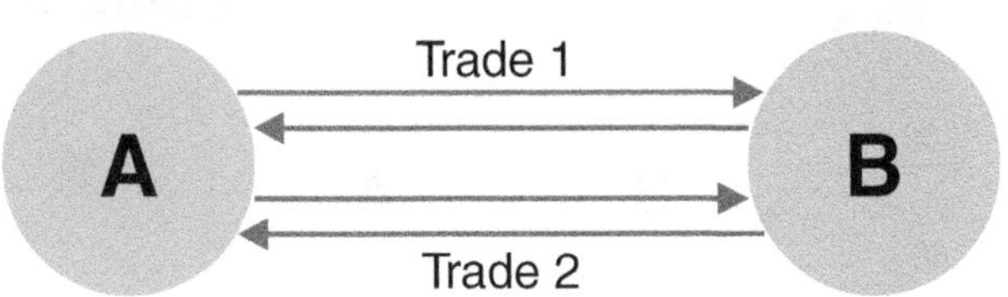

Figure 5.1 Illustration of the need for netting in bilateral markets.

Bilateral derivatives markets have historically developed netting methods whereby parties can offset what they owe to one another. The following two mechanisms facilitate this in relation to the two points raised above:

- *Payment netting:* This gives an institution the ability to net cashflows occurring on the same day even if they are in different currencies. This typically relates to settlement risk.
- *Close out netting:* This allows the termination of all contracts between the insolvent and a solvent counterparty, together with the offsetting of all transaction values (both in the solvent counterparty's favour and against it). This typically relates to counterparty risk.

5.1.2 Payment netting and CLS

Payment netting is illustrated in Figure 5.2, which shows cashflows occurring on the same day of 100 and 60 (converted to a given currency) being netted to a single payment of 40.

Payment netting covers the situation where an institution has to make and receive more than one payment during a given day and allows the combination of same day cashflows into a single net payment. This reduces settlement risk and enhances operational efficiency.

Settlement risk is also a major consideration in FX markets where the settlement of a contract involves a payment of one currency against receiving the other. In such situations, it is often inconvenient to settle the currencies on a net basis. Here there is another important innovation as most FX trades now settle through Continuous Linked Settlement (CLS),[1] which can be seen as a third-party system offering a safe settlement. For example, Bank A delivers 100 million Euros to CLS and Bank B delivers 125 million dollars to CLS. When both deliveries arrive then CLS make the payments to A and B. This is called payment versus payment (PVP). Parties still make the intended cashflows but CLS ensures that one cannot occur without the other (which is a risk if one counterparty defaults). CLS Bank also acts as a delivery versus payment (DVP) agent for certain credit default swap (CDS) transactions to provide multilateral netting of cashflows.

5.1.3 Close out netting

It is not uncommon to have many OTC derivative trades with an individual counterparty. Such trades may be simple or complex and may cover a small or wider range of products across different asset classes. A trade may be the reverse of another one if it is executed for the purpose of unwinding the first trade. Moreover, trades may constitute hedges (or partial

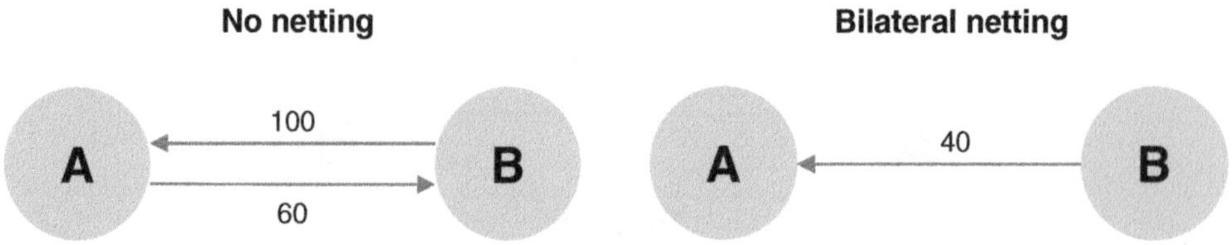

Figure 5.2 Illustration of the impact of payment netting.

[1] The largest multi-currency cash settlement system, see http://www.cls-group.com.

hedges) so that their values should naturally move in opposite directions. Alternatively, trades may be completely different (e.g. interest rate and FX trades) but again may have the potential to offset one another from a mark-to-market point of view.

Close out netting[2] comes into force in the event that a counterparty defaults. Its aim is to allow a timely termination and settlement of the net value of all trades with that counterparty. Essentially, this consists of two components:

- *Close out:* The right to terminate transactions with the defaulted counterparty and cease any contractual payments.
- *Netting:* The right to offset amounts[3] due at termination of individual contracts and determine a *net balance*, which is the sum of positive and negative transaction values, for the final close out amount.

Close out netting permits the offset of mark-to-market values in the event of default of one party as illustrated in Figure 5.3. Note that close out netting is completely general since it only depends on mark-to-market (MTM) values at the time of default and not matching cashflows.

Close out netting permits the immediate termination of all contracts between an institution and a defaulted counterparty, and the offset of the amount it owes a counterparty against the amount it is owed to arrive at a net payment. If the institution owes money then it makes this payment, whilst if it is owed money then it makes a bankruptcy claim for that amount. Close out netting allows the surviving institution to *immediately* realise gains on transactions against losses on other transactions and effectively jump the bankruptcy queue for all but its net exposure.

Netting is not just important to reduce exposure but also to reduce the complexity involved in the close out of trades in the event that a counterparty defaults. In OTC derivatives markets, surviving parties will usually attempt to replace defaulted trades. Without netting, the

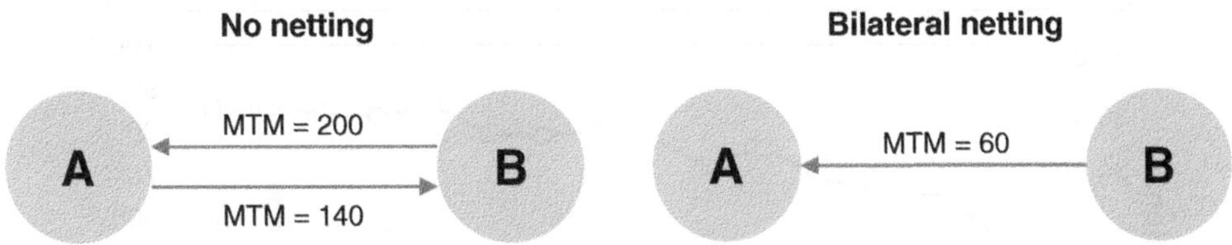

Figure 5.3 Illustration of the impact of close out netting. In the event of default of party A, without netting, party B would need to pay 200 to party A and would not receive the full amount of 140 owed. With netting, party B would simply pay 60 to party A and suffer no loss.

[2] Note that the related concept of 'set-off' is similar to close out netting and involves obligations between two parties being offset to create an obligation that represents the difference. Typically, set-off relates to actual obligations whilst close out netting refers only to a calculated amount. Set-off can be treated differently in different jurisdictions but is sometimes used interchangeably with the term 'close out netting'.

[3] The calculations made by the surviving party may be later disputed via litigation. However, the prospect of a valuation dispute and an uncertain recovery value does not affect the ability of the surviving party to immediately terminate and replace the contracts with a different counterparty.

total number of trades and their notional value that surviving parties would attempt to replace may be larger and hence may be more likely to cause market disturbances.

5.1.4 The ISDA Master Agreement

Most netting in the bilateral OTC derivatives market is supported by ISDA agreements. The International Swaps and Derivatives Association (ISDA) is a trade organisation for OTC derivatives practitioners. The ISDA Master agreement is a bilateral framework, which contains terms and conditions to govern transactions between parties. It is designed to eliminate legal uncertainties and to provide mechanisms for mitigating counterparty risk. It specifies the general terms of the agreement between parties with respect to general aspects such as netting, margin, definition of default and other termination events. Multiple transactions can be covered under a general Master Agreement, which essentially forms a single legal contract of indefinite term, covering many or all of the transactions traded. Individual transactions are incorporated by reference in the trade confirmation to the relevant Master Agreement. Trading then tends to occur without the need to update or change any aspect of the relevant ISDA agreement.

5.1.5 The impact of netting

Netting has been critical for the growth of the OTC derivatives market and, without it, the current size and liquidity of OTC derivatives would not exist. Netting means that the overall credit exposure in the market grows at a lower rate than the notional growth of the market it self. The expansion and greater concentration of derivatives markets has increased the extent of netting steadily over the last decade such that netting currently reduces exposure by close to 90% (Figure 5.4).

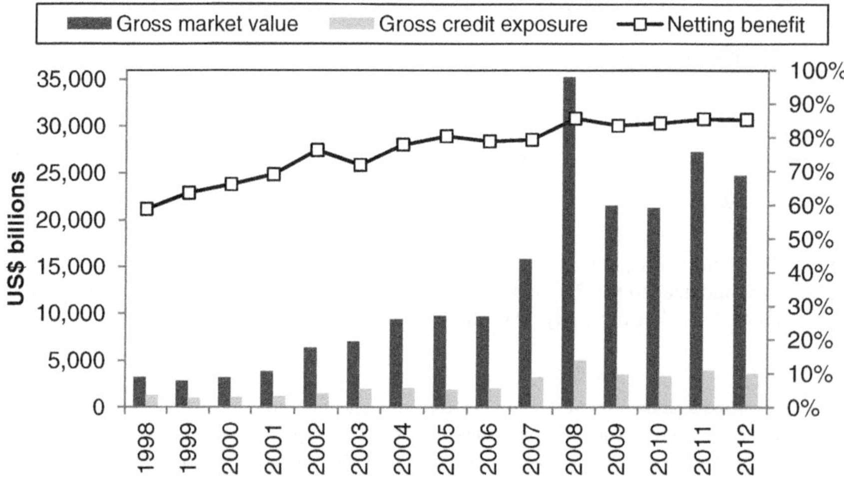

Figure 5.4 Illustration of the impact of netting on OTC derivatives exposure. The netting benefit (right-hand y-axis) is defined by dividing the gross credit exposure by the gross market value and subtracting this ratio from 100%. Source: BIS

Netting has some subtle effects on the dynamics of derivative markets. First, although the size of exposures are smaller, netted positions are inherently more volatile than their underlying gross positions, which can create systemic risk. Another problem with netting occurs when an institution wants to trade out of a position. In such a situation, the relative illiquidity of OTC derivatives may be problematic. If the institution executes an offsetting position with another market participant, whilst removing the market risk as required, they will have counterparty risk with respect to the original and the new counterparty. To offset the counterparty risk, it is necessary to trade with the original counterparty who, knowing that the institution is heavily incentivised to trade out of the position with them, may offer unfavourable terms to extract the maximum financial gain. The institution can either accept these unfavourable terms or trade with another counterparty and accept the resulting counterparty risk.

The above point extends to establishing multiple positions with different risk exposures. Suppose an institution wants both interest rate and foreign exchange hedges. Since these trades are imperfectly correlated then by executing the hedges with the same counterparty, the overall counterparty risk is reduced, and the institution may obtain more favourable terms. However, this creates an incentive to trade repeatedly with the same counterparty, leading to potential concentration risk.

An additional implication of netting is that it can change the way market participants react to perceptions of increasing risk of a particular counterparty. If credit exposures were driven by gross positions then all those trading with the troubled counterparty would have strong incentives to attempt to terminate existing positions and stop any new trading. Such actions would likely result in even more financial distress for the troubled counterparty. With netting, an institution will be far less worried if there is no current exposure (mark-to-market value is negative), which may in turn reduce systemic risk.

5.1.6 Netting impact outside OTC derivatives markets

It should be noted that close out netting may seem very beneficial in OTC derivatives markets where it reduces exposure and potentially leads to easier close out. However, for financial markets generally, it merely *redistributes* value to OTC derivatives creditors from other creditors. Consider the previous example (Figure 5.3) with parties A and B as before but now assume that party B has other creditors (OC) to whom it has a liability of 100 (Figure 5.5). Assume also that party B has other (non-derivative) assets of 40.

Party B defaults with total assets of 180 (140 derivatives and 40 other) whilst its liabilities total 300 (200 derivatives and 100 other). Without netting, assuming other creditors and derivative creditors have the same seniority,[4] a recovery of 60% (180/300) would apply and the payments would be as on the left-hand side of Figure 5.6. However, if the derivatives contracts are subject to netting as illustrated on the right-hand side of Figure 5.6, then the liabilities become 60 and 100 for derivatives and other creditors respectively against the assets of 40. This leads to a lower recovery of 25% (40/160) for the other creditors who receive 25. The derivatives creditors receive a total of 155, 140 from being able to net their assets and liabilities and 15 from recovery of their *netted* claim. This leads to an overall recovery of 77.5% (155/200) for derivatives creditors.

It is important to observe from the above example that bilateral netting of OTC derivatives merely increases the recovery for OTC derivatives counterparties (77.5% instead of 60% in the above example) but reduces the recovery of other creditors (25% instead of 60%). This

[4] OTC derivatives would typically be pari passu with senior debt, for example.

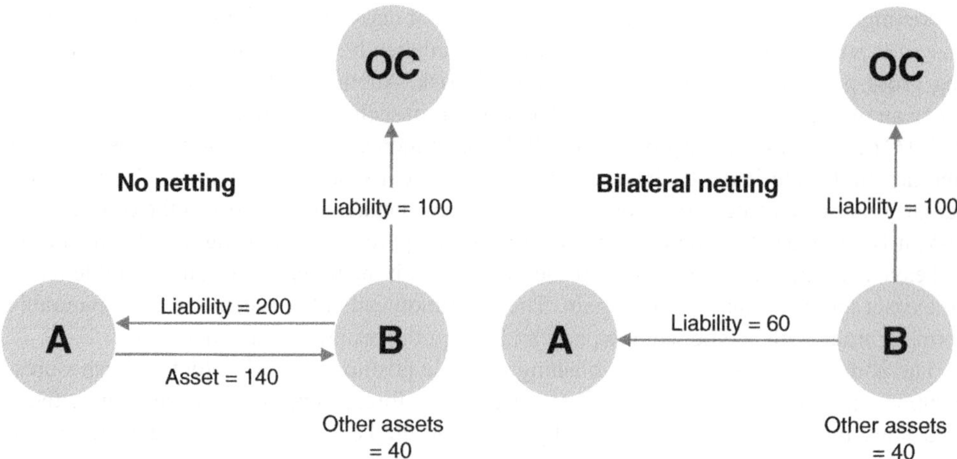

Figure 5.5 Example of bilateral derivatives netting including other creditors (OC).

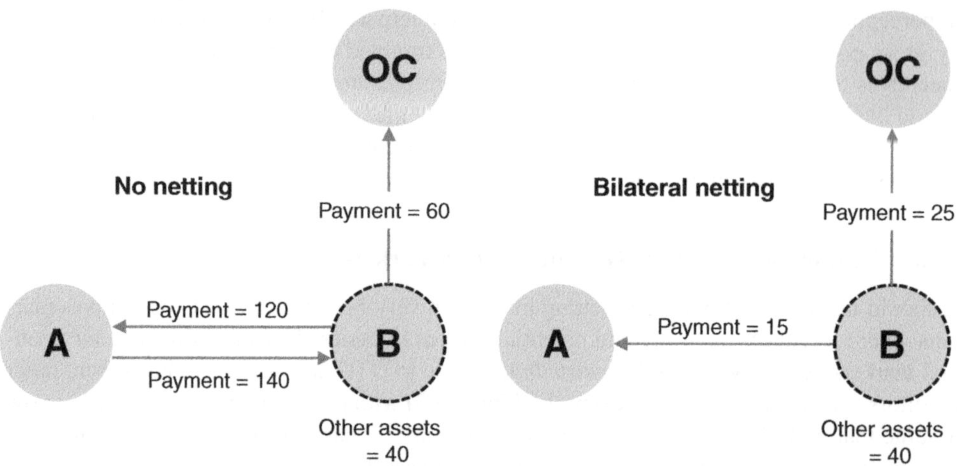

Figure 5.6 Example of bilateral derivatives netting including other creditors (OC) showing payments made in default of party B assuming party A and other creditors are paid the same percentage recovery.

potentially illustrates a much broader point, which is that certain benefits (netting, margin, central clearing) may be positive for OTC derivatives markets but not necessary for financial markets in general.

The above illustrates an important point, which is that derivatives netting cannot reduce risk overall and therefore simply redistributes it within a capital structure (Pirrong 2013). Netting may reduce exposure to OTC derivatives counterparties but increase exposure to other creditors (e.g. bondholders) who will demand a greater return as compensation for this. A bank may reduce its derivatives counterparty risk (and capital) through netting but this may induce changes in other parts of the balance sheet of the bank. This could pose the question as to whether reducing systemic risk in derivatives markets at the expense of increasing systemic risk elsewhere is a worthwhile trade-off.

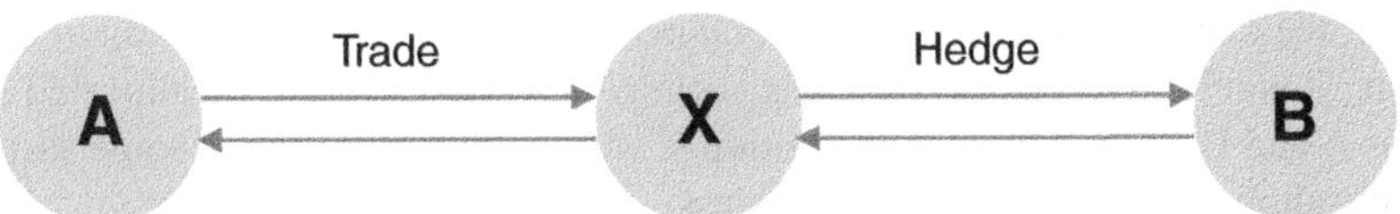

Figure 5.7 Illustration of the typical situation in which counterparty risk arises.

5.2 MULTILATERAL NETTING

5.2.1 The classic bilateral problem

The classic counterparty credit risk problem is illustrated in Figure 5.7, which supposes an institution X executes a trade with counterparty A and hedges this with counterparty B (for example, the institution could be a bank providing an OTC derivative trade to a client (A) and hedging it with another bank (B)). In this situation, if the trades are contractually opposite, the institution has no volatility of their overall mark-to-market and no market risk. However, they do have counterparty risk to both counterparties A and B since, if either were to default, this would leave exposure to the other side of the trade. Bilateral netting does not help in this example since the trade and hedge are executed with different counterparties.

5.2.2 Aim of multilateral netting

Standard netting arrangements like those described previously in this chapter are undertaken *bilaterally*, i.e. between two institutions only. Whilst bilateral netting has a significant impact on reducing overall credit exposure, it is limited to pairs of institutions within the market. Suppose that institution A has an exposure to institution B, whilst B has the same exposure to a third institution C that has another identical exposure to the original institution A. Even using bilateral netting, all three institutions have exposure (A has exposure to B, B to C and C to A). Some sort of trilateral (and by extension multilateral) netting between the three (or more) institutions would allow the exposures to be netted further as illustrated in Figure 5.8.

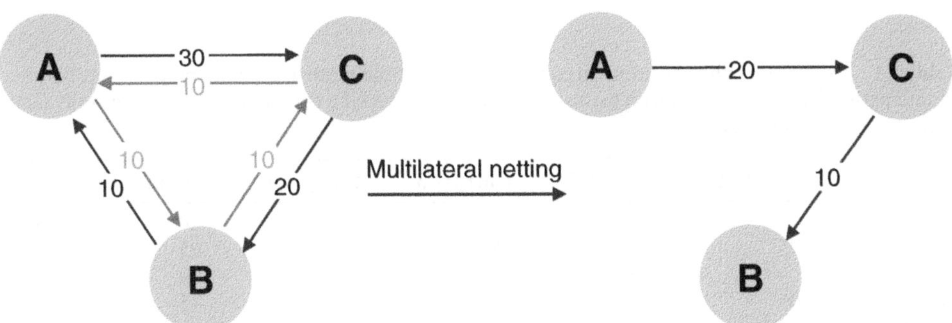

Figure 5.8 Illustration of the potential exposure reduction offered by multilateral netting. The black and grey exposures indicate positions in contractually identical (and therefore fungible) transactions, differing only in notional amount. The exposures in grey are removed completely whilst those in black are reduced by ten units.

However, the implementation of multilateral netting is not trivial. In addition to the operational costs, it would give rise to questions such as how losses would be allocated between institutions A and B if, for example, institution C were to default. Clearly, some sort of third party organisation needs to facilitate the process.

5.2.3 Trade compression

Bilateral markets have used trade compression as a way to achieve multilateral netting. This has developed since OTC derivatives portfolios grow significantly through time but contain redundancies due to the nature of trading (e.g. with respect to unwinds). This suggests that the trades can be simplified in terms of number and gross notional value but with an almost identical risk profile. This will reduce operational costs and minimise counterparty risk. It may also reduce systemic risk by lowering the number of contracts that need to be replaced in a counterparty default scenario. In order to understand trade compression, consider the example represented by the positions of five counterparties in Table 5.1. This shows position sizes[5] between different counterparties in certain fungible (interchangeable) products. Note that the total gross notional between counterparties is 1,250. A graphical depiction of this 'market' is shown in Figure 5.9.

The aim of compression is to reduce the gross notional in Figure 5.9 without changing the net position of any counterparty (last column of Table 5.1). However, this is likely to be a subjective process for a number of reasons. First, it is not clear what should be minimised. An obvious choice may be the total notional, although this would not penalise large positions or the total number of positions. Alternative choices could be to use the squared notional or the total number of positions which would reduce large exposure and interconnectedness respectively (O'Kane 2013 discusses this point in more detail). Second, there may need to be constraints applied to the optimisation such as the size of positions with single counterparties. In the above example, there is no trade between counterparties 1 and 3. It may be that one or both of them would like to impose this as a constraint on any 'compressed system'. There are many different algorithms that could be used to optimise the market above. Commercial applications have tended to follow relatively transparent approaches (for example, see Brouwer 2012). The example below, albeit for a very small market, will provide some insight on how they work in practice.

Table 5.1 Example showing positions in equivalent contracts between five counterparties. Note that the counterparties have no position with themselves and when reversing counterparties then the equivalent negative positions must be seen.

	Cntrpty 1	Cntrpty 2	Cntrpty 3	Cntrpty 4	Cntrpty 5	Total
Cntrpty 1	–	95	–	–105	20	10
Cntrpty 2	–95	–	85	–60	95	25
Cntrpty 3	–	–85	–	70	–20	–35
Cntrpty 4	105	60	–70	–	–75	20
Cntrpty 5	–20	–95	20	75	–	–20

[5] This will be referred to as notional but could represent exposure or another measure as it is the relative values that are important.

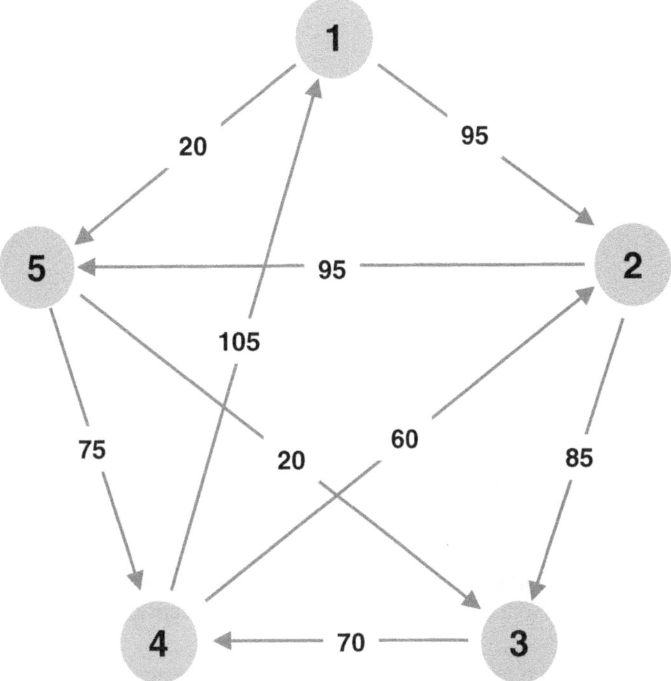

Figure 5.9 Illustration of the market represented by the positions in Table 5.1.

One obvious method to reduce the total notional is to look for opportunities for netting within rings in the market. A trilateral possibility occurs between counterparties 2, 3 and 4 as illustrated in Figure 5.10 where notionals of 60, 70 and 85 occur in a ring and are therefore be reduced by the smallest amount (assuming positions cannot be reversed) of 60. This leads to

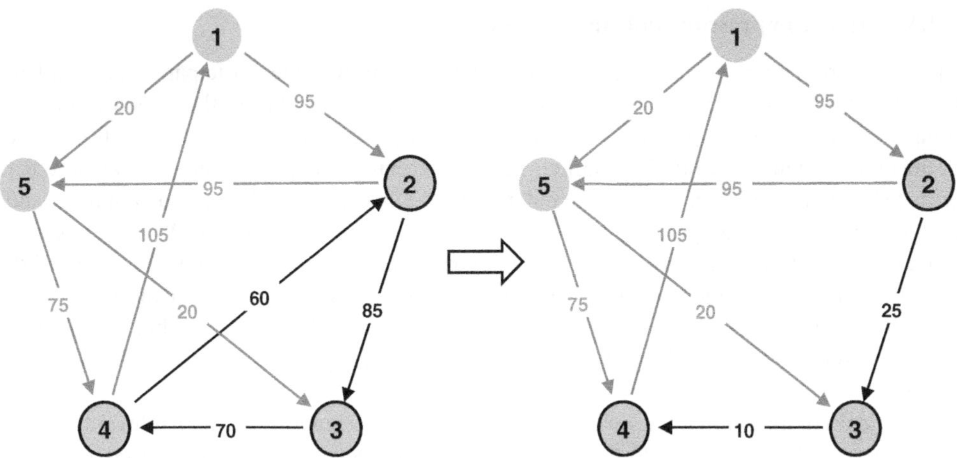

Figure 5.10 Illustration of using trilateral netting between counterparties 2, 3 and 4 to reduce the overall notional of the system shown in Figure 5.9.

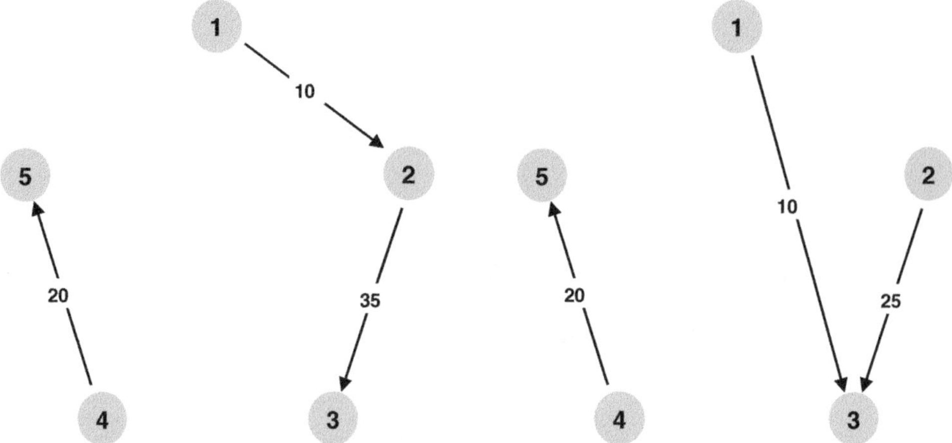

Figure 5.11 Illustration of two possible final results of compressing the original market in Figure 5.9 leading to total notionals of 130 (left-hand side) and 110 (right-hand side).

the total notional of the compressed system being reduced to 890 (from 1,250) on the right-hand side of Figure 5.10. Note that this is similar to the concept of clearing rings discussed in section 2.1.4.

Continuing a process such as the one above could lead to a number of possible solutions, two of which are shown in Figure 5.11. Note that the solution on the left hand side has reversed the exposure between counterparties 4 and 5, whilst on the right-hand side there is a trade between counterparties 1 and 3 where none existed previously. The latter solution has a lower total notional of 110 (compared to 130 for the former), however, this also illustrates that constraints imposed by counterparties (for example, 1 and 3 not wanting exposure to one another) will weaken the impact of compression. Figure 2.4 in Chapter 2 shows the impact of the much greater emphasis on compression in OTC derivatives in the last few years.

5.2.4 Trade compression and standardisation

Trade compression by its nature needs the cooperation of multiple participants and standard contracts, which are therefore fungible. OTC derivatives that do not fit the standard product templates cannot be compressed. A good example of producing standardisation of this type is the credit default swap (CDS) market. In the aftermath of the GFC, large banks together with ISDA made swift progress in standardising CDS contracts in terms of coupons and maturity dates to aid compression (and indeed facilitate central clearing). CDS contracts now trade with both fixed premiums and upfront payments and scheduled termination dates of 20 March, 20 June, 20 September or 20 December. This means that positions can be bucketed according to underlying reference entity (single name or index) and maturity but without any other differences (such as the previous standard where coupons and maturity dates would differ).

A typical compression cycle will start with participants submitting their relevant trades, which are matched according to the counterparty to the trade and cross-referenced against a trade-reporting warehouse. As shown in the example in the last section, an optimal overall solution may involve positions between pairs of counterparties increasing or changing sign.

Table 5.2 Simple illustration of trade compression for single name CDS contracts. An institution has three contracts with the same reference credit and maturity but traded with different counterparties. It is beneficial to 'compress' the three into a net contract, which represents the total notional of the long and short positions. This may naturally be with counterparty A as a reduction of the initial trade.

Reference Credit	Notional	Long/short	Maturity	Coupon	Counterparty
ABC Index	40	Long	20/12/2019	200	Counterparty A
ABC Index	25	Short	20/12/2019	150	Counterparty B
ABC Index	10	Short	20/12/2019	300	Counterparty C
ABC Index	**5**	**Long**	**20/12/2019**	**250**	**Counterparty A**

For this and other reasons, participants can specify constraints (such as the total exposure to a given counterparty, which may be related to internal credit limits of a participant). Participants must also specify tolerances since, whilst the aim of compression is to be totally market risk- and cash-neutral, allowing some small changes in mark-to-market valuations and risk profile can increase the extent of the compression possible. Based on trade population and tolerances, changes are determined based on redundancies in the multilateral trade population. Once the proposed terminations and replacement trades are accepted by all participants, the process is finished and all trade terminations and replacements are legally binding. Such changes can take effect by unwinding portions of trades, executing new trades and novating trades to other counterparties.

A simple example of the potential result of a CDS compression exercise for one market participant is given in Table 5.2. Here, the net long position resulting from trades with three counterparties is reduced to a single identical long position with one of the counterparties. Note that in this example, the coupons are assumed to be different and the weighted coupon is maintained.[6] This is not typically the case in the CDS market as mentioned above[7] but may be a problem for compression of other products such as interest-rate swaps which do not trade with upfront premiums.

Companies such as TriOptima[8] provide compression services covering major OTC derivatives products such as interest rate swaps (in all global currencies), credit default swaps (single-name, indices and tranches) and energy swaps. This has been instrumental in reducing exposures in OTC derivatives markets, especially in rapidly growing areas such as credit derivatives,[9] although compression is subject to diminishing marginal returns over time as the maximum multilateral netting is achieved, and the benefit from a new cycle relates only to changes in trading since the last cycle.

We also note that compression services are complementary to central clearing[10] as reducing the total notional and number of contracts cleared will be operationally more efficient and reduce

[6] $(40 \times 200) - (25 \times 150) - (10 \times 300) = (5 \times 250)$.

[7] Although CDS trade with at least two different coupons of 100 bps and 500 bps, which are standards for investment and speculative grade credits respectively. A credit or index could potentially have trades outstanding with both coupons used (for example, due to a significantly changing credit quality through time).

[8] www.trioptima.com.

[9] For example, 'TriOptima tear-ups cut CDS notional by $9 trillion', http://www.risk.net/risk-magazine/news/1505985/trioptima-tear-upscut-cds-notional-usd9-trillion. 'CDS dealers compresss $30 trillion in trades in 2008', Reuters, 12 January 2009.

[10] 'TriOptima and LCH.Clearnet terminate SwapClear USD interest rate swaps with notional principal value of $7.1 trillion' http://www.lchclearnet.com/media_centre/press_releases/2011-08-04.asp.

complexity in closing out positions in the event of a clearing member default. However, since trades are generally cleared very quickly after being executed, the trade compression process must be done at the CCP level. Indeed, LCH.Clearnet's SwapClear service offers a multilateral trade compression service (via a joint venture with TriOptima)[11] to reduce notional across clearing member's positions via tear-up of offsetting positions (discussed later in section 8.2.3).

Development of more advanced compression services that cover both bilateral and centrally cleared products is likely to become important in reducing the costs associated with clearing. This is discussed later in section 12.3.3.

5.2.5 Central clearing

It should be obvious from the example above and also those in section 2.1.5 that a CCP can provide multilateral netting benefits. As an example, consider the situation in Figure 5.12 where the arrows are probably best interpreted as cashflow or margin payments, as discussed in more detail below. This shows that although bilateral netting can reduce exposure significantly, central clearing can reduce it even more through multilateral netting.

As shown in Table 5.3, bilateral netting reduces the total exposure of the system in Figure 5.12 by a factor of three (360 to 120). This can be reduced further to 60 by central clearing, even if the exposure of the CCP is included (in practice this would be mitigated by margining).

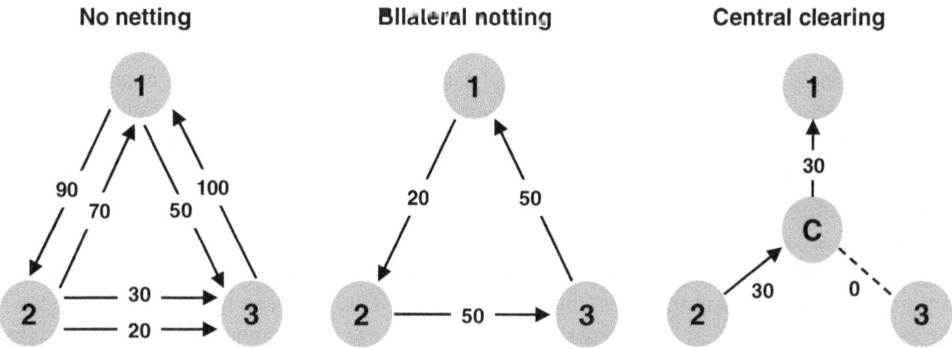

Figure 5.12 Comparison of no netting, bilateral netting and central clearing. The central counterparty is represented by C.

Table 5.3 Illustration of the reduction in exposure from bilateral netting and central clearing as shown in Figure 5.12.

	No netting	Bilateral netting	Central clearing
Cntrpty 1	170	50	30
Cntrpty 2	90	20	0
Cntrpty 3	100	50	0
CCP (C)	–	–	30
Total	360	120	60

[11] For example, see http://www.trioptima.co.uk/news/SwapClear-and-TriOptima-eliminate-cleared-interest-rate-swaps-.html.

Although the above example seems to be identical to compression, there are important differences. For compression, trades need to be standardised since this provides the fungibility so that contracts can be torn-up to represent the result of the compression cycle. Contracts also need to be standardised for central clearing, but for different reasons relating to operational costs, margin calculations and potential close out in the event of clearing member default. Such differences mean that multilateral netting benefits can be seen for centrally cleared trades that would not be achieved through trade compression.

To explain the above point differently, the multilateral netting benefits from central clearing will be seen in cashflow netting and reduction in margins (both variation and initial). For example, two different trades with different counterparties that are negatively correlated will have a strong netting benefit under central clearing but are not appropriate for trade compression due to not being interchangeable.

5.2.6 Multilateral netting increasing exposure

When promoting central clearing, a key point made by policymakers and regulators is often that CCPs facilitate multilateral netting, which can alleviate systemic risk by reducing exposures more than in bilateral markets. Whilst multilateral netting is clearly more beneficial when all trades are covered, in reality fragmentation will be a problem. Two obvious sources of fragmentation are non-clearable trades (which remain bilateral) and multiple CCPs. Such a situation is illustrated in Figure 5.13, where some of the positions are assumed to be cleared outside the CCP shown.

The quantitative impact of partial multilateral netting is shown in Table 5.4, which considers the total exposure under no netting, bilateral netting and partial central clearing. Even ignoring the exposure faced to and from the CCP itself (i.e. assuming the CCP is risk-free), the overall reduction in exposure is better with bilateral netting (total exposure 120) than with central clearing (total exposure 210). For example, with no netting, counterparty 1 has a total exposure of 170 (70 to counterparty 2 and 100 to counterparty 3) and under bilateral netting this is reduced to 50 (to counterparty 3 only). However, under partial central clearing, counterparty 1 gains in some multilateral netting of their positions with counterparties 2 and 3 but loses the bilateral netting of the two sets of positions.

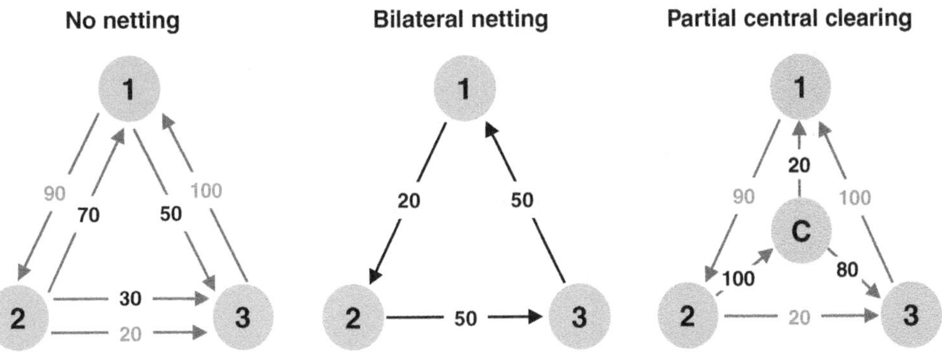

Figure 5.13 Comparison of no netting, bilateral netting and partial central clearing where only a subset of trades (black lines as opposed to grey ones) can be centrally cleared.

Table 5.4 Illustration of an increase in overall exposure caused by multilateral netting related to central clearing of only a subset of trades as shown in Figure 5.13.

	No netting	Bilateral netting	Partial clearing (excluding CCP positions)
Cntrpty 1	170	50	100
Cntrpty 2	90	20	90
Cntrpty 3	100	50	20
Total	360	120	210

Note that the above example could correspond to a situation where certain trades cannot be centrally cleared, or alternatively where they are cleared via a separate CCP to the one shown (although this could be helped by interoperability between the CCPs discussed in section 8.5.1 and cross-margining covered in section 9.5).

The above example illustrates that the loss of bilateral netting benefits may dominate the increase in multilateral netting ones and result in central clearing increasing the overall exposure in the market. This splitting of netting sets is analysed with some simple examples by Duffie and Zhu (2011). Their results are based on considering the netting benefit for trading a single class of contracts through a CCP as opposed to bilateral clearing. They show, using a simple model,[12] the required number of members trading through the CCP for a single asset class to achieve overall netting reduction. Results using Duffie and Zhu formulas are plotted in Figure 5.14 as a function of correlation and number of asset classes. For example, for four uncorrelated asset classes, there must be at least 15 members to make clearing a single asset class through the CCP valid (in terms of exposure reduction).[13]

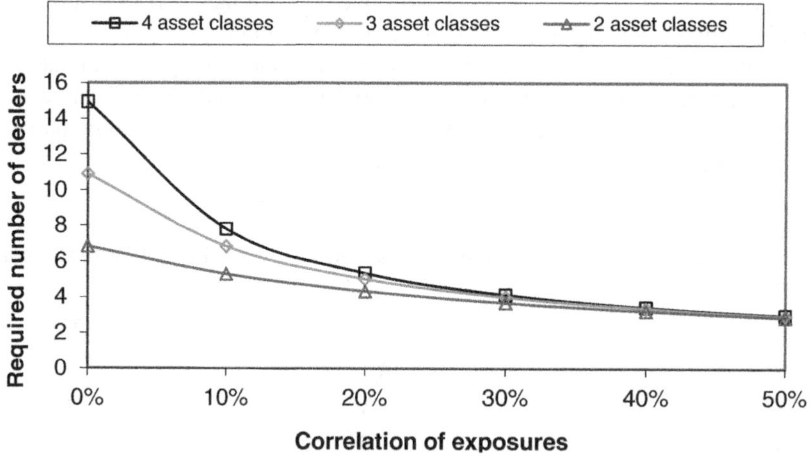

Figure 5.14 Required number of members for a single asset class CCP to improve netting efficiency calculated using the formula of Duffie and Zhu (2011).

[12] Simplifying assumptions of symmetry and equal variance of exposure are used in this case.

[13] Interestingly, the impact of correlation between asset classes makes a CCP more effective since bilateral netting is less effective in this case.

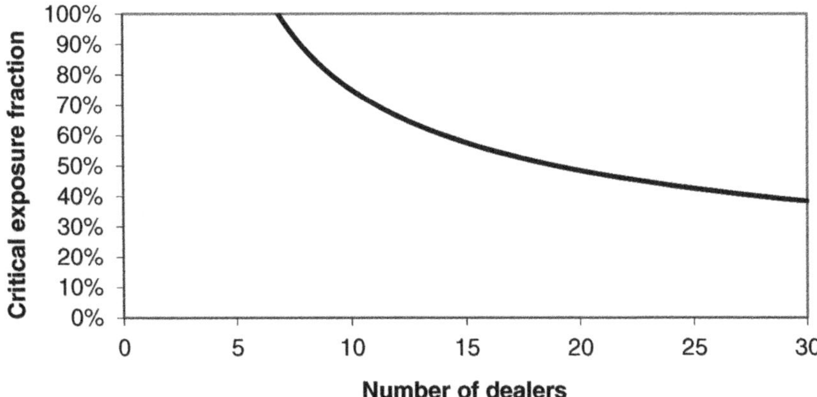

Figure 5.15 Required fraction of exposure attributed to a single asset class ('critical exposure fraction') to make a CCP for that asset class effective. The results as a function of the number of members are calculated using the formula of Duffie and Zhu (2011).

The above example assumes equal distribution of exposure across asset classes. Duffie and Zhu also consider a non-homogeneous case and derive an expression[14] for the fraction of dealer's exposure that must be concentrated in a particular asset class to make a CCP for that asset class viable. This fraction is shown in Figure 5.15. For example, with 10 dealers, using a CCP for a given class of derivatives will be effective only if three quarters of the dealers' bilaterally netted exposure resides in that class of products.

Overall, the Duffie and Zhu results illustrate that achieving overall netting benefits from central clearing (compared to bilateral trading) is not a foregone conclusion. Increased netting benefits can only be achieved by a relatively small[15] number of CCPs clearing a relatively large volume of transactions.

It should be noted however that the success of central clearing on OTC derivatives should be judged primarily on the reduction of systemic risk in financial markets. As discussed more in Chapter 14, this is not directly related to the reduction of exposure in OTC derivatives markets. Put another way, a CCP may increase exposure in an OTC derivative market and still be successful (and vice versa).

[14] This assumes independence between asset classes.

[15] See also the later comments on interoperability.

6

Margining[1]

A first-rate organizer is never in a hurry. He is never late. He always keeps up his sleeve a margin for the unexpected.

Arnold Bennett (1867–1931)

6.1 BASICS OF MARGIN

6.1.1 Rationale

Margin provides a means to reduce credit exposure and counterparty risk beyond the benefit achieved with other methods such as netting. Margin refers to an asset that offsets exposure in a legally enforceable way. The fundamental idea of margin is simply that cash or securities are transferred or pledged from one counterparty to another as security for a credit exposure. In the event of default, the surviving party may be able to keep their margin to offset losses that they may otherwise incur.

The basic idea of margining is very simple and illustrated in Figure 6.1. Parties A and B have one or more transactions between them and therefore agree that one or both of them will exchange margin in order to offset the exposure that will otherwise exist. The rules regarding the timings, amounts and type of margin posted should naturally be agreed before the initiation of the underlying trade(s).

Since exposures in derivatives are generally bilateral then margin is typically also posted bilaterally. Naturally, margin would reflect the mark-to-market of the underlying trades, which can generally be positive or negative from each party's point of view. This idea forms

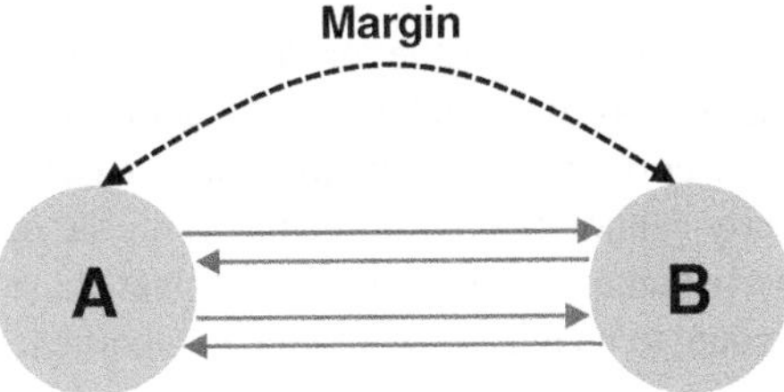

Figure 6.1 Illustration of the basic role of margin.

[1] In this chapter, as with the rest of this book, we use the word 'margin' uniquely. The term 'collateral' is often used instead of margin (especially in OTC derivative markets) but 'margin' is the commonly used term in relation to exchanges and central counterparties.

the basis of *variation margin* (sometimes called 'market-to-market margin'). Mark-to-market is used for variation margin calculations because it is the most obvious and easy way to define a proxy for the actual loss arising from the default of one of the parties. However, in an actual default scenario, the variation margin may be insufficient due to aspects such as delays in receiving margin and close out costs (e.g. bid-offer). For these and other reasons, additional margin is sometimes used in the form of *initial margin*. Figure 3.4 in Chapter 3 shows conceptually the roles of variation and initial margins.

6.1.2 Title transfer and security interest

In practice, there are two methods of margin transfer:

- *Title transfer:* Here, legal possession of margin changes hands but with potential restrictions on the use of margin.
- *Security interest:* In this case, the margin does not change hands but the receiving party acquires an interest in the margin.

The former method is beneficial for the margin receiver since they hold the physical assets and are less exposed to legal risk. The latter is preferable for the margin giver, especially when considering aspects such as segregation (see section 6.2.3).

6.1.3 Simple example

Margin can perhaps be best understood by a simple everyday example of a mortgaged house which also provides an insight into some of the risk arising from margining. The mortgage lender has *credit risk* since the mortgagor may fail to make future mortgage payments. This risk is mitigated by the house playing the role of margin and being pledged against the value borrowed. It is worth noting that there are a number of residual risks introduced in this arrangement:

- The risk that the value of the property in question falls below the outstanding value of the loan or mortgage. This situation is often known as 'negative equity' and corresponds to *market risk*. Note that this depends on both the value of the property (the margin) and the value of the mortgage (exposure).
- The risk that the mortgage lender is unable, or faces legal obstacles, to take ownership of the property in the event of a borrower default, and faces costs in order to evict the owners and sell the property. This corresponds to *operational or legal risk.*
- The risk that the property cannot be sold immediately in the open market, and will have a falling value if property values are in decline. To achieve a sale, the property may then have to be sold at a discount to its fair value if there is a shortage of buyers. This is *liquidity risk*.
- The risk that there is a strong dependence between the value of the property, and the default of the mortgagee. For example, in an economic downturn, high unemployment and falling property prices make this rather likely. This is a form of *wrong-way* risk.

Note that in the above example, there is no equivalent of variation margin (e.g. the mortgagor does need to post additional margin if their house price declines or if interest rates increase).

However, there is the equivalent of initial margin generally built-in, as the loan-to-value ratio of a mortgage is generally less than 100%.[2]

Margin posted against derivatives positions is, in most cases, under the control of the counterparty and may be liquidated immediately upon an event of default. This arises due to the laws governing derivatives contracts and the nature of the margin (cash or liquid securities). Exposure, in theory, can be completely neutralised as long as a sufficient amount of margin is held against it. However, there are legal obstacles to this and issues such as rehypothecation. Bankruptcies such as Lehman Brothers and MF Global have provided evidence of the risks of rehypothecation (see sections 6.2.2 and 6.4.5).

6.1.4 The margin period of risk

An important aspect with margin is the contractual frequency of margin calls. If they are frequent, this maximises the risk reduction benefit but may cause operational and liquidity problems. For variation margin, daily margining has become fairly standard in bilateral OTC derivatives markets, although longer periods do sometimes exist. In centrally cleared markets, daily margining is a standard with even intraday margining occurring in certain situations. Initial margins, where they exist, are generally adjusted on a less frequent basis.

The margin period of risk (MPR) is the term used to refer to the *effective* time between a counterparty ceasing to post margin and when all the underlying trades have been successfully closed out and replaced (or otherwise hedged) as illustrated in Figure 6.2. Even if a margin agreement is in place, a counterparty will still be exposed to market risk over the MPR.

In general, it is useful to define the margin period of risk as the combination of two periods:

- *Pre-default:* This represents the time prior to the counterparty being in default and includes the following components:
  - o The contractual period for making margin calls (often daily).
  - o Operational delays in requesting and receiving margin.

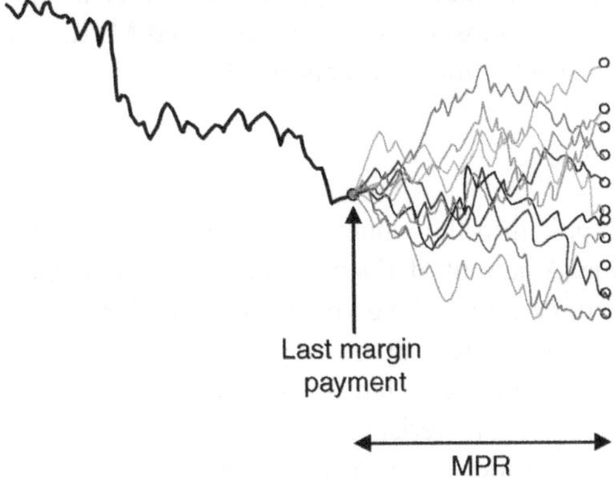

Figure 6.2 Illustration of the role of the margin period of risk (MPR).

[2] Except in highly risky mortgages such as the ones that partially led to the GFC.

  - o Disputes regarding the amount of margin.
  - o Settlement of non-cash margin.
  - o The grace period that must be given from a party failing to post margin to being deemed in default.
- Post-default:
  - o Close out of trades.
  - o Re-hedging and/or replacement of postions.
  - o Auction of trades (specific to CCPs).

CCPs reduce the pre-default period by making daily and potentially also intradaily variation margin calls in cash only (no settlement delays). They also have full authority over all calculations (no disputes allowed) and ensure that members can adhere to the operational requirement of posting margin and that they guarantee to post of the behalf of clients if necessary. Finally, CCPs have no requirement to provide a grace period before declaring a clearing member in default. In OTC markets, the pre-default period is more problematic due to the nature of the bilateral relationship.

CCPs also have better control over the post-default period thanks to mechanisms such as auctions, where a defaulted member's trades will be sold to other surviving CCP members. Nevertheless, for a large and relatively illiquid portfolio, this is not a trivial task. CCPs generally make assumptions regarding the MPR of around five business days. This is broadly consistent with the experience of the Lehman bankruptcy in relation to OTC derivatives portfolios, where CCPs had dealt with the majority of the risk (although not all) within a week (see section 4.1.4). By contrast, regulatory capital requirements for OTC derivatives under Basel rules require that the MPR must be at least 10 business days.[3]

The MPR illustrates the importance of initial margin. Assuming only variation margin, the *best-case* reduction of counterparty risk can be shown to be approximately half the square root of the ratio of the maturity of the underlying portfolio to the MPR (see more detailed discussion in section 7.2.4). For a five-year OTC derivatives portfolio, with a MPR of 10-business days, this would lead to an approximate reduction of $0.5 \times \sqrt{5 \times 250 / 10} \approx 5.6$ times. In reality, due to aspects such as thresholds and minimum transfer amounts, the improvement would be less than this and to reduce counterparty risk further would require initial margin. The choice of initial margin is closely tied to the assumed MPR, as is clearly illustrated in Figure 6.2. This will be discussed more in section 9.2.

6.1.5 Haircuts

A haircut is a discount applied to the value of margin to account for the fact that its value may deteriorate over time. A haircut of x% means that for every unit of that security posted as margin, only $(1 - x)$% of credit will be given, as illustrated in Figure 6.3. The margin giver must typically account for the haircut by posting more margin. Typically, cash margin in a major currency will require no haircut, but other securities will have pre-specified haircuts depending on their individual characteristics.

The important points to consider before assigning a haircut are:

[3] This assumes margin can be called for on a daily basis. Basel III requirements increase the MPR to 20 or more business days in certain situations.

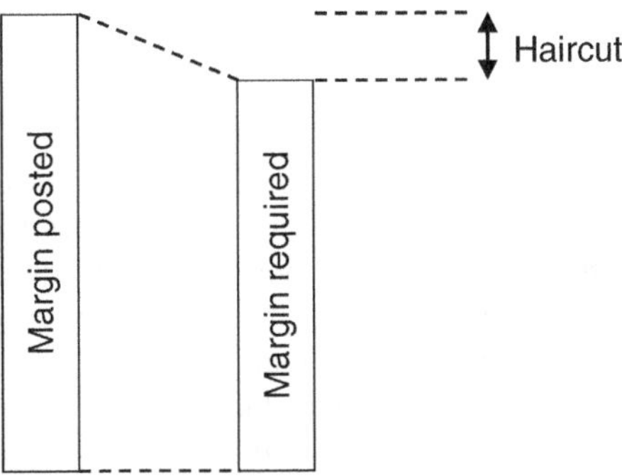

Figure 6.3 Illustration of haircuts applied to margin.

- Time taken to liquidate the margin.
- Volatility of the underlying market variable(s) defining the value of the margin.
- Maturity of the security.
- Default risk of the security.
- Liquidity of the security.
- Any relationship between the default of the counterparty and the value of the margin.

Haircuts are primarily used to account for market risk stemming from the price volatility of the type of margin posted. Even volatile assets such as equities or gold might be allowed as margin in bilateral markets (but probably not by CCPs), but with correspondingly large haircuts. However, securities that would have significant default and/or liquidity risks (and therefore could lose significant value) are often not allowed to be posted as margin (this is especially true for central clearing).

6.2 MARGIN AND FUNDING

6.2.1 Funding costs

The traditional role of margin for bilateral OTC derivatives has been as a counterparty risk mitigant. However, there is another role of margin, which is as provision of funding. Without margin, an institution could be owed money but would not be paid immediately for this asset. Since institutions are often engaged in hedging transactions this can create funding problems (for example, a bank not receiving margin on a trade may have to post margin on the associated hedge trade).

As margin has relevance in funding as well as counterparty risk reduction, one point to bear in mind is that different types of margin may offer different counterparty risk and funding benefits. An important distinction is that margin as a counterparty risk mitigant is by definition useful only in an actual counterparty default scenario. On the other hand, margin as a means of funding is relevant in all scenarios. For example, an entity posting their own bonds provides a funding benefit but is a poor counterparty risk mitigant. This balance between counterparty risk and funding is discussed in more detail in section 7.3.5.

6.2.2 Reuse and rehypothecation

A very important general concept with respect to margining is rehypothecation or reuse as the holder of margin is sometimes not the economic owner from a legal standpoint. Interest is typically paid on margin with reference to the overnight indexed swap (OIS) rate (for example, EONIA in Europe, Fed Funds in the US), sometimes with a spread adjustment. The receiver of margin must pass on coupon payments, dividends and any other cashflows.[4] This leads to the question of whether non-cash margin can be reused in another margin arrangement or elsewhere (for example the repo market). Margin delivered under title transfer (section 6.1.2) is intrinsically reusable, whereas that pledged under security interest would need to have the right of rehypothecation granted (in OTC derivative markets this right is normally given in documentation unless explicitly removed).

There is a clear and obvious need to rehypothecate or reuse margin in derivative markets. Participants generally have trades with one counterparty and hedges executed with another. If they have margin arrangements with both counterparties then they will clearly find it useful to rehypothecate or reuse margin, as illustrated in Figure 6.4. Here, margin received from counterparty A is posted directly to counterparty B. If counterparty B permitted only cash margin then securities received from counterparty A could be used via a repurchase agreement to provide this cash. However, if the margin in this case were underpledged under security interest and not permitted to be rehypothecated, it would create a potential funding problem since party X would have to find new margin to post to counterparty B.

Rehypothecation would seem to be obvious because it keeps the flow of margin moving around the financial system without any blockage. The question arises as to whether rehypothecating a security in this way creates additional risk due to the loss of control of margin. This is not a particular issue with variation margin since this will be posted against mark-to-market losses as shown in Figure 6.5. There is a risk that variation margin needs to be returned against a mark-to-market gain, but this is not usually a large problem due to frequent margin calls. Initial margin is the major issue since it represents an extra amount above any liability, and if it is rehypothecated by a counterparty then it may be lost in a default scenario.

Rehypothecation is not ideal from a pure counterparty risk reduction point of view, as illustrated in Figure 6.6. In this example, initial margin posted from party A is rehypothecated via counterparty B through a chain of other parties. A combination of default of B or any

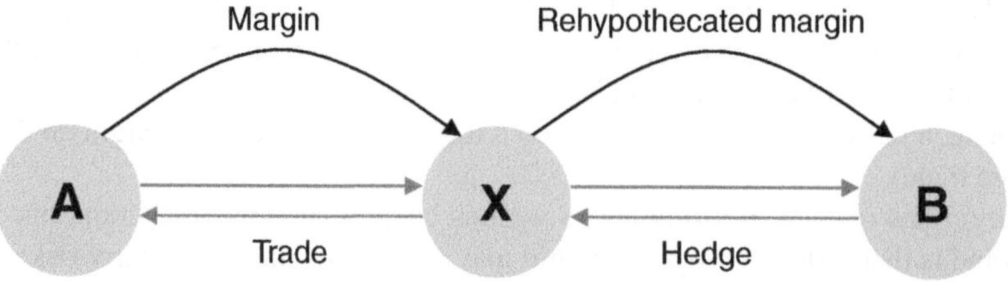

Figure 6.4 Illustration of the importance of rehypothecation of non-cash margin. Party X receives margin from party A and reuses (rehypothecates) this margin to party B. Note that cash and securities posted by title transfer can intrinsically be reused.

[4] A potential exception is where payment of a cashflow would trigger an immediate margin call in which case some or all of that cashflow can be retained in lieu of margin required.

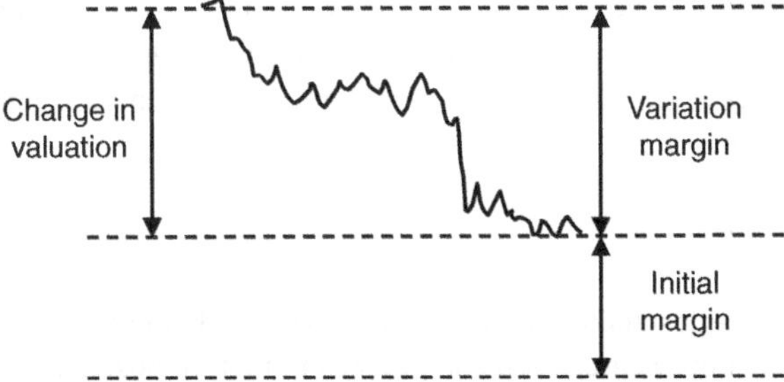

Figure 6.5 Illustration of the difference between variation and initial margins with respect to segregation and rehypothecation. Since variation margin is, in general, already owed then it does not require segregation and can be naturally rehypothecated. Initial margin requires the protection of segregation and no rehypothecation to avoid creating additional credit risk.

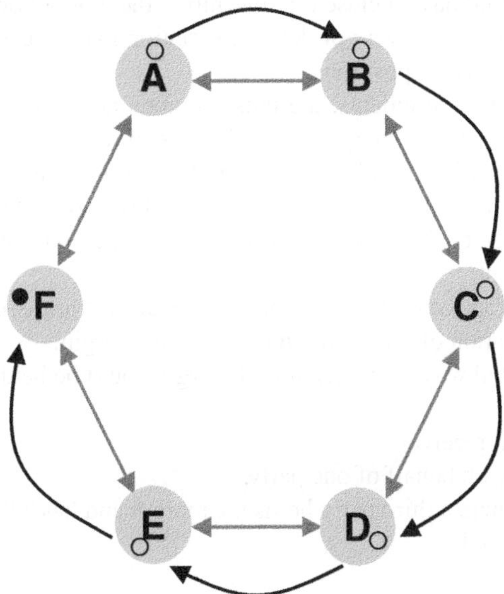

Figure 6.6 Illustration of the potential risks of rehypothecation of margin (empty circles indicate margin that has been rehypothecated, the dark circle represents the actual margin).

other party may represent a risk. This can be mitigated by legal requirements over the return of margin in the event of bankruptcy, but lessons from the GFC have shown this to be far from foolproof.

Prior to the GFC, the pledging, reuse and rehypothecation of margin was strongly encouraged to allow a 'velocity of margin' without creating excessive drag. This was viewed as being critical to the entire financial system (Segoviano and Singh 2008). However, the practice of rehypothecation probably became too widespread, especially in the interbank market (presumably, since there was little concern of actual bank defaults). The bankruptcy of Lehman Brothers illustrated the potential problems with rehypothecation. One example is that customers of Lehman Brothers Inc. (US) were treated more favourably than the UK customers of Lehman Brothers International (Europe), in terms of the return of rehypothecated assets (due to differences in customer protection between the UK and the US).[5] Not surprisingly, in the aftermath of the GFC, a significant drop in rehypothecation has been observed (Singh and Aitken 2009b).

6.2.3 Segregation

Segregation of margin is designed to reduce counterparty risk and is therefore contrary to the practice of rehypothecation. Segregation corresponds to margin posted being legally protected in the event that the receiving counterparty becomes insolvent. In practice, this can be achieved either through legal rules that ensure the return of any margin not required (in priority over any bankruptcy rules), or alternatively by a third party custodian holding the margin.

Generally, variation margin is not segregated (and can be rehypothecated as discussed in section 6.2.2), nor is this required by future regulation. This is because it does not represent over-margining, and should have a close relationship to the amount owed by the giver to the receiver (see Figure 6.5). In the event of default, variation margin can be retrieved via right of set-off against the underlying positions.

In addition to clearing requirements, the most obvious need for segregation arises from the practice of exchanging initial margins, as will be required for many non-clearable OTC derivatives. Where two parties A and B post each other initial margin, without segregation, the amounts posted may effectively cancel as they could post (cash) or rehypothecate (non-cash) back to the other party. As illustrated in Figure 6.7, the concept of segregation in this case is therefore important.

Not surprisingly, the regulatory requirements over margin (discussed later in section 6.5) generally require segregation of initial (but not variation) margin.

There are three potential ways in which initial margin could be held:

- Directly by the margin receiver.
- By a third party acting on behalf of one party.
- In tri-party custody where a third party holds the margin and has a three-way contract with the two parties concerned.

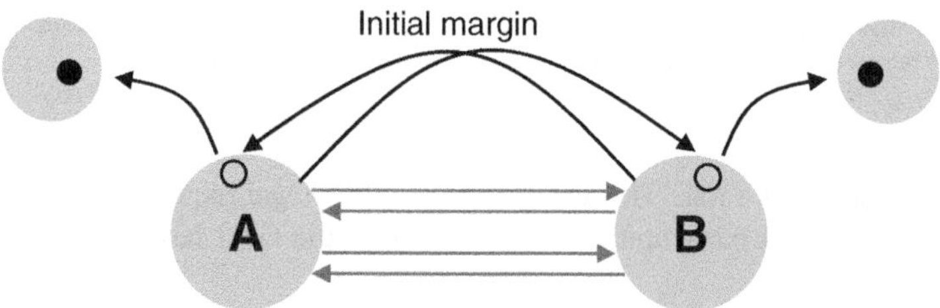

Figure 6.7 Illustration of the need for segregation of initial margins. Parties A and B post initial margin to each other, which needs to be segregated, which could be achieved (for example) via a third party.

[5] The liquidator of Lehman Brothers (PricewaterhouseCoopers) stated in October 2008, shortly after the bankruptcy, that certain assets provided to Lehman Brothers International (Europe) had been rehypothecated and may not be returned.

Since cash is fungible, it is difficult to segregate on the balance sheet of the margin receiver. Hence, a tri-party arrangement where the margin is held in a designated account, and not rehypothecated or re-invested in any way, may be desirable. On the other hand, this limits investment options and therefore makes it difficult for the margin giver to earn any return on their cash.

As mentioned in section 6.1.2, there are two methods of posting margin, namely title transfer and security interest. Segregation and non-rehypothecation of initial margin is practical in the latter case and difficult in the former. Title transfer leaves the margin giver as an unsecured creditor in the event of default of the margin receiver, since the underlying assets belong to the margin receiver at the time of transfer (and title is passed on in the event of rehypothecation). Around half of the OTC derivatives market is margined via title transfer, as it forms the basis of English law Credit Support Annexes (CSAs). Initial margin requiring segregation should therefore ideally be governed by a security interest type of margining relationship, or additional legal requirements.

Obviously, if margin is held with a third- or tri-party agent then it is important to consider potential default risk and relationship between the counterparty and third party, since there is a risk in case they become insolvent at the same time. There is also the issue of concentration risk with such third parties.

There is also a subtle case where the treatment may need to be different, and rehypothecation and segregation issues come together. Consider a situation as in Figure 6.8 where party X essentially acts as an intermediary for a trade between parties A and B. This could occur either because X does a bilateral trade with A and then executes a 'back-to-back' hedge with party B, or because X is clearing a trade for a client A with a party B being a CCP. In such situations, party X can realistically argue that they should be able to rehypothecate initial margin as shown. As described later, these cases may allow for rehypothecation under initial margining and central clearing rules. However, another issue that would arise in such a case is the legal protection and segregation that party A is affording with regards to its margin that resides with party B. This is a complex problem with several different potential setups and will be explained in more detail in Chapter 13.

Note that segregation, whilst clearly the optimal method for reducing counterparty risk, causes potential funding issues for replacing margin that would otherwise simply be rehypothecated. As we will discuss later in Chapter 13, this is at the heart of the cost/benefit analysis of central clearing mandates and bilateral clearing requirements.

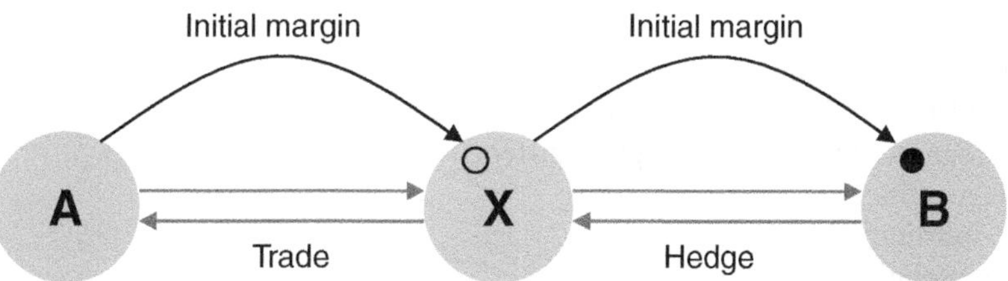

Figure 6.8 Illustration of the need for rehypothecation of initial margin, for example where party A executes a trade with party B but via party X (the empty circle indicates margin that has been rehypothecated, the dark circle represents the actual margin).

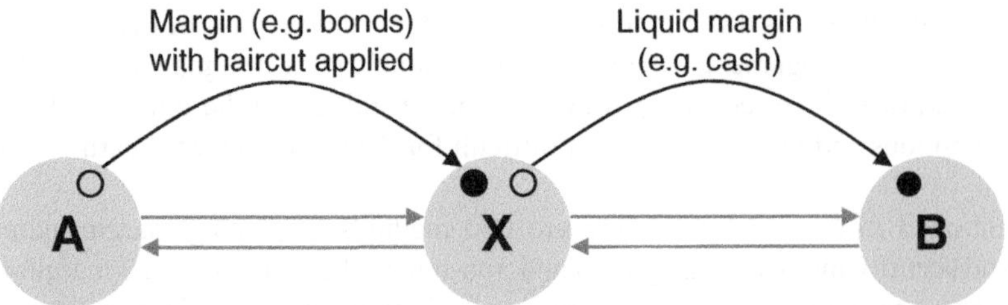

Figure 6.9 Illustration of margin transformation. Party A posts margin to party X who posts more liquid margin to party B (or back to party A). The obvious chain of A-X-B could be a client posting margin to a clearing member, who provides a transformation service in providing eligible (e.g. more liquid) margin to a CCP.

6.2.4 Margin transformation

Margin transformation refers to the conversion of one type of margin to another. Methods exist for this already such as repos, where a bond is exchanged for cash over a certain period. Margin transformation is likely to be an important tool in the clearing of OTC derivatives since CCPs generally enforce very high standards over margin liquidity (and indeed regulation tends to require this). Since many financial institutions may not have the relevant liquid margin to post, then it may be relevant to set up margin transformation possibilities illustrated in Figure 6.9. For example, a clearing member of a CCP may offer a service whereby their clients can post them relatively illiquid margin in lieu of more liquid margin, that the clearing member then posts to the CCP. The clearing member will charge a haircut on the illiquid margin, and/or a fee for providing this service. This is equivalent to the provision of a guaranteed rolling repo transaction.

6.3 MARGIN IN BILATERAL OTC DERIVATIVES MARKETS

6.3.1 The credit support annex (CSA)

There is no obligation in an OTC derivatives contract for either party to post margin. In bilateral markets, within an ISDA Master Agreement (section 5.1.4), it is possible to append a Credit Support Annex (CSA) to mitigate counterparty risk by agreeing to various margin posting. Most bilateral margin agreements are under ISDA documentation.[6] As with netting, ISDA has legal opinions throughout a large number of jurisdictions regarding the enforceability of the provisions within a CSA. The CSA is therefore at the centre of any margin agreement, as it governs the mechanics of margin with respect to issues such as:

- Method and timings of the underlying valuations.
- The calculation of the amount of margin that will be posted.
- The mechanics and timing of margin transfers.
- Eligible margin.
- Margin substitutions.
- Dispute resolution.
- Interest rate payments on margin.
- Haircuts applied to margin securities.

[6] The most recent figure is 87% as reported by ISDA (2013c).

- Possible rehypothetication (reuse) of margin securities.
- Triggers that may change the margin conditions (for example, ratings downgrades that may lead to enhanced margin requirements).

The process by which two counterparties will agree to margin their exposures can be summarised as follows:

- Parties negotiate and sign a CSA, containing the terms and conditions under which they will operate.
- Trades subject to margin are regularly marked-to-market, and the overall valuation including netting is agreed (unless this amount is disputed).
- The party with negative mark-to-market delivers margin (subject to minimum transfer amounts and thresholds as discussed later).
- The margin position is updated to reflect the transfer of cash or securities.
- (Periodic reconciliations should also be performed to reduce the risk of disputes).

CSAs must explicitly define all the parameters of the margin requirements and account for all possible scenarios. The choice of parameters will often come down to a balance between the workload of calling and returning margin versus the risk mitigation benefit of doing so. We will now analyse the components that make up the margin process in more detail.

6.3.2 Types of CSA

Due to the very different nature of OTC derivatives counterparties, different bilateral margin arrangements exist. Broadly speaking, these can be categorised into the following:

- *No CSA:* In some OTC derivatives trading relationships, CSAs are not used because one or both parties cannot commit to margin posting. A typical example of this is the relationship between a bank and a corporate, where the latter's difficult (for liquidity reasons) to post margin may mean that a CSA will not be used. A corporate typically prefers to pay up front for the counterparty risk they impose on the bank, via a credit value adjustment (CVA) charge (section 7.3.1), rather than posting margin to mitigate this charge.
- *Two-way CSA:* For two similar counterparties, a two-way CSA is more typical. Two-way CSAs with low thresholds are standard in the interbank market and are beneficial (from a counterparty risk point of view at least) to both parties.
- *One-way CSA:* In some situations, a one-way CSA is used, which is beneficial to only the margin receiver. A typical example is a high-quality entity such as a triple-A sovereign trading with a bank.

Another important point is that, historically, OTC derivative markets have sometimes linked margin requirements to parameters such as credit ratings. For example, prior to the financial crisis, triple-A entities, such as monoline insurers, traded through one-way CSAs, but with triggers specifying that they must post margin if their ratings were to decline. Such agreements can lead to rather unpleasant discontinuities, since a downgrade of a counterparty's credit rating can occur rather late with respect to the actual decline in credit quality, which in turn may cause further credit issues due to the requirement to post margin. This is exactly what happened with AIG and monoline insurers during the GFC (section 2.3.4) and is therefore a good argument against margins being linked to ratings or credit quality in general.

6.3.3 Thresholds and initial margins

The two key parameters that define the nature of a CSA are thresholds and initial margins, which are generally mutually exclusive.

A *threshold* defines the level of mark-to-market above which margin is posted, and therefore represents an exposure that cannot be mitigated. For example, if the threshold is 100 and the exposure is 250, then the amount of margin posted will be 150. If the exposure is less than 100 then no margin will be posted at all. The benefit of thresholds is that they generally reduce the operational burden of calling and returning margin. In a one-way CSA, the non-margin posting counterparty has a threshold of infinity.

Two other important terms used in CSAs are *minimum transfer amounts* and *rounding*. Margin cannot be transferred in blocks that are smaller than the minimum transfer amount, which avoids the operational costs associated with transferring small amounts. The minimum transfer amount and threshold are additive in the sense that the exposure must exceed the sum of the two before any margin can be called. A margin call or return amount may also be rounded to a multiple of a certain size to avoid non-standard amounts. Note that in central clearing, thresholds and minimum transfer amounts are typically zero.

The basis of OTC derivative margin agreements is variation margin (although it is not defined as such in a CSA). An initial margin (independent amount)[7] defines an amount of extra margin that must be posted independently to the valuation of the underlying trades. Initial margin is intended to cover the potential costs, above variation margin, in the close out of trades in the event of default. The aim is that with a sufficient initial margin a portfolio of trades will be well protected, just as a mortgagee is well protected if a house value significantly exceeds the value of the underlying loan. Note that mathematically an initial margin is the same as a negative threshold and vice versa. This is why thresholds and initial margins are not commonly used together. Initial margins have been historically used in OTC derivatives transactions to protect against:

- Delays inherent in the posting of variation margin.
- The period to close out the defaulted counterparties positions and associated market movements.
- Bid-offer costs in relation to close out.
- Aspects such as minimum transfer amounts that may lead to under-margining.

In bilateral markets, initial margins are typically expressed as fixed amounts, percentage of notional, or some quantitative (e.g. value-at-risk) calculation. The existence and size of initial margin is in general driven by a number of factors such as:

- The credit quality of the counterparty.
- The relationship of the counterparty (e.g. end user).
- The underlying leverage in the transaction.
- The nature (volatility, size) of underlying exposure.

Parties committing initial margins bilaterally are generally exposed since, in the event of the default of the receiver, they may be unable to retrieve their margin, which may have been

[7] This is the term usually used in OTC derivatives via CSAs, but we use the term 'initial margins' throughout to avoid confusion.

comingled or rehypothecated. This was illustrated in the Lehman Brothers bankruptcy where claims for the return of cash and securities representing initial margins were generally treated as unsecured claims on the Lehman estate. This led to market participants having a strong wish for initial margins to be held in such a way that they are remote from the bankruptcy of the receiver and immediately retrievable in the event of their default (segregation).

Initial margins are historically quite rare in OTC derivatives markets, except in certain cases such as banks trading with hedge funds. For example, BCBS-IOSCO (2012) reports that the total amount of initial margin held against non-centrally cleared derivative transactions represents €100 billion or approximately 0.03% of the gross notional exposure. Nevertheless, initial margins will become much more common in the future with central clearing and mandatory margin requirements for uncleared trades. The segregation issue mentioned above will also be a key issue.

6.3.4 Disputes

In bilateral OTC markets, margin requirements are typically based on mark-to-market prices that may differ significantly across market participants. In the event of a dispute between counterparties, the 'calculation agent' in the OTC derivatives contract usually gets to determine the price used for determining margin and settlement values. Given the non-transparent and decentralised nature of the OTC market, significant disagreements can occur about margin requirements, often arising from disputes over the prices used to calculate current mark-to-market values.

In OTC derivative markets, disputes over margin calls are common and can arise due to one or more of a number of factors:

- trade population
- trade valuation methodology
- application of netting rules
- market data and market close time
- valuation of previously posted margin

If the difference in valuation or disputed amount is within a certain tolerance specified in the margin agreement, then the counterparties may 'split the difference'. Otherwise, it will be necessary to find the cause of the discrepancy. Obviously, such a situation is not ideal and will mean that one party will have a partially unmargined exposure, at least until the origin of the disputed amount can be traced, agreed upon and corrected. The following steps are normally followed in the case of a dispute:

- The disputing party is required to notify its counterparty (or the third-party valuation agent) that it wishes to dispute the exposure or margin calculation, no later than the close of business on the day following the margin call.
- The disputing party agrees to transfer the undisputed amount and the parties will attempt to resolve the dispute within a certain time frame (the 'resolution time'). The reason for the dispute will be identified (e.g. which transactions have material differences in valuation).
- If the parties fail to resolve the dispute within the resolution time, they will obtain mark-to-market quotations from several market makers (typically four), for the components of the disputed exposure (or the value of existing margin in case this is the component under dispute).

Reconciliations aim to minimise the chance of a dispute by agreeing on valuation figures even though the resulting netted exposure may not lead to any margin changing hands. They can even be performed using dummy trades before two counterparties even transact with one another. It is good practice to perform reconciliations at periodic intervals (for example, weekly or monthly) so as to minimise differences in valuation between counterparties. Such reconciliations can pre-empt later problems that might arise during more sensitive periods. Reconciliations may be rather detailed and therefore highlight differences that otherwise may be within the dispute tolerance or that by chance offset one another. Hence problems that may otherwise appear only transiently should be captured in a thorough reconciliation. Around half of OTC derivatives portfolios are currently reconciled on a daily basis.[8]

In an attempt to improve dispute management, especially in light of margin requirements for non-cleared derivatives, ISDA has developed the 'ISDA 2013 EMIR Portfolio Reconciliation, Dispute Resolution and Disclosure Protocol',[9] which is based around European regulatory requirements.

The global financial crisis highlighted many problems in the margin management practices of banks. Regulators have reacted to this in the Basel III proposals for bilateral trades (section 4.2.1), which reduce (in some cases) the capital savings that can be achieved via margining. Margin management practices are improving substantially. One aim for the future should be STP (straight-through processing) of margin, i.e. sending and settling multiple margin calls without user intervention.

6.3.5 Standard CSA

A large amount of optionality exists in most bilateral CSAs since there are so many possibilities about the type of margin that can be delivered (and substituted) across currency, asset class and maturity. Knowing the cheapest-to-deliver margin in the future depends on many aspects, such as the future exposure, OIS rates in different currencies, cross-currency basis swap spreads, haircuts and substitution criteria. For these reasons, CSAs are generally being simplified and the concept of a standard CSA has been developed.

The ISDA Standard Credit Support Annex (SCSA) aims to achieve standardisation and greatly reduce embedded optionality in CSAs whilst promoting the adoption of standard pricing (for example, what is now typically known as OIS discounting). At the same time, the mechanics of a SCSA are focused on being closely aligned to central clearing margin practices. Additionally, the SCSA aims at creating a homogeneous valuation framework, minimising valuation disputes and making trading and innovation more straightforward. The SCSA is still being developed and the reader is referred to the ISDA website (www.isda.org) for the latest status.

In a typical CSA, a single amount is calculated at each period for a portfolio, which may cover many currencies. Cash margin may therefore be posted in different currencies and also typically in other securities. In addition, thresholds and minimum transfer amounts are commonly not zero. A SCSA greatly simplifies the process, requiring:

- Cash margin only (with respect to variation margin, any independent amounts will be allowed in other securities).

[8] Source: ISDA margin study (2013c).

[9] https://www2.isda.org/functional-areas/protocol-management/protocol/15.

- Only currencies with the most liquid OIS curves (USD, EUR, GBP, CHF and JPY) will be eligible.
- Zero thresholds and minimum transfer amounts.
- One margin requirement per currency (cross-currency products are put into the USD bucket).

The original intension was for the SCSA to require parties to individually calculate one margin requirement per currency per day, with delivery of cash in the relevant currency. However, this gives rise to settlement risk (section 7.1.3). To mitigate this, it was proposed to convert each currency amount into a single amount in one of seven "transport currencies", with an accompanying interest adjustment overlay (to correct for interest rate differences between the currencies, known as the "Implied Swap Adjustment Mechanism" or "ISA Method"). However, this method creates difficulty for the so-called leverage ratio of Basel III where cash margin can only be used if it is the same currency. This netting of currencies is problematic alongside forthcoming regulatory margin rules (see section 6.5.6). The current SCSA proposal has returned to the original concept and requires exchange of cash in 17 different currencies.

6.3.6 Margin practices in bilateral OTC markets

This section reviews market practice in the OTC derivative markets via the data from ISDA (2013c) and BIS (2013a).

Margin posting across the market is quite mixed depending on the type of institution (Table 6.1). The main reasons for counterparties posting lower margins are the difficulties in sourcing relevant high-quality securities and the operational workload associated with margin posting.

Despite this, margin usage has increased significantly over the last decade, as illustrated in Figure 6.10, which shows the estimated amount of margin and gross credit exposure. Gross credit exposures are adjusted for double counting of bilateral positions and are reported directly.[10] The ratio of these quantities gives an estimate of the fraction of credit exposure that is margined, which has grown year on year. Note that the overall number is a slightly misleading figure since is represents a combination of trades with no margin (no CSA, 0% margin), close to 100% margin (two-way CSA) and a relatively small number of cases of initial margins (greater than 100%).

Table 6.1 Margin posting by type of institution.

Institution type	Margin posting
Broker dealers, hedge funds	Very high
Sovereigns	Very low
Supranationals, local authorities, private equity funds, corporates	Low
Sovereigns	Very low

Source: ISDA (2013c).

[10] As discussed in BIS (2013a), there are two forms of double counting in the reported collateral amounts. The first is that margin may be counted twice by both the deliverer and receiver and this has been corrected for by halving the numbers. The second is the rehypothecation of margin for which there is no attempt to correct.

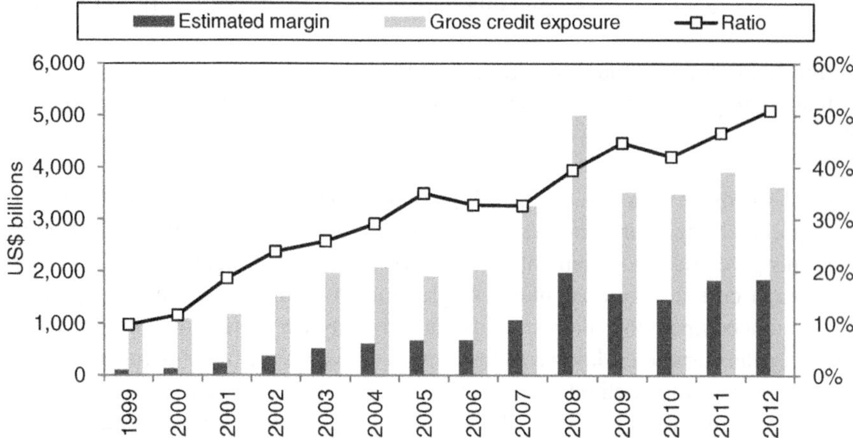

Figure 6.10 Illustration of the amount of margin compared to the gross credit exposure (i.e. after netting has been accounted for) and the ratio given the overall extent of margining of OTC derivatives. Source: BIS (2013a).

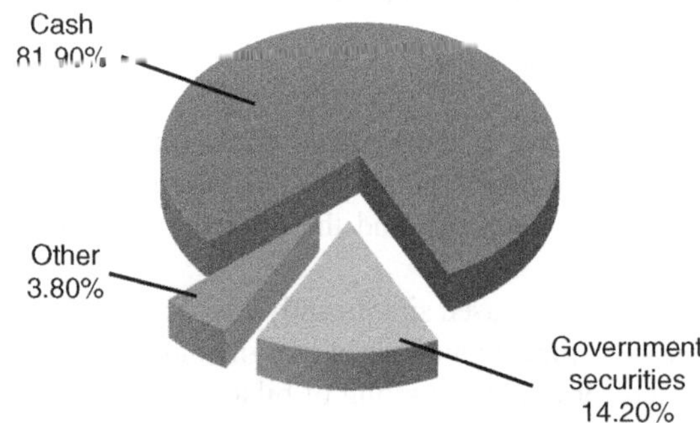

Figure 6.11 Breakdown of the type of margin used for OTC derivatives. Around 90% of cash is posted in USD and EUR currencies. The other category contains margin such as government agency securities, supranational bonds, US municipal bonds, covered bonds, corporate bonds, letters of credit and equities. Source: ISDA (2013c).

Cash is the major form of margin taken against OTC derivatives exposures (Figure 6.11). The ability to post other forms of margin is often highly preferable for liquidity reasons. However, the GFC provided stark evidence of the way in which margin of apparent strong credit quality and liquidity can quickly become risky and illiquid (for example, Fannie Mae and Freddie Mac securities and triple-A mortgage backed securities). Cash margin has become increasingly common over recent years, a trend which is unlikely to reverse, especially due to the cash variation margin required for centrally cleared trades.

Initial margins (known as independent amounts in ISDA documentation as mentioned previously), where received, are commonly not segregated, with around two thirds being comingled with variation margin. The amount of segregation has increased slightly over the last year. When initial margin is segregated then it is either held on the balance sheet of the margin receiver, with a custodian or in a tri-party arrangement.

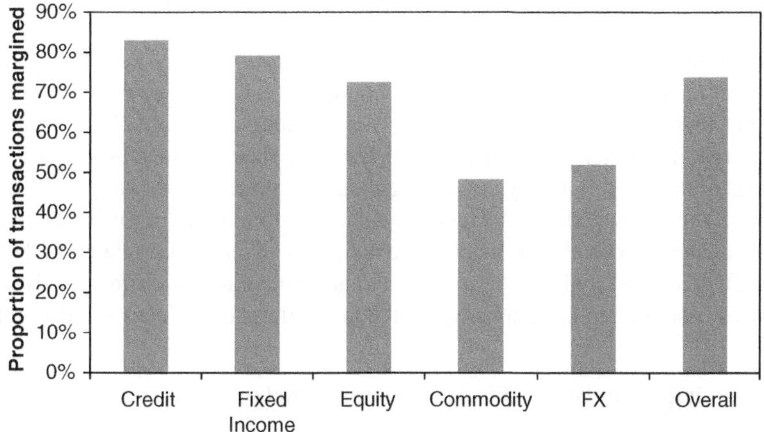

Figure 6.12 Illustration of the proportion of OTC derivatives margined shown by product type. Source: ISDA (2013c).

As illustrated in Figure 6.12, a large proportion of all OTC derivatives trade under margin agreements. The percentages are highest for credit derivatives, which is not surprising due to the high volatility of credit spreads[11] and the concentration of these trades with financial counterparties (as opposed to end users). Additionally, the fact that many FX transactions are short-dated explains the relatively low number for this asset class.

A final point that is important to note is in relation to margin reuse or rehypothecation. Where rehypothecation is allowed then this is often utilised, as seen from Figure 6.13, which is not surprising as this reduces funding costs and reduces demand for high-quality margin. However, it is also worth noting that a substantial proportions of margin is not eligible for rehypothecation.

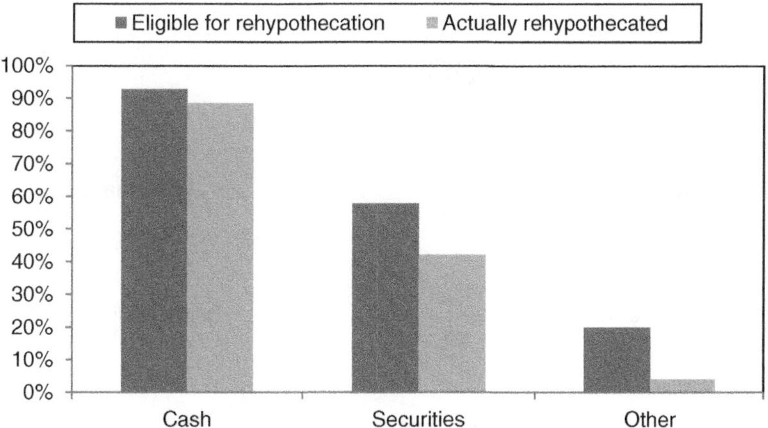

Figure 6.13 Illustration of rehypothecation of margin (large dealers only). Source: ISDA (2013c).

[11] In addition, the wrong-way risk embedded in credit derivatives may be driving this aspect.

6.4 THE RISKS OF MARGINING

Whilst margining is a useful mechanism for reducing counterparty risk, it has significant limitations that must be considered. It is also important to emphasise that margin, like netting, does not reduce risk overall but merely redistributes it. Essentially, margin converts counterparty risk into other forms of financial risk. The most obvious aspect is the linkage of margining to increased liquidity risk. Margining also gives rise to many other risks such as legal risk, if the envisaged terms cannot be upheld within the relevant jurisdiction. Other potential issues such as correlation risk (where margin is adversely correlated to the underlying exposure), credit risk (where the margin assets may default or suffer an adverse credit effects) and FX risk (due to margin being posted in a different currency) are also important.

6.4.1 Margin impact outside OTC derivatives markets

Similar to the example on netting in section 5.2.6, it is important to look at the impact of margin outside OTC derivatives markets. Figure 6.14 shows the impact of the posting of margin on an OTC derivative transaction. Assume that in default of party B, party A (either a bilateral counterparty, or a CCP) and the other creditors (OC) of B, have the same seniority of claim (pari passu). Party B owes derivatives creditors 50, and other creditors 100, and has assets of 100.

With respect to the amount of margin posted in Figure 6.14, it is useful to consider the following three cases:

- *No margining:* In the no margin case, the other creditors will have a claim on two thirds (100 divided by 150) of the assets of B, with the derivative claims of A receiving the remaining one third. The derivatives and other creditors will both recover 67% of their claims.
- *Variation margin:* If party B posts 50 variation margin to A against their full derivative liability, then this will reduce the value received by the OCs in default. Now the remaining assets of B in default will be only 50, to be paid to the other creditors (recovery 50%).

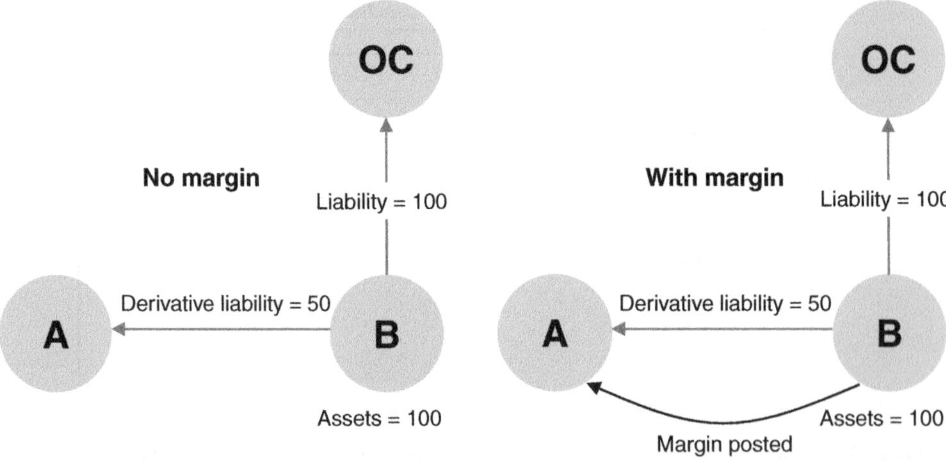

Figure 6.14 Example of the impact of derivatives margin on other creditors (OC). The margin posted (variation and possibly also initial) will reduce the claims of the other creditors.

- *Initial margin:* Suppose that B pays 50 variation margin and 25 initial margin and that the entire initial margin is used by A in the close out and replacement costs of their trades with B. In such a case, the OCs would receive only the remaining 25 (recovery 25%). (Of course, it could be argued that some or all of the initial margin may be returned, but a significant portion may be lost – the sceptical reader may wish to glance forward to section 10.2.1.)

Like the example on netting in the previous chapter, this again illustrates a redistribution risk within a capital structure, favouring derivatives counterparties at the detriment of other creditors. Margin does not reduce risk, it merely redistributes it (although possibly in a beneficial way).

6.4.2 Operational risk

The time-consuming and intensely dynamic nature of margining means that operational risk is a very important aspect. The following are examples of specific operational risks:

- missed margin calls
- failed deliveries
- computer error
- human error
- fraud

The following is a non-exhaustive list of points to consider in relation to operational risk:

- Legal agreements must be accurate and enforceable.
- IT systems must be capable of automating the many daily tasks and checks that are required.
- The regular process of calls and returns of margin is complex and can be extremely time-consuming, with a workload that increases in markets that are more volatile.
- Timely accurate valuation of all products is of fundamental importance.
- Information on initial margins, minimum transfer amounts, rounding, margin types and currencies must be maintained accurately for each counterparty.
- Failure to deliver margin is a potentially dangerous signal and must be followed up swiftly.
- Auction protocols (for CCPs) should be well defined.
- Fire drills (for CCPs) should be performed regularly to identify any potential weaknesses.

6.4.3 Liquidity risk

Margining leads to demanding liquidity requirements. Indeed, this is why some counterparties historically have not traded under CSAs. One of the most obvious manifestations of this liquidity risk occurs when margin has to be liquidated following the default of a counterparty and the underlying trades need to be simultaneously replaced. First, the surviving institution faces transaction costs (bid-offer) and market volatility over the liquidation period. Second, there is the risk that by liquidating an amount of a security that is large compared with the volume traded in that security, the price will be driven down and a potentially large loss incurred. If one chooses to liquidate the position more slowly, in small blocks, then there is exposure to market volatility for a longer period. It is also important to avoid concentration risk such as margin being in highly correlated securities or a single large issue.

6.4.4 Funding liquidity risk

The above considerations only come into play when a counterparty has actually defaulted. A more significant aspect of liquidity risk stems from the funding needs that arise due to margin terms, especially when margin needs to be segregated and/or cannot be rehypothecated. We refer to this as funding liquidity risk.

The problem with margin is that it converts counterparty risk into funding liquidity risk. This conversion may be beneficial in normal, liquid markets where funding costs are low. However, in abnormal markets where liquidity is poor, funding costs can become significant and may put extreme pressure on an institution. Chapter 13 will be dedicated to discussing this problem in more detail.

6.4.5 Segregation risk

The case of MF Global provides a good illustration of the potential risks of segregation. MF Global was a major derivatives broker that filed for bankruptcy in October 2011. The aim of segregation is to limit rehypothecation and make initial margins safe in the event of default of the margin receiver. This may be viewed as very safe since violation of segregation rules can be subject to both civil and criminal penalties.

Unfortunately, it became clear that prior to bankruptcy, MF Global had illegally transferred a total of US$1.6 billion of segregated customer margins to third parties. These margins had been passed to banks and trading partners of MF Global to meet overdrafts and margin calls. This was obviously a serious problem: for example, client positions could not be transferred to alternative solvent entities because the margin to support their risks was not available. Note that the problem was not investment losses in the pool of segregated assets (which could be considered another potential risk) but funds actually transferred out of the segregated pool. There are civil lawsuits and numerous private lawsuits in relation to this case (although no criminal lawsuits).

In the case of MF Global, segregation was not effective and customers lost money as a result. This raises questions about the enforcement of segregation, especially in times of stress. Note that the extreme actions from senior members of MF Global in using segregated customer margins were caused by desperation to avoid bankruptcy. It is perhaps not surprising that in the face of such a possibility, extreme and even illegal actions may be taken. There is obviously the need to have very clear and enforceable rules on margin segregation.

6.5 REGULATORY MARGIN REQUIREMENTS

This section outlines the regulatory margin requirements for bilateral OTC derivatives not subject to central clearing, as given in BCBS-IOSCO (2013b), and is discussed further in section 9.4.

6.5.1 Background

As discussed in section 4.2.5, in addition to already formulated rules for mandatory central clearing of standardised OTC derivatives and higher capital requirements for non-cleared trades, G20 leaders agreed in 2011 to add bilateral margin requirements for non-clearable

OTC derivatives. These margin requirements cover both variation and initial margins, with the latter being more significant due to being quite rare in bilateral markets. Such bilateral initial margins are intended to reduce systemic risk and to bridge the divide between clearable and non-clearable trades (which could otherwise encourage regulatory arbitrage).

The margin rules for non-cleared OTC derivatives are controversial, with concerns that they may create large funding liquidity problems. The Working Group on Margining Requirements (WGMR) has responded to concerns by watering down the final rules described in BCBS-IOSCO (2013b). Most notably, in addition to various exemptions, there is a threshold below which initial margin does not need to be exchanged. A quantitative impact study (QIS) developed by the WGMR estimated that, with this threshold, the initial margin requirements would require a relatively modest €700 billion in liquid assets. However, most participants in the QIS interpreted the threshold as applying to each entity, whereas the WGMR define this against a consolidated group (which could in some cases contain many different entities). This effect is estimated to increase the aforementioned value to around €1 trillion.[12]

Note that the US regulators such as the Federal Reserve, the Commodity Futures Trading Commission and Securities and Exchange Commission have each proposed margin rules in relation to the institutions they regulate which differ from those defined by BCBS-IOSCO. However, the US has been heavily involved in the development of the BCBS-IOSCO requirements, and would not therefore be expected to deviate substantially.

6.5.2 General requirements

Initial and variation margin requirements will apply to financial entities and systemically important non-financial entities ('covered entities'). The rules do not apply to the following entities:

- Sovereigns
- Central banks
- Multilateral development banks
- The Bank for International Settlements
- Other non-financial institutions that are not systemically important

The precise definition of covered entities is likely to have some slightly different interpretations in different regions. Intra-group transactions are treated at the discretion of the local regulator and should be subject to appropriate regulation concerning initial and variation margin, in a manner consistent with each jurisdiction's legal and regulatory framework. In addition to the exemption of various entities, certain products are also exempt, notably FX forwards and swaps, and repos and security lending transactions. A transaction can be exempt either due to the nature of one of the entities trading *or* the transaction type itself.

The concepts of variation and initial margin are intended to reflect current and potential future exposure respectively. With respect to each, standards state that covered entities for non-centrally cleared derivatives must exchange:

[12] For example, see 'WGMR proposals raise procyclicality fears', Risk, 5 April 2013, http://www.risk.net/risk-magazine/feature/2257285/wgmr-proposals-raise-procyclicality-fears.

- Variation margin:
  - Must be exchanged bilaterally on a regular basis (e.g. daily).
  - Full margin must be used (i.e. zero threshold).
  - The minimum transfer amount must not exceed €500,000.
- Initial margin:
  - To be exchanged by both parties with no netting of amounts.
  - Should be bankruptcy-protected.
  - Should be based on an extreme but plausible move in the underlying portfolio value at a 99% confidence level (at least).
  - A 10-day time horizon should be assumed on top of the daily variation margin exchanged (this is broadly consistent with Basel capital requirements for margined transaction).
  - Can be calculated based on internal (validated) models or regulatory tables.

Since initial margin is required to be segregated, this will be held separately from variation margin. A standard CSA would be modified to represent separate initial and variation margin amounts, with segregation rules over the former.

For covered entities and transactions, appropriate margin practices must be in place for all non-CCP derivative transactions. Variation margins will be required on all relevant trades from the same date. Initial margin requirements will be phased in by the use of declining thresholds from 1 December 2015, as shown in Table 6.2 (potentially also dependent on local regulator). Rigorous and robust dispute resolution procedures should be in place in case of disagreements over margin amounts. This is an important point since risk-sensitive initial margin methodologies will be, by their nature, quite complex (see Chapter 9) and likely to lead to disputes.

The principals therefore create a phasing in of requirements and allow an institution to be exempt if they have a total notional of less than €8 billion (for example, this would exempt small and medium-sized pension funds and hedge funds).

Table 6.2 Timescales for the implementation of margin requirements for covered entities and transactions based on aggregate group-wide month-end average notional amount of non-centrally cleared derivatives (including physically settled FX forwards and swaps), newly executed during the immediately preceding June, July and August.

Date	Requirement
1 December 2015	Exchange variation margin with respect to new non-centrally cleared derivative transactions
1 December 2015 to 30 November 2016	Exchange initial margin if average aggregate notionals exceed €3 trillion
1 December 2016 to 30 November 2017	Exchange initial margin if average aggregate notionals exceed €2.25 trillion
1 December 2017 to 30 November 2018	Exchange initial margin if average aggregate notionals exceed €1.5 trillion
1 December 2018 to 30 November 2019	Exchange initial margin if average aggregate notionals exceed €0.75 trillion
From 1 December 2019	Exchange initial margin if average aggregate notionals exceed €8 billion

Regarding the quality of initial margin, the margin should be 'highly liquid' and in particular should hold its value in a stressed market (accounting for the haircut). Risk-sensitive haircuts should be applied and margin should not be exposed to excessive credit, market or FX risk. Margin must not be 'wrong-way', meaning correlated to the default of the counterparty (for example, a counterparty posting their own bonds or equity). Examples of satisfactory types of margin are:

- Cash
- High-quality government and central bank securities
- High-quality corporate/covered bonds
- Equity in major stock indices
- Gold

As mentioned above, FX swaps and forwards are exempt from initial margin rules, which followed lobbying from the industry. This, like a similar exemption over clearing, is controversial. On the one hand, such FX products are often short-dated and more prone to settlement risk than counterparty risk. On the other hand, FX rates can be quite volatile and occasionally linked to sovereign risk, and cross-currency swaps are typically long-dated.

6.5.3 Threshold

To manage the liquidity impact associated with margin requirements, it is possible to use an initial margin threshold (not to be confused with the threshold defined in a CSA discussed in section 6.3.3). The introduction of this threshold followed the results of a quantitative impact study (QIS) which indicated that such a measure could reduce the total liquidity costs by 56% (representing over half a trillion dollars).[13] This would work in much the same way as a threshold in a typical CSA in that initial margin would not need to be posted until this threshold is reached, and above the threshold only the incremental initial margin would be posted. For example, for a threshold amount of 50 and a calculated initial margin of 35 no margin is required. However, if the calculated margin is 65 then an amount of 15 needs to be posted. The threshold can be no larger than €50m and must apply to a consolidated group of entities where relevant. This means that if a firm engages in separate derivatives transactions with more than one counterparty, but belonging to the same larger consolidated group (such as a bank holding company), then the threshold must essentially be *shared* in some way between these counterparties.

The threshold rules imply that a firm must have in place a system to identify the exposure to a counterparty across an entire group. It would then be necessary to decide how to identify the benefit created by the threshold. It could be allocated across entities a priori or used on a first-come-first-served basis. With respect to the threshold and minimum transfer amount (mentioned in the last section), there may also be the problem of conversion between currencies. Trades not denominated in the currency that the threshold is set may lead to the threshold being breached for FX reasons.

[13] http://www.bis.org/press/p130215a.htm.

6.5.4 Segregation and rehypothecation

Variation margin can be rehypothecated (see discussion in section 6.2.2) and netted. Initial margin should be exchanged on a gross basis (i.e. amounts posted between two parties cannot cancel) and must be immediately available to the collecting party in the event of their counterparty's default and also subject to arrangements that protect the posting party under the applicable law in the event that the collecting party enters bankruptcy. Furthermore, initial margin should not be rehypothecated, re-pledged or reused. These requirements mean initial margin needs to be completely segregated so as to provide the maximum protection against counterparty risk. As discussed in section 6.2.3, this is a problem under an English law CSA where title transfer of margin securities occurs and it would therefore be impossible for the client to have a first priority claim over the margin. Another problem arises from cash margin, which, since it is fully fungible, is more difficult to segregate than other assets. The use of a third party to achieve such segregation will create further credit risk to that party. Third-party custodians would most likely offer the most robust protection, although this does raise the issue as to whether such entities (the number of which is currently quite small) would become sources of systemic risk with the amount of margin they would need to hold.

Arrangements for segregation will vary across jurisdictions depending on the local bankruptcy regime and need to be effective under the relevant laws, and supported by periodically updated legal opinions. In general, there would seemingly need to be significant changes in market practice to accomplish the protection of clients from the rehypothecation of their initial margins.

Regarding client transactions, an entity entering into an uncleared transaction with a client must:[14]

- Notify the counterparty that they have the right to require the segregation of initial margins.
- Segregate these margins if this is the wish of the counterparty.
- Use an independent third-party custodian for this segregation.

However, in relation to the previous discussion in section 6.2.2 (see Figure 6.4), there is a question as to whether rehypothecation should be allowed in very limited situations where the trade is a hedge of a client position and will be suitably protected once rehypothecated with the client having a priority claim under the relevant insolvency regime. In the following limited circumstances, rehypothecation is allowed:

- The transaction(s) in question are solely for the purpose of hedging the firm's derivatives position arising out of transactions with the client (note that the definition of a hedge is not given and ambiguity exists over whether this would need to be an exact hedge or whether this could be a proxy hedge for example).
- The client's rights in the margin are protected.
- The client has been informed of its right not to permit rehypothecation and made aware of the risks associated with rehypothecation in the event of the insolvency.
- The client has been given the option to individually segregate its margin.

[14] Dodd–Frank also requires similar disclosure, see http://www.cftc.gov/ucm/groups/public/@newsroom/documents/file/ucs_qa.pdf.

- The client gives 'express consent in writing' to the rehypothecation, is told of the fact of any rehypothecation and, where it has chosen individual segregation, can be informed of the value of the margin that has been rehypothecated.
- Initial margin is treated as a segregated customer asset until rehypothecated to a third party (and once returned to the firm by the third party to which it was rehypothecated).
- Rehypothecation can only take place by a firm which is subject to regulation of liquidity risk.
- Rehypothecation can only take place to a regulated and unaffiliated third party firm pursuant to a directly enforceable agreement.
- Once rehypothecated to a third party, the third party treats the margin as a segregated customer asset and agrees not to further rehypothecate the margin.
- Both the firm and the third party must keep appropriate records to show that all relevant conditions have been met.

6.5.5 Initial margin methodologies

There is then the question of how to define initial margin amounts for portfolios. Rules require that initial margins should be calculated separately for different asset classes with the total requirement being additive across them. It is not therefore possible to benefit from potentially low historic correlations between risk factors in these assets. The relevant asset classes are defined as:

- Currency/rates
- Equity
- Credit
- Commodities

Separate calculations must also be made for derivatives under different netting agreements. The calculation of initial margins for covered entities can be done via two methods:

- Regulatory defined margin schedules.
- Entities own or third party quantitative models (that must be validated by the relevant supervisory body).

There can be no 'cherry picking' by mixing these approaches based on which gives the lowest requirement in a given situation (although it is presumably possible to choose different approaches for different asset classes as long as there is no switching between these approaches).[15]

Where an entity uses their own quantitative model for calculating margin this should be calibrated to a (equally weighed) period of not more than five years which includes a period of financial stress. These requirements, in particular the use of stress period, are aimed at avoiding procyclicality of margins and will be discussed further in Chapter 9. Large discrete

[15] The precise wording here from BCBS-IOSCO (2013b) is 'Accordingly, the choice between model- and schedule-based initial margin calculations should be made consistently over time for all transactions within the same well defined asset class'.

Table 6.3 Standardised initial margin schedule as defined by BCBS-IOSCO (2013b).

	0–2 years	2–5 years	5+ years
Interest rate	1%	2%	4%
Credit	2%	5%	10%
Commodity		15%	
Equity		15%	
Foreign exchange		6%	
Other		15%	

calls for initial margin (as could presumably arise due to procyclicality of the margin model) should be avoided as these tend to produce cliff-edge effects.

For entities not using their own models for margin calculations, a standardised initial margin schedule can be used (Table 6.3). The quantities shown should be used to calculate gross initial margin requirements by multiplying by the notional amount.

To account for portfolio effects, the well-known[16] NGR (net gross ratio) formula is used, which is defined as the net replacement divided by the gross replacement of transactions. The NGR is used to calculate the net standardised initial margin requirement via:

$$\textit{Net standardised initial margin} = (0.4 + 0.6 \times \textit{NGR}) \times \textit{Gross initial margin}$$

NGR gives a simple representation of the future offset between positions, the logic being that 60% of the current offset can be assumed for future exposures. For example, consider two 4-year interest rate products with notional values of 100 and 50 and respective mark-to-market (replacement cost) valuations of 10 and –3. This means that the NGR is 70% (the net exposure of 7 divided by the gross exposure of 10). From Table 6.3, the gross initial margin of the two trades would be 2% of 150 multiplied by NGR, which would then lead to a net initial margin of 2.1.

The choice of either internal models or standardised margin schedules is a difficult one. The latter are very simple and transparent but will yield more conservative requirements (for example, ISDA estimates that without thresholds the total amount of initial margin would be around six times higher than internal models). However, the design of internal models is open to substantial interpretation and would inevitably lead to disputes between counterparties and a large amount of regulatory approvals of different models. Disputes in OTC markets are often for relatively simple reasons (e.g. disagreement on trade population or valuation issues). This implies that disputes over initial margin calculations (which are much more complex and subjective) will be extremely common. ISDA has been developing a standard industry margin model (SIMM)[17] in an attempt to avoid a proliferation of margin models and reduce the number of disputes. This approach is discussed in more detail in section 9.4.5. However, such a model would have to have general approval, potentially within all jurisdictions, for all institutions wanting to use the model.

[16] NGR is used in bank capital requirements and the definition can be found in Annex IV of the Basel capital framework, paragraph 969(iv), Part 5, Basel II: International Convergence of Capital Measurement and Capital Standards: A Revised Framework (available at: www.bis.org/publ/bcbs128d.pdf).

[17] See 'Dealers plan standard margin model for WGMR regime', Risk, 21 June 2013, http://www.risk.net/risk-magazine/news/2276485/dealers-plan-standard-margin-model-for-wgmr-regime.

6.5.6 Non-netting across asset class

As mentioned above, BCBS-IOSCO rules require margins to be additive across asset classes, which would suggest that a separate initial margin model can be created for each asset class and the results treated additively. On the one hand, this simplifies matters as inter-asset dependencies (e.g. interest rate and credit spread correlations) do not need to be specified. On the other hand, this creates difficulties, an obvious problem being how to define to which asset class a given product should be assigned. This not only applies to relatively rare hybrid products as, for example, even a simple credit derivative transaction has interest rate as well as credit risk. Another problem is that separating asset classes may mean that hedged positions (e.g. a CDS position and an associated interest rate hedge) would not be seen as such and lead to higher margin requirements.

One way to get around the above problems is to divide risk factors and not products across asset classes (note this is also proposed by ISDA (2013b) in the standardised initial margin methodology discussed later in section 9.4.5). This would require a general margin methodology covering all risk factors and products. However, such a methodology would not need to model the correlations across asset classes. Risk factors in each asset class would then be shocked separately and independently of each other with the results being added. In such an approach, a given product would potentially create margin requirements across more than one asset class if it had sensitivity to the relevant risk factors. Additionally, offsetting products would be seen as such as they would not be potentially split up into different asset class categories. Indeed, a new product would not need to be assigned to any asset class, potentially avoiding another source of subjectivity and potential disputes.

The one disadvantage of the above approach is that it requires a generic risk factor methodology. This does not allow one asset class to use a proprietary model and another the standardised margin schedule.

6.5.7 Haircuts

As in the case of initial margin models, approved risk-sensitive internal or third party quantitative models can be used for establishing haircuts so long as the model for doing this meets regulatory approval. BCBS-IOSCO defines that haircut levels should be risk-sensitive and reflect the underlying market, liquidity and credit risks that affect the value of eligible margin in both normal and stressed market conditions. As with initial margins, haircuts should be set so to mitigate procyclicality and to avoid sharp and sudden increases in times of stress. The time horizon and confidence level for computing haircuts is not defined explicitly but would likely follow those for clearing (see later discussion in 9.2.1). The time horizon for computing a haircut could be argued to be less (say 2–3 days) than the horizon for initial margin since the margin may be liquidated independently and more quickly than the portfolio would be closed out.

Instead of model-based haircuts, an entity is allowed to use standardised haircuts as defined in Table 6.4.

In relation to the SCSA discussed in section 6.3.5, it appears that margin in a different 'transport currency' may attract an 8% haircut. This has been recently confirmed by European regulators.[18]

[18] See 'EU applies 8% haircut to margin-currency mismatches', Risk, 17 April 2014, http://www.risk.net/risk-magazine/news/2340270/eu-rules-levy-8-haircut-on-margin-currency-mismatches.

Table 6.4 Standardised haircut schedule as defined by BCBS-IOSCO (2013b). Note that the FX add-on corresponds to cases where the currency of the derivative differs from that of the margin asset.

	0–1 years	1–5 years	5+ years
High-quality government and central bank securities	0.5%	2%	4%
High-quality corporate/covered bonds	1%	4%	8%
Equity/Gold	15%		
Cash (in the same currency)	0%		
FX add-on for different currencies	8%		

6.5.8 Criticisms

As with the criticisms of mandatory central clearing, those against mandatory bilateral margin requirements cite costs as the key issue (based on the comments to the original consultative paper). More specially, the very large liquidity cost when initial margins cannot be rehypothecated is a key point, and it is suggested that the costs for end users (e.g. pension funds) may be very problematic. The following are representative comments:[19]

> We fully agree that the proposal to require all financial firms and systemically important non financial entities that engage in non-centrally cleared derivatives to exchange initial and variation margin on a 'universal two-way' basis would, as acknowledged by the consultation paper, incur the most substantial liquidity costs of all possible proposals in this area. We do not however, agree that it would best achieve the policy goal of reducing systemic risk and promoting central clearing.
>
> Any requirements to segregate margin with third party custodians and not allow the conservative reuse of margin will further exacerbate both the liquidity demands of the proposals and concentration risks in the financial system via the reliance on a small number of third party custodians. As a result of the potential effects above, the proposals are likely to increase the procyclicality of the financial system and leave market makers less willing to provide liquidity in non-centrally cleared derivatives when demand is greatest.
>
> The proposal contains, in our view, four elements which we consider to create significant costs to the industry and which are likely to disincentivise the use of OTC derivatives for risk management purposes: (i) the requirement for two-way posting of the full amount of initial margin (IM) on a gross basis (ii) mandatory full IM segregation without the possibility to rehypothecate or reuse the margin posted (iii) restrictions on margin eligibility (iv) the proposed treatment of transactions with affiliates.

An estimate of initial margin requirements is made by ISDA (2012), who state that total initial margin requirement could range from US$1.7 trillion to US$10.2 trillion (depending on the use of internal models and standard margin schedules, and the level of thresholds). They also suggest that in stressed market conditions, initial margin requirements could increase dramatically, perhaps by a factor of three. Whilst, the threshold of US$50 million

[19] http://www.bis.org/publ/bcbs226/comments.htm.

would relieve the liquidity strain created via the margin requirements, it would increase the procyclicality problem as margins would be even more sensitive to market conditions.

The overall thrust of criticisms seems to be twofold. First, initial margin requirements will be very costly and cause banks to find new ways of funding, diverting funding from other areas (e.g. lending businesses) or simply withdrawing from OTC derivatives markets. Second, initial margin requirements will create liquidity risk and give rise to procyclicalities where margin requirements could increase sharply in a crisis.

A number of respondents to the proposals on margin requirements make the suggestion that initial margins are unnecessary, suggesting instead that variation margin and regulatory capital requirements are sufficient to ensure systemic resilience.

Some other problems arise in relation to leverage ratio requirements for banks. In calculating the ratio, cash margin is included whilst non-cash margin is not. This seems to incentivise the use of non-cash margin.

7

Counterparty Risk in OTC Derivatives

By definition, risk-takers often fail. So do morons. In practice it's difficult to sort them out.
Scott Adams (1957–)

7.1 INTRODUCTION

This chapter is an introduction to relevant aspects of counterparty credit risk and other related topics such as credit value adjustment (CVA). We will review concepts such as credit exposure and valuation adjustments, and look at the impact of margin on counterparty risk. These topics are covered in more detail in other places (e.g. Pykhtin and Zhu 2007, Gregory 2012). The concept of funding value adjustment (FVA) can be seen as being related to counterparty risk reduction and will also be introduced.

7.1.1 Background

Traditionally, credit risk can generally be thought of as lending risk. One party owes an amount to another party and may fail to pay some or all of this due to insolvency. This can apply to loans, bonds, mortgages, credit cards and so on. Lending risk is based on relatively deterministic exposures (e.g. the size of a mortgage) and is unilateral (e.g. a mortgagor does not incur credit risk to a mortgagee).

Counterparty credit risk (often known just as counterparty risk) is the credit risk that the entity with whom one has entered into a financial contract (the counterparty to the contract) will fail to fulfil their side of the contractual agreement (e.g. they default). With counterparty risk, as with all credit risk, the cause of a loss is the obligor being unable or unwilling to meet contractual obligations. Counterparty risk is mainly relevant in derivative contracts and in particular OTC derivatives contracts. Two aspects may differentiate contracts with counterparty risk from traditional credit risk:

- The value of the contract in the future is uncertain, in most cases significantly so. The value of a derivative at a potential default date will be the net value of all future cashflows required under that contract. This future value can be positive or negative and is typically highly uncertain (as seen from today).
- Since the value of the contract can be positive or negative, counterparty risk is typically *bilateral*. In other words, in a derivatives transaction, each counterparty has risk to the other (although this risk, of course, will be asymmetric).

7.1.2 Origins

Counterparty risk arises in the following situations:

- Exchange-traded financial transactions, for example:
  - futures
  - options
- Securities financing transactions, for example:
  - repos and reverse repos
  - securities borrowing and lending
- OTC (over the counter) derivatives, some well-known examples being:
  - interest rate swaps
  - FX forwards
  - credit default swaps

Counterparty risk is generally not considered a significant problem in the first two areas. Exchanges typically only deal with liquid and short-dated products, and have a central clearing function with margining requirements to mitigate any residual risk from the default of a member of the exchange. Security financing transactions, such as repos, tend also to be short-dated and are usually over-margined via haircuts (e.g. a repo has an implicit initial margin due to the haircut making the value of the asset greater than the cash amount).

This leaves OTC derivatives as the major source of counterparty risk due to:

- *Size of the market:* Whilst not the best measure of risk, the total gross notional amount outstanding of OTC derivatives was estimated at US$668 trillion in mid-2013.[1] This is almost an order of magnitude larger than the total world GDP (gross domestic product). It is also many multiples of the total notional of exchange-traded derivatives (see Figure 2.4).
- *Long-dated products:* Many OTC products are long-dated due to the hedging needs of participants (e.g. pension funds). Products with maturities of several decades are not uncommon.
- *Unsecured exposures:* Some OTC derivative counterparties are unable or unwilling to post margin to secure the exposures they have. For example, entities such as sovereigns, supranationals and development banks typically do not post margin in OTC derivatives contracts (partially mitigated by their relatively strong credit quality), and other 'end users' such as corporates may at most provide only partial margin. Finally, even financial institutions only post margin based on the current mark-to-market of a contract (via a so-called zero threshold two-way CSA discussed in section 6.3.2). This creates potential exposure over the 'margin period of risk' (MPR) as discussed in section 6.1.4.

7.1.3 Settlement and pre-settlement risk

A derivatives portfolio contains a number of settlements equal to multiples of the total number of trades (for example, a swap contract will have a number of settlement dates as cashflows are exchanged periodically). Counterparty risk is mainly associated with pre-settlement risk, which is the risk of default of the counterparty prior to expiration (final settlement) of the

[1] See 'Statistical release: OTC derivatives statistics at end-June 2013', November 2013, http://www.bis.org/press/p131107.htm.

contract. However, we should also consider settlement risk, which is the risk of counterparty default *during* a settlement process.

- *Pre-settlement risk:* This is the risk that a counterparty will default prior to the final settlement of the transaction (at expiration). Counterparty risk refers to this component. Many derivatives contracts are short-dated and the pre-settlement period is, as the name suggests, short. In longer-dated transactions, especially common in OTC derivatives, the term 'pre-settlement' may be confusing. This one of the reasons that it is normally referred to as counterparty risk.
- *Settlement (Herstatt)*[2] *risk:* This arises at settlement if there are timing differences between each party performing its obligations under the contract. Generally, this settlement refers to the maturity of the contract (e.g. the exchange of currency payments in an FX forward). However, some derivatives, particularly over-the-counter (OTC) ones, may exchange periodic cashflows which can give rise to settlement risk on discrete days prior to maturity.

The difference between pre-settlement and settlement risk is illustrated in Figure 7.1.

Whilst settlement risk gives rise to much larger exposures, default prior to expiration of the contract is substantially more likely than default at the settlement date. However, settlement risk can be more complex when there is a substantial delivery period (for example, in a commodity contract where one may be required to settle in cash against receiving a physical commodity over a specified time period).

Clearing reduces both counterparty (pre-settlement) and settlement risks. Generally, settlement risk is the more significant component in short-dated (e.g. classical exchange-traded) products whilst counterparty risk is more important for longer-dated (e.g. OTC derivatives) products. Furthermore, there are well-established methods for reducing settlement risks in

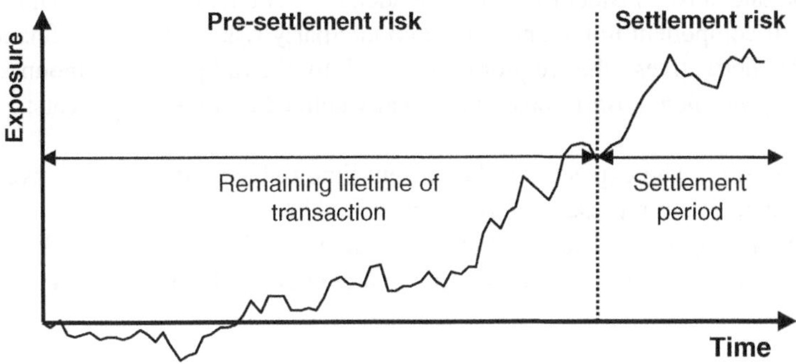

Figure 7.1 Illustration of pre-settlement and settlement risk. Note that the settlement period is normally short (e.g. hours) but can be longer in some cases. The pre-settlement period may be small for some derivatives with short maturities but larger for those with longer maturities such as many OTC products.

[2] This is named after a well-known example of settlement risk arising from the failure of a small German bank, Bankhaus Herstatt. Some of Herstatt Bank's counterparties had paid Deutschemarks to the bank during the day believing they would receive US dollars later in the same day in New York. However, Herstatt defaulted and as a result, all outgoing US dollar payments from their account were suspended.

OTC markets such as Continuous Linked Settlement (CLS) for FX transactions (section 5.1.2). All of this makes counterparty risk a key concern for OTC derivative markets.

Bilateral and centrally cleared markets manage settlement risk by netting (section 5.1.3) cashflow payments (at least those in the same currency). CCPs can further avoid settlement risks by requiring that payments be received before paying out. However, this potentially creates a funding problem for market participants.

FX transactions represent the most problematic form of settlement risk as payments often need to proceed in their respective currencies. The exemptions given to FX trades under central clearing and initial margining mandates (section 4.2.6) are due to the fact that they are relatively short-dated (minimal counterparty risk) and have settlement mechanisms such as CLS (minimal settlement risk). However, it should be noted that cross-currency swaps do not typically benefit from either of these aspects, and yet may still benefit from exemptions from clearing and bilateral margining requirements (in the latter case for only their FX component).

7.2 EXPOSURE

7.2.1 Definition

Credit exposure (hereafter often simply known as exposure) defines the loss in the event that a counterparty defaults. Exposure is characterised by the fact that a positive value corresponds to a claim on a defaulted counterparty, whereas in the event of negative value an institution is still obliged to honour their contractual payments. This means that if an institution is owed money and their counterparty defaults then they will incur a loss, whilst in the reverse situation they cannot generally gain[3] from the default by being somehow released from their liability.

Exposure is a very time-sensitive measure since a counterparty can default at any time in the future and one must consider the impact of such an event many years from now. Exposure is a non-trivial component in the analysis of counterparty risk as, for many financial instruments (notably derivatives), the creditor is not at risk for the full principal amount of the trade but only the *replacement cost*. Exposure is broadly defined by two components:

- *Current exposure:* The exposure at the present time (which should be relatively straightforward to define as it represents only the current value).
- *Potential future exposure:* The possible future value, which depends on market movements and other effects such as contractual terms in a contract and is therefore more difficult to define.

A defining feature of counterparty risk arises from the asymmetry of potential losses with respect to the value of underlying transaction(s). In the event that a counterparty has defaulted, an institution may close out the relevant contract(s) and cease any future contractual payments. Following this, they may determine the net amount owing between them and their counterparty, and take into account any margin that may have been posted. Note that margin

[3] Except in some special and non-standard cases that are discussed in Gregory (2012) and also in case of replacement costs as discussed in the next section.

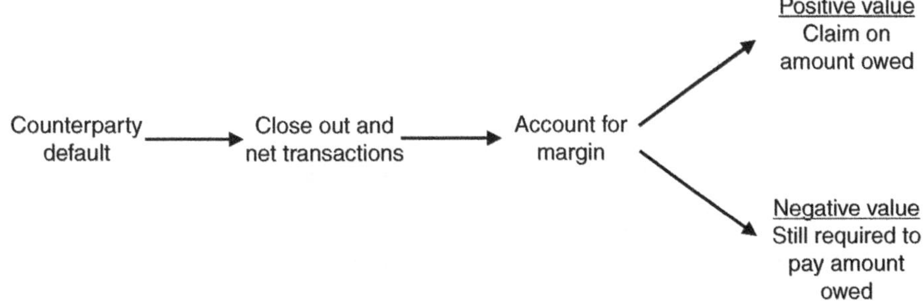

Figure 7.2 Illustration of the impact of a positive or negative value in the event of a counterparty default.

may be held to reduce exposure but any posted margin may have the effect of increasing exposure (although only to the extent that it is in excess of amounts already owed).

Once the above steps have been followed, there is a question as to whether the net amount is positive or negative. The main defining characteristic of exposure is related to whether the effective value of the contracts (including margin) is positive (in an institution's favour) or negative (against them), as illustrated in Figure 7.2:

- *Negative value:* In this case, an institution is in debt to its counterparty and is still legally obliged to settle this amount. Hence, from a valuation perspective, the position appears essentially unchanged.[4] An institution does not gain or lose from their counterparty's default in this case.
- *Positive value:* When a counterparty defaults, they will be unable to undertake future commitments, and hence an institution will have a claim on the positive value at the time of the default, typically as an unsecured creditor. They will then expect to recover some fraction of their claim, just as bondholders receive some recovery on the face value of a bond. However, this unknown recovery value is, by convention, not typically included in the definition of exposure.

The above feature (an institution loses if the underlying value is positive and does not gain if it is negative) is a defining characteristic of counterparty risk. One can define exposure simply as max(*value*, 0), where the term *value* should be adjusted for netting and margin effects as discussed in the previous two chapters.

A current valuation of all relevant positions and margin will lead to a calculation of current exposure (admittedly with some uncertainty regarding the actual close out amount). However, it is even more important to characterise what the exposure might be at some point in the future. This concept is illustrated in Figure 7.3, which can be considered to represent any situation from a single trade to multiple netted trades, with some margin arrangement possibly also associated to them. Whilst the current (and past) exposure is known with certainty, the future exposure is defined probabilistically by what may happen during the transaction

[4] Although the actual close out valuation of the transaction may differ significantly, especially for non-standard and illiquid transactions. This is discussed more in the next section.

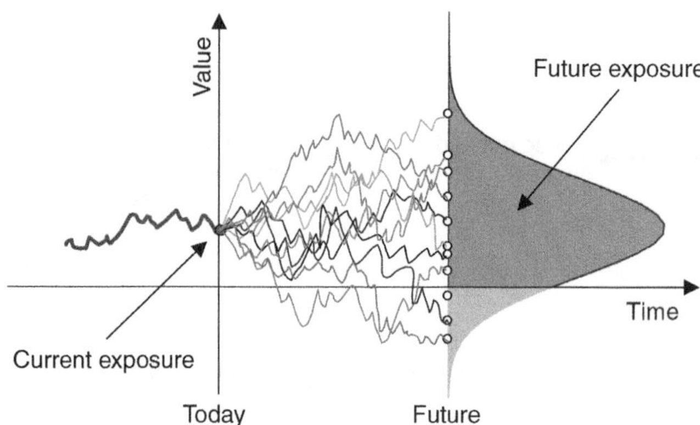

Figure 7.3 Illustration of future exposure with the grey area representing exposure (positive future values). The white area represents negative values which generally do not lead to losses.

lifetime in terms of market movements and contractual features, both of which are uncertain. Hence, in understanding future exposure one must define the level of the exposure and its underlying uncertainty.

7.2.2 Mark-to-market and replacement cost

In the event of a counterparty default then OTC derivative contracts would normally be replaced, and it is this 'replacement cost' that actually characterises any losses. Indeed, contractual definitions of actions in default scenarios typically refer to replacement costs. Future replacement costs are therefore the appropriate measure to use to define exposure.

However, a problem with future replacement costs are that they depend on a number of aspects, such as the nature of the market at the default time and any charges levied by a replacement counterparty for credit and liquidity components. For reasons of simplicity, the mark-to-market value of a transaction is often used in quantification as a reasonable proxy for the replacement cost. This is the case in determining the amount of (variation) margin to be paid and, in quantitative models, for determining exposure. One role of initial margin is therefore to provide a buffer for any losses resulting from replacement cost at close out being higher than the theoretical mark-to-market at default.

In bilateral transactions, the replacement cost is often difficult to define and can lead to legal cases in large bankruptcies (Lehman Brothers being a particularly significant example). CCPs remove such problems as they effectively define the replacement cost via the auction or other method they use to close out and hedge positions. However, this may in turn lead to additional problems where defaulted clearing members or clients claim that the prices achieved by the CCP in closing out their portfolios are not representative (as discussed later in section 10.2.1).

7.2.3 Non-margined exposure

Although this book deals with margined transactions, either bilateral or centrally cleared, it is informative to understand the nature of exposure without any margining in place. The

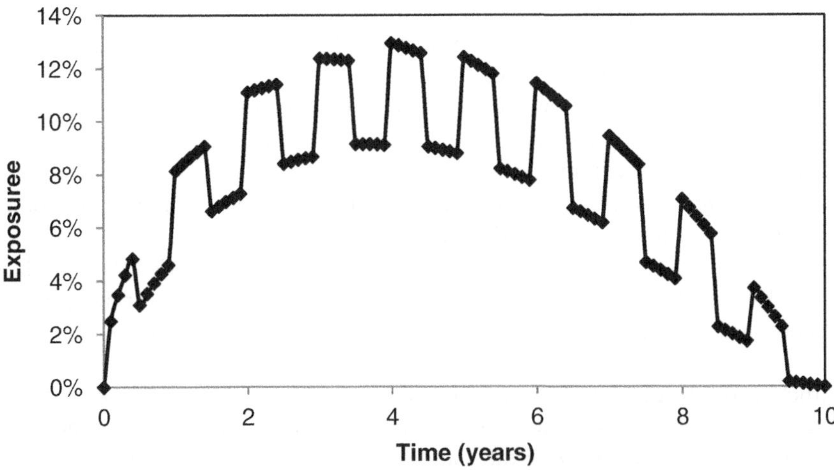

Figure 7.4 Illustration of the exposure (defined as a worst-case measure and in percentage of notional) for a 10-year swap with unequal cashflows and no margin agreement.

potential future exposure of an OTC derivative without any margin exchange depends broadly on three different aspects:

- *Market movements:* Market movements are increasingly uncertain moving further into the future. This will have the effect of increasing exposure approximately according to the 'square root of time rule'[5] meaning that, all other things being equal, a two-year exposure will be approximately $\sqrt{2} = 1.41$ times larger than a one-year exposure.
- *Time to maturity:* As transactions approach maturity, they may have less sensitivity to market movements leading to a reduction in exposure.
- *Contractual effects:* Standard components of derivative contracts such as cashflow payments and exercise decisions may change exposure, often discretely. Less common contractual terms such as early termination triggers (where a transaction may be contractually cancelled based on certain conditions) can also have an impact on exposure.

All of the above effects are illustrated in Figure 7.4, which represents an exposure for a 10-year interest rate swap over its lifetime. The exposure initially increases due to the uncertainty of market movements but then declines due to the approaching maturity. Also seen are jumps, since the swap pays semi-annually but receives on a quarterly basis.

7.2.4 Margined exposure

In the event that margin is posted against an exposure, the magnitude and structure changes significantly. This is because a potentially long-dated exposure is essentially converted into a short-dated one. A margined exposure is essentially defined by the following two components:

[5] This is relevant for independently and identically distributed (i.i.d.) random variables only but is a useful rule of thumb in practice.

- *Contractual effects:* Typically, margin agreements contain clauses relating to how much margin should be posted at a given point in time. The most important are a threshold and an initial margin defined in section 6.3.3. A threshold specifies that margin is posted only against exposure *above* a certain level whereas an initial margin represents additional margin above the exposure. Clearly, increasing the threshold will increase exposure whereas increased initial margin will reduce exposure.
- *Delay in receiving margin:* The effective time taken to receive margin is the other key component in determining to what degree margin reduces exposure. This effective delay in receiving margin is often known as the margin period of risk (MPR), introduced in section 6.1.4. The MPR is typically set to be around 10 business days or more in bilateral transactions and less (e.g. five business days) in centrally cleared transactions.

It is instructive to consider the case of a margin agreement with a zero threshold but no initial margin. Figure 7.5 illustrates the approximate impact of a strong margin agreement (daily variation margin exchange with zero threshold but no initial margin) on exposure. The main source of risk is the inability to receive margin for a time equal to the MPR. This means that the exposure is defined by a potential increase in the value of the contracts over this period and is proportional to the variability of these contracts. Many portfolios will also 'age' over time due to the maturity of transactions and payment of cashflows. This will have the impact of making the exposure reduce as the time horizon approaches maturity.

Regarding the overall reduction in exposure, this clearly depends broadly on the length of the MPR compared to the original maturity of the portfolio in question. Since risk scales approximately with the square root of time, this should be applied to calculate the appropriate scaling factor. A more precise calculation that actually shows the approximate reduction for a swap like portfolio (meaning that the non-margined exposure peaks as in Figure 7.4) is $0.5 \times \sqrt{T / \tau}$ (this is explained in Appendix 7A). So, for example, if a 5-year portfolio were margined with an assumed MPR of 10 business days then the approximate average reduction

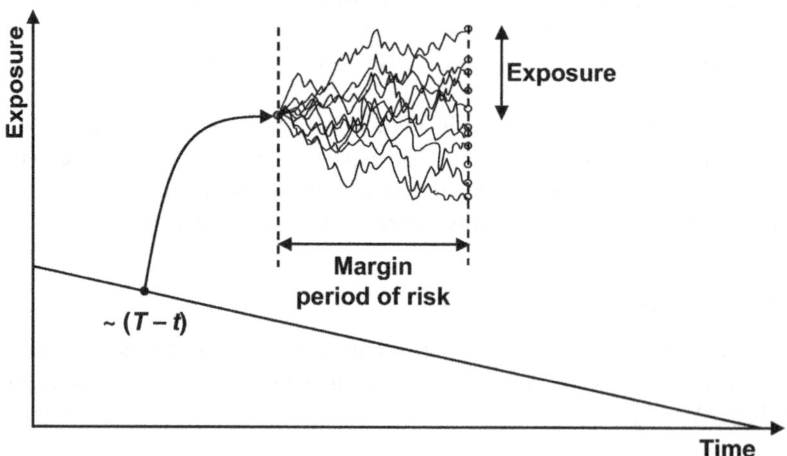

Figure 7.5 Illustration of the impact of a strong margin agreement (daily exchange with zero threshold but no initial margin) on exposure. *T* represents the final maturity date and *t* the current date.

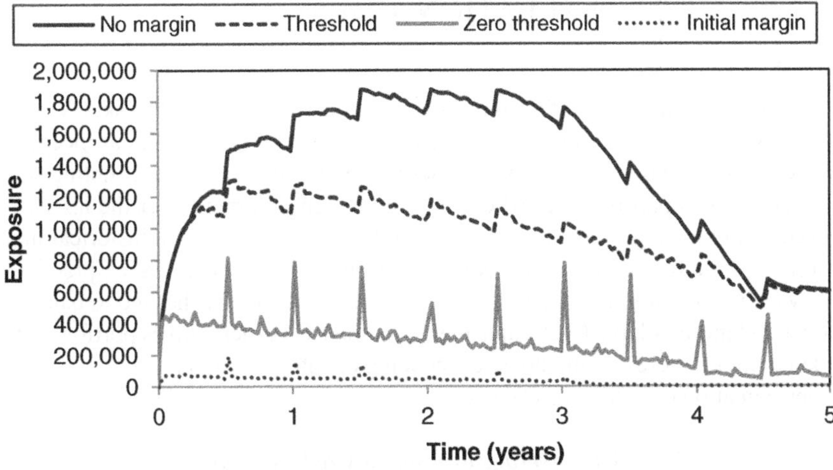

Figure 7.6 Illustration of the exposure of a 5-year portfolio for different margin cases. The margin period of risk is assumed to be 10 business days.

in exposure would be expected to be $0.5 \times \sqrt{250 \times 5 / 10} = 5.6$. In reality, a strong variation margin agreement would be expected to be slightly worse than this due to aspects such as the need to post margin as well as receive it,[6] and the effect of other margin terms such as minimum transfer amounts.

Figure 7.6 illustrates the exposure calculated for a 5-year portfolio under different margining terms. Compared to the no margin case, margining with a zero threshold reduces the exposure by a significant amount, on average around a factor of 5, consistent with the approximate calculation above. The case of a positive threshold increases the exposure compared to the zero threshold, since it prevents margin from being received below a certain level. However, initial margin allows the exposure to be reduced beyond the zero threshold value since it acts as a buffer to absorb potential moves during the MPR. Referring to Figure 7.5, it would seem natural to define the initial margin via some quantified worst-case move during the MPR. This is indeed the case with the use of value-at-risk (VAR) approaches with specific confidence levels and time horizons to define bilateral or CCP initial margins amounts as discussed in more detail in Chapter 9.

One final point to note about the margined exposures in Figure 7.6 is that the impact of cashflow payments that are characteristic of many long-dated derivatives portfolios are important. If a party makes a significant cashflow payment (such as the netted fixed against floating leg on a swap), then the exposure will essentially jump at this point since the margin to cover this cashflow cannot be received immediately. This is an important consideration for the margining of OTC derivative portfolios.

[6] Since margin posted and then required back will be at risk, as this is typically not protected in a bilateral margin (CSA) agreement. Furthermore, as variation margin is not segregated, as discussed in section 6.2.3, it can be at risk under margining rules.

7.3 VALUATION ADJUSTMENTS

7.3.1 CVA

Credit value adjustment (CVA) refers to the quantification of counterparty risk. CVA has been used by banks for many years to price the new counterparty risk in trades at inception. Reporting of CVA is also now a requirement under international fair value accounting standards (IFRS 13) and is also part of Basel III capital requirements. A trend over the last few years has evolved from viewing CVA as an actuarial style reserve based upon historical inputs, to an adjustment to the fair value based upon market-implied parameters. Such practices have been catalysed via requirements such as IFRS 13 and Basel III. This has led to banks having much larger and more volatile CVA adjustments for their OTC derivatives portfolios. In turn, this has led to more interest in methods for reducing counterparty risk.

The approximation definition of CVA is:

$$CVA = Average\ exposure \times Credit\ spread$$

where the average exposure represents the entire lifetime of the transaction or portfolio in question (this is often known as EPE or expected positive exposure). The credit spread represents the benchmark credit risk of the counterparty as observed from market prices such as credit default swaps or bonds. If the credit spread of a counterparty cannot easily be observed directly (quite common for many counterparties) then another counterparty or a credit index may be used as a proxy for estimation.

7.3.2 Impact of margin on CVA

It is interesting to consider the impact of margining on the reduction of CVA. We first show CVA for the strong CSA case as a function of the MPR in Figure 7.7. The CVA increases approximately with the square root of the increasing MPR, as expected from the simple analysis presented in section 7.2.4, tending towards the no margin case. What is clear is that even a

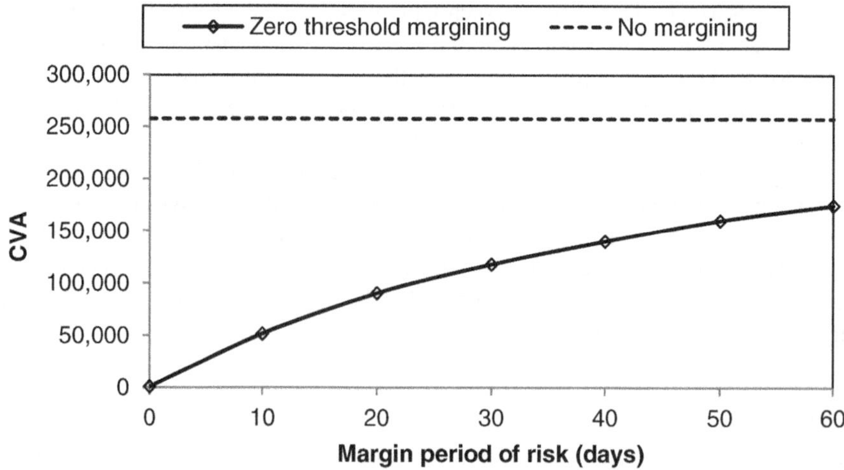

Figure 7.7 Illustration of the CVA of a 5-year portfolio as a function of the margin period of risk (MPR) in business days.

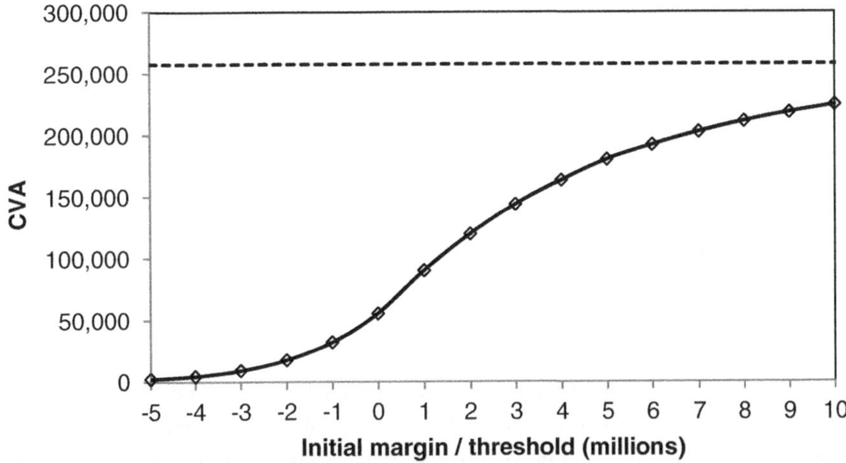

Figure 7.8 Illustration of the CVA of a 5-year portfolio as a function of threshold and initial margin for a margin period of risk (MPR) of 10 business days.

relatively short MPR causes a material CVA number. This could be viewed as a clear need for initial margin so as to mitigate the residual CVA caused by the MPR.

CCPs do not compute or charge CVA. Instead, they charge financial contributions and have loss allocation rules so they do not have any material counterparty risk (or at least that is the aim). A simplistic but useful way to look at the initial margin required by a CCP, is that it is the amount required to make the CVA become practically zero.

It is interesting to consider the impact of (received) initial margin on CVA. Mathematically, an initial margin is the same as a negative threshold. Intuitively, this can be understood since a positive threshold means that margin is not received until this level is reached and so a negative threshold must imply that margin is held even at an exposure of zero. Figure 7.8 shows CVA as a function of threshold (positive values) and initial margins (negative values) for a fixed MPR. As the threshold reduces, the CVA decreases from the no margin value to a value around five times smaller, as discussed previously in section 7.2.4. With an increasing initial margin, the CVA reduces towards zero.

Although the above illustrates the impact of initial margin reducing CVA to potentially close to zero, there is a clear law of diminishing returns. The greatest rate of reduction in CVA comes when the threshold is lowered towards zero. Thereafter, it takes progressively more initial margin to achieve the same amount of CVA reduction. Hence, whilst initial margin can indeed neutralise CVA completely, it appears to be a very costly process. Put differently, initial margins should be large enough to safely mitigate counterparty risk but no larger. The true cost of margin is seen when looking at other valuation adjustments such as DVA and FVA.

7.3.3 DVA and FVA

Alongside CVA, it is also important to consider other valuation related components. Debt value adjustment (DVA) is the opposite of CVA and refers to the benefit that a party achieves when they default since they do not pay liabilities in full. The use of DVA has been mainly

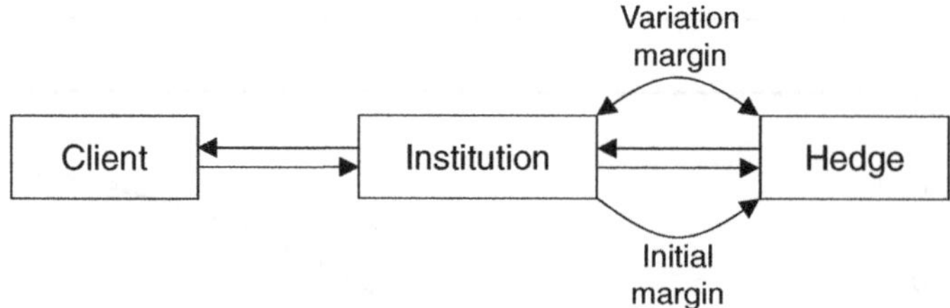

Figure 7.9 Illustration of the need to price funding costs into transactions. A non-margined client trade is hedged with a transaction under a margin agreement, which requires variation margin and potentially initial margin posting.

driven by fair value accounting requirements (e.g. IFRS 13). Since the goal is to define the 'exit price' of a transaction, DVA must be included in valuation as representing the counterparty's CVA. For example, if a party unwinds a transaction with a counterparty then this counterparty may include an assessment of their CVA in the price and this is represented by the party's own DVA component. However, DVA is controversial since it creates an increasing profit for a party with declining credit quality (e.g. see Gregory 2009).

Another commonly used component in derivatives pricing is funding value adjustment (FVA). This represents the funding costs and benefits that a derivative contract can create. FVA represents the funding imbalance caused by non-margined transactions as illustrated in Figure 7.9. Here, an institution has a transaction with a client without a margin agreement, which is hedged via a margined transaction.[7] Hence the institution will have a funding cost (benefit) when they post (receive) margin on the hedge. This represents, for example, a common situation when a bank does a transaction with a typical end user.

There are two distinct forms of FVA arising from the above setup:

- *Variation margin FVA:* This is a symmetric funding component arising from the posting and receipt of variation margin.
- *Initial margin FVA:* A one-way funding cost related to the need to post initial margin on the hedge, for example due to mandatory clearing or margining rules. Even if initial margin was also received then this would not offset this cost due to the need for segregation (section 6.2.2).

The first term above has been widely discussed in the literature of recent years and has, like DVA, proved controversial. Hull and White (2012) argue that variation margin FVA should not be valued into transactions or reported in financial statements. The argument of Hull and White can be expressed simply that, since variation margin only represents a payment of what is owed already, then any apparent funding costs or benefits will not exist when the entire balance sheet of an institution is considered. Despite this, arguments exist for the use of FVA alongside CVA and DVA, for example Burgard and Kjaer (2011). Current market practice seems to be that most banks price some sort of funding component linked to variation margin requirements alongside CVA adjustments (see Deloitte-Solum 2013).

[7] Note that there are other ways to explain the existence of funding costs and benefits and some may argue with the need to explain funding arising due to the hedge of the trade. However, this is a simple and intuitive explanation of FVA.

The FVA represented by initial margin is not controversial as this represents an additional margin in excess of any amount owed and therefore is not offset by any balance sheet benefit. This is also enforced via segregation: whereas variation margins may be rehypothecated and reused, initial margins by their very nature must be segregated and therefore offer no funding benefit (section 6.2.3). Hence, whilst CVA can be reduced to zero with a substantial initial margin (Figure 7.8), the cost of this will be an increasing FVA cost. We will return to this discussion of the potential cost of margining in Chapter 13

7.3.4 Wrong-way risk

Wrong-way risk (WWR) refers to an adverse relationship between the credit quality of a counterparty and the exposure to them. In the GFC, the potential dangers of WWR were illustrated, for example, when banks lost billions of dollars due to largely non-margined trades with monoline insurance companies (e.g. see Gregory 2008).

Broadly speaking, as defined by the BCBS (2011a), there are two distinct types of WWR, which could apply to either exposure, or margin-related linkages:

- *General WWR:* This arises from macroeconomic relationships (such as interest rates being correlated to credit spreads) and as such is an unavoidable consequence of trading and margining in financial markets. It can be mitigated via the correct calculation of initial margins and haircuts. Indeed, one of the requirements for initial margin in CCP and bilateral markets is to be liquid and of strong underlying credit quality. This can be seen as partially mitigating any WWR concerns.
- *Specific WWR:* This generally arises from 'poorly structured transactions' (BCBS 2011a) such as counterparties posting their own assets as margin. Such cases are probably best avoided altogether and indeed may be prevented by the rules of a CCP.

In the context of clearing and margining, there are two possible WWR effects to consider:

- *Exposure WWR:* This occurs when the exposure of a transaction is adversely related to the credit quality of the counterparty, meaning that the exposure is likely to be high when the credit quality of the counterparty deteriorates. An example could be a counterparty paying a floating rate of interest in a swap that is more likely to default in a high interest rate regime (general WWR). A more extreme example is a bank selling credit default swap protection on another bank domiciled in the same country (specific WWR).
- *Margin WWR:* This would refer to a situation where the value of margin has a dependency on the credit quality of the counterparty posting the margin. An example of this could be a counterparty sensitive to a high interest rate regime posting treasury bonds (general WWR). A stronger example would be a sovereign posting their own bonds as margin (specific WWR).

Central clearing can potentially disguise exposure WWR since the CCP replaces the counterparties to a trade. For example, suppose a bank sells CDS protection on another similar bank domiciled in the same geographical region. This is a classic WWR situation, but under central clearing the CCP will effectively replace the bank counterparty and be the seller of protection. The wrong-way risk is essentially absorbed by the CCP and may not be quantified properly, leading to insufficient margins and default funds being held against the risk (see also section 8.4.6).

On the other hand, exposure WWR can be mitigated by the initial margin and default fund requirements of CCPs which, unlike bilateral markets, could be increased for identified WWR situations. Furthermore, margin WWR may be prevented by CCPs having strong standards over admissible margin. In a bilateral market, due to the flexibility of CSAs, an entity may be able to post margin with a price highly correlated to their own credit quality (e.g. a bank posting bonds of the sovereign of the region in which they are located). However, a CCP may not allow such margin to be posted and will therefore mitigate the potential WWR in such a case.

7.3.5 The balance between counterparty risk and funding

There is an important balance between counterparty risk (CVA) and funding (FVA). An obvious example is with respect to initial margins: increasing initial margin reduces counterparty risk but increases funding costs. For received margin to be useful in reducing counterparty risk, it must not have any adverse margin WWR as defined above. Margin posted will create additional counterparty risk unless segregated. On the contrary, for margin to be useful and/or not costly from a funding point of view then it needs to be rehypothecable and/or not segregated. Following this, it is possible to identify that different types of margin have different characteristics when considered from a counterparty risk or funding perspective. Some examples of such characteristics are shown in Table 7.1.[8]

An entity posting their own bonds is clearly bad (although not completely useless)[9] from a counterparty risk reduction point of view. However, if such bonds can be rehypothecated[10] then they are still beneficial from a funding point of view (e.g. they can be repoed or posted in another margin agreement). A bank posting cash in their local currency will be a similar situation: the wrong-way nature is problematic from a counterparty risk but not a funding point of view. Segregated initial margin represents the reverse situation: it reduces counterparty risk effectively but is costly from a funding perspective, as it cannot be reused in any way.

A practical example of the balance represented in Table 7.1 is the move by some sovereigns and supranationals away from their beneficial one-way CSAs to post margin. Given the different impact of margin on counterparty risk and funding (section 6.2.1), the most optimal

Table 7.1 Comparison of the benefits of different types of margin from counterparty risk and funding points of view.

	Counterparty risk	Funding
Cash	Good	Good
Entity posting own bonds (that can be rehypothecated)	Bad	Good
Cash from major bank in their local currency	Fair	Good
Initial margin (segregated)	Good	Bad

[8] Note that this considers the general aspects for both payer and receiver of margin.

[9] Even in default, the bonds will have some recovery value. Additionally, it may be possible to call for more margin as the bond price declines, although the benefit will depend on how quickly the counterparty credit quality deteriorates.

[10] Or are re-used under title transfer.

outcome is probably for such entities to post their own bonds as margin.[11] This mitigates the funding cost they would otherwise impose on banks and therefore reduces the FVA charge they have to pay. It is not as effective at reducing counterparty risk and therefore CVA and CVA capital charges but since such entities have triple-A ratings then this is not a major concern anyway.

In terms of defining admissible margins, CCPs and mandatory margin requirements focus on the reduction of counterparty risk. The implication is that this may create funding strains in the market. Such strains are the heart of the cost/benefit analysis of clearing and bilateral margin rules. We will discuss the costs and impact of margining in more detail in Chapter 13.

APPENDIX 7A: SIMPLE FORMULA FOR THE BENEFIT OF A MARGIN AGREEMENT

This formula looks to define the approximate reduction that a 'strong margin agreement' would have on mitigating credit exposure. The assumptions in deriving this formula are zero threshold, current mark-to-market of zero and a one-way CSA in the parties' favour (since there is no incorporation of the impact of posting margin although this may only create a small effect anyway).

Incorporating the impact of future uncertainty and duration, a reasonable proxy for the uncertainty of a non-margined portfolio (see Figure 7.5) is $\sqrt{t}\,(T-t)$, where T is the (longest) maturity in the portfolio. Note that this considers the portfolio will gradually decay over time as cashflows are paid and transactions mature. This term should be multiplied by a term to represent the volatility of the portfolio but this is ignored since the same volatility would occur in the margined case. Integrating this term between now and the final maturity gives:

$$\int_0^T \sqrt{t}\,(T-t) = \frac{4}{15}T^{\frac{3}{2}}$$

In the margined case, as explained in section 7.2.4, a reasonable proxy for the standard deviation is $\sqrt{\tau}\,(T-t)$, where τ is the so-called margin period of risk (MPR) or time to receive margin. Integrating this in a similar manner gives:

$$\sqrt{\tau}\int_0^T (T-t) = \frac{1}{2}\sqrt{\tau}T$$

Taking the ratio of the above terms would give a factor of:

$$\frac{8}{15}\sqrt{T/\tau} \approx 0.5\sqrt{T/\tau}$$

Hence a useful ballpark estimate of the impact of margin on reduction of exposure (and CVA) would be by a factor of $0.5\sqrt{T/\tau}$. The ratio is not surprising since the margin agreement has the impact of reducing the risk horizon from T to τ. The factor of 8/15 is due to the non-margined profile being assumed to have a classic humped shape (e.g. see Figure 7.6).

[11] For example, see 'KfW now using two-way CSAs, dealers claim', Risk, 2 February 2011, http://www.risk.net/risk-magazine/news/2023483/kfw-csas-dealers-claim.

Part III

Structure and Mechanics of Clearing

8
The Basics of CCP Operation

These will be entities that are too-big-to-fail on steroids.

Andrew Haldane[1] (1967–)

This chapter provides an overview of CCP operation, covering aspects such as basic functions, operation, risk mitigation and default management. Chapters 9 to 11 will then explore in more detail aspects around margining, loss allocation and client clearing.

8.1 CCP SETUP

8.1.1 CCP ownership

CCP ownership and operation tends to work broadly via either a vertical or horizontal setup with competing structures coexisting. These structures are outlined below:

- *Vertical (e.g. Eurex and CME):* In this approach, the CCP is usually a division of, and owned by, an exchange. The CCP is essentially tied to the exchange and provides clearing only for products traded on that exchange. Such a CCP is typically one of a number of entities that provide services from trading to settlement of transactions that are all embedded within a single organisation and infrastructure. This model has generally developed over the years for futures exchanges, and arose as the exchanges evolved and developed a central clearing function.
- *Horizonal (e.g. LCH.Clearnet and OCC):* Horizontal CCPs are separately owned (typically by their clearing members), have their own financial backing and can therefore clear trades across multiple markets and asset classes. They generally exist as separate entities. This may be more appropriate for bilateral OTC, as opposed to exchange-traded, transactions.

The relative merits of vertical and horizontal models are given in Table 8.1. A vertical CCP can be highly specialised to a particular type of product, which may lead to stronger risk management. Such structures are also typically more efficient and therefore cheaper. However, such a setup is more likely to create monopolies leading to a less competitive marketplace, and the need to consider how CCPs clearing different products would be interoperable. Horizontal structures have an open model and can clear multiple products across different platforms. This can be beneficial for an institution trading on multiple exchanges having potentially only a single CCP relationship and single point of contact for clearing. This also encourages market competition but is less operationally efficient and more expensive. Vertical structures will also obviously lead to a larger number of CCPs than horizontal structures,

[1] Executive Director of Financial Stability at the Bank of England.

Table 8.1 Comparison of vertical and horizontal CCP setups.

	Advantages	Disadvantages
Vertical	• The CCP is specialised to the particular market (e.g. credit derivatives) • More operationally efficient and less costly	• Less competition as it is harder for new CCPs to gain market share leading to a limited choice for users • Need for interoperability
	Requires multiple CCPs	
Horizontal	• Better choice for users – encourages competition and supports new market entrants • Interoperability and cross-margining is less of a problem	• High operational costs from connections to multiple markets
	Could be supported by a single or a small number of CCPs	

although consolidation of CCPs/exchanges can lead to a wider vertical coverage that offers more of the benefits of horizontal clearing structures.

Whilst historically CCPs have generally followed a vertical structure (for exchanges), horizontal CCPs are more common in the OTC derivative clearing world. Regulation appears to favour the increased competition that horizontal clearing allows with rules calling for CCPs to be 'open'. For example, the European Commission (EC) under MiFID II Article 29 proposes to give CCPs access rights to trading venues, which would allow market participants to use a CCP other than the one defined by an exchange or other trading platform. This is seen as important to increase competition between CCPs, thereby reducing costs and improving the quality of clearing services.

It may be that certain asset classes are more suited to vertical CCP structures whilst others are better served by a horizontal structure. One obvious factor is the amount of offset that exists: if this is high then the cross-margining benefits that are more easily attainable under a horizontal structure may favour this setup. Smaller and domestic markets may find a vertical structure more beneficial due to the relative concentration of products and market participants.

Related to the above discussion is the ideal total number of CCPs in the market, which represents a subtle balance. In order to maximise netting benefits, a smaller number of CCPs is preferable, but this clearly increases the systemic risk associated to a CCP failure. A large number of CCPs will bifurcate netting benefits and could lead to excessive competition and a 'race to the bottom', as seen with rating agencies prior to the GFC. Cross-margining (section 9.5) can achieve netting benefits across CCPs but this can create legal and operational issues across jurisdictions.

8.1.2 Fees

CCPs have a number of explicit and implicit methods to effectively charge for their service, including:

- *Flat fees:* For example, maintenance fees charged on a monthly or quarterly basis to maintain a given portfolio of cleared positions. This could be based, for example, on the percentage of the notional of the cleared portfolio.

- *Fees per trade:* For example, a clearing fee charged at trade inception.
- *Margin related fees:* A CCP may charge fees for the safekeeping of non-cash margin.
- *Income generated on margins held:* Thanks to being able to invest margins and other financial resources at higher rates than paid to those posting the margins (clearly this may lead to a CCP taking credit and liquidity risks as discussed in section 8.3.4).

Investment income may be hard to achieve due to the need for segregation and to invest margins and default funds (which may be needed at short notice) in liquid, non-credit risky assets. CCPs would therefore generally rely on a combination of fixed fees paid on a periodic basis and per trade (by notional) fees. They may also make specific charges via clearing and risk processing fees, booking or maintenance fees. Whilst there may be different tariffs that effectively give discounts for large volumes of trades, CCPs can benefit from fees that increase linearly compared to risk that generally increases sub-linearly due to portfolio effects.

Clearing members that clear trades for clients may pass on fees directly (or even increase them). They may also charge additional fees such as a balance sheet utilisation fee (for example to cover increased default fund or default fund capital charges) or fees for providing additional services to their clients (for example, intraday liquidity of margin upgrading as discussed in section 11.1.4).

8.1.3 What needs to be cleared?

It is important to note the significant concentrations of assets classes and products within the OTC derivatives market. From Figure 2.5 and Table 2.2 in Chapter 2, it can be seen that interest rate products make up about 80% of the gross notional within the OTC derivatives market. The remaining amount is made up primarily of foreign exchange (10.6%) and credit default swaps (3.5%). Given the aforementioned exemption for clearing of foreign exchange trades (section 4.2.6), this explains the OTC clearing effort being focused around interest rate products and credit default swaps.

Of course, gross notional can be misleading. For example, a significant component (15.4%) of the gross notional in the interest rate market is forward rate agreements (FRAs). However, since these are relatively short-dated, they are not as significant as this figure suggests from a counterparty risk perspective.[2] Another important area where notional is misleading is credit default swaps. The high volatility of credit spreads and their wrong-way risk (section 7.3.4) makes them more significant than this notional figure suggests.

8.1.4 Important OTC derivative CCPs

CCPs have existed for many years, for example, both CME and LCH had clearing functions in late 19th century. What is relatively recent is central clearing of OTC derivatives. The global association of CCPs (CCP12)[3] currently has 31 member CCP organisations across Africa, the Americas, Asia, Australia and Europe operating in exchange-traded and/or OTC markets. Globally, banks clear trades through tens of CCPs, but a much smaller number of CCPs focus on OTC derivative products. A list of some of the most important OTC CCPs

[2] Indeed, Table 2.2 gives the ratio of gross market value to gross notional for interest rate products at 2.7%. This ratio for FRAs is only 0.2%. Source: BIS.

[3] www.ccp12.org.

Table 8.2 Products cleared by a variety of significant OTC derivative CCPs. A tick indicates that the CCP has an active function to clear the product in question. A question mark indicates that the CCP intends to offer a clearing service for the product or has a service that has not yet cleared a significant notional amount.

		IR	**CDS**	**FX**	**Equity**	**Commodity**
US and Canada	CME Clearing US	✓	✓	✓		✓
	ICE Clear Credit		✓			
	LCH.Clearnet Ltd*	✓				
	Int'l Derivatives Clearing Group (IDCG)**	✓				
Europe	CME Clearing Europe	✓		?		✓
	ICE Clear Europe		✓			✓
	LCH.Clearnet Ltd†	✓		✓	✓	✓
	Eurex Clearing AG	✓	?		?	
	LCH.Clearnet SA		✓			
	NASDAQ OMX (Sweden)	✓			✓	✓
Australia	ASX	?				
Brazil	BM&FBovespa	?				
Hong Kong	HKEx Clearing	?		?		
Japan	Japan Securities Clearing Corporation	✓	?			
Singapore	Singapore Exchange Ltd (SGX)	✓				

* SwapClear US.
** Converted to futures contracts.
† SwapClear.

is shown in Table 8.2, together with an indication of the asset classes for which they offer clearing (IR represents interest rates, CDS credit default swaps and FX foreign exchange).

Currently, the biggest players in OTC derivative clearing are:

- *LCH.Clearnet:* LCH.Clearnet is a major independent CCP and was the first CCP to clear significant amounts of OTC transactions through SwapClear, which is dominant in the interbank interest rate swap market. Originally SwapClear focused only on about 20–30 large banks but since 2009 have allowed their membership to expand significantly to around 100 currently.[4] SwapClear have also facilitated client clearing since 2009. LCH. Clearnet SA also offers clearing of CDS.
- *ICE:* ICE (Intercontinental Exchange) offers clearing for energy products. ICE Clear Credit offers clearing for some CDS products (where it is the clear market leader), having around 30 members at the time of writing.[5]
- *CME:* CME ClearPort acts as a CCP for OTC energy derivatives and also offers an interest rate swap clearing service. CME Clearing offers CDS clearing (although the volumes have been small).
- *Eurex:* Clears OTC derivatives mainly in the equity space but including interest rate swaps. Eurex Credit was launched in 2009 to clear CDS but has had very little volume and is not being actively developed.

[4] As of June 2013, there were 170 LCH.Clearnet Ltd members in total. Membership details for SwapClear and the other clearing platforms are given at http://www.lchclearnet.com/membership/ltd/current_membership.asp.

[5] As of June 2013, ICE Clear Europe Ltd has 69 members. A list can be found at https://www.theice.com/publicdocs/clear_europe/ICE_Clear_Europe_Clearing_Member_List.pdf.

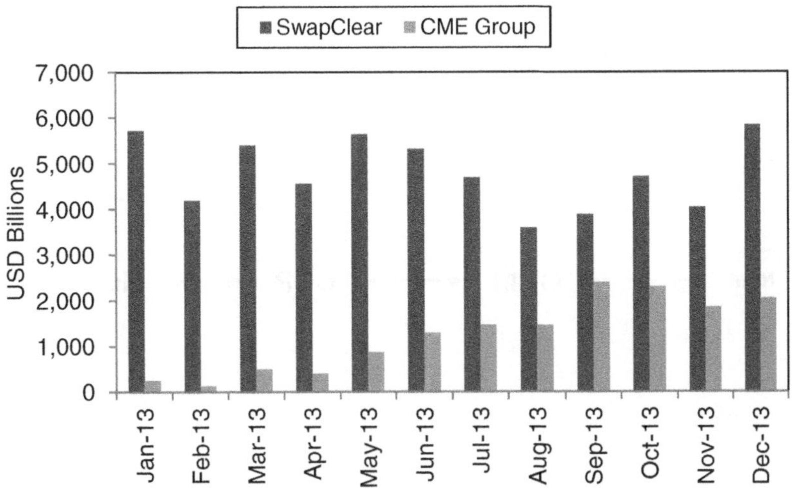

Figure 8.1 Monthly notionals cleared by SwapClear and CME Clearing for interest rate client trades. Source: LCH.Clearnet (http://www.swapclear.com/what/clearing-volumes.html) and CME Group (http://www.cmegroup.com/trading/interest-rates/cleared-otc/#data).

Note that there is some division between clearing and client clearing. For example, LCH SwapClear has become dominant in the IRS market thanks to inter-dealer trades, which represent the majority of the market. This can be seen by the total notional of interest rate swap volume reported by SwapClear as €419 trillion at the time of writing.[6] However, client clearing shows a more even balance and SwapClear is not as dominant in the smaller client clearing interest rate swap market, which is shared with other CCPs such as CME Group and Eurex. For example, Figure 8.1 shows the total notional cleared by SwapClear and CME Clearing for interest rate based client trades only.

8.2 CCP OPERATION

8.2.1 CCP members and non-members

From the point of view of clearing through a CCP, one can consider (at least) three types of participant:

- *General clearing member (GCM):* This member of the CCP is able to clear for third parties, as well as their own trades. The term used in the US is FCM (Futures Commission Merchant).
- *Individual clearing member (ICM):* These members can clear only their own trades.
- *Non-clearing member (NCM):* A non-member institution has no direct relationship with the CCP and therefore clears trades through a GCM.

[6] See http://www.swapclear.com/what/clearing-volumes.html. As of close of business 17 January 2014.

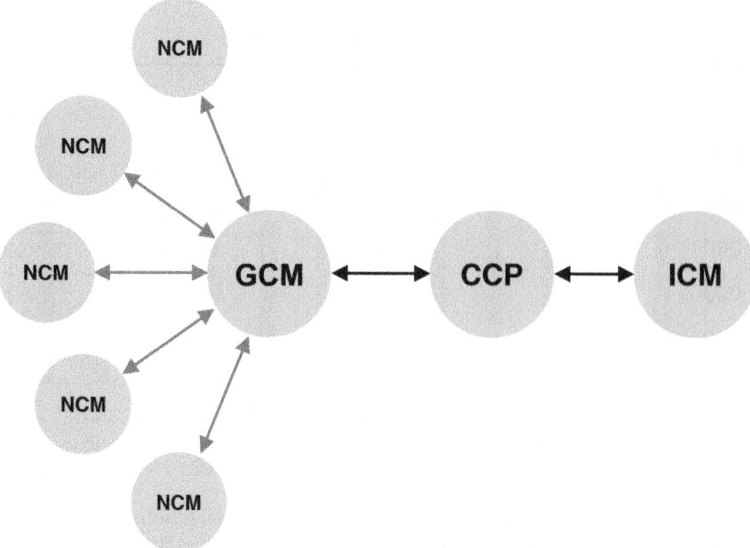

Figure 8.2 Illustration of the relationship between CCPs, clearing members and clients.

These relationships are illustrated in Figure 8.2. (Note that terminology differs; the above terms are used, for example, to denote SwapClear members.) A GCM or ICM will typically be a large bank or dealer who has a large number of counterparties. An NCM is more obviously characterised by a smaller player or end user of OTC derivatives. Whilst these are the more obvious roles of members, they are not the only characterisations. For example, a GCM may in fact be another CCP and an NCM may be a regional bank. Note that relationships should be considered to be bilateral: an NCM will probably trade under a traditional bilateral CSA with the GCM who will have a similar ISDA type legal arrangement with the CCP (see section 11.1 for more detail).

Generally, only clearing members have a direct relationship with the CCP. Trades by NCMs ('clients') of GCMs must be guaranteed by a clearing member, and that clearing member is liable to the CCP for any outstanding payment obligations that its clients cannot satisfy. By clearing through a GCM, an NCM can gain benefits from central clearing even though they are not a clearing member. Furthermore, since clearing members are subject to membership requirements, default fund contributions and ongoing monitoring, the CCP ensures that it has exposure only to firms that it can monitor carefully and from whom it can take adequate financial resources.

Although not shown in Figure 8.2, there may also be the concept of indirect clearing. This adds another layer via 'clients of clients', for example clients of regional banks who themselves are NCMs clearing trades through global banks who are GCMs. Regulation may also force this effect, for example if a European bank has clients wanting to clear through a US CCP. The European bank cannot be an FCM[7] and so may be an NCM of a US bank that is an FCM (interoperability is another solution as discussed in section 8.5.1). In theory, building extra layers is not problematic as all relationships are essentially bilateral ones and the CCP only cares about the GCMs (or ICMs).

[7] Recall that in the US CCP members must be registered Futures Commission Merchants (FCMs).

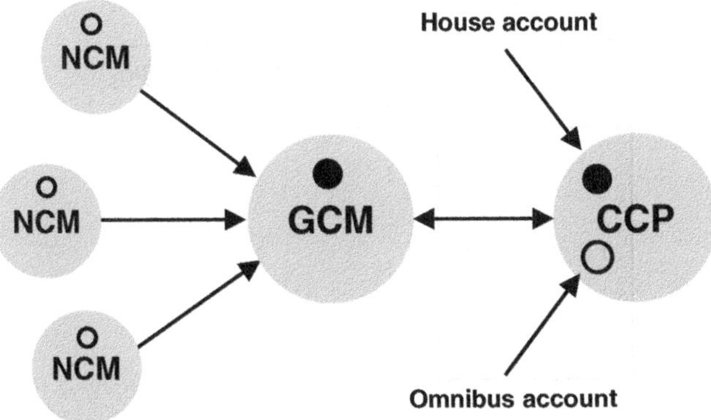

Figure 8.3 Illustration of the house account (of a general clearing member) and omnibus account representing their non-clearing members (clients).

Regarding the account structure for a GCM with respect to their clients, a common practice is to separate client accounts from those of the GCM (the latter is commonly known as the 'house' account) but to comingle client funds in an 'omnibus' account as shown in Figure 8.3. This is operationally efficient but does expose clients to each other as discussed further in section 11.3.1. The omnibus structure has been common in futures markets but OTC products, prompted by regulation, are generally being given greater levels of protection. Such approaches such as LSOC (section 11.3.3) reduce the risk for clients but are more expensive both operationally and in terms of margin requirements.

8.2.2 Process of clearing

In OTC markets trade execution is generally still on a bilateral basis. Central clearing is then a subsequent process and bilateral counterparty risk will exist for a period. Some trades that are 'backloaded' (section 4.2.4) or 'frontloaded' (section 4.2.6) may be bilateral for a period and then be moved to clearing. Other trades may be cleared almost immediately, for example due to the clearing mandate. The process of clearing can be outlined by the following steps:

- *Trade execution and confirmation:* This occurs normally, as it does in bilateral markets which are not cleared.
- *Trade submitted for clearing:* The CCP will normally have been pre-agreed at the time of the trade (except in the cases of backloading or frontloading). Large banks will typically be members of multiple CCPs to allow clients choice on which CCP to use. Note that a client does not need to clear through the counterparty they traded with and can choose a different GCM if they wish. On the other hand, some banks may offer more competitive rates if they are used for execution and clearing.
- *CCP acceptance:* CCPs have to accept trades (or not) quickly[8] (for example, the CFTC requires FCMs to accept or reject within 60 seconds). This does not allow a bank enough time to discuss with a client and understand the nature of the trade (and if it may be fol-

[8] See for example http://www.thejavelin.com/press-releases/javelin-and-cme-execute-and-clear-41-billion-of-interest-rate-swaps-in-real-time.

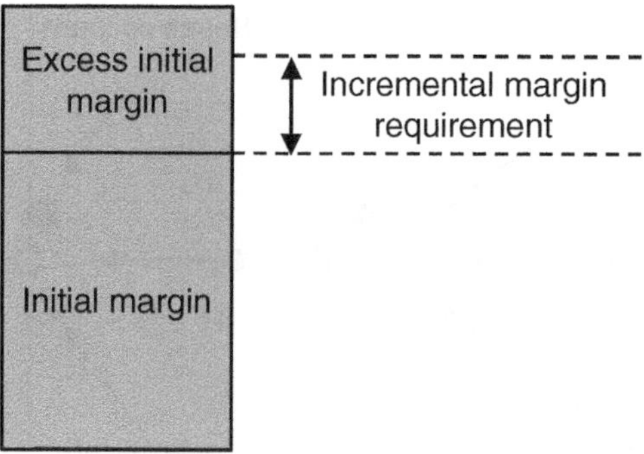

Figure 8.4 Illustration of the use of excess initial margin to prevent the need for an additional margin requirement for a transaction (as long as the incremental requirement is less than the excess held by the CCP). Any incremental requirement above the excess initial margin may lead to an intradaily requirement.

lowed by other risk reducing trades, for example). In order to accept the trade, the CCP will have to check the impact on risk limits.

- *Margin calls:* The CCP will need to re-calculate the initial margin that is required. Since there may be offsets with other existing trades, this margin calculation is not trivial. Sometimes sensitivity approaches are used to estimate margin requirements (without needing to re-run the margin model) and an intraday margin call is made. Alternatively, a pre-funded initial margin is used and up to a limit, trades can occur without requiring additional margin (Figure 8.4). The incremental initial margin required for a client (NCM) trade will depend on the level of segregation used.
- *Cash management:* Due to margining, cashflow payments and other aspects, CCPs perform an important cash management function. This is partly operational, for example, the collection and payment of margins, payment of cashflows and transfer of securities. CCPs also have treasury functions, such as the investment of cash and securities held as margin, and for other purposes such as the payment of interest on margin accounts.

8.2.3 Compression

As noted in section 5.2.4, cleared trades can still make use of multilateral trade compression. It may seem that compression of cleared trades is less relevant, as compression aims not to change the market risk characteristics of portfolios and would not (for example) be expected to lead to a significant reduction in margin requirements. Despite this there are clear benefits of reducing the number of trades and total notional cleared by a given CCP relating to efficiency, including:

- Operational (e.g. cashflow payments and reporting)
- Computation burden (e.g. for margin calculation)
- Simplifying the auction process (fewer trades to close out)

An illustration of the impact of compression on clearing is given in Figure 8.5. This shows the total notional (all currencies) of interest rate swaps cleared by SwapClear, together with the compressed notional that has been essentially removed. The compression is done by

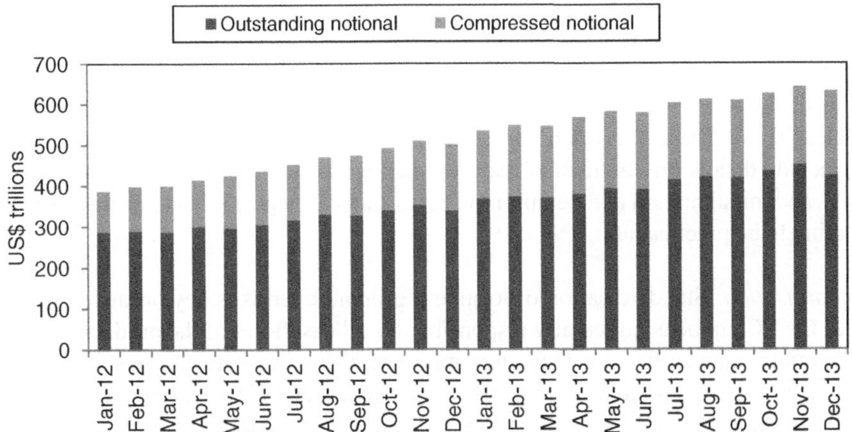

Figure 8.5 Illustration of SwapClear interest rate swap notional outstanding and compressed notional. Source: LCH.Clearnet (http://www.swapclear.com/what/clearing-volumes.html)

TriReduce[9] via the joint venture between SwapClear and TriOptima described previously in section 5.2.4.

Compression involves tearing up trades and potentially also replacing them with new ones. One important feature of compression is that portfolios must be processed together rather than in batches. In the latter case, step-by-step processing of a portfolio may calculate that initial margins are insufficient at some point during the processing because later offsetting trades have not been seen. This is the reason that LCH.Clearnet's SwapClear compression service had to be stopped for a period[10] because trades processed in batches did not meet CFTC rules on real-time (e.g. no longer than seconds) registration of trades.

8.2.4 Requirements for products to be cleared

Looking at the potentially large number of products in the OTC derivatives market, it is clear that many of them are not close to being, and indeed may never be able to be, centrally cleared. That said, a significant proportion of the market could be cleared via a relatively small number of products. For example, the total OTC derivatives notional was US$693 trillion as of June 2013 (Figure 2.4), of which US$370 trillion is made up of interest rate swaps which (aside from a relatively small fraction of transactions in illiquid currencies) can already be cleared through a number of CCPs (indeed around half of the interest rate swap market is cleared already, mainly through LCH.Clearnet's SwapClear service).

In terms of the interest rate market in particular (as the major OTC asset class to experience clearing over the last decade or so), the products currently cleared are:

- Fixed-to-floating interest rate swaps
- Basis swaps (floating to floating interest rate swaps)
- Overnight index swaps
- Forward rate agreements (FRAs)

[9] http://www.trioptima.co.uk/services/triReduce.html.

[10] See 'SwapClear to restart compression in leverage boon for banks', November 2013, http://www.risk.net/risk-magazine/news/2309337/swapclear-to-restart-compression-in-leverage-boon-for-banks.

This leaves interest rate caps and floors as well as swaptions as the next obvious products that might be cleared in this area.

Clearly, some OTC products will not be cleared because CCPs will not consider the business that such clearing will bring as sizable enough to cover the cost of building the capability to clear them. There are a number of hurdles to overcome for products to be cleared. These include details on contractual features such as cashflow payments, robust valuation methods, and initial margin and default fund assessment. The general characteristics required for clearing to be practical are:

- *Standardisation:* Standardisation of legal and economic terms is key because clearing requires the CCP to be contractually responsible for all cashflows of the product in question. Furthermore, standardisation facilitates multilateral netting between identical contracts and makes it easier to replace contracts in the event that a clearing member defaults. Finally, for standard products, it is easier to have robust trade capture, confirmation and processing methods that are important for the smooth operation of central clearing. For example, prior to 2009 there was a standardisation of CDS contracts (section 5.2.4), which was a prerequisite to any migration to CCPs.
- *Non-complex:* Exotic or complex derivatives (even if standardised)[11] create a number of hurdles to central clearing. Products that are more complex are more subjective to value for variation margin purposes, and initial margin requirements are very difficult to determine. This means that under- or over-margining is likely the former case leading to excessive risk and the latter to high costs. Adverse selection would also be a problem where clearing members understand the risks of the products better than the CCPs themselves which is likely since much of the proprietary knowledge on pricing complex products exists within large banks. Market participants who have a better understanding of the underlying risk of a product can trade it more (less) depending on whether the CCP has over (under) estimated the risk as seen for example via margin requirements.
- *Liquid:* Centrally cleared products need to be liquid for a number of reasons. First, liquidity brings accurate pricing information for variation margin purposes and provides rich historical time-series price data to use to calculate initial margins. Second, liquid products can be more efficiently replaced in default scenarios as illiquid trades will have high bid offer spreads and may be more likely to be subjected to large risk premiums and negative price moves in turbulent markets. It should be noted that liquidity might be *transient* as in many OTC derivatives, liquidity tends to decline over time and yet these positions are guaranteed by the CCP for a long time.
- *Wrong-way risk.* Ideally, centrally cleared products would not be subject to wrong-way risk (WWR). This occurs when the default of a counterparty is linked adversely to the value of the underlying contract, which in turns means that the value of the contract will potentially decline rapidly at the time of the counterparty default. These negative implications for default management are therefore quite important. This is a subtle point in relation to credit default swaps, as based on this point their clearing is difficult and yet it was precisely these products that catalysed the regulatory requirements in the first place.
- *Market volume:* There is significant effort for a CCP to build the relevant processes, models and systems to be able to clear a given product. If the size of the market for this particular product is not sufficiently large, then presumably clearing will not be beneficial as the CCP will be unable to recoup fully the expenditure in the product development process.

[11] Note that an exotic product can have standard terms but the valuation complexity would still exist.

Not all OTC derivatives are suitable at present for central clearing and some may never be. In particular, those that are difficult to clear because they are more likely to exhibit poor liquidity and jumps in valuation, cannot be managed with traditional CCP methods of risk management. The above requirements also restrict clearing and impose costs. For example, standardisation prevents customisation, which facilitates derivatives users to trade products that closely fit their particular risk management needs. Having to hedge with standard products via CCPs then creates basis risk.

Hull (2010) defines four classes of derivatives from the point of view of clearing:

- Plain vanilla with standard maturities
- Plain vanilla with non-standard maturities
- Non-standard but with well-established models
- Highly exotic

At the current time, only some of the first category above is covered by CCPs. It could be argued that they could all be covered eventually with the possible exception of highly exotic derivatives, which have in any case been in decline in recent years. There are ways in which some of the apparent hurdles to clearing less standard and complex products can be overcome. For example, a method such as RFQ (request for quotation) potentially allows, via the number of price quotations given, the market to determine the set of OTC contracts that can be cleared. However, a key question is whether the auction process would function smoothly following the default of a major market participant (which would likely be accompanied by a period of severe market stress). If there would be insufficient market liquidity to close out a given product in such an environment then it is hard to envisage clearing of that product as a successful risk mitigation process.

Whilst it is possible to clear more products, CCPs as commercial organisations will prefer to focus on only clearing the most profitable high volume and standardised contracts. The increasing risk and the law of diminishing returns from the overheads to clear lower volume products may well stifle the clearing mandate, and leave only a small fraction of products (although not notional amounts) centrally cleared. This point gives rise to an important question: should exotic products (such as those that helped cause the GFC) be left outside CCPs due to their excessive risks, or are they precisely the products that need to be cleared?. A CDS index contract may seem standardised and liquid, and is indeed already centrally cleared at several CCPs (and arguably falls into the first category defined by Hull above). However, in line with the Merton (1974) ideas on the pricing of credit risk, a CDS contract is equivalent to an out-of-the-money American style barrier option.[12] Such a product (more in line with the last Hull category) should be a long way from clearing. The point is that it is not even trivial to define whether a product is complex or not.

8.3 CCP RISK MANAGEMENT

8.3.1 Overview

A CCP stands between buyers and sellers and guarantees the performance of trades. In a centrally cleared market, counterparty risk is centralised within the CCP that is legally obliged to

[12] Merton draws the analogy between default and the hitting of a barrier. The out-of-the-money and American style attributes arise from default being relatively unlikely but potentially occurring at any point.

perform on the contracts it clears. There is consequently no need for the original counterparties to monitor one another in terms of credit quality as they are only exposed to the overall credit quality of the other members.[13] This clearly puts the emphasis on the operation and resilience of the CCP itself.

In order to perform counterparty risk mitigation, a CCP actually performs a number of related functions:

- *Multilateral netting:* Due to the centralisation of trades, a CCP can provide netting benefits for trades that originated with different counterparties. This can reduce exposure although it depends on the coverage of clearing (see section 5.2.6).
- *Margining and default funds:* A CCP will collect both variation and initial margins from its members to cover potential default losses. It will also hold default fund contributions from its members to cover possible extreme losses in excess of margins. Initial margins and default funds will be driven by factors such as volatility, correlation and size of the cleared portfolio.
- *Default management:* A CCP will manage a member default. This will include hedging and auctioning the underlying positions, allocation of any losses in excess of the margins held and transferring or 'porting' (section 11.1.7) client trades to solvent clearing members.

In order to manage the risk that they take, CCPs have a number of mechanisms to ensure their financial health. These are critical, as even the perception that a large CCP may fail could be catastrophic for financial markets.

- *Membership requirements:* A CCP has strict admission criteria imposed on its members to ensure they have a low probability of insolvency and have the necessary operational abilities to engage in clearing. This ensures that it is rare that the CCP will face the default of a member.
- *Margining:* In the unlikely scenario that a CCP does suffer a member default, member-specific financial resources are held to cover losses and therefore manage the default without affecting other clearing members. This prevents losses spilling over and creating potential knock-on effects via imposing losses on other clearing members. These member-specific financial resources are the margins (variation and initial) and default fund contributions.
- *Auction and hedging:* In the event of a member default, the CCP will use methods such as holding a centralised auction of positions and macro-hedging key risks in the defaulting member's portfolio. This aims to ensure a rapid re-balancing of markets risks and minimises the chance of losses.
- *Loss waterfall:* In the hopefully unlikely event that the CCP does not have enough margin and other financial resources from a defaulter to cover associated losses, it applies a pre-defined waterfall to absorb losses and ensure that it can remain solvent.

The above aspects will be covered in more detail below and in later chapters.

[13] There may be certain methods of loss allocation (section 10.3) that may lead to some sensitivity to the credit quality of a specific counterparty.

8.3.2 Membership requirements

CCPs employ robust membership requirements to ensure clearing members do not bring undue risk to the CCP (although such restrictions should on the other hand not be anti-competitive). In general, membership requirements are based around:

- *Creditworthiness:* The probability of default of the clearing member, as assessed by external or internal methods.
- *Liquidity:* The ability of the member to meet liquidity requirements such as the need to meet margin calls at short notice.
- *Operational:* The ability to adhere to the CCP rules such as those pertaining to auctions.

New applicants will undergo due diligence covering their business model, financial results, regulation, operations, risk management and planned clearing activities. More specific requirements may include:

- *Capital base:* Members are required to have a minimum core capital base in order to be GCMs or ICMs. This may need to be higher in the former case of clearing members also clearing for clients. Note that in the US, the Commodity Futures Trading Commission limits the CCP capital requirements for member dealers to a maximum of US$50 million. The intension of this ruling is to open CCPs up to smaller members and prevent the largest banks from being dominant. SwapClear and ICE Clear Credit members require a minimum adjusted net capital of US$50 million which applies outside the US also.
- *Rating:* A CCP may impose a minimum rating for clearing members such as single A. Due to the potential problems with external ratings, highlighted by the GFC, CCPs may use internal ratings instead. For example, SwapClear uses an internal credit score based on market data as well as external ratings.
- *Operational requirements:* A clearing member must conform to the operational requirements of processing trades and have all the necessary banking arrangements in place to support margin payments.
- *Default fund contributions:* A clearing member must contribute to the CCP default fund (e.g. SwapClear members must contribute a minimum of £10 million per member). Members are also required to make future additional contributions to the default fund ('rights of assessment'), which are often capped at their current contribution. Members clearing for clients may have to contribute more to the default fund.
- *Regulatory approvals:* The clearing member must typically have at least one entity licensed by authorities in the US or European Union, or other competent authority in another region.
- *Default management:* Clearing members must undertake to periodically participate in 'fire drills' and demonstrate their capability in a default scenario to capture and bid on a large set of trades (potentially in the region of hundreds of thousands) in a timely fashion (usually a few hours). In the event of an actual default, the clearing member is expected to actively participate in the default management process, for example by sending a senior trader and bidding in the resulting auctions.

The overall threshold for CCP membership is a balance. A high bar on membership will mean that CCPs will experience fewer member defaults but will concentrate membership amongst a few large systemic banks. This in turn means that when a default does occur it will by definition represent an extreme situation. A lower bar for membership may arguably allow weaker clearing members to join which could make the CCP more risky in general (this is the dilemma SwapClear was faced with when opening up membership in 2009 as discussed in section 8.1.4). The key question is whether having a small number of large strong credit quality members is the best solution, or if a larger number of smaller and possibly less creditworthy members may be preferable.

Not all parties can be direct clearing members. In particular, many buy side and smaller financial institutions may not qualify as direct clearing members and therefore will clear through an existing clearing member. Alternatively, an institution could be able to become a clearing member but may find the indirect clearing route more efficient (for example, due to not being required to commit to operational procedures and contribute to the CCP default fund).

A clearing member wanting to leave a CCP typically needs to first flatten their position and then go through a formal process resigning their membership. Alternatives to this are becoming a client of another clearing member or switching trades back to being bilateral (assuming this is allowable and noting the likely initial margins that will be required). If the member also cleared client positions then these would need to be 'ported' (transferred) to another member or closed out. Some large dealers are including a provision in contractual terms with clients such that they can effectively be able to cease providing clearing services.

Finally, note that expulsion rules will not mirror membership requirements. Expelling a clearing member would represent a major event that could cause significant knock-on effects for the market and the clearing member's clients. For example, a change in SwapClear rules[14] was made recently to avoid potentially leaving a large investment bank just one notch away from expulsion. Presumably, casting out a clearing member, especially one with a large portfolio, would only be done as a last resort.

8.3.3 Margining

CCPs take margin from their members against the risk of the portfolios they clear. Variation margin represents mark-to-market changes in the value of the portfolio and is calculated via a revaluation of all underlying positions on at least a daily basis. These valuations will be made on the basis of:

- Third party sources
- Price submissions by members
- The CCP's own valuation models

The last case is particularly important for OTC products due to their relative illiquidity and long maturities. Variation margining clearly requires timely and reliable price data for all cleared derivatives and, where price data is not directly available, market standard valuation methods. Such methods may sometimes need to evolve with market practice, a good example being the move from LIBOR to OIS discounting for interest rate swaps.[15]

[14] For example see SwapClear changes expulsion rules, http://www.risk.net/risk-magazine/news/2172414/swapclear-changes-expulsion-rules.

[15] See 'LCH.Clearnet adopts OIS discounting for $218 trillion IRS portfolio', June 2010, http://www.lchclearnet.com/media_centre/press_releases/2010-06-17.asp.

Typically, only cash is accepted as variation margin but other liquidity securities (e.g. US treasury bonds) may be admissible for initial margins. Variation margin and settlement amounts from clearing members' other clearing activities in a single currency may be netted, resulting in a single payment or receipt per day. Usually, there is no netting of different currencies for variation margin purposes (see discussion in section 9.1.1). Furthermore, initial and variation margin amounts will typically not be offset by netting.[16] In some cases, especially in volatile markets, intraday variation margins may be called for.

Initial margin is intended to cover potential close out losses in the event of a default by that clearing member. Typically, it is calculated using different scenarios for possible price movements over an assumed close out period or liquidation period (known as the 'margin period of risk' in bilateral markets, see section 6.1.4), such as five days. Initial margin exists for the life of the trade and can be increased or reduced depending on market conditions and the remaining risk. Unlike variation margin, initial margin need not necessarily be in cash. Acceptable types of margin in this context may include:

- Cash
- Government treasury bonds and government agency securities
- Sovereign debt
- Gold
- Certain mortgage backed securities
- Equity indices
- Bank issued letters of credit
- Money market and mutual funds
- Certificates of deposit

The general aim of margin rules is that, after the application of haircuts, the CCP is not exposed to significant credit, market and liquidity risks. Securities must be sufficiently liquid, such as having price data available on a frequent basis and with low credit risk. Another important factor is that the credit quality of the member and value of the margin do not have an adverse 'wrong-way' relationship. An extreme example of this would be an entity posting their own equity or bonds, but more subtle and difficult to identify cases may also arise (see section 7.3.4).

Regarding the denomination of cash and securities, acceptable currencies may be those where the issuing sovereign has a reasonable credit quality and an FX market exists to convert and hedge the resulting currency risk. For cash margin, there must also be no legal problems associated to holding the currency.

In the case of client clearing, it is important to note that clearing members must pay required margin to a CCP irrespective of whether or not they have received it from their clients, and may implicitly offer short-term liquidity by posting margin in advance of receiving it.

8.3.4 Margin interest rates

CCPs will hold large amounts of margin. This offers a possibility for income to balance the interest rates that CCPs may contractually agree to pay. Most CCPs will pay interest

[16] For example, a clearing member required to post variation margin but with a reduced initial margin requirement would have to first pay the variation margin and later receive the initial margin benefit.

to clearing members on excess cash deposited as initial margin. Typically, this may be set at a level with respect to a short-term deposit rate (e.g. LIBID[17] minus 25 bps). Clearing members may not fully pass on the benefits of interest rates paid on margin (for example, a clearing member receiving LIBID minus 25 bps may pay to their client the same rate minus 50 bps). This may partly compensate the clearing member for the short-term liquidity they may provide in margin posting. Variation margin may also be adjusted for price alignment interest (PAI) which reflects an interest rate to compensate for an overnight funding cost/benefit (section 9.1.3). The PAI rate will be set by the CCP and may therefore not align with the actual funding cost associated to the variation margin. Margin interest rates depend on not only the CCP but also the underlying currency of the transaction.

Since CCPs will pay interest rates on some margin received, they need to generate a return on the margin they hold. However, margin also needs to be invested extremely carefully so as to avoid creating material additional risk for the CCP. In increasing riskiness, a CCP may invest margins as follows:

- *Deposit with a central bank:* This is the safest choice but is likely to pay only a small (less than OIS) interest rate.
- *Deposit with a commercial bank:* This will likely provide a better rate of return than above, but is more risky. It may also increase systemic risk if the bank is a significant clearing member.
- *Invest in high-quality assets:* Investing margins in a high-quality diversified portfolio. This may give the possibility for reasonable returns but without significant risks.

Investment of margins can make clearing cheaper but has the potential to expose clearing members and clients to increased risks and increase the likelihood of CCP failure. Some obvious guidelines for the investment portfolio of a CCP are:

- Minimal market and credit risk.
- Low liquidity risk (margin can be liquidated quickly without driving prices down and creating losses).
- Investments in financial companies or companies highly correlated to financial markets are limited/avoided.
- Maturity of transactions is carefully considered to ensure a CCP can meet cashflows without needing to exit transactions that may be difficult to liquidate.

CCPs may also mix investments, having a portion of margins tied up in relatively long-dated and illiquid instruments, but enough readily available to meet cashflow needs even in a stressed scenario.

There is clearly risk of investment losses in relation to margin. There is a subtle balance between generating returns, which for instance can provide a means of income for a CCP, and preserving capital. CCPs generally have the latter as a priority and would typically use cash in relatively safe activities such as deposits with commercial banks, tri-party repos, or to purchase high-quality securities. Investments are typically subject to minimum credit rating, counterparty or issuer specific limits and concentration limits. Repo investments need to have appropriate haircuts, and the maturity of investments needs to be aligned with liquidity

[17] The London Interbank Bid Rate.

requirements. Whilst CCPs investment strategies are likely to be highly conservative, it is important to note that risk taking offers a way to be more competitive on clearing costs. Furthermore, there have been illustrations of the risk of this type of activity (for example in the default of MF Global or 'London Whale' trade losses of J.P. Morgan).

8.4 DEFAULT MANAGEMENT

In the event of a clearing member default, CCPs have general rights in relation to managing the risk of that member's portfolio. These rights include suspension of trading, closing out positions, transferring client positions and liquidating margin. The privileged position of a CCP (compared to a bilateral counterparty) should enhance its ability to deal with a default in an efficient manner.

8.4.1 Declaring a default

One of the principles of central clearing is that the CCP takes both sides of every trade and therefore, through having a 'matched book', has no market risk. What a CCP does have though is 'contingent market risk' (Figure 8.6). This is because it will still have to pay variation margin to non-defaulters who have made a valuation gain that would have been otherwise offset by variation margin received from the defaulting counterparty.

The first stage is for the CCP to deem a clearing member in default. This may occur if that clearing member is insolvent, fails to make a margin payment or misses a contractual cashflow payment to a CCP. Whilst this should, in theory, happen as soon as the member fails to perform, in actuality there may be more flexibility than this. However, CCPs do typically have complete discretion over this decision. Example wording under CCP rules is 'the CCP can declare a default in respect of a member who appears to the CCP to be unable or likely to become unable to meet its obligations in respect of one or more contracts'. Presumably, a CCP would not deem a clearing member in default in certain situations, such as an operational problem with posting margin. However, this does pose the question of how much grace would be given to members whose insolvency may or may not be permanent.

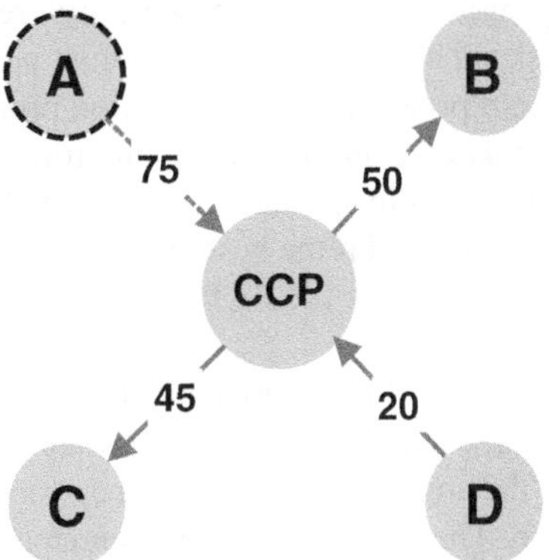

Figure 8.6 Illustration of the contingent market risk faced by a CCP. A market move creates changes in valuation and the resulting flows of variation margin as shown. If clearing member A defaults then the CCPs position is unbalanced due to still having to pay variation margin to members B and C.

8.4.2 Close out process

Once a default is declared, a CCP has the right to manage the market risk associated with the outstanding contracts of the defaulted member, and will aim to return to a matched book as quickly as possible without imposing additional costs on members. Importantly, a CCP has more flexibility than counterparties in bilateral markets, and essentially has a privileged position with respect to bankruptcy law. The CCP has the ability to macro-hedge risk, close out and transfer the positions of defaulted members and of their clients without any required consent. Moreover, the CCP has the discretion to determine if the prices achieved during these actions are economically reasonable. In a bilateral market, the methodology for closing out trades and the macro-hedging the positions of a defaulted counterparty prior to close out may be challenged by the bankruptcy administrators.[18]

In order to assist in the close out period, the CCP will form a default management group of some sort. This group will contain not only key personnel from the CCP, but also senior traders from member firms who may be seconded on a revolving basis. There will be a firewall between seconded traders and other members of their firm. The first stage of the default management process is typically to macro-hedge any significant risk in the book so that it is less exposed to market moves during the rest of the close out period. The CCP's advantageous position compared to bilateral counterparties makes such actions possible without the danger of the defaulted member challenging the nature of any losses incurred.

The CCP could cancel or tear-up the other halves of all the relevant trades and compensate or charge the other clearing members for any price change since the last variation margin adjustment. However, due to the nature of derivatives markets, the clearing members would likely seek to replace their cancelled trades, which may well then be centrally cleared with the same CCP. A simpler route therefore, is for a CCP to execute replacement trades directly with CCP members.

8.4.3 Auction

The auction process provides a suitable mechanism for a CCP to close out positions in a non-destabilising manner. Surviving CCP members will submit two-way prices for subportfolios (divided, for example, by currency) and the member bidding the best price will win a given portfolio. The macro-hedging will assist in this process by creating portfolios that do not have significant directional risks. The CCP members, whilst not legally required to participate, have some incentive to help proactively in the auction process since they stand to bear losses if it is inefficient, or fails. The default management group have the discretion to accept any bid in the auction, even if it results in sizeable losses for the CCP. On the other hand, they may also deem that the auction has failed if the best bid is not high enough. In such a case, an auction could be rerun at the discretion of the CCP or other methods of loss allocation may occur (see Chapter 10).

In order to maximise the efficiency of a potential auction, this process is practiced via periodic (e.g. twice a year) 'fire drills' where clearing members submit prices. New CCP members will also be required to take a 'driving test' to show that they can deal with the operational requirements posed by the auction. These operational requirements revolve around the ability to process, price and bid on relatively large portfolios of trades in a short timescale (a few hours).

---

[18] For example, suppose a party hedges risk in a defaulter's portfolio but prior to close out these hedges lose money against gains in the value of the portfolio. The defaulting counterparty will likely claim that they should not be exposed to losses on the hedges.

In the case of a clearing member default, their initial margin and default fund contributions are available to the CCP to hedge the portfolio and cover losses in the auction. The default management group has the discretion to split the portfolio into subportfolios, apply relevant market risk hedges and auction trades in the manner they consider optimal.

With respect to the above, as discussed previously in section 4.1.4, SwapClear reported 90% of their Lehman risk was neutralised in one week and all 66,000 trades were auctioned within three weeks.

8.4.4 Client positions

Client positions are most efficiently ported to a surviving clearing member. Indeed, clients may have agreements with backup members in place specifically for such a purpose. However, porting requires the surviving clearing member to accept the portfolio and associated margin in question. This in turn will depend on the way in which client margin has been charged and segregated. In the event porting is not possible then the client trades (of the defaulted member) will be managed in the default process together with the member's own portfolio. Chapter 11 provides further detail.

8.4.5 Loss allocation

The viability of a CCP depends on its ability to withstand the default of one or more clearing members. As in bilateral markets, the first line of defence for a CCP in such a scenario will be to close out all positions for the member in question and apply netting of such positions. By construction, any variation margin held should at best offset existing netted mark-to-market losses (except in the unlikely event that the trades in question have made a sudden profit). Initial margin (including any excess) will then cover any further losses due to aspects such as bid-offer costs and adverse price moves during the close out process. The CCP can also utilise the default fund contribution of the defaulter.

In case the initial margin and default fund contributions prove insufficient, and/or the auction fails, then the CCP has other financial resources to cover the losses. In general, a 'loss waterfall' defines the different ways in which resources will be used. Although they differ from CCP to CCP, a typical loss waterfall is represented in Figure 8.7.

In extreme scenarios, where the initial margin and default fund contributions of the defaulted member(s) have been exhausted, further losses may be taken from some equity contribution of the CCP (for example, current annual profits) which would still allow the CCP to continue to function. This ensures that the CCP has 'skin in the game' and is incentivised to have initial margins and default funds which are large enough. As long as these are sufficient then the 'defaulter pays' approach is fulfilled. This skin in the game is not written into all CCP rules. For example in 2014, a futures broker on the Korea Exchange (KRX) defaulted as a result of an algorithmic trading error. KRX mutualised a loss of US$4.3 million to the default fund contributed by their members without suffering any loss themselves. The KRX rules determined that they would suffer a loss only after the default fund of around US$200 million had been exhausted.[19]

After the defaulter pays point, the financial resources contributed by other members via the remaining default fund contributions are used. This is the point at which moral hazard

[19] Banks launch clearing review after Korean broker default, *Financial Times*, 7 March 2014, http://www.ft.com/cms/s/0/14b59838-a4d6-11e3-9313-00144feab7de.html#axzz2xeKF5nQP.

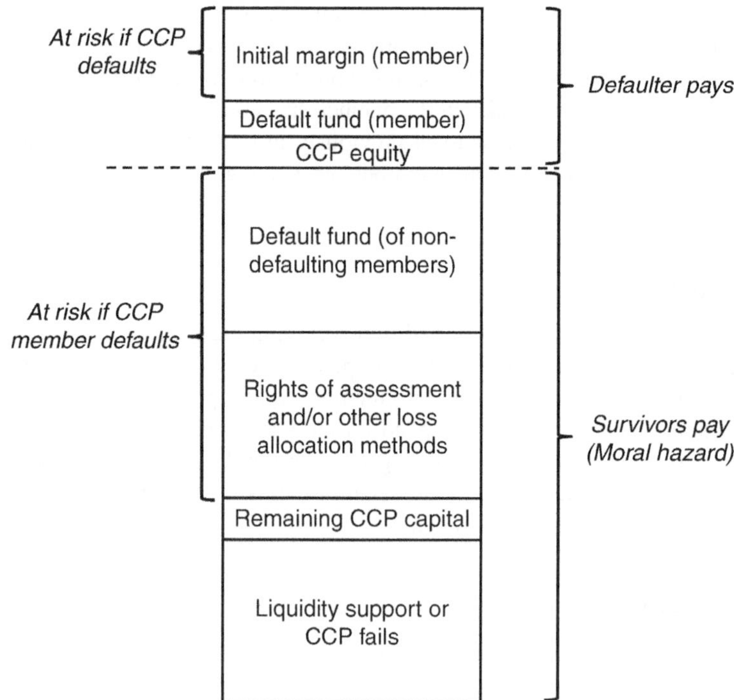

Figure 8.7 Illustration of a typical loss waterfall defining the way in which the default of one or more CCP members is absorbed.

appears as other members are paying for the failure. Indeed, it is possible for a clearing member to lose some of their default fund when another member, with whom they have avoided trading, defaults.

Losses wiping out a significant portion of the default fund of a CCP are clearly envisaged to be exceptionally unlikely. However, if this does happen then the surviving members of the CCP are required to commit some additional default fund to support the CCP, which is often called rights of assessment. This contribution is not unlimited and is usually capped (often in relation to a member's initial default fund contribution) as a means to mitigate moral hazard.

A CCP may have other methods besides an auction at their disposal. Methods such as selective tear-up of trades or variation margin haircutting are possible mechanisms (discussed in more detail in Chapter 10). Compared to absorbing losses via a default fund, such methods may produce a more heterogeneous allocation of losses (for example, clearing members with opposite positions to the defaulter may suffer more). Whatever loss allocation method is used, it should be fair and create incentive for all clearing members to actively help in the auction process, and therefore avoid losses permeating far down the loss waterfall.

After rights of assessment and other loss allocation methods, the remaining capital of the CCP would be used to cover losses. At this point, assuming losses persist, the CCP will fail unless they receive some external liquidity support (via a bailout from a central bank for example). We should note that, in order to reach the bottom of the loss waterfall, many layers of financial support must be eroded. Hence, although unquantifiable to any precision, this should be an extremely low probability event.

Some CCPs may have other components in the waterfall. For example, lines of credit with banks and financial guarantees provided by insurance companies. Having such liquidity 'on tap' is costly but this cost may be justified since CCPs could be very exposed in the event of a large negative asset price move, or the default of a clearing member and possible withdrawal of other clearing members.

8.4.6 Wrong-way risk

Wrong-way risk (WWR) can be a significant problem in some OTC derivatives and is often a key feature of counterparty risk losses in a financial crisis (e.g. the Asian crisis from 1997 onwards, and the global financial crisis from 2007 – see Gregory 2012). WWR is often ignored in the assessment of counterparty risk and CCPs tend to be no exception.

Exposure WWR (section 7.3.4) relates to an adverse linkage between market risk (exposure of transactions and margin held) and credit risk (default probability of counterparty). CCPs in general treat these components separately; market risk is mitigated by initial margins and credit risk by aspects such as membership requirements. A qualitative treatment of WWR by CCPs is probably important, especially in products such as credit default swaps (CDSs). For example, if a bank sells CDS on a bank domiciled in the same region and this trade is then centrally cleared, then the nature of clearing hides this WWR.

8.5 CCP LINKAGE

A theoretical ideal (e.g. Duffie and Zhu 2010) based on maximising netting involves just a single global CCP. However, it seems likely that jurisdictional issues and product segregation will create a relatively large number of OTC CCPs. It is therefore not surprising that linkages between different CCPs sometimes exist as mechanisms to get closer to the single CCP ideal in a multi-CCP world. Such linkages come in different forms and involve cross-margining, mutual offset and interoperability. The benefits include reduced costs, increased CCP competition and circumvention of regulatory barriers. The drawbacks are that CCPs become connected, leading to channels for systemic risk as well as legal and operational risks between the interlinked CCPs. It should also be noted that CCPs develop a substantial amount of development around their product offerings and may not wish to enter into linkages, which may involve sharing this intellectual property.

8.5.1 Interoperability

Interoperability via a link arrangement could allow two clearing members, say CM1 and CM2, to be able to clear via their own respective CCPs, CCP1 and CCP2, without any contractual relationship between CM1 and CCP2 or CM2 and CCP1. This would allow parties to concentrate their portfolio at their CCP of choice. One example of the need for interoperability is the need for a linkage between a global and local CCP so as to support trading between a global bank with a local bank. Another example would be a linkage between two CCPs clearing different products to provide margin benefits via cross-margining (section 8.5.4). Interoperability offers two obvious tangible benefits:

- *Netting:* Clearing members could gain from multilateral netting between products cleared via different CCPs, and would see this benefit via the need to be clearing members in fewer CCPs. This may potentially lead to lower overall fees, initial margins and default fund contributions. This would also potentially permit a clearing member to close out a position via a trade with a different CCP.

- *Regulatory:* Counterparties could clear trades with each other even when local regulators require them to use CCPs domiciled in their own region. Whilst regulation in the US and EU facilitates cross-border clearing via recognition or exemption of non-domestic CCPs, it may still be desirable to get around regulatory constraints confining parties to certain CCPs.

Interoperability would involve novating the original contract into three, rather than two, contracts. In addition to the usual contracts between clearing members and CCPs, there would need to be a contract between the two CCPs. If a CCP fails then the surviving CCPs in a link arrangement would be responsible to fulfil the contractual obligations resulting from that linkage. This opens up the issue of how the CCPs mitigate the risk they have to each other. This potentially requires an alignment of regulatory regimes and bankruptcy rules. Furthermore, depending on the form of interoperability, a tri-party arrangement may have to be in place so that, for example, the clearing member agrees that initial margin posted to one CCP can be used to offset losses by the other.

The benefits of interoperability would be seen in lower operational costs (less need to be a member of multiple CCPs), lower margin costs (smaller initial margins and potential variation margin offset), and higher netting benefits as well as circumventing potential regulatory issues where banks must clear through their own regional CCP. Interoperability can also facilitate cross-margining between CCPs as discussed in section 8.5.4. Interoperability may also lead to greater competition between CCPs.

The obvious negative aspect of interoperability is that CCPs will be linked, potentially creating channels for risk propagation and increasing systemic risk as the failure of one CCP can adversely influence another. It also increases legal risk for CCPs under different jurisdictions and operational risk due to CCPs being dependent on each other's systems. At the current time, only a small number of CCP interoperability arrangements exist.

8.5.2 Participant and peer-to-peer models

The simplest form of interoperability is the 'participant' model illustrated in Figure 8.8. In this arrangement, CCP2 is a clearing member of CCP1 and has the same contractual requirements and rights as any other clearing member. This may naturally occur if CCP1 is in a stronger position than CCP2 who is more in need of the interoperability arrangement. CCP2 would have to contribute initial margin and default fund contributions to CCP1 and is

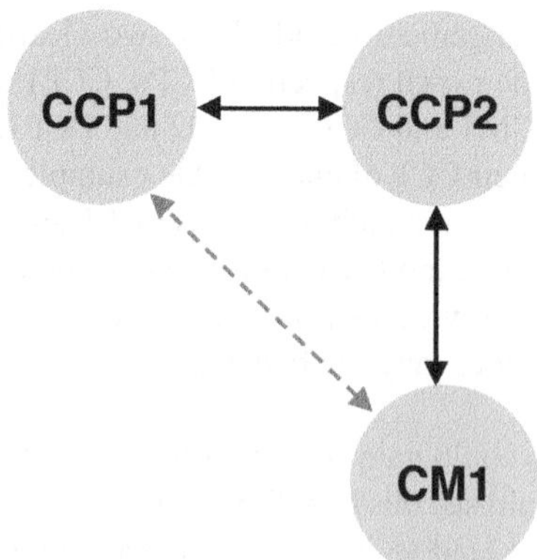

Figure 8.8 Illustration of participant interoperability between CCPs. CCP2 is a member of CCP1.

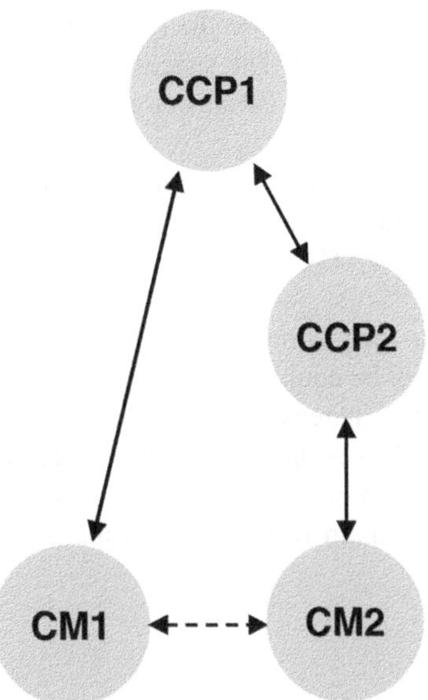

Figure 8.9 Illustration of peer-to-peer interoperability between CCPs. The original bilateral trade between CM1 and CM2 (dotted line) can be centrally cleared via different CCPs.

therefore exposed to a potential failure by CCP1. CM2 would essentially been seen by CCP1 as a client of CCP2. This approach is simple, and does not require CCPs to have a new bilateral contractual arrangement and to harmonise their risk management procedures for clearing members. Whilst it would circumvent regulatory cross-border issues, since the relationship between CCPs is unilateral, it does not allow for cross-margining (discussed in section 8.5.4) since CCP1 sees CM1 and CCP2 as different clearing members (due to segregation via house and omnibus segregation as discussed in section 8.2.1) and charges initial margin on their positions independently.

Figure 8.9 illustrates a more sophisticated form of interoperability known as the 'peer-to-peer' model. Here, two or more CCPs would need to enter into a contractual arrangement and share information about each other's positions in order to clear trades on a mutual basis. This is not trivial to do, especially across different jurisdictions where aspects such as regulation and bankruptcy laws may differ. The advantage of peer-to-peer interoperability is that it facilitates two counterparties clearing trades with each other whilst remaining members of only their original CCPs. The CCPs would also ideally need to be well harmonised in terms of their contractual terms to avoid difficult asymmetries. The CCPs will then need to exchange margin between each other, potentially including initial margin.

In peer-to-peer interoperability, linked CCPs will share information and where they see offsetting exposures, they can reduce the margin requirements accordingly. Part of their contractual arrangement must define how this initial margin will be calculated (knowing that the portfolios of CM1 and CM2 are not perfectly correlated), held and subdivided in the event of a default.

A recent paper suggests another route for interoperability, which does not cause the potential adverse linkages between CCPs.[20] It argues that CCPs do not post margins or default

[20] 'Guidelines and Recommendations for establishing consistent, efficient and effective assessments of interoperability arrangements', European Securities and Markets Authority, 10 June 2013.

funds to each other, but rather both increase their default funds from clearing members to reflect the risk they have to one another. The success of the clearing would then depend on the netting benefits and therefore lower initial margins dominating this increase in default fund requirements.

Interoperability arrangements are currently in place between some CCPs in Europe (clearing equity) and also linked several US CCPs. Some commentators argue that interoperability will be much harder to achieve in OTC derivatives due to more complex margin standards and default fund requirements.

Interoperability gets closer to the theoretical ideal (e.g. Duffie and Zhu 2010) of having just a single global CCP but it cannot be equivalent to a single CCP solution due to crossing multiple jurisdictions. Moreover, the increased netting benefits, lower costs and circumvention of regulatory hurdles does need to be balanced against negative aspects, such as increased interconnectivity leading to systemic, legal and operational risks.

We now describe two of the main results of interoperability, namely mutual offset and cross-margining.

8.5.3 Mutual offset

A mutual offset arrangement permits clearing members to clear a transaction at one CCP but then close it by clearing the opposite trade through another CCP, or alternatively to transfer positions between CCPs. This allows trading the same position across markets (and time zones). The CCPs involved will have exposures to each other since they must create an offsetting position between themselves, as illustrated in Figure 8.10. However, since the trades offset perfectly, this arrangement is the simplest form of CCP linkage.

8.5.4 Cross-margining

Clearing the same product in multiple CCPs causes fragmentation and limits the benefits of clearing, especially in terms of multilateral netting (section 5.2.6). Interoperability can lead to a form of cross-margining to improve this situation. The aim of cross-margining[21] is for

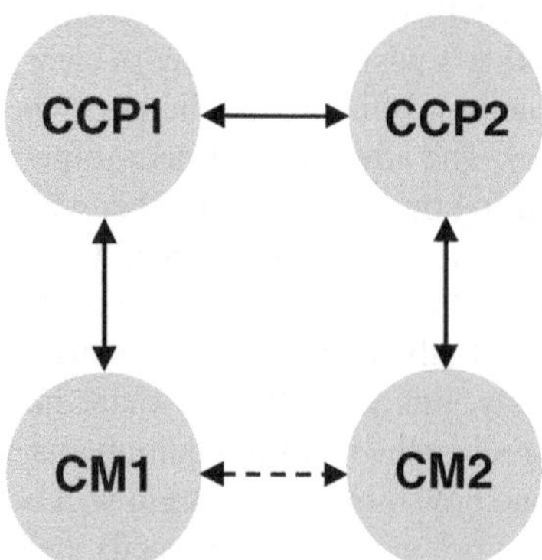

Figure 8.10 Illustration of mutual offset where the clearing member (CM1) can offset a trade cleared through CCP1 with another cleared through CCP2.

[21] Note that cross-margining is also used to mean the portfolio benefits that are achievable through clearing different products at the same CCP.

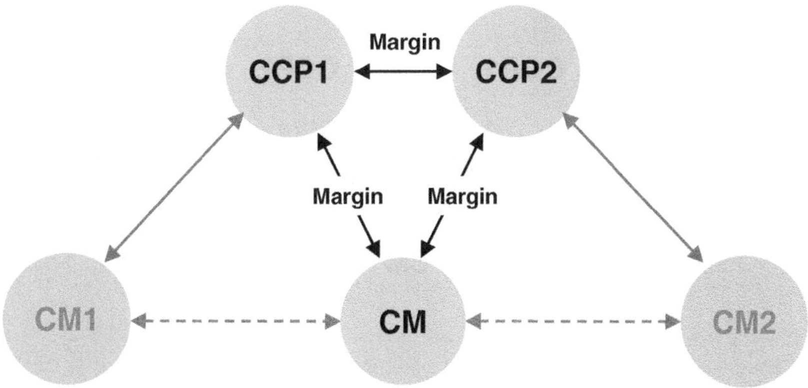

Figure 8.11 Illustration of cross-margining of CM's positions with CCP1 and CCP2. CM1 and CM2 show the other side of the two trades that would also be cleared by the CCPs.

different CCPs to share risk management arrangements such that they can utilise the offsets between positions to reduce margin requirements to members clearing through both CCPs (noting, for example, that clearing through different CCPs will impose an additive total initial margin implicitly assuming perfect positive dependency). Generally, this is only done for strongly negatively correlated positions where the margin gains can be significant (e.g. interest rate futures and offsetting swaps). If two such trades were cleared at the same CCP, then the margin requirements would be lower thanks to their offsetting nature. Cross-margining allows such margin offsets to be generated even via trades cleared at different CCPs.

In order to achieve cross-margining, CCPs have to share trade information and agree on margin calculations, as illustrated in Figure 8.11. In the event of a default by the clearing member denoted by CM, then the CCPs can offset gains and losses but they need to agree how to subdivide margin. With variation margin this should be straightforward as positions will be additive but complexities will arise for initial margin. The most cost-effective arrangement would be for CCPs to share a single agreed initial margin amount, which is held by one of the CCPs or with a third party custodian. If a CM defaults on its obligations to either or both CCPs, then the margin can be liquidated and shared in a pre-defined way. However, there is an exposure between CCPs, as each is exposed to the joint default of the other CCP and clearing member in the event of losses on the cross-margined positions that they hold.

There are two subtly different forms of cross-margining. In the first, which already exists in practice, negatively correlated positions (e.g. short futures position against a long call option) are cross-margined. In such situations, it is structurally highly probable that losses on one position will correspond to gains on the other. Hence, the CCPs can share initial margin knowing that in a default scenario, it is likely that only one of them will require it (assuming close out costs are not significant). A more difficult cross-margining would be applied in the situation where the correlation is not necessarily negative but offset still exists (e.g. interest rate swaps and credit default swaps). There may be some natural offset between these two portfolios, but they could both plausibly experience losses in a default scenario. In this case, the co-operation is more sensitive to the pre-defined margin sharing rules and any cross-border issues, since both CCPs may need to use initial margin to cover losses.

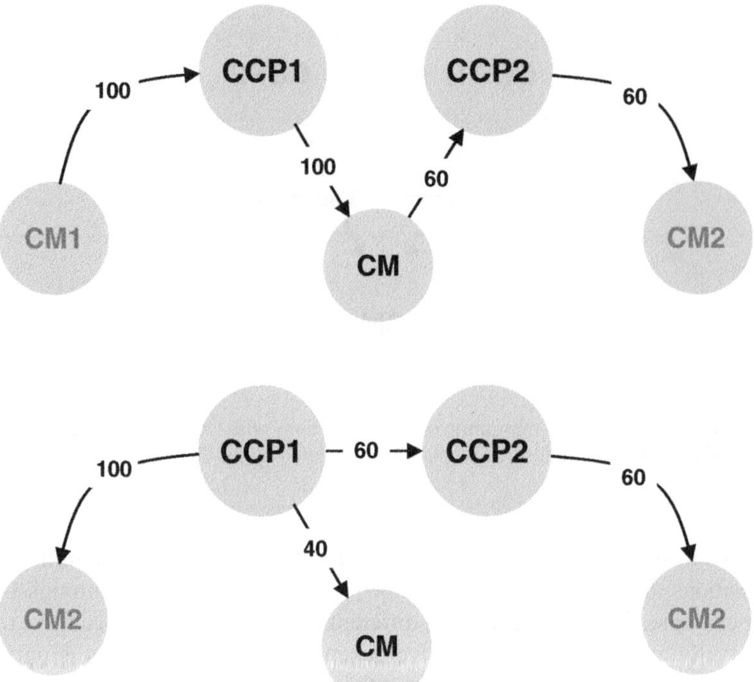

Figure 8.12 Illustration of a potential variation margin move for the cross-margining relationship shown in Figure 8.11 assuming that the CM's trade with CCP1 loses 100 and their trade with CCP2 gains 60.

Cross-margining can also extend to variation margins, which allows a single net payment which can reduce the volume of payments needing to be made. Suppose that CM in Figure 8.11 has partially offsetting trades with CCP1 and CCP2, the former gains 100 with the latter losing 60. The flow of variation margin needs to be as shown in the bottom of Figure 8.12. Margin passes between the CCPs and CM makes only the net margin payment due to offsetting positions. Note that in practice, such an arrangement typically requires the CCP holding joint accounts for variation margin payments. This creates a more continuous dependence between the CCPs and exposes them to each other's default.

There is historical evidence of the potential benefits of being able to offset variation margins in this way. In the stock market crash of 1987, a clearing member at the Chicago Mercantile Exchange (CME) had long positions in index futures offset by options position cleared at OCC (see also discussion in section 14.2.5). The clearing member was struggling to make very large variation payments to one CCP, which would have been significantly offset from margin received from the other. However, the timing gap caused problems. Within two years, CME and OCC had started to develop plans for cross-margining.

Cross-margining with respect to initial margins is discussed more in section 9.5 in the next chapter.

9
Margin and Default Fund Methodologies

In the business world, the rear view mirror is always clearer than the windshield.

Warren Buffett (1930–)

This chapter describes margining in more detail. In particular, we focus on the methodologies for determining variation and initial margins, and default fund contributions. Initial margin methodologies for both CCP and bilateral markets are discussed. Cross-margining aspects are also considered.

9.1 VARIATION MARGIN

Variation margin is relatively simple conceptually, being just an adjustment for the change in mark-to-market value of the relevant positions at frequent periodic intervals. Valuation is relatively straightforward since a prerequisite for clearing is that the underlying trades are standardised and liquid. Variation margin will typically be cash in the trade currency. As a counterparty to all trades, CCPs are calculation agents, valuing all positions and collecting or paying respective margin amounts.

9.1.1 Valuation

Clearly, a CCP needs to have in place clear procedures for defining data sources and price quotes. However, OTC derivatives represent a greater challenge for variation margin calculations because valuations will potentially need to be generated by pricing models rather than being observed directly as market prices. One of the reasons for this is that longer-dated products do not remain liquid throughout their lifecycle and hence need to be marked-to-market based on models calibrated to similar liquid instruments. Often this is not highly complex and amounts to little more than an interpolation, but it does introduce some subjectivity into valuations.

Furthermore, OTC derivative pricing models, even for standard and liquid products, may change and be refined over time. This may lead to the need for discrete changes in valuation practices, which in turn may lead to jumps in variation margin requirements. Furthermore, the pricing may become more complex and subjective as markets change and put a strain on variation margin calculation methodologies for a product that may already be cleared in high volume.

A good example of the above is the move from LIBOR to OIS discounting for interest rate products. Prior to the global financial crisis (GFC), LIBOR was generally viewed as the 'correct' discount rate due to the perceived almost total lack of credit risk within this unsecured lending rate. However, in recent years, the so-called overnight indexed swap (OIS) rate is considered the relevant discount rate for margined transactions (Piterbarg 2010). This greatly complicated matters for a number of reasons. In the past, pricing a single interest rate swap used the same rate (LIBOR) for both projecting the future cashflows and discounting them. Now, it is considered necessary to account for the difference between contractual rates (e.g. LIBOR) that include credit risk, and the rates for discounting which should be risk-free (OIS). This is often known as 'dual curve'[1] pricing or 'OIS discounting'. The difference between LIBOR and OIS discounting can be material, especially for off-market trades.

LCH.Clearnet's SwapClear service switched to OIS discounting (for USD, GBP and EUR currencies) in 2010.[2] Many large swaps dealers made this change at the same time, but some smaller banks still use LIBOR discounting. The OIS story illustrates how variation margin calculations can still rely on relatively complex valuation models and be subject to methodology changes through time. Whilst CCPs can effectively define mark-to-market valuations for margin purposes, they clearly need to have methodologies that are robust and market standard. This is a challenging point as more complex products (e.g. vanilla interest rate swaptions) may become cleared.

9.1.2 Frequency of margin calls

The frequency of variation margin calls represents a difficult balance. On the one hand, they should occur often in order to minimise the 'margin period of risk' (section 6.1.4). Indeed, since a larger time between margin calls creates more risk for the CCP then it would require higher costs, probably via larger initial margin requirements. On the other hand, frequent margin posting is operationally challenging (for both CCPs and clearing members) and increases potential liquidity risks (see discussion in section 14.2.5).

Historically, in the bilateral OTC derivatives markets margining has sometimes been infrequent (e.g. weekly, monthly), but daily posting requirements have increasingly become the norm. Centrally cleared OTC markets generally work on a daily basis, with variation margin requirements typically published overnight (e.g. 2 a.m. for ICE Clear Europe) and required to be paid at the beginning of the trading day (10 a.m. for ICE Clear Europe).

However, CCPs will potentially make intraday margin calls in special situations when large price movements breach internal thresholds (such calls can be partially mitigated by a clearing member having excess margin in their account, see Figure 8.4 in the previous chapter). For example, both LCH.Clearnet and ICE will make intraday margin calls in 'special circumstances' and such calls will require margin posting very quickly (e.g. within the hour). Intradaily margining is becoming increasingly common and is supported by technological advances. Indeed, LCH.Clearnet makes seven variation margin calculations throughout the trading day and may call for intraday margin in the event of a material mark-to-market move based on pre-determined credit thresholds.

9.1.3 Convexity and price alignment interest

The periodic exchange of variation margin creates a convexity effect similar to that well characterised in futures contracts. To understand this effect, consider the clearing of an

---

[1] Noting that dual curve pricing is relevant for a single interest rate transaction and different currencies and cross-currency products will require many curves incorporating the various tenor basis and cross-currency basis effects.

[2] 'LCH.Clearnet adopts OIS discounting for $218 trillion IRS portfolio', 17 June 2010, http://www.lchclearnet.com/media_centre/press_releases/2010-06-17.asp.

interest rate swap paying the fixed rate ('payer swap'). As interest rates rise, the value of this position increases and the entity (CCP or clearing member) would receive variation margin in cash equal to the mark-to-market of the position (assume this cash is then invested, for example, on short-term deposit). Now suppose that interest rates fall again such that the swap returns to its previous value and the same variation margin has to be returned. The entity will have made a profit due to the investment return on the margin held. Of course, the reverse can be true where the entity would have to post margin. However, there will be an overall profit since margin is received (paid) in high (low) interest rate scenarios. This profit is essentially a convexity effect due to the correlation between the value of the swap and the interest rate. This means that a cleared payer (receiver) swap would be more (less) valuable than the equivalent uncleared swap.[3]

Ideally, a cleared swap would not deviate from its equivalent uncleared version as in the above example. CCPs have therefore developed methods to correct for the deviations. For example, LCH's SwapClear uses the concept of price alignment interest (PAI) on variation margin with the intention 'To minimise the impact of daily cash variation margin payments on the pricing of interest rate swaps, the Clearing House will charge interest on cumulative variation margin received and pay interest on cumulative variation margin paid in respect of these instruments'.[4] The PAI rate is typically set to the relevant overnight (e.g. Fed Funds in the US) rate and is intended to adjust for the (overnight) cost of funding variation margin (although this does not, of course, mean it will match the actual funding requirement of the party posting it).

An alternative way to attempt to correct for the difference between cleared and uncleared trades is via the conversion of OTC products into futures contracts or 'futurisation'. This is discussed later in section 12.3.1. Cont et al. (2011) provides a more technical discussion of these issues.

9.1.4 Variation margin and liquidity risk

The benefit of intraday margin calls is risk reduction, for example, LCH.Clearnet called for US$40 million of margin from Lehman Brothers on Friday 12 September 2008. This margin would not have been forthcoming on the following trading day since Lehman by then had filed for bankruptcy. It could also be argued that there is no liquidity cost associated with variation margin. For example, BCBS-IOSCO (2013b) state (emphasis added):

> In the case of variation margin, the BCBS and IOSCO recognise that the regular and timely *exchange of variation margin* represents the settlement of the running profit/loss of a derivative and *has no net liquidity costs* given that variation margin represents a transfer of resources from one party to another.

The above statement is referring to bilateral markets and even in such a context it could be challenged (see section 13.1.2). Moreover, in centrally cleared markets, variation margin *is* costly due to the asymmetries in margin posting that are skewed in the CCPs favour. CCPs

---

[3] A similar effect can be seen between the prices of interest rate futures (exchange-traded) and forward rate agreements (OTC).

[4] LCH.Clearnet limited update to section 3.5.2 price alignment interest (PAI) rate, 17 November 2008, http://www.lchclearnet.com/images/section%203_tcm6-47191.pdf.

may make one or more intradaily margin calls per day and typically only return margin once a day. Such effects would be most pronounced during volatile markets where large price moves may cause CCPs to ask for very large intraday margins from some participants covering their losses, whilst possibly not returning immediately the equivalent margin against gains of other clearing members (see section 14.2.5). This creates liquidity risk for clearing members, not just for their own positions but also for those of their clients, since they will generally need to fund the posting of client margin in these situations.

9.2 INITIAL MARGIN

Initial margin is perhaps the key aspect that defines the effectiveness of clearing. It represents an additional margin required to cover the largest projected loss on a given transaction or portfolio. However, determining initial margin is a complex quantitative task and represents a difficult balance: under-margined trades impose excessive risk on a CCP whereas excessive margins raise the costs of trading OTC derivatives. The methodology and assumptions used to compute initial margins will obviously have a significant impact on margin demands as shown, for example, by Duffie et al. (2014).

9.2.1 Close out period

In the event that a clearing member defaults, there will be a delay since the last variation margin has been received. There will then be a further delay until the clearing member's portfolio has been completely closed out. The total length of time for this to happen will be known as the margin period of risk (MPR), which is a term that originated in bilateral OTC markets (section 6.1.4). A CCP is exposed to market risk for the length of the MPR and will need to quantify this for risk management purposes. Clearly, estimating the MPR is quite complex, product/market specific and subjective.

Figure 9.1 illustrates schematically the components of the MPR for a CCP. Recall that, as discussed in section 8.4.2, the CCP has greater authority and control over this process than a typical counterparty in a bilateral OTC trade. The MPR is defined by three general periods:

- *No action:* This is the period from when the clearing member last posted margin until remedial action is taken. It will correspond to the delay between margin calls and any additional delay before the CCP declares the clearing member in default and starts to act. In this period, the CCP is exposed to the full volatility (and likely downward pressure) of the underlying portfolio.
- *Macro-hedging:* The CCP may first seek to neutralise key sensitivities of the underlying portfolio via macro-hedges. This should cause the overall risk of the portfolio to drop significantly, although the portfolio will be still subject to aspects such as curve risks, basis risks and bid-offer costs.
- *Auctions:* The CCP will then arrange and hold one or more auctions to trade out of the underlying portfolio. During this time, the risk will gradually drop to zero although the CCP may be exposed to costs in auctioning the positions. It should be noted that the macro-hedges executed in the previous step should be helpful in the auction process because the portfolios auctioned will be the defaulter's trades together with the macro-hedges. Since these will have less sensitivity to market moves, it should be easier for clearing members to put in reasonable bids, even in volatile markets.

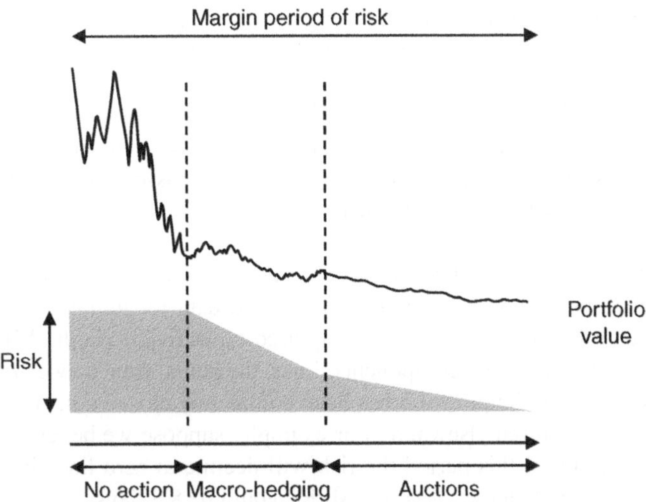

Figure 9.1 Illustration of the margin period of risk for a CCP.

Assessing the MPR is complex, not only because of the length of the above periods but also for 'wrong-way risk' reasons. Wrong-way risk refers to a linkage between default probability and exposure (section 7.3.4). This means that the MPR should be assessed under the assumption that the member in question is in default. For example, if a member's default is expected to produce particular volatility in the relevant market, then this should be considered. There are several general aspects to incorporate:

- *Volatility:* The market volatility over the period is likely to be higher than normal market volatility, especially if the clearing member in default is large and/or systemically important. For example, Pykhtin and Sokol (2013) estimate that the volatility of CDS index spreads in the aftermath of the Lehman bankruptcy was around four to five times bigger than over the period prior to their failure. Extending the MPR to compensate for this increased volatility could be significant, as a doubling of volatility would approximately equate to an MPR four times longer.[5]
- *Risk reduction:* During the close out process, the actual risk of the portfolio declines as illustrated in Figure 9.1, and this would suggest a shortening of the MPR (see discussion on the Lehman close out by LCH.Clearnet in section 4.1.4). For example, being exposed to a portfolio with its risk reducing linearly for 10 days is approximately equivalent to being exposed to the full portfolio for about four days.[6]
- *Downward pressure:* In addition to the market volatility, there could also be downward pressure on prices, especially if the underlying portfolio is large. For example, Pykhtin and Sokol (2013) report a significant 'upwards jump' in CDS spreads after the Lehman

[5] Based on the well-known square root of time scaling that is relevant for independently identically distributed (i.i.d.) random variables.

[6] If we consider for simplicity that we are exposed to a portfolio for a total of n days but that the portfolio risk declines by a fraction of $1/n$ at the end of each day, then in variance terms this is equivalent being exposed to the full portfolio for $1+n/3\times(1-1/n)\times(1-1/2n)$ days.

bankruptcy, which would have created a significant negative mark-to-market move for a CDS portfolio that was net long credit risk (luckily, of course, CDS contracts were not centrally cleared at this time).

- *Costs:* As mentioned above, any specific bid-offer or other costs experienced in the auctions will contribute further losses. For example, there have been claims of profiteering by clearing members in auction processes, which imposes losses on the defaulted member and potentially also the CCP (see section 10.2.1).

The important point is that the above effects are not *generally* modelled in specific detail by CCPs (one obvious exception is the use of stressed data for initial margin calculations, discussed later) and therefore should all be captured collectively via the MPR choice. The MPR is therefore defined by two components. First, the actual time between the last margin payment and the time that the portfolio has been completely closed out, and second, adjustments for effects not captured elsewhere. For example, suppose we believe the actual MPR is five days but that during this period the risk will decline to zero linearly and the market volatility will be double, then the 'effective MPR' would be 8.8 days.[7]

In exchange-traded futures markets, the MPR used is generally one day (or sometimes two days) due to the underlying liquidity allowing rapid close out. In OTC products, a longer period of typically five days is used, although sometimes slightly longer periods are used for client portfolios (SwapClear uses seven days). These estimates certainly seem reasonable for the actual MPR, but it is not clear if they really reflect what we have defined above as the effective MPR, which in certain situations could be argued to be significantly higher. Note that the choice of MPR is partially at the discretion of the CCP in question whereas initial margin requirements for uncleared bilateral trades must use a 10-day horizon (section 4.2.5).

9.2.2 Coverage

The purpose of initial margin is to cover the adverse mark-to-market moves illustrated in Figure 9.1. This cannot, of course, be done with certainty but initial margins are intended to cover a very large proportion of potential price moves (99% or more when explicitly quantified) during the MPR. There is a clear balance in setting initial margin levels; too low will imply the CCP is taking excessive risk whilst too high and clearing costs may become excessive. A CCP must balance the need to be competitive by incentivising central clearing (low margins) with maximising their own creditworthiness (high margins). Not surprisingly, high margins have been shown empirically to have a detrimental impact on trading volumes (for example, see Hartzmark 1986 and Hardouvelis and Kim 1995). Brady (1988) discusses the crash of 1987 and its impact on some CCPs arising in an extreme market event with associated liquidity problems (see also section 14.2.5).

Clearing members will also want to be comfortable with the basic initial margin calculation methodology, as any lack of comfort with risk measurement methodologies could erode confidence in the CCP. Whereas variation margin relates to the current exposure, initial margin provides coverage for the future exposure. Initial margin is, by contrast to variation margin, much more complex and more subjective.

[7] Using the formula given in footnote 6 reduces the MPR from 5 days to 2.2 days, which then needs to be quadrupled to reflect the approximate effect of doubled volatility.

In general, the following components are important considerations in deciding on initial margin:

- *Volatility:* The most obvious aspect is the volatility of the portfolio in question. This is driven by the volatility of the underlying market variable(s) and the maturity. OTC derivatives, especially those that are long-dated, are likely to have significant initial margins.
- *Tail risk:* Whilst volatility typically measures continuous price variability, some products, especially CDS, can suffer from tail risk due to jumps or gaps in the underlying market variables.
- *Dependency:* Since CCP members typically hold a variety of trades with a CCP, it is important to understand the offsetting nature of such trades. If correlation between the price moves of different trades is small (or even negative), then clearly the overall portfolio is less risky and the benefit of this is that less margin needs to be charged. However, the interdependencies within and between asset classes are notoriously difficult to quantify and can change significantly through time.

It should be noted that initial margin is intended to cover a worst-case scenario but may not capture some of the more extreme behaviour such as very heavy tailed distributions or strong dependencies. Such effects, where relevant, may be better captured by default fund contributions.

9.2.3 Linkage to credit quality

Initial margin depends primarily on the market risk of the centrally cleared trades and only a small component, if any, is linked to the credit quality of the clearing member. This means that, at least from a margin point of view, the members of a CCP are essentially treated equally. This has the obvious implication that CCP members must be rather similar in credit quality. Even then, there are asymmetric information problems since weaker members will be gaining at the expense of stronger members. Indeed, Pirrong (1998) argues that the delay in adopting central clearing on certain exchanges was related to stronger credit quality members not wishing to subsidise weaker ones.

Some CCPs do base margins partially on credit ratings, for example, by requiring more when a member's rating falls below a certain level.[8] Unfortunately, linking initial margins to external credit ratings is clearly problematic since these are imprecise and granular measures of credit quality. Furthermore, due to increasing margin requirements when clearing members are already under financial pressure, they are potentially destabilising. These triggers also can create systemic risk (for example, see discussion on monolines in section 2.3.4) via so-called cliff-edge and death spiral effects. Indeed, SwapClear dropped multipliers in response to the significant threat that some clearing members would be downgraded and their margin requirements increased significantly (and indeed potentially even expelled).[9] Other OTC CCPs (e.g. ICE Clear Europe)[10] do not link margins to external credit ratings. This may also be sometimes prohibited by regulation. For example, the Commodity Futures

[8] For example, see http://www.lchclearnet.com/membership/sa/market_capital_requirements.asp.

[9] See 'SwapClear changes expulsion rules', 4 May 2012, Risk, http://www.risk.net/risk-magazine/news/2172414/swapclear-changes-expulsion-rules.

[10] See https://www.theice.com/publicdocs/clear_europe/ICE_Clear_Europe_Risk_FAQ.pdf.

Table 9.1 Summary of the advantages and disadvantages of linking initial margins to credit quality.

	Advantages	**Disadvantages**
Credit linked initial margins	• Less moral hazard • CCP margins naturally rise in a crisis	• Cliff edge and death spiral effects
No credit linkage in initial margins	• Encourages smaller counterparties to be clearing members • No cliff edge and death spiral effects	• Bad credits are subsidised (moral hazard)

Trading Commission's latest derivatives clearing organisation rules prohibit membership requirements (such as external credit ratings) that would have the effect of excluding or limiting clearing membership of certain types of market participants.

OTC CCPs, such as LCH.Clearnet and ICE do still use internal rating scales to measure the relative credit quality of clearing members on a qualitative and quantitative basis. Based on these scales, multipliers or other remedies (such as limiting trading activity) may be applied. As with many aspects of central clearing, the advantages and disadvantage of credit sensitivity margin requirements (Table 9.1) are balanced.

Another related aspect to this is the linkage of haircuts to credit quality. This was illustrated quite clearly via the MF Global default. MF Global held US$6.4 billion of European sovereign debt (which was financed through repo trades). When, due to the declining credit risk of the issuers, haircuts on these assets were increased, this created a negative asset shock that helped to catalyse the decline of MF Global. Whilst CCPs should ideally increase haircuts to mitigate declining credit risk in such situations,[11] there is a clear danger that it increases systemic risk, especially when done suddenly. Even if the CCP is better off from such a move (which is debateable since they may push the clearing member into default), it is unlikely that the market as a whole would benefit.

9.2.4 Haircuts and non-cash margins

Whereas variation margins are generally cash-only, CCPs allow initial margins to be posted in other securities. This raises the issue of whether the value of the initial margin assets held would decline during the close out period. In general, a CCP will mitigate this risk in two distinct ways:

- *Eligible securities:* Securities eligible for initial margin will be restricted to those without any significant credit or liquidity risks that could cause extreme adverse price moves. Moreover, securities that might be adversely correlated to the credit quality of a clearing member would not be accepted.
- *Haircuts:* Given the above, the CCP should be concerned only with the market risk, which can be mitigated by the appropriate choice of haircut. Indeed, even assets such as gold and equity indices are potentially acceptable as they have large market risks that can be mitigated by accordingly large haircuts and probably do not suffer from other sources of adverse price moves, such as illiquidity.

[11] For example, see 'LCH Raises Margin Costs for Trading Spanish Government Bonds', 20 June 2012, http://www.bloomberg.com/news/2012-06-19/lch-lifts-margin-costs-for-trading-most-spanish-government-bonds.html.

Haircuts, as discussed previously, are generally defined to cover the majority of detrimental price moves over a representative liquidation period (for example, a two-day price movement and a 99.7% confidence level). Note that the assumed period may be shorter than for initial margin calculations because selling margin securities is not dependent on the successful completion of an auction or other default management functions. Haircuts may also be applied to cash margin in illiquid currencies with similar assumptions over liquidation period and confidence level, and can be relatively significant.[12]

9.2.5 The SPAN methodology

Outside OTC clearing, the market standard approach for margin calculations is the so-called SPAN (Standard Portfolio Analysis of Risk)[13] methodology, originally developed by the CME in the 1980s. SPAN was licenced by the CME and by 2008 was being used by more than 50 exchanges and CCPs globally. The introduction of SPAN was revolutionary at the time since it allowed margins for futures and options to be calculated based on the overall portfolio risk. A typical example would be the margining of a portfolio containing offsetting exposure to different equity indices (e.g. S&P 500 and NASDAQ) where the high correlation would create beneficial margin reduction.

SPAN works by evolving individual risk factors (e.g. spot price, volatility) combinatorially based on movements in either direction at a certain confidence level. Products with the same underlying market variable will share risk factors (e.g. futures and options on the same equity index). A series of shifts are applied to each risk factor, which are intended to be representative of one- or two-day moves in the underlying variables. Some more extreme shifts may also be applied (which may be particularly relevant, for example, for an out-of-the-money position). The portfolio is then revalued under the different moves and the worst scenario is normally used to define the initial margin. An example of SPAN shifts applied to an option position is shown in Figure 9.2.

The strong standardisation of exchange-traded transactions (e.g. where the number of expiration dates or strikes for a given product is small) supports a relatively simple method such as SPAN. SPAN is quite well suited to risk assessment on simple portfolios such as futures and options, which are generally of low dimensionality. Whilst SPAN-type methods work well and are tractable for simple portfolios, they have drawbacks. Most notably, they do not scale well to a large number of dimensions (as the number of combinations of moves grows exponentially). OTC derivatives portfolios are typically of high dimensionality, with many more risk factors than for exchange-traded markets. For example, even a single interest rate swap is sensitive to the full term structure of interest rate moves, and cannot be represented as a single parallel shift in rates since this implies unrealistically that rates for different tenors are perfectly correlated. SPAN also makes relatively simplistic assumptions on implied volatility changes, normally expressed as a single volatility shift, which will not capture volatility risk in portfolios sensitive to more subtle changes in the volatility surface. SPAN approaches give results which are relatively static through time and also do not clearly attach an underlying probability to the scenario defining the initial margin, and are therefore not especially risk-sensitive. Finally, the up and down moves that define the

[12] For example, with the two-day time horizon and 99% confidence level and assuming an FX volatility of 15%, a haircut would be $\phi^{-1}(0.99)\times\sqrt{2/250}\times 15\% = 3.1\%$.

[13] 'SPAN Overview – CME Group', http://www.cmegroup.com/clearing/files/span-methodology.pdf.

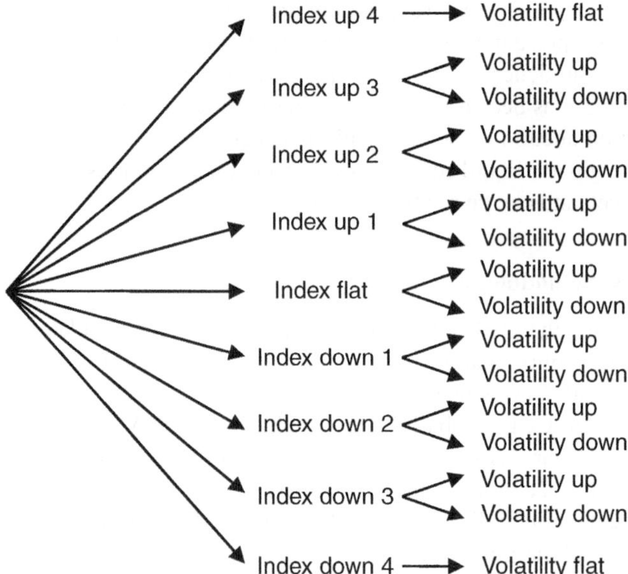

Figure 9.2 Illustration of risk factor shifts applied for determining the initial margin of an option position using SPAN. The underlying index is shifted up and down by four different amounts and single up/down volatility shifts are applied to each (note the fourth index shift is an extreme scenario intended for deep out-of-the-money options).

worst move of a given market variable are somewhat subjective and a specific probability cannot be readily attached to the result. This is why OTC derivatives CCPs have been moving towards more VAR-like methods for initial margin calculation, as discussed below.

9.3 VAR AND HISTORICAL SIMULATION

Given the drawbacks of SPAN for more complex and potentially multi-dimensional derivatives portfolios and the general usage of value-at-risk (VAR) models for market risk applications, it is not surprising that CCPs (e.g. LCH, CME and Eurex) have moved towards more risk-sensitive VAR-type approaches for initial margin calculations for OTC products. Such approaches are suited to, for example, high dimensionality multi-currency swap portfolios. Furthermore, the definition of VAR is very intuitive, which is a key reason why it became so widely adopted within banks. It is therefore relevant to review VAR approaches and then describe more specifically the approaches taken by CCPs.

9.3.1 Value-at-risk and expected shortfall

VAR is a key approach for quantifying financial market risk that has been developed by large banks over the last two decades. A VAR number has a simple and intuitive explanation as the worst loss over a target horizon to a certain specified confidence level. The VAR at the $\alpha\%$ confidence level gives a value that will be exceeded with *no more* than a $(1 - \alpha)\%$ probability. An example of the computation of VAR is shown in Figure 9.3. The VAR at the 99%

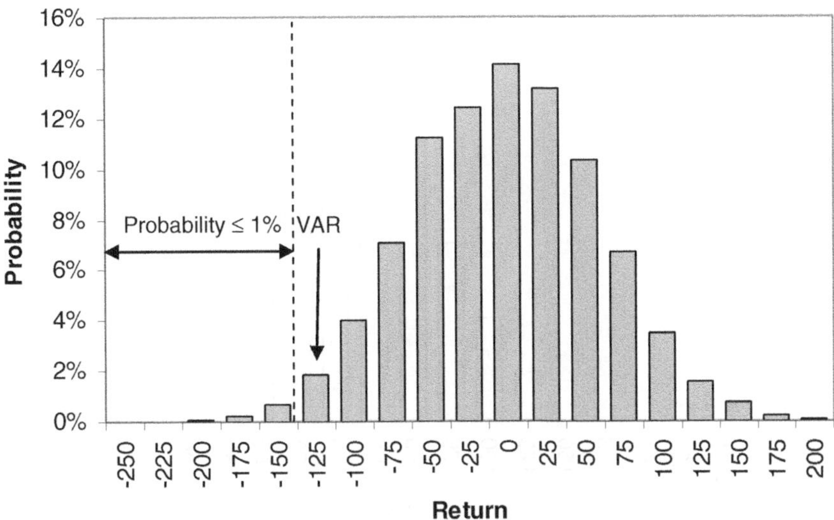

Figure 9.3 Illustration of the value-at-risk (VAR) concept at the 99% confidence level. The VAR is 125, since the chance of a loss greater than this amount is no more than 1%.

confidence level is −125 (i.e. a loss) since the probability that this will be exceeded is no more than 1% (it is actually 0.92% due to the discrete[14] nature of the distribution). To find the VAR, one finds the *minimum* value that will be exceeded with the specified probability.

VAR is a very useful way in which to summarise the risk of an entire distribution in a single number that can be easily understood. It also makes no assumption as to the nature of distribution itself, such as that it is a Gaussian.[15] It is, however, open to problems of misinterpretation since VAR says nothing at all about what lies beyond the defined (1% in the above example) threshold. To illustrate this, Figure 9.4 shows a slightly different distribution with the same VAR. In this case, the probability of losing 250 is 1% and hence the 99% VAR is indeed 125 (since there is zero probability of other losses inbetween). We can see that changing the loss of 250 does not change the VAR since it is only the *probability* of this loss that is relevant. Hence, VAR does not give an indication of the possible loss outside the confidence level chosen. Over-reliance upon VAR numbers can be counterproductive as it may lead to false confidence.

Another problem with VAR is that it is not a *coherent* risk measure (Artzner et al. 1999), which basically means that in certain (possibly rare) situations it can exhibit non-intuitive properties. The most obvious of these is that VAR may not behave in a sub-additive fashion. Sub-additivity requires a combination of two portfolios to have no more risk than the sum of their individual risks (due to diversification). This could translate into the requirement that the initial margin, when clearing a large portfolio through a single CCP, would be no greater

[14] For a continuous distribution, VAR is simply a quantile (a quantile gives a value on a probability distribution where a given fraction of the probability falls below that level).

[15] Certain implementations of a VAR model (notably the so-called variance-covariance approach) may make normal distributions assumptions, but these are done for reasons of simplification and the VAR idea itself does not require them.

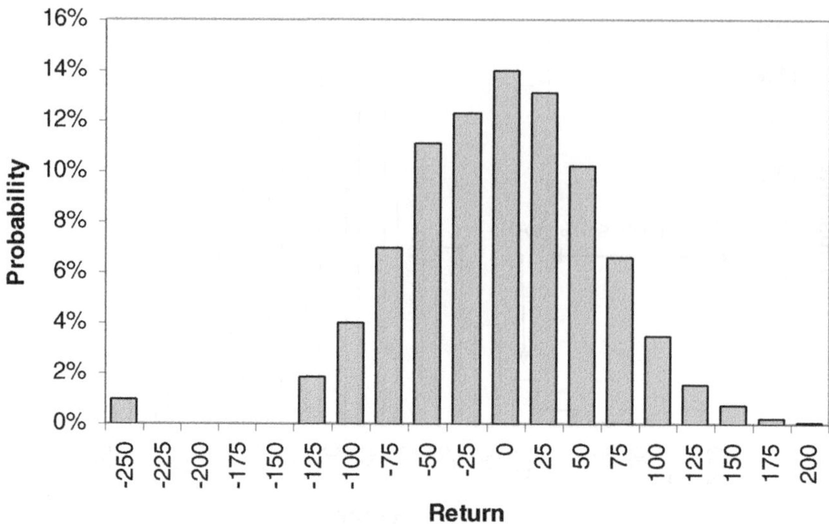

Figure 9.4 Distribution with the same VAR as Figure 9.3.

than the total initial margin when clearing the same portfolio as subportfolios through different CCPs.[16] Such properties cannot be guaranteed when using VAR as a risk measure.

A slight modification of VAR is often known as expected shortfall (ES). Its definition is the average loss equal to or above the level defined by VAR. Equivalently, it is the average loss knowing that the loss is at least equal to the VAR. ES does not have quite as intuitive an explanation as VAR, but has more desirable properties such as not ignoring completely the impact of large losses (the ES in Figure 9.4 is indeed greater than that in Figure 9.3). Furthermore, ES is a coherent risk measure and this would guarantee that, for example, cross-margining between CCPs would always lead to lower initial margin requirements (a feature not guaranteed with VAR). An example of the lack of sub-additivity of VAR is shown in Table 9.2. Here the 80% VAR[17] is defined by the fourth highest loss, which is higher in the combined portfolio (90) than in the sum of the two individual portfolios (80). ES is an average of the highest two values and does not exhibit this problem.

Table 9.2 Example showing the sub-additivity properties of VAR and ES metrics. The scenarios corresponding to the VAR are shown in bold.

	Portfolio 1	Portfolio 2	Total portfolio
Scenario 1	10	30	40
Scenario 2	30	**40**	70
Scenario 3	**40**	30	70
Scenario 4	10	90	100
Scenario 5	80	10	**90**
VAR (80%)	40	40	90
ES (80%)	60	65	95

[16] Assuming the CCPs use the same initial margin approach.

[17] A low confidence level is required due to the small number of scenarios shown.

9.3.2 Historical simulation

The most common implementation of VAR and ES approaches is using historical simulation. This takes a period (usually several years) of historical data containing risk factor behaviour across the entire portfolio in question. It then re-simulates over many periods how the current portfolio would behave when subjected to the same historical evolution. For example, if 4 years of data were used, then it would be possible to compute around 1,000 different scenarios of daily movements for the portfolio. If a longer time horizon is of interest then quite commonly the 1-day result is simply extended using the 'square root of time rule' (section 7.2.3). For example, in market risk VAR models used by banks, regulators allow the 10-day VAR to be defined as $\sqrt{10}=3.14$ multiplied by the 1-day VAR.

VAR models can be 'backtested' as a means to check empirically their predictive performance. Backtesting involves performing an *ex-post* comparison of actual outcomes with those predicted by the model. VAR lends itself well to backtesting since a 99% number should be exceeded once every hundred observations.

There are a number of questions and potential problems when using historical simulation such as:

- *Data relevance:* The success of the method as a risk management tool relies on history being a good guide to the future.
- *Data window:* The choice of how long to make the data window is subjective. A long window or 'look-back period' (e.g. 10 years) will provide more data points but *might* contain old and irrelevant data. A short window may contain more recent relevant data but will contain fewer points overall and be subject to noise, and may cause procyclicality (section 9.3.5).
- *Autocorrelation:* This refers to the fact that data over sequential time horizons may be quite dependent (such as during quiet or volatile periods).

9.3.3 Look-back periods

The look-back period refers to the historical range used for defining risk metrics such as VAR. Choosing the look-back period is quite subtle: a very long period may use old and meaningless data, whereas a short period may lead to unstable results. Banks have typically used between one and three years for the purposes of VAR models for capital calculations and not usually more than five years. Typically, shorter look-back periods are more problematic as very volatile periods (such as the period in the aftermath of the Lehman default) drop out of the data set. One way to smooth such effects is to use 'exponential damping' where the weights of historical scenarios decline the further back they go. This means that large price moves drop gradually out of a data set. Under the so-called Basel 2.5 changes (BCBS 2009) implemented from the end of 2011, banks were required to include a one-year stressed period in their VAR calculations. Practically this has meant that data around the Lehman bankruptcy would remain in the VAR data set long after it had dropped out of the look-back period.

9.3.4 Relative and absolute scenarios

Relative returns have traditionally been used in historical VAR approaches. This means that a move in interest rates from 3% to 3.6% is interpreted as a 20% increase. In a low interest rate

Table 9.3 Comparison of historical simulation using absolute and relative returns.

	Historical data			Historical simulation	
	Initial rate	**Final rate**	**Change**	**Initial**	**Simulated**
Absolute	3.0%	3.6%	0.6%	1.0%	1.6%
Relative	3.0%	3.6%	20%	1.0%	1.2%
Absolute	4.0%	3.2%	–0.8%	1.0%	0.2%
Relative	4.0%	3.2%	–20%	1.0%	0.8%

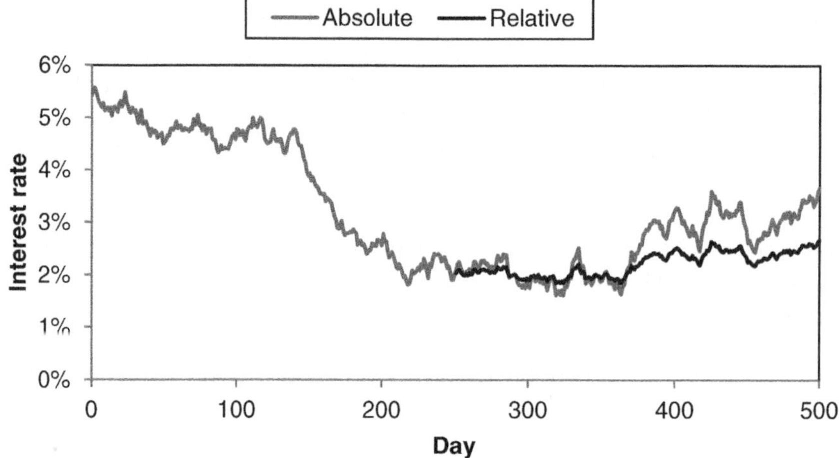

Figure 9.5 Illustration of historical simulation for an interest rate process using absolute and relative scenarios. The simulation begins at the 250-day point.

environment, where rates are 1%, this would translate into quite a small upwards move to only 1.2%. If instead the absolute rate change were used, then the equivalent move would be to 1.6%. This is illustrated in Table 9.3, which shows two different scenarios. It is also worth noting that absolute returns may produce negative interest rates (which may be unrealistically large) whilst relative returns cannot (unless interest rates themselves become negative).

Whether absolute or relative scenarios are most appropriate depends on the current rates regime. Absolute moves are more conservative in a falling interest rate environment as illustrated in Figure 9.5. On the other hand, the reverse will be true during a period of rising rates. This is a well-known problem in the area of interest rate models where behaviour can move between normal (absolute shifts) and log-normal (relative shifts).

9.3.5 Procyclicality

In relation to VAR models, the concept of procyclicality will potentially cause VAR to be high in crisis periods but low in stable periods. This is now a well-known problem as it encourages high leverage in bullish market environments, leading to sudden and extreme crises. Strong procyclicality of initial margins is clearly problematic since it could lead to dangerously low initial margin requirements during good economic periods. To have an idea

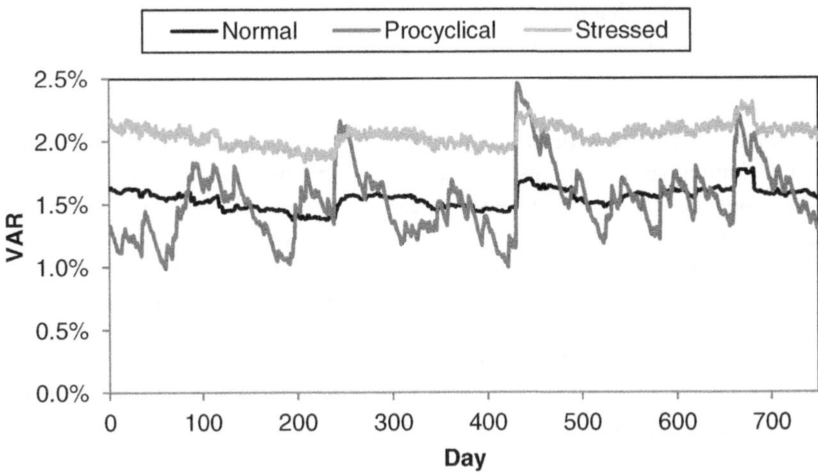

Figure 9.6 Illustration of normal, procyclical and stressed VAR calculations through time.

of how significant such an effect could be, Heller and Vause (2012) estimate that without any adjustment for procyclicality, initial margins for interest rate swaps could increase by around a factor of two times between a low and high volatility regime, and CDS could show an impact of approximately an order of magnitude.

The impact of procyclicality on VAR is illustrated in Figure 9.6 (this example is for interest rate swaps). The procyclical VAR can change sharply whilst the normal one stays reasonably constant. We also show the impact of including some conservative or stressed assumptions, which will be discussed below. In the normal scenario, the VAR is quite stable but is potentially too low in volatile markets due to an averaging effect. Procyclical VAR does increase more in markets that are volatile but does so suddenly. Stressed VAR is both stable and more appropriate in volatile markets but at the cost of being potentially much too high for the majority of the time.

There are a number of choices that can influence initial margin procyclicality:

- *Historical time series:* The choice of look-back period is a key input. If the period is short then it may arguably contain the most relevant recent data but it will also lead to margins moving rapidly through time as turbulent days move in and out of the data set and cause rapid oscillations (see procyclical example in Figure 9.6). Using a long history will tend to smooth out such effects as given periods will have less overall impact on the measure calculated (similar to the normal result in Figure 9.6).
- *Volatility scaling:* Certain VAR methods use various ways to capture volatility clustering in financial data. A simple example is to use exponentially weighted moving average (EWMA) historical data,[18] which means that the data points have less impact the further away they occur. A more sophisticated and commonly used approach is filtered historical simulation (FHS). Whilst these approaches all arguably get closer to the realities of

[18] For example, this is used by LCH in the PAIRS methodology used for SwapClear, see http://www.lchclearnet.com/images/lch.clearnet_limited_swapclear_im_model_changes_tcm6-63320.pdf.

financial markets (e.g. that there are long periods of small market moves followed by short periods of strong moves), they potentially lead to greater procyclicality and would cause initial margins to increase quickly at the start of a crisis but then drop quickly as the crisis averts.

- *Autocorrelation:* VAR approaches sometimes use overlapping returns to maximise the number of individual data points. This creates problems since overlapping data will by definition show dependencies, and a single extreme event will show up in several overlapping periods and have a large impact. The only simple methods to prevent autocorrelation are to either use the worst-case single loss or non-overlapping returns.
- *Risk measure:* The choice of risk measure has some impact on procyclicality. For example, suppose the worst-case scenario in a five-year window is used to calculate VAR. When this day drops out of the data window then the initial margin will drop potentially significantly. If on the other hand the initial margin is the average of the worst few days (see SwapClear changes described in section 9.4.2) then one day dropping out will have a smaller impact.

The GFC showed up various deficiencies in bank's VAR approaches for measuring market risk capital. This led to various regulatory changes such as the need to calculate a 'stressed VAR' from a 12-month period of 'significant financial stress relevant to the bank's portfolio' (BCBS 2009). The stressed result of Figure 9.6 is clearly most advantageous in terms of being stable and not underestimating VAR in volatile periods. However, it is clearly also the most conservative approach. In addition, the fundamental review of the trading book (BCBS 2012a) has recommended a move from VAR to ES for bank market risk capital requirements as a more coherent risk measure (see section 9.3.1). Both the use of stressed data and ES type approaches have recently made their way into initial margin methodologies as discussed in the next section.

9.4 INITIAL MARGINS FOR OTC DERIVATIVES

9.4.1 Requirements for initial margin approach

The VAR approaches developed for characterising market risk in banks over the last two decades have more recently been applied to initial margin calculations used by CCPs. In this respect, the following general aspects are important when designing an initial margin model:

- *Forecasting:* The model can produce a reasonable forecast of potential exposures of the portfolio, accounting for all relevant risk factors and incorporating aspects such as non-Gaussian (fat-tailed) behaviour.
- *Dependencies:* Dependencies between different risk factors are modelled appropriately to capture (but not overstate) the diversification between different products. This is especially important for calculating the benefit achieved by cross-margining (section 9.5).
- *Procyclicality:* The margin approach is designed to avoid procyclicality as much as possible. This may require incorporating different regimes of market data such as stressed periods.
- *Margin period of risk:* The margin period of risk is based on the liquidity, market size and specific characteristics of the product(s) in question.

9.4.2 OTC CCP initial margin approaches

Until recently, a typical approach for OTC derivatives may have been to use historical simulation with up to five-years of data and defining the initial margin via a VAR type measure (e.g. 99.7%). Methods such as EWMA and FHS (section 9.3.5) have been used. However, initial margin approaches have also been evolving based on lessons generally learned from the drawbacks of VAR approaches that have been highlighted over the years, especially during the GFC. Furthermore, regulation around CCPs and initial margins has not surprisingly focused on some of the shortcomings of potential VAR approaches. The Committee on the Global Financial System (CGFS 2010), for example, has recommended 'through-the-cycle' margins. Under CCP standards in Europe (ESMA 2012), CCPs must limit procyclicality in one or more of the three following ways:[19]

- Applying a margin buffer equal to at least 25%.
- Assigning at least 25% weight to stressed observations in the look-back period.
- Ensuring that its margin requirements are not lower than those that would be calculated using volatility estimated over a 10-year historical look-back period.

As an example of the above evolution, SwapClear in 2013 made the following changes to their methodology:[20]

- *Absolute increments:* Relative changes in market variables were modified instead to use absolute changes in market variables. This is more conservative in a low interest-rate environment (see Figure 9.5).
- *Data history:* This has been increased from 5 years to 10 years to give a more stable estimator. Without this, the data around the Lehman default would have dropped out of the history and almost certainly caused a significant drop in margins. In addition, the decay factor used for damping historical scenarios (see discussion on EWMA in section 9.3.5) has been recalibrated.
- *Expected shortfall:* The initial margin is now defined as an ES since it uses the average of the six worst scenarios out of a total of 2,500 business days. This represents a confidence level of over 99.7%. As discussed above, ES has better properties than VAR, and this approach will therefore be coherent and is likely to be more stable.

Other CCPs have made similar changes, for example, CME uses a stressed period in order to comply with the ESMA requirement mentioned above. This is in line with the stressed VAR requirement in bank's capital requirements mentioned above and potentially deals with the drop-out problem more elegantly (since using a 10-year window simply delays this effect).

Initial margins may change due to:

- *Time series changes:* Old data will drop out of data windows and new market events will be included.
- *CCP methodology decision:* CCPs will change their margin methodologies (e.g. changing the data window or moving from VAR to ES).

[19] The deadline for changes was 15 September 2013, five years after the Lehman bankruptcy.

[20] See http://www.lchclearnet.com/images/lch.clearnet_limited_swapclear_im_model_changes_tcm6-63320.pdf.

Ideally, margins should be stable through time but they should also respond to new data and methodological advances. Certain changes can be regarded as only short-term fixes. For example, the move from relative to absolute returns becomes inappropriate when rates begin to rise. Furthermore, shifting to a 10-year horizon prevents the market data around the Lehman bankruptcy from dropping out of the data set, but it will still drop out eventually.

Of course, initial margins cannot avoid procyclicality entirely. Indeed, it is potentially useful that CCPs can adjust margins in response to changes in market conditions, as this limits their vulnerability (Pirrong 2011). Highly sensitive approaches, prone to procyclicality, will also probably lead to lower average margin requirements (although these will rise significantly in a crisis). However, market conditions can change quickly and large margin changes can influence prices through effects such as causing forced liquidations of assets. Of course, the safest approach is for initial margins to be conservative but, as illustrated in Figure 9.6, this is also the most expensive solution. Whilst regulation and pressure from members[21] will prevent margin methods from becoming excessively aggressive, competition between CCPs will encourage this to some degree.

CCPs may include additional components in the initial margin calculation. It is also important to account for FX risks for positions denominated in different currencies. CCPs may also use 'margin multipliers' which will lead to increased margins for excessive amounts of liquidity, credit, concentration and sovereign risks. These may account for the fact that the liquidation of a reasonably large and/or complex OTC portfolio would be subject to substantial bid-offer costs, and could move the market. Client trades may also attract a larger margin requirement.

Table 9.4 contrasts the initial margin assumptions used for interest rate products at three significant OTC CCPs. It can be seen that there is a reasonable convergence on aspects such as historical simulation methods, liquidation periods, volatility scaling and liquidity charges. Differences still exist, in terms of methods to avoid aspects such as procyclicality and autocorrelations, which is seen by the use of different data windows and measures used. Given the small differences, the methods would be expected to give reasonably material (e.g. 10–20%) differences on a stand-alone basis. However, this may be blurred by portfolio effects in the actual initial margin calculation. Not all CCPs are as closely aligned in terms of methodology assumptions, for example, NASDAQ OMX uses a three-factor principal component analysis (PCA) approach for interest rate products.[22]

The above analysis has focused largely on interest rate products since these represent a high proportion of OTC derivatives clearing to date. The other main asset class that is important for OTC CCPs is credit derivatives. Calculating initial margin requirements for credit default swaps represents greater challenges. This is due to a sparseness of data and the fact that credit spread distributional changes can be highly complex and especially prone to aspects such as fat tail effects.

For the above reasons, CDS initial margin methodologies tend to differ from historical simulation approaches. ICE Clear uses a proprietary Monte Carlo simulation to evaluate a large 5-day decline in portfolio value based on 20,000 simulations and incorporating asymmetric distributional assumption and co-movements in relation to credit spreads. LCH.

[21] See for example, 'Member revolt forces SwapClear to revamp margin model', Risk, 5 December 2012, http://www.risk.net/risk-magazine/news/2229594/member-revolt-forces-swapclear-to-revamp-margin-model.

[22] http://www.nasdaqomx.com/digitalAssets/87/87719_cfm-margin-guide---methodology.pdf.

Table 9.4 Comparison of initial margin methodologies for interest rate products.

	LCH.Clearnet (SwapClear)	**CME**	**Eurex**
Name	PAIRS*	HVaR**	PRISMA†
History	10-year	5-year	3-year + 1-year stress period
Measure	Expected shortfall (average of 6 worst)	99.7% VAR (4th largest loss)	At least 99% (average of five VAR measures non-overlapping returns)
Returns	Absolute	Relative	Absolute
Volatility scaling	Filtered historical simulation incorporating volatility scaling	EWMA with volatility scaling and subject to volatility floor	Filtered historical simulation
Liquidity period	5 days (7 days for clients)	5 days	5 days
Addition charges	Credit risk and liquidity risk	Liquidity charge	Historical correlation breaks and liquidity costs

* http://www.lchclearnet.com/risk_management/ltd/margining/swapclear.asp.
** http://www.cmegroup.com/trading/interest-rates/files/OTC-IRS.pdf.
† http://www.eurexclearing.com/clearing-en/risk-management/eurex-clearing-prisma.

Clearnet use a modified SPAN approach[23] (CDS SPAN®) which works on the basis of a 99.7% confidence level using fat-tailed distributional assumptions. Both LCH and ICE include additional components to capture effects such as bid-offer costs and concentration risks of large portfolios.

9.4.3 Competition

An obvious concern over CCP initial margin methodologies is that of competition. CCPs competing on pricing could be beneficial by offering lower initial margins, which may in turn lead to a 'race to the bottom'. CCPs have also been compared to rating agencies (Kenyon and Green 2012) in that their competition may create systemic risk and in turn contribute to a financial crisis.

Clearing members may want initial margins to be small to make clearing cheaper. However, they also need to be sure that the CCP is suitably covered for the risk it faces. Moral hazard suggests that strong CCP members will lose at the expense of the weaker ones (see comment on historical experience of the LME in section 2.1.5). The change from using relative to absolute returns at LCH.Clearnet, mentioned above, was catalysed by member lobbying.[24] Strong members should want initial margin to cover as large a portion of the overall risk as possible to reduce moral hazard. This also makes it easier to pass costs to clients transparently since non-clearing members do not make default fund contributions.

However, there have been claims of CCPs being 'over-competitive' on initial margin requirements. For example, SwapClear accused a rival CCP, International Derivatives Clearing

[23] http://www.lchclearnet.com/Images/risk%20mgt%20overview%20-%20public%20var_tcm6-64637.pdf.

[24] See footnote 21.

Group (IDCG), of having initial margin requirements that were 'bordering on reckless'.[25] This was related to IDCG's 'futurisation' of the contracts (see section 12.3.1). It should be noted that IDCG denied such claims, which were made at a time when both CCPs were competing for the clearing of huge portfolios from Fannie Mae and Freddie Mac.

The above evidence seems to suggest that some competition between CCPs will exist, and the more competitive ones may be correspondingly more risky. However, the evidence also suggests that dramatically divergent behaviour leading to overly aggressive pricing may be corrected by market forces such as clearing member pressure.

9.4.4 Computation considerations

It is not surprising that initial margin methodologies for OTC derivatives have become broadly based on simulation methods. These methods are the most accurate as they are the only way to incorporate important effects such as irregular probability distributions, time changing volatility and multidimensionality. They are also the only generic approaches, which makes product development and cross-margining more practical.

However, these relatively sophisticated approaches are also costly. Margin calculations are portfolio-based and therefore to calculate the initial margin on a new trade, the incremental effect vis-à-vis the entire portfolio must be calculated. Such incremental effects will be important to clearing members (and clients) when deciding where to clear trades and whether to backload trades to CCPs. Even with pre-computations and parallel processing, an incremental calculation is often not achievable in real time and therefore cannot be part of the execution process for a new trade (as discussed in section 8.2.2, regulation may require trades to be accepted for clearing in narrow time windows such as 60 seconds). Furthermore, clearing members and clients will want to be comfortable with approaches and understand the magnitude of initial margins for various trade and portfolio combinations. One obvious way to optimise computation times is to use sensitivities ('Greeks') to approximate the change in value of each trade rather than resorting to a 'full revaluation'. Given the number of scenarios generated, full revaluation generally tends to be time-consuming, especially for complex derivatives, which require relatively sophisticated pricing models.

Given the above, CCPs have developed tools for calculating approximate initial margins without the need for full re-simulation. An example is the SwapClear Margin Approximation Risk Tool (SMART), which is available also on Bloomberg.[26] Regarding treatment of initial margins for new trades, CCPs will either calculate these approximately in real-time or rely on initial margin buffers intended to cover the risk until the true margin impact can be calculated (probably overnight). This incremental risk may also be covered by an additional component of the default fund, which could be based on the relative utilisation by a clearing member over the most recent period. This means that a member clearing large volumes of trades may have to make a relatively large additional contribution to the default fund to cover the intraday risk such trades are generating.

[25] See 'LCH.Clearnet CEO calls rival "reckless" as Fannie, Freddie clearing battle heats up', Risk, 15 April 2010, http://www.risk.net/risk-magazine/news/1601290/lch-clearnet-ceo-calls-rival-reckless-fannie-freddie-clearing-battle-heats and 'LCH.Clearnet warns of loose standards', Financial Times, 16 April 2012, http://www.ft.com/intl/cms/s/0/0458dc94-48ef-11df-8af4-00144feab49a.html#axzz2htSDhLrA.

[26] http://www.bloomberg.com/pressroom/bloomberg-integrates-margin-calculator-for-swap-participants/.

9.4.5 Standard initial margin model (SIMM)

As discussed in section 6.5, regulation is being introduced to require that initial margins be posted against bilateral (non-cleared) trades. Although some institutions and products are exempt, and the requirement is being phased in and subject to thresholds, the initial margins resulting from this requirement will be significant. These requirements seem particularly high under the simple standardised margin schedule described in section 6.5.5 (ISDA 2012 estimate over US$8 trillion for schedule-based margins). This suggests that applying a more sophisticated methodology for initial margin calculations could be quite important to prevent requirements being overly conservative. Obviously, VAR methods such as those described above and used already for initial margin calculations by CCPs would be the natural choice.

However, an important difference in bilateral markets is that parties need to agree on quantities such as margins (compared to centrally cleared markets where the CCP has the right to enforce their own calculation). More complex margin calculation methodologies, such as VAR-based, should be expected to lead to significant disputes. Indeed, in bilateral markets, even variation margin calculations (based on current exposure) have often led to significant valuation disputes. It is therefore inconceivable that initial margin calculations (based on future exposure estimates) would not lead to more disputes over what is by its nature a highly subjective and complex estimation. It seems impractical that an institution would replicate the margin model and data set used by all of their bilateral counterparties. On the other hand, they would probably be unwilling to agree blindly to initial margin requirements generated by such a model.

Given standardised margin schedules are too conservative and proprietary models will lead to major dispute problems, there is an obvious need for a standard model that is risk-sensitive but can be agreed by all parties across bilateral OTC markets. ISDA has been perusing this initiative with input from market participants. The standardised initial margin model (SIMM) is an idea to develop a uniform methodology for calculating bilateral initial margins.[27] ISDA (2013d) broadly described a proposal for the structure of such a model based on the following important characteristics:[28]

- *Non-procyclicality:* Margins should not be subject to continuous changes linked to market volatility, which could exacerbate stress in volatile market conditions. It is proposed that margins are not explicitly linked to market levels or volatility. It is also suggested that scenarios should be updated periodically and not continuously.
- *Ease of replication:* To mitigate problems arising from potential disputes, a transparent methodology and data set must be used.
- *Transparency:* It must be possible to understand the drivers of the methodology and therefore drill down to understand discrepancies and avoid disputes.
- *Quick to calculate:* The calculation must be quick (e.g. seconds) to facilitate fast pricing checks.
- *Extensible:* It should be easy to extend to cover additional risk factors in order to facilitate the addition of new products.
- *Predictibility:* Initial margin results must be predictable in order for institutions to price correctly and allocate capital.

[27] Noting that this therefore does not give any opinion on initial margins calculated by CCPs.

[28] Note that this is the author's own description of the characteristics given by ISDA (2013d).

- *Costs:* The cost to buy or build the model must not be prohibitive so it does not restrict access.
- *Governance:* Regulators should approve the model and calibration and review this on a periodic basis.
- *Margin appropriateness:* Margin should be risk-sensitive and give appropriate reduction for offsetting positions.

To adhere to the above, ISDA define a general model based on the relevant risk factors for all underlying products in the portfolio. Market scenarios shocks (10-days or equivalent scaled amount) are then applied to each risk factor via 'factor models' or methods such as historical VAR. This still leaves a significant amount of detail to be decided in terms of the precise description of risk factors, the data set to be used and the method chosen to generate scenario shocks (e.g. principal component analysis or historical simulation) from this data.

The other main methodology choice suggested is the use of pre-computed Greeks, instead of full revaluation, to recalculate the value of a portfolio with respect to different risk factor shocks. Although such an approach can underestimate margin for complex and/or partially hedged positions, this would seem to be pragmatic given the likely need for rapid incremental margin calculations in order to make trading decisions.

Finally, ISDA propose that to meet the requirement of separating margin calculations across asset classes, shocks are applied to each asset class separately. As discussed in section 6.5.6, this may be preferable to a product separation by asset class, as it better represents trades subject to risk factors in different asset classes (e.g. interest rate and credit) and partially hedged positions. Furthermore, a product does not need to be classified as belonging to a particular asset class, as it will be subject to all different asset class shocks.

9.5 CROSS-MARGINING

9.5.1 Rationale

Cross-margining is a general term that refers to margin calculations made on a portfolio, rather than on a product-by-product basis. The advantage of this is that margins will be more competitive as they will benefit from reductions due to offsetting positions. Indeed, Gemmill (1994) illustrates the diversification offered to CCPs from clearing several markets that are not highly correlated. Cross-margining offers the following interrelated benefits:

- *Lower margin costs:* Lower initial margins due to the diversification benefit between positions.
- *More efficicent liquidations:* In the event of a default scenario, all cross-margined positions could be liquidated together as an offsetting or hedged portfolio. This could minimise close out costs and reduce the systemic impact of the default.
- *Reduced legal and operational risk:* Since initial margin represents funds not actually owed to counterparties, this also provides a reduction of exposure to losing margins in the event of non-segregation, fraud or operational problems.
- *Regulatory transparency:* Regulators may have, through CCPs, a better aggregate view of the positions of clearing members.

CCP members and their clients will be actively looking to receive the benefits of such favourable dependencies in the form of lower initial margins. In particular, some sophisticated financial institutions use a variety of different transactions and often execute combinations of positions that are partially hedged. In such situations, the cross-margining benefits would be expected to be particularly significant.

There are a number of different ways in which cross-margining can be applied, some of which are already common and some that may develop as OTC clearing develops:

- Within a given product type (e.g. different currencies of interest rate swaps).
- Between products within a given asset class (e.g. fixed to floating interest rate swaps and basis swaps or index and single name credit default swaps).
- Between products in different asset classes (e.g. interest rate swaps and credit default swaps).
- Between exchange-traded and OTC products (e.g. interest rate futures and interest rate swaps).
- Between regions for a given CCP (e.g. CME US and CME Europe).
- Between different CCPs.

Some of the above are more challenging, for example, due to the need to develop sophisticated models to represent the dependencies in a portfolio, for operational reasons (e.g. futures vs. OTC products) or jurisdiction differences (between CCPs in different regions). However, particularly as OTC clearing becomes more widespread, the possibility to achieve lower margins through cross-margining will become increasingly important for market participants.

There is also some evidence that clearing multiple asset classes may be useful in default management. For example, Lehman traded a combination of interest rate, equity, agriculture, energy and FX positions on the CME and whilst they suffered losses on two out of five of these asset classes, this was covered by excess margin from the other three (Pirrong 2013), meaning that the *overall* initial margin was sufficient. LCH.Clearnet's diversified spread of business was a help in the same default, with the CEO stating: 'Without this degree of diversification it is doubtful whether we would have had the time to identify and transfer the client positions. Instead we would have had no option but to close out all the positions in the house account, leaving many clients unhedged'.[29]

9.5.2 Cross-margining within a CCP

Historically, CCPs have tended to avoid extending cross-margining excessively. This is not surprising as in the presence of cross-margining, initial margin methodologies will have to be more complex and represent dependencies and basis positions, which would not be important for silo-based portfolio calculations. However, as CCPs expand and cover more product types (especially in the OTC space), this issue will become more important and will be subject to competitive pressures.

There are inherent dangers with cross-margining though. Probably the most difficult aspect in understanding and quantifying financial risk is that of dependency between different financial variables. It is well known that historically estimated correlations may not be a good representation of future behaviour, especially in a more volatile market environment,

[29] Wall Street Journal, 'How LCH.Clearnet got clear of Lehman', 14 October 2008, http://online.wsj.com/article/SB122392821573229759.html.

or crises, where correlations have a tendency to become very large on an absolute basis. It is also important to note that, unlike volatility, it is not immediately obvious how to stress a correlation value as the underlying sensitivity of a portfolio may be positive or negative and may not even be monotonic. Therefore, whilst multidimensional modelling of risk factors can lead to increased benefits from margin offsets, it also increases the underlying model risk.

Note also that clearing members often require more margin from their clients than is required by CCPs. Cross-margining benefits obtained via a CCP may not necessarily be fully passed on by clearing members, although competitive pressures will likely again play an important role to give clients access to offsets.

9.5.3 Exchange-traded and OTC products

As OTC clearing increases, one development that can reduce costs is cross-margining between exchange-traded (e.g. futures) and OTC products. Indeed, this has already started with, for example, CME offering cross-margining benefits between Eurodollar and Treasury futures contracts and OTC interest rate products since 2012.[30]

However, such a coming together is not completely trivial, as illustrated in Table 9.5. First, initial margins for futures products have typically used SPAN methodologies whereas OTC products are treated in a historical VAR framework. Second, the assumed liquidation period for more liquid futures products is shorter (typically one or two days) than their OTC counterparts (typically five or more days). Third, margin account structures for these products may differ: futures positions have generally used omnibus accounts structures (section 8.2.1) whereas OTC products are being given greater segregation of margins via methods such as LSOC ('legally segregated by operationally comingled' – see section 11.3.3). A final potential problem could be regulatory driven, for example, in the US where futures products are regulated by the SEC and OTC by the CFTC.

Cross-margining requires treating both sets of products under a unified methodology which, given their greater complexity, needs to be OTC-based. This is generally achieved via the movement of futures from SPAN based methods to OTC approaches. This means that futures positions will probably be treated more conservatively in terms of liquidation period than if they were margined alone. This could be important as OTC positions are generally long-dated and futures shorter dated, and so margin offsets may be expected to be only moderate at best in some cases. This implies that it will be important to characterise the likely offset between two portfolios, before moving to cross-margining, to ensure that the offsets will overcome any more conservative treatment of futures products. Practical challenges and only moderate benefits are seemingly hindering the growth of futures and OTC cross-margining.[31]

Table 9.5 Comparison of methodologies for margining futures and OTC-cleared products.

	Futures	**OTC products**
Initial margin methodology	SPAN	Historical VAR
Assumed liquidation period	One or two days	Five days
Account structure	Omnibus account	OTC segregated account (e.g. LSOC)

[30] See http://www.cmegroup.com/trading/interest-rates/cleared-otc/files/portfolio-margining-capital-efficiencies.pdf.

[31] For example, see 'Cross-margining at CME slowed by practical challenges', Risk, 1 August 2013, http://www.risk.net/risk-magazine/news/2284938/crossmargining-at-cme-slowed-by-practical-challenges.

9.5.4 Cross-margining between CCPs

Cross-margining benefits are clearly hindered by the regional and product specialisation of CCPs. Interoperability of CCPs (section 8.5.1) provides a way to increase efficiency further by having CCPs sharing margins. In such a situation, there is a contractual agreement between two (or more) CCPs to jointly margin transactions in certain products. This creates a potential diversification benefit such as that achieved when clearing different asset classes through a single CCP. Cross-margining agreements may be limited to certain specified products or may extend to the entire product coverage of the CCPs in question.

Cross-margining between CCPs can take the form of a one- or two-pot arrangement as illustrated in Figure 9.7. In a two-pot arrangement, each CCP nets internally and has its own separate account for the initial margin required. The benefits of this are limited, an example being that CCPs may offset some residual risk and in the event of a default, an excess at one CCP may be allowed to cover losses at the other. In a one-pot arrangement, there is greater efficiency as positions would be closed out together in the event of a default. Accordingly, all such positions are treated at the same time using one single methodology, leading to potentially significant savings. However, a one-pot arrangement requires CCPs to agree on the joint account setup, the margin methodology to be used and the way in which the single margin account would be sub-divided in the event of a default. It also requires an alignment of bankruptcy, customer protection and regulator regimes and may require a single default management methodology to be agreed between the CCPs.

Cross-margining arrangements are not new (for example, OCC began a cross-margining programme in 1989[32] and another example is between ICE Clear US and OCC for equity index products). Cross-margining examples relevant to OTC-cleared products are:

- *Credit default swaps:* There is a cross-margining arrangement between ICE Clear Credit (US) and CME (US)[33] covering single-name and index CDS positions.
- *Interest rate products:* An initiative known as Project Trinity would see a combined margining of SwapClear's interest rate trades together with US Treasury bonds and bond futures cleared by NYSE Liffe US and the DTCC.
- *OTC/exchange-traded:* ICE and DTCC for OTC derivatives (ICE) and cash products (DTCC).

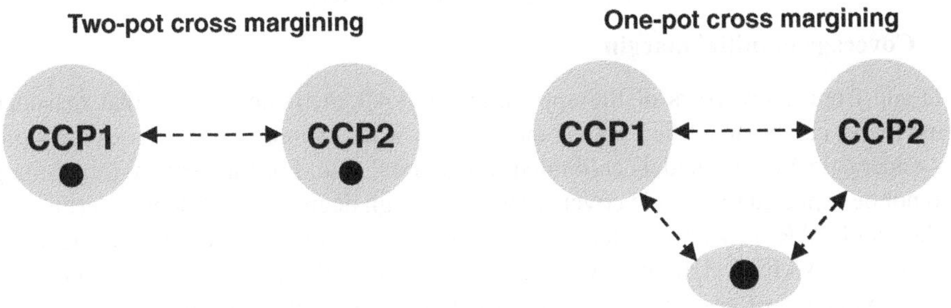

Figure 9.7 Comparison between one- and two-pot cross-margining arrangements.

[32] http://www.optionsclearing.com/about/press/releases/2009/10_06.jsp.

[33] See, for example, 'Clearinghouses Seek to Merge Margin Accounts for CDS Clients', Dow Jones Newswires, 7th October 2011.

9.5.5 Methodologies for cross-margining

Increasing cross-margining will require more sophistication around initial margin calculation methodologies. Whilst methods such as VAR are ideally suited for multidimensional portfolios, there are challenges represented by more cross-margining:

- *Representation of dependencies:* Increasingly, broad cross-margining requires a cross-representation of correlations, curve and basis positions. Relying on historical behaviour can be dangerous as they can be notoriously unstable over time and change rapidly (especially in a crisis period). It may therefore be appropriate to limit cross-margining, and avoid using correlation parameters that are potentially too favourable.
- *Risk metric used:* The quantitative measure used for determining initial margin is very important in a cross-margining environment. It is well known, for example, (section 9.3.1) that VAR is not a 'coherent' risk measure whereas expected shortfall is. The impact of using a non-coherent risk measure such as VAR could be that the initial margin requirement for two cleared portfolios which are cross-margined could actually be higher than the sum of the two individual components (although this is unlikely for the joint distribution of risk factors occurring in most actual cases).
- *Allocation:* For one-pot cross-margining between CCPs, there needs to be an agreed methodology for allocating the shared margin in the event of a default. Such a problem is not trivial since it amounts to allocating the portfolio diversification effect back to the contributing subportfolios. One obvious idea is to use the concept of 'marginal VAR' (for example, see Jorion 2007, Chapter 7).
- *Computational speed:* Cross-margining will lead to larger portfolios and therefore more time-consuming calculations. These calculations need to be fast as it is clearly desirable to be able to represent cross-margining benefits and allocations on a close to real-time basis.
- *Account setup:* Setting up one-pot cross-margining accounts is a complex problem with regional and regulatory issues involved. CCPs must each have a claim on their allocation of the margin in the shared account. Clients must also have protection over amounts given via cross-margining arrangements between CCPs. Differences in regulatory and bankruptcy regimes can add to the difficulty in achieving this.

9.6 DEFAULT FUNDS

9.6.1 Coverage of initial margin

One lesson from many years of the application of VAR methodologies is that reasonably extreme losses can be quantified with some success, whereas more severe losses are significantly underestimated by models calibrated to historical data. For this reason, initial margin should not be expected to provide coverage to a very high degree of confidence. Furthermore, a weakness of VAR measures is that they only specify the probability, and not the size, of losses above the VAR level. In other words, in 99% of cases, the initial margin may be enough but in the other 1% of scenarios, there is no guarantee that losses are not extremely large. Expected shortfall is not significantly superior in this respect as it only gives the *average* loss above the VAR. Issues such as this have been understood for many years. For example, Bates and Craine (1999) estimated that following the 1987 crash, the expected losses conditional on a margin call being breached, increased by an order of magnitude.

The intended coverage of CCP initial margin for OTC derivatives seems to be at above the 99% confidence level and 5-day liquidation period (e.g. CPSS-IOSCO 2012). The European Securities and Markets Authority (ESMA) have specified a minimum confidence level of 99.5% for CCPs clearing OTC derivatives (compared to exchange type products, which are 99%). Initial margins seem to be generally intended to cover 'normal market conditions'; this is sometimes explicitly mentioned and is otherwise implicit due to the use of historical data[34] for initial margin methodologies. There is, of course, no suggestion that initial margin is sufficient to ensure the safety of a CCP. In their analysis of the 1987 crash, Bates and Craine (1999) comment, 'But focussing on tail probabilities alone is an inadequate criterion for survival, and for clearinghouse regulation.' Whilst the assumptions of a 99% confidence level or more together with the potential inclusion of stress periods of data and liquidity adjustment may seem reasonably conservative, initial margin breaches are clearly possible. Furthermore, experience with VAR models over many years suggests that the likelihood and, more importantly, severity of breaches are much worse than expected.

A CCP remains exposed to tail risk if a participant defaults and market conditions are more extreme than anticipated in the margin calculations. Although it is not feasible to cover all such tail risks, a CCP should maintain sufficient financial resources to absorb some part of them. The magnitude of such financial resources can be quantified via stress scenarios in relation to member defaults and related market conditions. The ability of a CCP to survive such extreme losses, potentially arising from default of more than one member, is critical. This is the role of the default fund (also known as the guarantee fund) which is a shared pool to be used to cover losses in excess of initial margins.

9.6.2 Role of the default fund

The role of the default fund is to absorb extreme losses not covered by margins as illustrated qualitatively in Figure 9.8. The distribution of losses is likely to be very heavy-tailed,

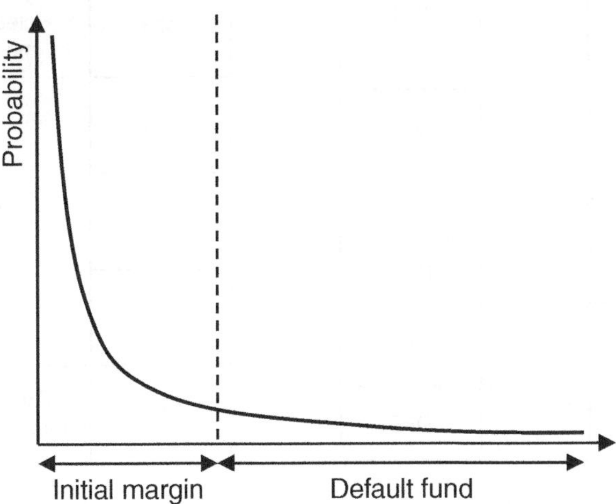

Figure 9.8 Representation of the relationship between initial margin and default fund.

[34] Although the historical data may include a stressed period, this period may be averaged and so not contribute fully to defining the initial margin.

meaning that if the margin is breached then very large losses are possible (as discussed in section 14.2.5, a historical loss of around one hundred times a CCP default fund has been observed). In order to provide coverage of these improbable but potentially large losses, an amount far beyond the initial margin is required. This is the classic problem of insurance and can only be mitigated by a pooling of risk. The default fund is therefore shared amongst the CCP members. The loss mutualisation inherent in the default fund is a key point, since it spreads extreme losses from the failure of a single counterparty across all other clearing members. This has the potential to ameliorate systemic problems but also creates other risks.

9.6.3 Default fund vs. initial margin

The default fund is a key component of clearing. Since it is mutualised, it provides a much higher coverage of losses than initial margin, which avoids the cost of clearing being prohibitive (since in reality paying for one's own default is not possible). For example, the size of the SwapClear default fund is approximately £2.1 billion as of June 2013 whilst the total initial margin held at that time was around ten times higher than this. Hence, the contribution to a default fund may seem reasonably small compared to initial margin requirements, but may provide much greater loss absorbency due to mutualisation.

In order to understand this, consider the split of initial margins and default funds shown in Figure 9.9. In all three cases, the same loss absorbancy exists. Smaller initial margins and correspondingly larger default funds are cheaper but increase moral hazard, as there is less chance of the 'defaulter pays' being followed.

The above shows the subtle balance between initial margins and default funds. High initial margins will be expensive (since larger amounts will be needed to provide the same size of buffer, as seen from Figure 9.9) but will reduce moral hazard, as members are more likely to

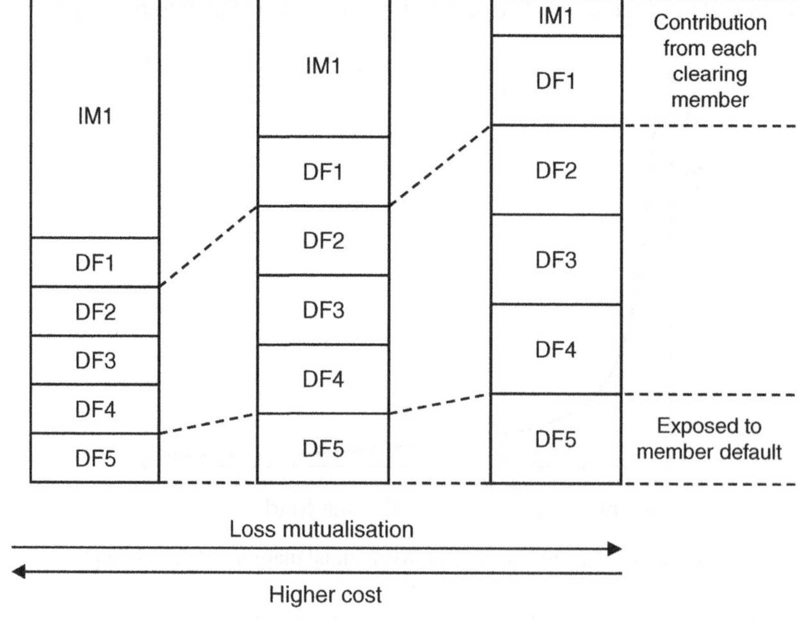

Figure 9.9 Comparison of different choices of initial margin and default fund proportions.

Table 9.6 Summary of the strengths and weaknesses between higher and lower initial margins and default funds.

	Higher initial margin **Lower default fund**	**Lower initial margin** **Higher default fund**
Cost	• Higher	• Lower
Client clearing	• Clients pay for their own risk via initial margin • Promotes portability	• Clients do not pay for their own risk directly • Portability may be difficult
Moral hazard	• Lower	• Higher

pay for their own defaults. High default funds make clearing cheaper but require a large mutualisation of risk, which reduces incentive for strong risk-mitigating behaviour on the part of the CCP members (and their clients). Using default funds instead of initial margins requires clearing members to subsidise each other. The right mix between initial margins and default funds is a balance, which is product- and market-specific, and depends on the assessment of the overall shape of the distribution illustrated in Figure 9.8. A given member's default fund contribution will likely be significantly smaller than their initial margin requirement (perhaps even an order of magnitude), reflecting a mutualisation benefit.

Another consideration is that non-clearing members do not contribute to the default fund of a CCP. This means that clients only contribute *directly* to the risk of their own portfolio via the initial margin that the CCP imposes on their clearing member (which in turn will likely be imposed on them). Hence, default funds not only mutualise the default of clearing members, but also of their clients. A related point is that large default funds and smaller initial margins will disincentivise clearing members from providing portability (see section 11.1.7). Portability refers to the transfer of client positions from one clearing member to another. Without enough initial margin, this becomes difficult, especially since the clearing member accepting the positions may have to pay more into the CCP default fund. The balance in choice of default funds is summarised in Table 9.6.

Putting more financial contributions into initial margins generally incentivises better behaviour, whereas putting more into default funds provides greater overall loss absorbency and therefore makes clearing cheaper at the expense of moral hazard.

9.6.4 Size of the default fund

It is worth remembering that a default fund being hit is a very rare event. For example, in the LCH.Clearnet history, seven defaults have occurred to date. All of these defaults have been managed within the initial margin of the defaulter, and therefore without any impact on other clearing members or markets.[35] That said, OTC CCPs in the future will be larger and will have to take on more complex and risky financial products compared to the past.

Clearly, the default fund has the role of making clearing cost-effective by using loss mutualisation to cover potential tail risk over the initial margins. It can also compensate for aspects such as model risk in initial margin calculations. However, working out the appropriate size of the default fund is extremely difficult to assess due to the very fact that it is covering

[35] See http://www.lchclearnet.com/Images/LCH%20Clearnet's%20default%20history%20May-13_tcm6-63482.pdf.

risk arising from extreme events. Calculating the potential exposure above initial margins is plagued by problems, such as fail tail behaviour, complex interdependencies and wrong-way risk. The actual probability of a CCP exhausting their default fund is impossible to quantity with any accuracy as it is linked to events involving default of one or more clearing members together with extreme market movements and illiquidity.

For the above reasons, CCPs typically calibrate the size of the *total* default fund qualitatively via pre-defined stress tests. This may then be allocated to clearing members in a relatively simplistic way, such as pro rata with initial margins (maybe averaged over a time period) or based on the total size of positions (potentially also subject to a floor). The total default fund size is typically framed in terms of the number of defaults a CCP can withstand (usually one or two). For example, SwapClear aims for their default fund to cover potential losses from the largest two Clearing Members[36] using a set of extreme, but plausible, theoretical and historical stress test scenarios that are tailored specifically for the interest rates market. Contributions to the SwapClear default fund by clearing members is then calculated on a pro-rata basis with respect to initial margins. The ICE default fund provides protection against two clearing member defaults and three additional CDS reference entities defaulting.

Recent regulation is also defining default fund coverage. For exchange-traded derivative CCPs this has often been the default of the largest counterparty whereas for OTC derivatives the requirements are more rigorous. For example, CPSS-IOSCO (2012) states:

> In addition, a CCP that is involved in activities with a more-complex risk profile or that is systemically important in multiple jurisdictions should maintain additional financial resources sufficient to cover a wide range of potential stress scenarios that should include, but not be limited to, the default of the two participants and their affiliates that would potentially cause the largest aggregate credit exposure to the CCP in extreme but plausible market conditions.

The apparent two largest default requirement above is potentially quite significant. For example, Heller and Vause (2012) study G14 dealers and estimate that CCP default funds may need to be about 50% larger to cover losses that could arise from default of the two most important IRS or CDS dealers, rather than just the single most important dealer. However, it is not surprising that OTC CCP default funds are viewed as needing to be more resilient. They would only be hit during a serious crisis when one or more clearing members had failed. It follows that the failed clearing members may be large systemically important financial institutions, and that financial markets would be extremely turbulent at this point. Furthermore, since the failed counterparties are likely to be members of several CCPs, the chance of this causing a severe systemic disturbance is high. Only very large default funds can guarantee the financial integrity of CCPs and provide the necessary confidence and stability to prevent a major crisis in such a situation.

9.6.5 Splitting default funds

Another question in the design of CCP risk management is the coverage of default funds across asset classes. A single mutualised default fund would offer high coverage and therefore

---

[36] http://www.lchclearnet.com/Images/LCH.Clearnet%20Limited%20Rules%20and%20Regulations%20-%20Amendments%20to%20the%20SwapClear%20Service%20Self%20Certification_tcm6-61298.pdf.

be a more cost-effective solution. However, split default funds could mitigate moral hazard issues and prevent a more risky asset class being subsidised by others. At some CCPs, a single default fund covers all product categories. Alternatively, separate default funds are used to cover clearing in different products. Eurex clearing applies one combined default fund for all exchange and OTC products with the exception of Eurex Credit Clear, which is covered via a separate default fund.[37] ICE maintains a separate default fund for CDSs cleared in the US and Europe.

LCH.Clearnet recently split their default fund into three, the first two covering interest rate swaps and FX transactions, and the third covering collectively equities, cash bonds, and repos. For example, a member clearing only futures would not be exposed to loss mutualisation from OTC products (or perhaps in the future, the default of a CDS clearer would not influence clearers of other OTC products). This was partly precipitated by US regulation from the CFTC (see section 8.3.2) that prevents any OTC CCP from setting as a membership requirement a level in excess of US$50 million of capital.

[37] See http://www.eurexclearing.com/clearing-en/resources/faqs/. Eurex also provides some separation of other asset classes via Clearing Fund Segments (CFS).

10
The Loss Waterfall and Loss Allocation Methods

I'll tell you what happens when a CCP goes bust. There is mayhem – possibly greater mayhem than if the biggest dealers and banks in the world go bust.[1]

Sir Paul Tucker (1958–)

10.1 POTENTIAL CCP LOSS EVENTS

This chapter defines the CCP loss waterfall in more detail. It also considers the potential loss allocation methods that CCPs may use when the financial resources within the waterfall cannot absorb a default. The capital requirements for the exposure that clearing members (and clients) have to CCPs (and each other) are also discussed.

10.1.1 Review of the loss waterfall

CCP insolvency would clearly represent a highly contagious event and it is therefore important for there to be a robust mechanism for wind-down or recovery. In contrast to formal bankruptcy, CCP loss allocation potentially allows a timely and orderly resolution of an extreme loss event that is likely preferable to CCP failure. However, determining the allocations of losses in a fair and transparent fashion is not trivial. Clearing members may be exposed to some combination of having to top-up exhausted default funds, be returned less margin than they are owed, having some or all of their trades torn-up (terminated) or even being forced to accept new trades at prices defined by the CCP. Such measures should be clearly written into CCP rules so as to provide clarity to mitigate systemic concerns and allow members to manage their risk to the CCP and allocate capital appropriately.

Figure 10.1 shows again the loss waterfall (see section 8.4.5) and a potential liquidation scenario causing losses that exhaust the default fund over the close out period or margin period of risk (section 9.2.1). In this extreme situation, the CCP needs to apply other methods of loss allocation. We will use the definitions 'first loss' and 'second loss' to denote the defaulter pays and remaining shared financial resources (survivors pay) respectively.

Since initial margins are designed to provide coverage to a high confidence level, it is likely that any sizeable hit to the mutualised default fund would only arise due to an adverse combination of a number of underlying factors. Whilst such a scenario is by construction unlikely, there must be a well-defined allocation of losses and/or recapitalisation of the CCP

[1] Comment made when deputy governor of the Bank of England, see http://www.risk.net/risk-magazine/news/2119514/bofes-tucker-weak-ccp-recovery-plans-risk-mayhem.

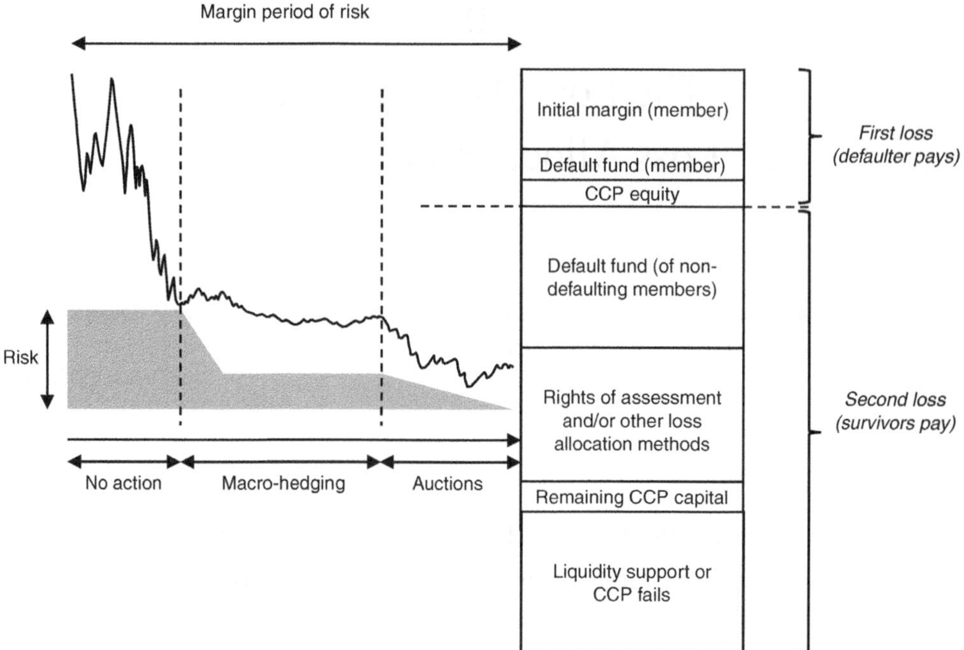

Figure 10.1 Illustration of the loss waterfall and potential risk in the event losses exceed the primary financial resources of the CCP.

as part of the CCP 'rule book'. Indeed, the mere existence of such a well-specified waterfall may add stability to the CCP since members will be better able to measure and manage their own risk if the CCP rules are clearly defined.

Most CCPs have 'rights of assessment' or 'capital calls' which represent an unfunded obligation to contribute additionally to a default fund that has been depleted by losses. Typically, such a recapitalisation will be invoked if a significant fraction (e.g. 25%) of the default fund is used. If this right were unlimited then the CCP would be unlikely to fail (unless all their clearing members did so). However, this would create large moral hazards and unlimited exposure for clearing members. Furthermore, it may de-stabilise markets as members would be required to contribute to default funds at the worst possible time. For these reasons, rights of assessment are generally capped. There therefore need to be alternative ways to allocate losses and prevent the CCP from failing. An insolvent CCP would create losses borne by the members in what would likely be a disorderly, lengthy and uncertain process. A well-defined and transparent loss allocation process may give more certainty and fairness and allow the CCP to continue to function.

Once losses exceed initial margins, plus the relatively small defaulted member's default fund and the CCPs equity contribution, moral hazard exists since stronger credit quality members will implicitly subsidise weaker ones. It is important to consider the possible side effects of this moral hazard and knock-on effects.

Broadly speaking, a CCP could fail for one of two reasons:

- Losses from a clearing member default.
- Loss for other reasons such as investment losses or fraud.

The first scenario is the one that may seem more likely and one in which clear loss allocation methods can be constructed. The second outcome is hopefully unlikely and the nature of resulting losses is impossible to predict, therefore a priori loss allocation is difficult to design. We will consider both possible potential avenues for losses but (like CCPs themselves) pay more attention to the former.

10.1.2 Clearing member default losses

For a CCP to recover from a member default they need to re-establish a matched book. This is normally achieved by replacing the defaulter's positions, for example by selling long positions to (or buying short positions from) surviving participants through an auction process. In a severe scenario, an auction may not clear at prices consistent with the CCP remaining solvent. In other words, the best prices demanded by surviving clearing participants to take on the defaulter's positions may exceed the financial resources available to the CCP. In an extreme scenario, it may be that the CCP received no price at all for one or more subportfolios.

There are a number of interrelated reasons why a default may lead to losses that may in turn breach the financial contributions of the defaulted member, and cause losses in the mutualised default fund (and beyond). These are:

- *Delay since last variation margin was received:* The delay before last receiving variation margin prior to the clearing member being declared in default. Due to variation margin practices of CCPs being at a minimum daily, and potentially also intradaily, this period is intended to be short. However, it should be considered how long a CCP might delay before putting a large clearing member in default.
- *Market volatility in hedging period:* Whilst macro-hedging the risk, the CCP will be exposed to further market volatility and potential bid-offer hedging costs for large positions. For more complex portfolios, such as OTC derivatives, such hedging costs may be significant.
- *Auction costs:* Finally, in attempting to auction the positions of the defaulted member, the CCP may be exposed to liquidation costs (although as noted in section 9.2.1, the above hedges should improve the auction process by creating less directional portfolios). This could be related to bid-offer costs, but in more extreme situations there might be severe downward price movements due to 'fire sale'-like dynamics. An extreme case of this could be a failed auction, where a CCP does not consider it has received reasonable bids for one or more portfolios. In liquid markets, such as exchange-traded ones, even large portfolios can be closed out relatively easily. For OTC derivatives, such a resolution could take at least a few days and may even be simply unachievable.

There is a key difference between losses due to market volatility and risk premiums experienced as liquidation costs. Market volatility may lead to losses for a defaulted member but these must lead to equivalent gains for surviving clearing members. This means that within the set of positions cleared by the CCP, there are possible ways to consider offsetting losses, for example by not posting margin against the gains of surviving members. On the other hand, when a CCP experiences bid-offer costs and/or risk premiums, these are costs that are not balanced by equivalent gains in the opposite cleared trades. The result of this is that loss allocation is likely to be more problematic. Put another way, highly volatile products may clearly present a challenge but illiquid products (or those that become illiquid in the aftermath of a major default) will be even more difficult.

10.1.3 Non-default related losses

There are possible associated issues that could create losses for the CCP even without a member default or that may contribute to losses in a default scenario, especially one in which market conditions are fragile:

- *Margin losses:* Any losses on assets held as (initial)[2] margin, as a result of market risk, credit risk or liquidity risks, including potential FX risk. These aspects are partially mitigated via haircuts.
- *Investment losses:* Losses arising from investments of cash or securities held as margin. This should be mitigated by any investment of initial margin and other financial resources being only in short-dated assets with strong credit quality and liquidity.
- *Operational risks:* Operational risks such as delayed margin calls, the inability to make relevant valuations in a timely fashion or investment losses arising from an operational error or serious fraud (e.g. a rogue trader).
- *Members leaving the CCP:* Members resigning their positions from the CCP may create market instability and reduce the number of participants in an auction.

As mentioned above, it is clearly extremely difficult to estimate the probability and size of the above losses and be sure that any loss allocation method will work. Additionally, the only obvious way to allocate losses would be via a pro-rata allocation of default funds and rights of assessment.

10.2 ANALYSIS OF CCP LOSS STRUCTURE

It is important to analyse the loss structure of a CCP and the way in which this may influence the behaviour of clearing members in the aftermath of a significant CCP loss event. Of particular interest is the way in which a CCP member may be encouraged to help a CCP in an extreme scenario, such as by actively participating in the hedging and auctioning of a defaulted member's portfolio.

The general way in which losses above defaulter's recourses are handled is either:

- Call for additional financial resources from clearing members (rights of assessment).
- Reduction of the claims of the clearing members.

Ideally, loss allocation rules will create the correct incentives both before and during the default management process.

10.2.1 Second loss exposure

The first point to note is that surviving clearing members have a 'second loss' position, or equivalently are short an out-of-the-money option which represents their possible losses via their default fund contributions (Figure 8.7). This means that clearing members are not incentivised to behave well within an auction if they believe that the 'defaulter's resources' (initial margin and default fund) will provide sufficient loss absorbency. Put differently,

[2] Since variation margin is usually required in cash.

auction bidders may take on positions at a profit knowing that the defaulter's resources that are held by the CCP will pay for such a profit. Indeed, the clearing members optimal strategy is to utilise 100% of the defaulter's resources, which otherwise will only be returned to the bankruptcy administrator.

There is some evidence of the above optimal behaviour in practice. For example, in the Lehman bankruptcy, there were claims that CME members profited from participating in the auction.[3] It should be noted that taking on large (and potentially relatively illiquid) portfolios in the aftermath of a large default creates substantial risks that cannot easily be hedged. It is therefore not unreasonable for clearing members to be conservative when bidding prices, thereby giving a cushion for the market and liquidity risks they face. Nevertheless, these CME related transactions have been alleged as fraudulent, although the CCP is likely to be protected from any legal claims due to having a privileged position with respect to bankruptcy law.[4] Such effects will be a significant detriment to other creditors, as illustrated previously in section 6.4.1.

If members believe that losses may exceed the 'defaulter pays' (Figure 10.1) financial resources and be mutualised back to them via the default fund, then this clearly incentivises better behaviour. However, there is now a more subtle behavioural problem often referred to as the prisoner's dilemma. This arises since members who believe that the loss allocation process may treat them relatively favourably are still not incentivised to help the CCP (for example, they may not actively participate in the auction).

10.2.2 The prisoner's dilemma

Participating in an auction exposes clearing members to the risks of positions they take on as, even though these risks can be hedged or offset, there is still exposure to market moves during this period. This risk may be especially problematic for large and relatively illiquid OTC derivatives positions. If an auction does not run smoothly then it may escalate problems and expose a CCP to an extended close out period, as well as increased market volatility and illiquidity.

Once losses move into the survivor pays region, moral hazard becomes a problem and there is a danger of certain gaming behaviour by CCP members. The prisoner's dilemma refers to a situation where it is in the individual interests of each party to take a particular course of action, but damaging for a large number of parties to take this route simultaneously. This could apply, for example, to the behaviour of CCP members who may not show cooperative behaviour even though it is in their best interest to do so. Such non-cooperative behaviour could be manifested in actions such as resigning from a CCP. Indeed, it could be argued that special measures may need to be applied in preventing members leaving a stricken CCP. The prisoner's dilemma also applies to clearing members participating actively in an auction process. Collectively they should do this but individually there may be gains from trying to avoid, or from bidding conservatively in the auction.

As long as they believe that initial margin may not be sufficient, it is collectively in the interests of the surviving clearing members to participate actively in an auction to ensure that

[3] For example, see 'Firms reaped windfalls in Lehman auction: examiner', Reuters, 15 April 2010, http://uk.reuters.com/article/2010/04/15/us-lehman-examiner-idUSTRE63D57U20100415.

[4] Wall Street Journal, 'CME, Lehman Book Bidders Likely Protected From Lawsuits', 15 April 2010, http://online.wsj.com/news/articles/SB10001424052702303348504575183893970883282.

the CCP can close out the portfolio most efficiently so as to minimise losses to the default fund. On the other hand, as in the prisoner's dilemma, an individual member potentially has the incentive not to participate actively in the auction in the hope that the other members instead devote their time and balance sheets to ease the problem. Of course, when all members adopt this view then the situation can become highly destabilising. Hence the CCP should have alternative methods to close out positions and allocate the resulting losses. Ideally, these methods would also go so far as to penalise members behaving outside the bounds of the common good. This would then in turn incentivise good behaviour in the auction.

10.2.3 Unlimited default fund contributions

Loss allocation methods are typically needed in the event that the default waterfall, including recourse to a CCPs own resources, has been exhausted and the CCP is therefore faced with insolvency. In principal, a CCP could simply require members to make an unlimited contribution to the default fund to avoid such an eventuality. In practice, this would create moral hazard and may still force a CCP into failure via a cascade of members resigning or defaulting. Furthermore, such a situation would also leave clearing members with a potentially unlimited exposure to a CCP, which would be extremely problematic. Finally, regulation may prohibit unlimited default fund contributions, for example, EMIR[5] requires cash calls by CCPs on clearing members to be limited. Default fund contributions are usually capped, for example, CME caps default fund contributions at a size that provide enough resources in the event of default of the four clearing members to which the CCP is most exposed.[6]

Since a default fund cannot be bottomless, it is necessary to have other loss allocation methods. These range from those that are less dramatic but may ultimately fail, to those that will always succeed but are extreme in nature. These will be covered in section 10.3.

10.2.4 Default fund tranches

The first part of loss allocation involves the allocation of the finite default fund to cover losses. Some CCPs may operate separate default funds to align the losses of members with the products they clear. This would ensure, for example, that clearing members clearing only futures would be protected from default losses resulting from a OTC derivatives portfolio being cleared with the same CCP. Furthermore, some CCPs may allocate losses within a default fund in tranches to mitigate the prisoner's dilemma and incentivise members to act in the common good.

An example of the above concepts is provided by Auction Incentive Pools (AIPs) used by LCH.Clearnet.[7] With AIPs, each member's default fund contributions are allocated proportionally to a currency-specific bucket, in an amount that reflects that relative risk that the member contributes in that currency. These currency-specific default funds will be used to absorb losses in auctions for products in each currency respectively. If a loss exceeds the AIP in a currency, this will be allocated to the remaining default funds in other AIPs and any unallocated default funds. This means that, for example, a regional bank clearing only products in their own currency would be partially protected in the event of the default of a European bank clearing mainly Euro-denominated products.

[5] EMIR 2013, article 43(3).

[6] Note that the current default fund would typically be sized to cover the two largest defaults.

[7] See LCH.Clearnet Ltd Default rules section 2.4, available at www.lchclearnet.com.

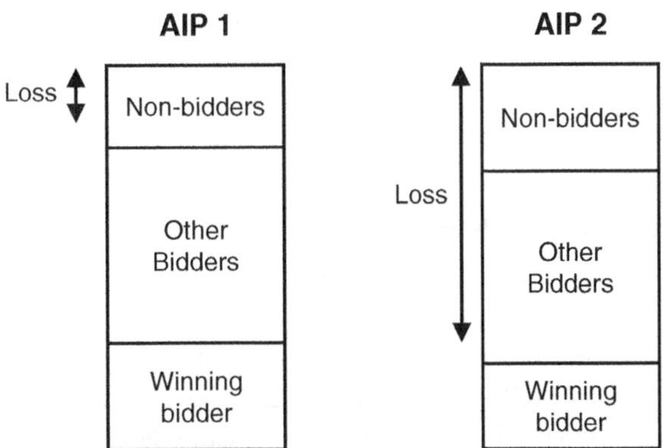

Figure 10.2 Illustration of tranching of default fund losses via auction incentive pools (AIPs).

Another feature of AIPs referring to the allocation of losses in tranches is related to members bidding in an auction for a particular currency. Losses in each LCH.Clearnet AIP are distributed in sequence according to the competitiveness of members bidding in the auction, according to:

- Non-bidders
- Other bidders
- Winning bidder

An illustration of the AIP concept is shown in Figure 10.2. This shows relatively small losses on the default fund for AIP1 and larger losses on that for AIP2. This means that all bidders on AIP1 would be protected from default fund losses which would be absorbed by non-bidders. Moreover, the relatively large losses on AIP2 would not cause losses for members clearing trades only in AIP1. However, note that the bidders in AIP1 could experience losses in two ways: first, via larger losses on AIP1 and second, via losses in excess of the total AIP2 default fund. In the latter case, this is because, as mentioned above, losses in excess of an AIP can be absorbed by the remaining default fund (either unallocated or allocated to other AIPs).

The aim of the above is clearly to give clearing members the incentive to participate actively in the auction process within the currencies they clear. Note that a member not clearing a given currency need not bid in that auction as they will not have any default fund allocated to that AIP. The CCP may inform members of their relative contribution to an AIP (compared to other members), which may incentivise them to bid in the auction aggressively if they have a large position.

10.3 OTHER LOSS ALLOCATION METHODS

Other loss allocation methods go beyond the idea of simply using default funds on a pro-rata basis. They have the ability to deal with a more extreme default scenario but also lead to additional risks and different incentives.

The basic idea of other loss allocation methods is that defaulting members with out-of-the-money positions will be unable to pay variation margin to the CCP, and this will therefore be offset by some reduction in the claims of the other surviving members. Differences arise in how the surviving members are treated on a relative basis. This could be pro rata, could affect only those with in-the-money positions or take some other form. In turn, different approaches may lead to different results and incentives for surviving clearing members.

10.3.1 Variation margin gains haircutting

Previously, Figure 8.6 illustrated that a CCP had a balance in terms of variation margins paid/received that was disturbed by a clearing member default. Variation margin gains haircutting (VMGH) is probably the most common alternative loss allocation concept (for example, see ISDA 2013b). The idea of VMGH is that gains which have accumulated since the start of the default management process (including any variation margin not received from the defaulter) can be reduced pro rata so as to absorb the amounts owing to the CCP by the defaulted member. This means that clearing members whose positions have increased in value since the default[8] will not receive the full margin to cover their gain, whilst those owing money to the CCP will still be required to pay in full. There may possibly be a cap on the variation margin haircut that can be applied.

An illustration of VMGH is shown in Figure 10.3. This shows a CCP owed variation margins of 5 and 15 by members B and D, the latter being in default. Correspondingly, the CCP owes the same total (20) of variation margin to two other members (A and C) in the amounts 12 and 8. Since the defaulter's initial margin and default fund contributions (10) are exceeded by the net amount owed (15), then the CCP must allocate a loss of 5. In the absence of any rights of assessment (or after such rights have been exhausted),[9] this could be allocated via haircutting the variation margin owed to members A and C on a pro rata basis as shown. Note that this uses the entire initial margin and default fund contribution. Depending on where

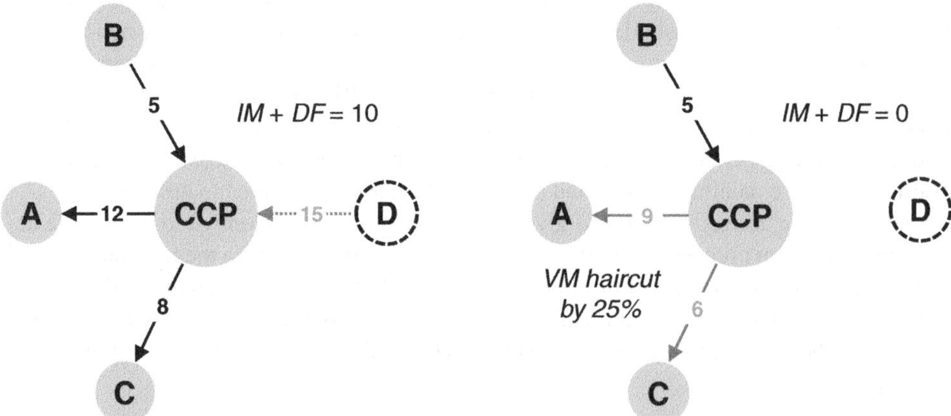

Figure 10.3 Illustration of variation margin gains haircutting. The diagram on the left-hand side depicts the initial situation where financial resources are not balanced, and the right-hand side represents the balancing of resources by using the defaulter's initial margin and (mutualised) default funds with VMGH.

[8] Strictly speaking, the last point at which the defaulted member paid variation margin.

[9] For example, if the default fund was only five and the rights of assessment were capped at 100%.

VMGH occurs in the waterfall, this could refer to only the financial resources of the defaulted member, or could include the mutualised default fund.

If VMGH allows a CCP to cover losses and resume normal service, then clearing members would probably need to replenish default funds (or resign membership if they have closed out all their positions and met obligations and no other defaults have occurred). The CCP can then, in theory, continue to operate albeit with some reputational damage. Presumably, members would at the very least expect management and/or methodology changes in such a case.

VMGH creates a limited exposure for CCP members, who can at most lose the total gains on their open positions since the last margin transfer. It also avoids forcing clearing members to replace positions. Another interesting feature is that it mimics the economics of insolvency in bilateral markets since parties with claims on the defaulter lose in a pro rata fashion. Clearing members on the other side of the defaulter's trades, and likely to incur VMGH, may actively bid in auctions to avoid this. Since VMGH mimics the dynamics of bilateral markets where gaining parties pay more, members with the largest trading activity with a defaulted member are likely to suffer most. Whilst this violates the idea that clearing creates a homogenous credit system, it does create some incentive not to trade with less creditworthy counterparties, even when such trades will definitely be cleared.

On the other hand, VMGH is potentially random and unfair and a clearing member may lose simply because the market moved in their favour at the time of a default. It may not be fair to penalise a member just because they were on the correct side of a market move. Note also that a clearing member may not have made an overall profit as their gains may be offset by losses associated to bilateral trades or those at another CCP (or they may be client trades). This raises the possibility that VMGH could force a clearing member into default, which in turn will affect other CCPs and bilateral counterparties with whom this member has traded. Complications also arise in non-derivatives clearing, where variation margin does not need to be exchanged daily or where there is physical settlement.

If a CCP can auction a defaulter's portfolio at mid-market prices and suffers no other losses (e.g. investment), then VMGH (without any cap) is guaranteed to work as the losses from the defaulter must be matched by equivalent gains for other CCP members. However, this does assume that the CCP would not pay out variation margin to non-defaulters after a defaulter had ceased making variation margin payments. This is probably a reasonable assumption since CCPs tend to be asymmetric over margin payments, e.g. they may request more margin for losses on an intradaily basis but only return margins corresponding to gains on the following day. However, it does raise the issue of whether a CCP giving a small amount of grace to a member who ultimately defaults may lead to a failure of VMGH since during the period of grace the CCP will still be paying out variation margin to other members.

The obvious reason why VMGH may fail in practice is if the CCP has to close out at a significant premium to mid-market prices. In such a case, unless the risk premium required can be covered by the member's initial margin and default fund contribution, then VMGH will fail. Any non-default losses or caps in VMGH may create the same effect. Since the survival of the CCP cannot be guaranteed, then it may be necessary to consider other more extreme methods of loss allocation.

10.3.2 Partial tear-up and forced allocation

The default of a clearing member leaves a CCP with unmatched positions. If the resulting exposure cannot be neutralised via an auction, then one other option is for the CCP to 'tear-up'

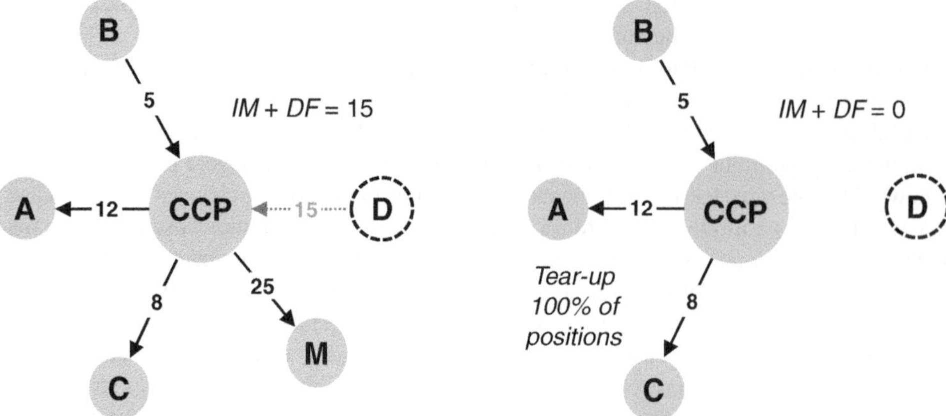

Figure 10.4 Illustration of tear-up. The diagram on the left-hand side depicts the initial situation where financial resources are not balanced, and the right-hand side represents the balancing of resources by using the defaulter's initial margin and (mutualised) default funds together with tear-up. M denotes the auction market where a risk premium of 25 is included in the price and therefore represents an extra cost for the CCP. Tear-up prevents the need to pay this risk premium.

unmatched contracts with surviving clearing members. Such contracts could be terminated with a cash settlement based on the current mid-market price or the equivalent price when the default occurred or variation margin was last exchanged. There may also need to be a pro rata reduction if the CCP is unable to pay such prices in full. The aim of the tear-up is to return a CCP to a matched book by terminating the other side of a defaulter's trades (or at least those than cannot be auctioned). All other contracts (possibly the majority of the total contracts cleared) could remain untouched. As with VMGH, this option as a backstop may incentivise active bidding in an auction when members fear they may otherwise have contracts torn-up.

The major difference with tear-up compared to VMGH is that the CCP is not exposed to any risk premium in auctioning transactions as it pays (at most) only the current mid-market value of the transaction. To understand this, consider the illustration in Figure 10.4, which is similar to the VMGH example above except that it is assumed that in the auction there is a risk premium of 25 charged (represented as a payment to the market represented by M). This risk premium means that VMGH will fail since, even if the haircut is 100%, the CCP's total financial resources (20) are insufficient to pay the risk premium. In this scenario, an alternative would be to tear-up all the underlying trades with members A and C and avoid the risk premium. Note that the CCP can pay the full (mid-market) amount owed to A and C without any haircut or other reduction (such as using a valuation when margin was last posted).

A CCP may reasonably attempt to tear-up the smallest subset of trades that will return it to a matched book and incur no financial losses. In the above example, it is necessary to tear-up 100% of the trades. However, if there were an additional 5 of financial resources (for example, the CCP had a larger mutualised default fund) then it would only be necessary to tear-up 80% of the positions.[10] Furthermore, if the CCP pays out less than the current market value of the contracts being torn-up, then the tear-up fraction can be lower. CCPs can obviously balance these considerations to attempt to minimise the impact on the market.

[10] This assumes linearity but in reality, the close out of a smaller portfolio may be easier and the resulting risk premium smaller.

In a real example with many more clearing members, there are likely to be choices for identifying which trades to tear-up. This could be done in the following ways:

- *Voluntary basis:* Clearing members could accept trades of their own volition ('voluntary tear-up'). This would seem to be unlikely given the circumstances in which a CCP may need to consider this loss allocation method.
- *Original counterparties:* Positions could be identified as the original opposite trades to the defaulters (assuming they can be distinguished). This choice represents a direct mimicking of bilateral markets.
- *By bidder.* Depending on the bids received in the auction.
- *Other:* Trades could be simply identified arbitrarily from the portfolio of any clearing member(s) with offsetting positions to the defaulter. This is the simplest route but is obviously potentially random and unfair.

As with VMGH, tear-up may change the behaviour of clearing members who may identify in the auction that they hold opposite positions to those of the defaulter. Since such positions are more likely to be torn-up, these members may be incentivised to bid more competitively in the auction.

Tear-up represents a dramatic loss allocation process and has a number of important disadvantages:

- *Unlimited liability:* Non-defaulting members theoretically face an unlimited liability since the amounts they are paid for torn-up trades will differ from the market prices at which these members can enter into replacement transactions.
- *Replacement impact:* Whilst tear-up avoids the CCP needing to replace trades via the auction, a similar dynamic may occur where clearing members have to hedge their risk from trades subject to tear-up. Such replacement hedges could create market instability, especially since the CCP has failed to execute similar trades via the auction. A clearing member could even be sent into default because of tear-ups.
- *Portfolio bifurcation:* Partial tear-up may alter the balance of surviving member's portfolios and therefore the exposure to the CCP. This in turn may trigger additional initial margin requirements if the tear-up results in a less diversified portfolio.

There are other loss allocation methods that are similar to tear-up. One is 'forced allocation' or 'invoicing back', where clearing members are obliged to accept certain portfolios at prices determined by the CCP. This has a similar effect since instead of tearing-up an existing trade, a CCP might impose the reverse trade on a member. However, forced allocation may be more flexible as any member can be allocated positions, whereas tear-up requires a member to have the appropriate trades in their portfolio (for example, a CCP may forcibly allocate to the worst bidder in the auction). Unlike tear-up, it would not be possible for a CCP to pass on the impact of forced allocation to its clients (see section 10.3.5).

10.3.3 Complete tear-up

In an extreme scenario, a final resort is a complete tear-up where all affected contracts are terminated. The CCP would then calculate the net obligation to all its members (including compensation for aspects such as previous haircuts to variation margins) and cash settle these amounts pro-rata. A complete tear-up seems incompatible with the objective of CCP survival. In theory, the CCP could resume business and accept new contracts for clearing once it is no longer encumbered with losses. However, it is unlikely that members would wish to use the CCP anymore. Hence, complete tear-up would likely be followed by the closure of the CCP, in which case they would return initial margins to surviving members (and default funds contributions although these would have likely been used up at this point).

A complete tear-up might avoid the portfolio bifurcation problem mentioned above that could leave participants without hedges and therefore with an unbalanced portfolio. However, members could still have unbalanced portfolios if hedges had been executed via another CCP.

10.3.4 Other methods

Initial margin haircutting has been suggested as a possible means to allocate losses (Elliott 2013), but has not been used in practice and it has a number of problems. First, clearing members would have to contribute additional initial margin and this would seem to be similar to rights of assessment. Second, regulation may prevent it, for example, EMIR forbids CCPs from using initial margin of non-defaulted members to cover default losses.[11]

Other methods may be used in an extreme scenario where a CCP may intend to shut down but aims to do this in the least destabilising fashion. A CCP could attempt to novate trades to another more stable CCP. It would seem unlikely that another CCP would agree to port what would be a very large portfolio of positions, without charging significant fees and margin requirements. A CCP could also execute a reverse clearing function and return trades to being bilateral. Such bilateralisation would potentially not be permitted by regulation and so would require at least a temporary waiver from regulatory authorities. It would also require a determination of the appropriate price that should be used. This may create further problems if two members do not have relevant bilateral documentation that would define aspects such as margin posting. Finally, it could lead to the appearance of unusual effects such as wrong-way risk, for example, a member buying protection on a sovereign may have a bank in that country as their new bilateral counterparty.

10.3.5 Impact on client trades

It is important to consider the impact of loss allocation on the clients of clearing members. As with other aspects, such as margin requirements, it is likely that clearing members will aim to align their bilateral relationship with a client to the clearing rules. This implies that clients could be exposed to loss allocation methods employed by the CCP. Indeed, regulation may encourage this to be the case.[12]

On the positive side, clients may not need to experience exactly the same effect as their clearing member, as shown for VMGH in Figure 10.5. Here, the CCP needs to haircut the variation margin payment owed to the general clearing member (GCM) by 33% from 15 to 10. However, since the GCM has client positions in different directions then it only needs

[11] EMIR article 45(4) 'A CCP shall not use the margins posted by non-defaulting members to cover the losses resulting from the default of another clearing member'.

[12] For example, under the EU's Capital Requirement Regulation article 306(1)(c), a clearing member will have to pass on the impact of actions such as VMGH to get appropriate capital relief.

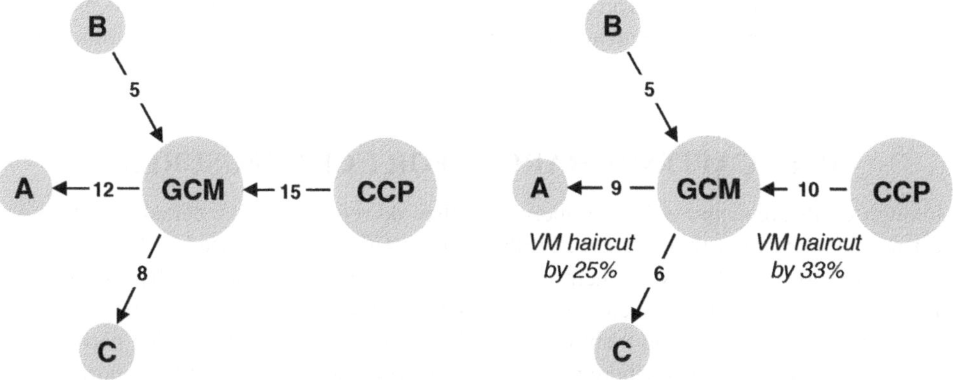

Figure 10.5 Illustration of the impact of VMGH on clients. The CCP haircuts the variation margin paid to the GCM by 33% but the margin payments owed to clients A and C need only be reduced by 25% due to the offset with client B.

to reduce the variation margin owed to clients A and C by 25%, due to receiving variation margin from client B.

The dynamic explained above would not work for a more severe loss allocation method such as tear-up. Here, a client would not have any way of knowing if a trade is a likely candidate since this would depend on the overall position of their clearing member and the defaulted portfolio, neither of which they have access to. Hence, the tear-up of a client trade would appear to be completely arbitrary and would be particularly problematic to end users who have one-directional hedges on. Clients may prefer methods such as forced allocation where the clearing member cannot pass on loss allocation methods directly.

10.3.6 Methods used in practice

Table 10.1 shows the current loss allocation methods used by some important OTC CCPs. The prevention of a CCP failure, leading to central bank support and ultimately a cost to taxpayer, ultimately requires loss allocation to be extreme if necessary. Indeed, the general trend in Table 10.1 to use VMGH and then complete tear-up in addition to the preceding default funds and rights of assessment, would seem to ensure that a CCP could not fail (except perhaps for losses not stemming from clearing member default). However, CCP rules and related supervisory guidance require clear limits on the allocation of losses to non-defaulting clearing members.

Table 10.1 Summary of different loss allocation methods used by major OTC derivatives CCPs.

CCP	Product	Methods
CME Clearing	Interest-rate swaps	Complete tear-up
CME Clearing Europe	Interest-rate swaps	VMGH and complete tear-up
LCH.Clearnet Ltd	Interest-rate swaps	VMGH (capped at the maximum of €100 million and 100% of the default fund contribution) and complete tear-up
LCH.Clearnet SA	Credit default swaps	

Source: Elliott (2013).

Unlimited rights of assessment and tear-up procedures that could have the effect of imposing unlimited liability on surviving members are being discouraged (e.g. see reference in footnote 5). However, this will in turn make CCP default a more distinct possibility.

10.4 CAPITAL CHARGES FOR CCP EXPOSURES

Although CCPs are supposedly extremely safe, they do represent some default risk to their clearing members (and their clients). Furthermore, a CCP does not need to fail for clearing members to suffer losses via their default funds contributions. Additionally, exposure to other loss allocation methods such as rights of assessment and VMGH may impose losses on both clearing and non-clearing members. Such losses are likely to occur during particularly volatile and illiquid markets, where resilience of clearing participants will be important and CCP exposures should be capitalised appropriately. Moreover, the methodology for computing the capital charges should be coherent (for example if a CCP increases the size of their default fund then the capital requirements for their members should reduce in line with their decreasing risk). There should also be a distinction between different CCPs, which will have different levels of riskiness. Capital requirements should also reflect the relative safety of central clearing compared to bilateral markets and offer relative capital savings.

Prior to Basel III, regulatory capital requirements allowed all CCP-related exposure to be given (explicitly or not) a zero capital charge. Clearly, this gives out the wrong message and potentially leads to moral hazard problems and the assumption that a CCP would therefore never be allowed to fail (or even impose losses on participants). In light of mandatory OTC clearing, there is a need to have a formal capital charge for CCP exposures. As with all capital requirements, the methodology ideally needs to be both relatively simple and transparent but also risk sensitive and not giving rise to perverse incentives. Due to the complexity of the CCP loss waterfall (discussed earlier in this chapter), this is clearly not an easy task.

In July 2012, preceded by two consultative documents (BCBS 2010 and BCBS 2011b), the Basel Committee published interim rules for the capitalisation of bank exposures to CCPs (BCBS 2012b). A year later, another consultant document was published proposing different requirements due to the results obtained from a quantitative impact study (BCBS 2013c). Following another quantitative impact study, a final set of rules was published (BCBS 2014b), which will apply from the beginning of 2017. The final rules in turn rely partly on a new methodology for calculating exposure (the SA-CCR discussed below). The interim rules and consultations illustrate the pressure to define rapidly CCP capital requirements in support of a pending clearing mandate.

The forthcoming discussion will therefore explain the 'interim rules' (BCBS 2012b) and the 'final rules' (BCBS 2014b), highlighting also some of the criticisms directed towards them. The reader is also referred to ISDA (2013a) for an alternative proposal for a risk-sensitive capital treatment for clearing member exposure to central counterparty default funds.

10.4.1 Qualifying CCPs

A qualifying CCP (QCCP) complies with the CPSS-IOSCO principles and is licensed to operate as a CCP (including via an exemption) in relation to the clearing services offered. A QCCP must also provide their members with information required to calculate their capital requirements (see section 10.4.4). Exposures to QCCPs will receive preferential capital treatment, as opposed to exposures to non-qualifying CCPs, which will be treated more conservatively (e.g. as bilateral exposures). However, banks should consider whether they should need to hold capital in excess of the regulatory requirements. Additionally, regional supervisors can still require banks to hold higher capital against CCP exposure if they deem it relevant. If a QCCP loses its 'qualifying' status, it will have a grace period of three months before higher non-qualifying CCP capitalisation rules apply.

The above initiative implies that there will need to be a globally coordinated, central list of QCCPs. Such a list could be defined via a consistent application of the CPSS-IOSCO principles. There is also presumably the problem that regulation may deem a CCP as non-qualifying even though it is deemed a QCCP by its own regulator (in a different region). At the time of writing, these problems remain unresolved.[13]

There are also potential cross-border issues with the definition of a QCCP. For example, the European Securities and Markets Authority (EMSA) require non-European CCPs to register and apply to be recognised as a 'third-country CCP' (in order for their European members to qualify for the more beneficial QCCP capital charges). Such a CCP would then be required to comply with certain aspects of the European Market Infrastructure Regulation (EMIR), for example, with respect to margin and default fund contributions (there is a grace period of 180 working days from the application date where a CCP could be recognised as a QCCP until June 2014). Under US rules, in order to service US clients, a CCP must either apply to the CFTC to become a derivatives clearing organisation (DCO) or obtain an exemption. The latter would only be granted if the CFTC believes that the CCP is subject to comparable regulation in their own region. Exemptions aside, these requirements are potentially controversial as a region may impose standards on a CCP based in another region that are viewed as being irrelevant to that region and its market participants.[14] However, despite differences between U.S. and EU regimes, some progress is being made on regulatory harmonisation.[15]

10.4.2 Trade and default fund related exposures

Most of the discussion below concerns QCCPs with reference made to non-QCCPs where relevant. The description is also non-mathematical, with more technical detail given in Appendix 10A. The first complexity in defining the exposure and capital requirements for a CCP is the two fundamentally different exposures that arise:

- *Trade exposures:* These exposures arise from the current mark-to-market exposure and variation margin together with the potential future exposure (PFE) and also the initial margin posted to the CCP. Such an exposure is only at risk in the case of the CCP failure (not the failure of other CCP members).
- *Default fund exposures:* This covers the exposure via the contribution made to the CCP's default fund, which is at risk even if the CCP does not default. This exposure is problematic to quantify since it is possible for a CCP member to lose some or all of their default fund contribution, due to the default of one or more CCP members or other events such

[13] For more discussion see ISDA's comments to the CPSS-IOSCO on Qualifying Central Counterparties at http://www2.isda.org/functional-areas/risk-management (15 February 2013) and also the Basel III FAQ which answers a question relating to the determination of whether or not a CCP is qualifying at http://www.bis.org/publ/bcbs237.pdf.

[14] For example, see 'Asia regulators attack EU over clearing house standards', Financial Times, 3 December 2013.

[15] 'Statement by the CFTC and the European Commission on progress relating to the implementation of the 2013 Path Forward Statement', 12 Feburary 2014, http://www.cftc.gov/PressRoom/PressReleases/pr6857-14

as operational or investment losses, even if the CCP itself does not fail. Furthermore, it may be necessary to contribute additionally to the default fund (rights of assessment) in the event of relatively large losses from the default of other members. The fact that each CCP sets default fund contributions itself further complicates this approach as this implies that each CCP will represent a specific risk. Finally, the potential application of other loss allocation methods, which may also be experienced by clients of clearing members, complicates this still further.

10.4.3 Capital requirements for trade exposures

Trade exposures consist of the following components:

- *Current exposure:* The mark-to-market position (adjusted for variation margin posted or received).
- *Potential future exposure (PFE):* The potential increase in the exposure in the future calculated in a similar way to other bilateral derivatives positions.
- *Initial margin:* The initial margin posted to the CCP unless this has been posted in a manner which makes it bankruptcy-remote. This includes margin given to a CCP in excess of the minimum amount required where the CCP may prevent the return of this margin.

Capital requirements for trade-related exposures are defined in a simple and non-risk-sensitive way. For a QCCP, this component attracts a capital charge based on a relatively low risk weight of 2% (0.16% capital charge). In the case of initial margin being bankruptcy-remote (e.g. held with a third party custodian), so that if the CCP defaults then the clearing member does not lose it, then a 0% risk weight can be applied to this component.

Regarding the calculation of PFE, under the interim rules a clearing member must use the method they use for the calculation of capital requirements to bilateral counterparties. This will be either the current exposure method (CEM), standardised method (SM) or internal model method (IMM)[16]. The final rules require the use the new replacement to the CEM and SM, known as the standardised approach (for counterparty credit risk) referred to as SA-CCR (BCBS 2014a), which is intended to be a more risk-sensitive capital methodology for banks without IMM approval.

A clearing member trading with a non-qualifying CCP is required to capitalise its exposure in accordance with the bilateral framework for calculating capital. This will result in a minimum 'standardised' risk weight of 20% (the lowest risk weight under Basel capital rules, others being 50% and 100%). This creates the possibility of a 'cliff edge effect' due to a large jump in capital if a CCP loses its qualifying status.

BCBS (2013c) has also proposed options for a more risk-sensitive approach to initial margin capital requirements. These could lead to potentially higher capital costs with a risk weight potentially as high as 20%.

[16] This includes the so-called 'shortcut method'. The changes to the IMM method introduced in Basel III will apply. However, for IMM banks the margin period of risk (MPR) may be allowed to be shorter than under bilateral rules.

10.4.4 Capital requirements for default fund exposures

There is much greater complexity around the capital treatment of default fund exposures and, in a sense, this represents 'capital on capital'. Some of the important features of a methodology to capitalise default fund contributions are:

- The charge should reflect the fact that default funds do not increase or reduce risk per se, but reallocate it. So if a CCP is taking a greater default fund contribution from clearing members then these clearing members will not need to hold as much capital themselves.
- The different characteristics of CCPs and their relative riskiness should be captured so as to create the correct incentives. A CCP with a smaller default fund (all other things being equal) should impose larger capital charges on its members.
- The default fund exposure broadly consists of two components: the current or 'pre-funded' contribution, which is known, and rights of assessment of other loss allocation methods ('unfunded'), which are more uncertain.
- The charge should not lead to higher capital costs than for an equivalent bilateral trade.

The interim rules (BCBS 2012b) proposed two possible methods to capitalise default fund exposures named as method 1 and method 2 (which banks can choose between). Method 2 (which was intended more as a fallback) subjects default fund exposures to a risk weight of 1250%, which (due to the 8% used to define the capital charge) means that there would be a unit of capital (dollar for dollar) required for each unit of default fund contributed. However, in this method there is a cap applied to both the trade and default fund related capital charges of 20% of the trade-related exposure (defined in the previous section). Method 1 is more complex and attempts to quantify the capital in relation to the financial resources of the CCP in a risk sensitive manner but the dollar for dollar capital requirement also forms the basis of this approach.

These rules were criticised for a number of reasons. First, method 1 relied on a simple capital methodology known as the current exposure method (CEM) to define the hypothetical capital required by the CCP. CEM was generally designed for simple and fairly directional portfolios of banks and is arguably too conservative for the more diverse portfolios of CCPs (although a greater netting benefit within the CEM formula is allowed as discussed below). The dollar for dollar capital requirement forming the basis of the approaches was also viewed as too conservative. An impact study also found quite significant differences between CCPs, which were not easy to justify.

The criticisms of the above interim rules have led eventually to the final rules (via two other approaches proposed in BCBS 2013c known as the tranches approach and the ratio approach). The final rules have followed a simple approach similar to method 2 but with some risk sensitivity as in method 1. We describe below method 1 and method 2 of the interim rules (which are relevant until 2017) and then the final rules (which are relevant thereafter).

Where a default fund is segregated between different products then separate capital calculations must be made for each product type. In case the CCP's default fund contribution is shared between such products then the CCP will have to allocate this to the relevant buckets.

For non-qualifying CCPs, banks must apply a one-to-one capital charge based on both the funded and unfunded (i.e. rights of assessment) default fund contributions. Where the unfunded requirements are unlimited then their effective size for the purpose of capital calculations should be determined by the national supervisor. For a QCCP, the total capital charge may be capped by the total charge that would be calculated if the CCP were non-qualifying.

10.4.5 Method 1 (interim rules)

This calculates the capital requirement with respect to a CCP default fund exposure in three stages:

1 Calculation of the hypothetical capital for the CCP.
2 Calculation of the aggregate capital requirements of the CCP.
3 Allocation of aggregate capital to clearing members.

First, the hypothetical capital requirement is defined by assuming the CCP is a bank and calculating its derivatives exposures to all of its clearing members and their clients (collectively known as the CCP counterparties). For this purpose, the CCP must use a risk weight of 20% (at least) and use the CEM methodology[17] for determining exposure. The hypothetical capital calculation must be calculated by the CCP at least on a quarterly basis. One major criticism of the CEM formula is its treatment of netting: in the interim rules the netting benefit given in the CEM formula is increased from 60% to 85% to reflect the diversification that may be present in cleared portfolios. Nevertheless, this aspect was one of the major contentious points with respect to the interim rules and was one of the reasons for the development of the SA-CCR (BCBS 2014a) used in the final rules. The initial margin and default fund of each CCP counterparty is subtracted from the calculated exposure.

Method 1 capitalises the total default fund contribution of all counterparties based on the aggregative capital requirements (K_{CCP}) assuming a scenario where two average clearing members are in default (and therefore their default fund contributions cannot be used). The CCP prefunded default fund from surviving clearing members (i.e. corrected for the two in default) is given by DF'_{CM} and the CCP's own resources used to cover losses *before* this default fund are defined by DF_{CCP}. The sum of these terms represents the total prefunded default fund size.

The precise specification is based on three potential situations (Figure 10.6) of declining riskiness:

- *Case 1.* The total pre-funded CCP default fund (DF_{CCP}) is less than the hypothetical capital (K_{CCP}). In such a case, clearing members are essentially charged the sum of:
  - A one-to-one capital charge (100%) on their contribution to the default fund.
  - An additional capital covering the 'hole' in the default fund with an even higher capital charge of 120%.
- *Case 2.* In this situation, the total default fund is larger than the hypothetical capital but the CCP's own resources are smaller than this amount. The capital charge is then made up of:
  - A one-to-one charge for the part of the default fund that can be seen contributing to reach the hypothetical capital (after the CCP's own resources are accounted for).
  - A smaller charge of 1.6% or less for the part of the default fund which is in excess of the hypothetical capital requirement.

[17] This applies for derivatives transactions. For securities financing transactions (SFTs) such as repos, standard supervisory haircuts apply.

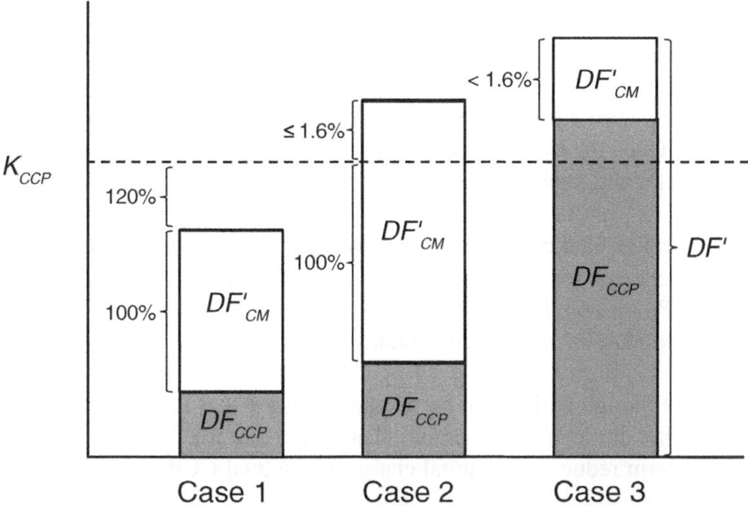

Figure 10.6 Illustration of tranches approach for CCP capital requirements. DF_{CCP} represents the CCP own resources used prior to the mutualised default fund and DF'_{CM} represents the total default fund contribution from the surviving clearing members.

- *Case 3.* In this case, the clearing member's own resources alone exceed the hypothetical capital. The capital charge is defined by a multiplier of less than 1.6%.

The above penalises heavily default fund contribution which (according to the hypothetical capital calculation) are expected to be mutualised but gives a low charge to those that are essentially above the hypothetical capital requirement. This creates a clear benefit from increasing the size of the CCP default fund in the form of lower capital charges for clearing members. More quantitative detail is given in Appendix 10A.

10.4.6 Method 2 (interim rules)

Method 2 is based on the one-to-one capital requirement defined by a 1250% risk weight but with a cap on the overall capital charge (including also the trade level exposure). As such, the capital charge for the CCP exposure (both trade level and default fund related) is defined by the *smaller* of the following:

- A 0.16% charge applied to the trade level exposure and a 100% charge applied to the default fund exposure;
- A 1.6% charge applied to the trade level exposure.

This defines a one-to-one capital charge subject to a cap, which would be relevant in the case that the initial margin contribution is rather large compared to the default fund contribution.

10.4.7 Final rules

The final rules (intended to apply from 1 January 2017) also define a hypothetical capital requirement but via the SM-CCR approach instead of the CEM approach discussed above. A MPR of 10 days is used within the SM-CCR formulas to define the CCP's exposure to its clearing members. Once the hypothetical capital of the CCP has been defined then the capital requirement for a clearing member is the higher of the following two terms:

- the prefunded default fund contribution multiplied by a ratio representing the hypothetical capital requirement divided by the actual total default fund size (both from clearing members and the CCPs own contribution);
- a 2% charge applied to the prefunded default fund.

The second term, although unlikely to be relevant, ensures that the more risky default fund contribution does not attract a lower capital charge that that for the initial margin (2% risk weight). The first term reduces the capital charge as the total CCP default fund increases in relation to the hypothetical capital requirement.

10.4.8 Example and discussion

Figure 10.7 gives an illustration of the total clearing member capital requirement as a function of the QCCP's own contribution to the default fund for method 1, method 2 and the final rules. In method 2, we assume that the second term (20% risk weight applied to the trade level exposure) is larger than the first term, so the first term defines the capital. In final rules, we assume that the first term defines the capital and therefore that the second term is smaller.

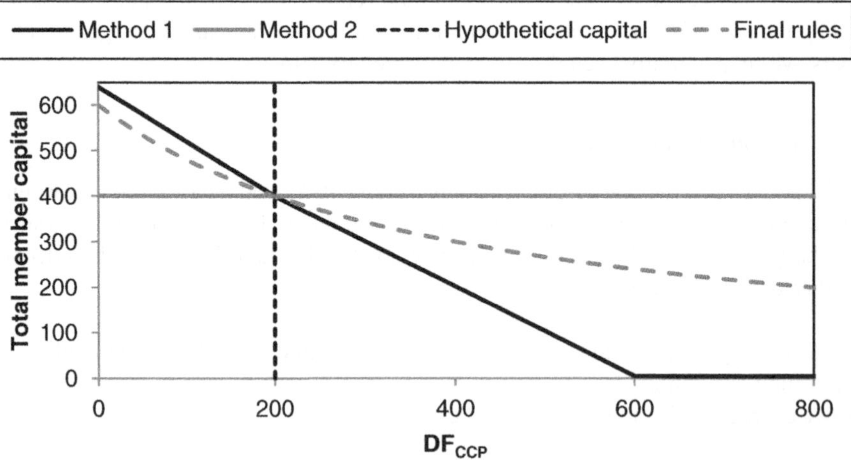

Figure 10.7 Example of the interim (method 1 and method 2) and final rules for CCP capital requirements as a function of the CCP contribution to the default fund (which may need to be junior to the other default fund components). The total clearing member contribution to the default fund is assumed to be 400 and the hypothetical capital requirement is 600. This means that the total capital reaches the hypothetical capital level when $DF_{CCP} = 200$ (shown by the dotted black line).

Both of these assumptions are likely in practice. By looking at the total capital requirement for all clearing members, we do not consider the granularity adjustment in method 2.

The dotted black line shows the point at which the total capital requirement meets the hypothetical capital, at which point there is a one-for-one capital requirement in all approaches. Most real cases would obviously be expected to be to the right of this point. Both method 1 and the final rules generate approximately the correct qualitative behaviour where the larger CCP default fund relates to a smaller clearing member capital requirement. For a given hypothetical capital, the final rules are not as beneficial as method 1, which leads to lower requirements for a well-capitalised CCP when the CCP default fund exceeds the hypothetical capital (although the final rules benefit from the use of the SA-CCR as described above).

The main contentious point is the baseline one-for-one capital requirement that is a core assumption in all approaches (although method 1 and the final rules do benefit from the fact that the CCPs actual capital will likely be substantially more than the hypothetical capital). Given CCPs are supposed to be safe and well protected by operational procedures such as auctions and the loss absorbency of initial margins, such a high capitalisation of the default fund may seem excessive. Indeed, the one-to-one default fund capital requirement seems to imply that it is a likely event that a QCCP will suffer a loss to its default fund equal to the hypothetical capital requirement. In reality, such a loss should be extremely unlikely since it is protected by:

- The initial margins of the defaulted member(s) calculated with at least a 99% confidence level in mind.
- The default fund(s) of the defaulted member(s).
- Any junior contribution by the CCP to the default fund.

In response to such a criticism, the BCBS (2013c) have commented that using risk weights below 1250% would threaten the ability of clearing members to absorb default fund losses in times of stress. On the other hand, they also accept that a 100% capital charge for default fund contributions may result in excessive charges that are inconsistent with the clearing mandate.

10.4.9 Client clearing and bilateral aspects

Client clearing refers to the situation where a non-clearing member clears a trade indirectly with a CCP as a client of a clearing member, as illustrated in Figure 10.8. As discussed in more detail in the next chapter, the specific involvement of the clearing member can differ but that is not important for the capital treatment described below.

There are two situations to consider in the client clearing case:

Figure 10.8 Illustration of client clearing facilitated by a general clearing member (GCM). Note that the precise relationship between the client and CCP (which is discussed in more detail in the next chapter) is not relevant for this discussion.

- *Clearing member point of view:* The GCM can be seen as having exposures to both their client and the CCP. As such there is the question of the capitalisation of these two exposures.
- *Client point of view:* The client position (assuming of course the client is a bank and subject to capital charges) and whether they are exposed to the CCP or the GCM (or both).

Regarding the latter situation, under certain conditions, if a bank is clearing through another clearing member, they may capitalise the transactions as a CCP exposure (rather than a bilateral one). This applies whether the bank is a client of the clearing member or if the clearing member is guaranteeing the CCP's exposure to the bank (these different client relationships, known as principal-to-principal or agency, are discussed in the next chapter in sections 11.1.2 and 11.1.3 respectively). The conditions required for this treatment to apply are:

- The transactions must be identified by the CCP as client transactions.
- Margin to support the transactions must be held by the CCP and/or the clearing member such that the client is protected from the insolvency of the clearing member and any of the clearing member's other clients (see further discussion on this in section 11.3). Legal opinions must support this margin protection.
- The relevant transactions must be highly likely to continue to be transacted through the CCP in the event of insolvency of the clearing member. This refers to the likelihood that the transactions can be 'ported' (see section 11.1.7) to another surviving clearing member in such a default scenario.

Where the above conditions are met, but a client is not protected from losses in the case that the clearing member and another client of the clearing member jointly default (fellow customer risk – see section 11.3.1), then a higher risk weight of 4% is applied. If this is not the case then the client must assume a bilateral capital charge to their clearing member.

Turning to the clearing member point of view, a clearing member must capitalise both exposures as shown in Figure 10.9 since it is exposed to both the client and CCP in this situation. These capital charges will be calculated as follows:

- *Client trade:* This must be treated as a usual bilateral trade (irrespective of whether the clearing member guarantees the trade or simply acts as an intermediary between client and CCP) as the CCP provides no support in the case of the client defaulting. This means

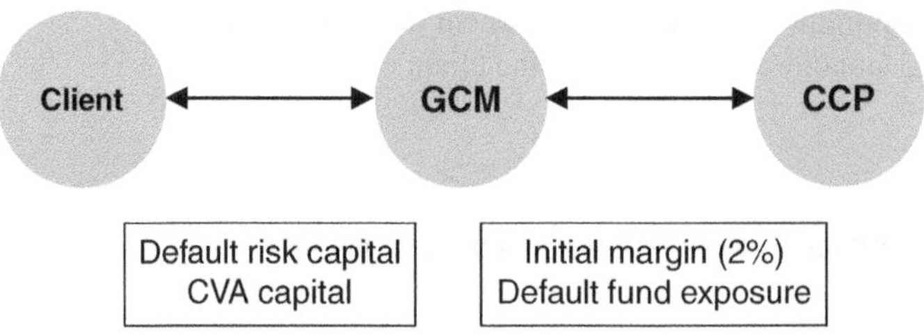

Figure 10.9 Illustration of capital charges faced by a clearing member clearing trades for a client.

that there will be a capital charge in relation to default risk and CVA (see section 7.3.1) as is usual in these circumstances.[18] These capital charges will be reduced by the margin (including initial margin) that the client is obliged to post (the benefit will depend on which capital model the bank uses for counterparty risk). The only difference compared to a pure bilateral trade is that it is possible to use a smaller margin period of risk which can be reduced from a minimum of 10 days to 5 days to reflect the shorter close out periods for cleared transaction. This reduction can either be modelled directly or a simple multiplier of 0.71 can be applied (see discussion in section 7.2.4).

- *CCP trade:* A clearing member must also apply the 2% capital charge to their trade exposure to the CCP even for a client trade. This is relevant since the clearing member is generally obligated to cover any losses the client would face due to the failure of the CCP. They will also have a charge on any additional contribution to the default fund that is required due to their client trades (although often CCPs do not require this).

APPENDIX 10A: TECHNICAL DETAILS ON THE INTERIM AND FINAL RULES

The description below is based on the notation and specification in BCBS (2012b) and BCBS (2014b) with some additional figures, analysis and explanation.

Hypothetical capital requirement (method 1)

The CCP's hypothetical capital requirement due to its counterparty credit risk exposure to all its clearing members (and clients) is:

$$K_{CCP} = \sum_i \max\left(EBRM_i - IM_i - DF_i, 0\right).RW.Capital\ Ratio$$

$EBRM_i$ is the exposure to counterparty i under the CEM approach (for derivatives) but with an enhanced netting benefit of 85%. IM_i and DF_i represent the initial margin and default fund contributions from that counterparty. RW is a risk weight of (at least) 20% and the capital ratio is 8% as usual.

Aggregate capital requirements for all clearing members (method 1)

In this method, DF'_{CM} denotes the prefunded default fund contributed by all surviving clearing members (having the default funds of two average members subtracted) and DF_{CCP} is the CCP's own contribution to the default fund used prior to this amount. The sum of these terms represents the total available default fund $DF' = DF'_{CM} + DF_{CCP}$. The capital requirements are then distinguished by three cases as shown in Figure 10.10.

The three cases shown in Figure 10.10 lead to a total capital charge across clearing members as shown in Table 10.2.

[18] These capital charges are discussed in more detail in Gregory (2012).

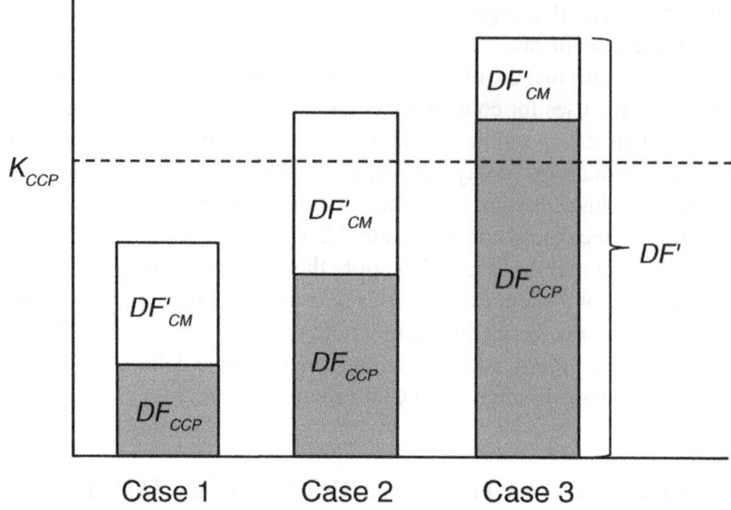

Figure 10.10 Illustration of method 1 for CCP default fund capital requirements. DF_{CCP} represents the CCP's own resources used prior to the mutualised default fund and DF'_{CM} represents the total default fund contribution from the clearing members corrected for two average members being in default.

Table 10.2 Summary of capital charges in method 1.

Condition	Aggregate capital requirement	Case
$DF' < K_{CCP}$	$c_2.\mu.(K_{CCP} - DF') + c_2.DF'_{CM}$	Case 1
$DF_{CCP} < K_{CCP} \leq DF'$	$c_2.(K_{CCP} - DF_{CCP}) + c_1.(DF' - K_{CCP})$	Case 2
$K_{CCP} \leq DF_{CCP}$	$c_1.DF'_{CM}$	Case 3

In the above, $c_2 = 100\%$ (a one-for-one capital charge), $\mu = 1.2$ and c_1 is a decreasing capital factor between 0.16% and 1.6% defined by:

$$c_1 = max\left\{\frac{1.6\%}{\left(DF' / K_{CCP}\right)^{0.3}}, 0.16\%\right\}$$

Aggregate capital requirements for all clearing members (method 1)

The aggregate capital required of the previous calculation is then allocated to according to individual clearing members in proportion to their contribution to the total default fund using a factor of:

$$\left(1+\beta.\frac{N}{N-2}\right).\frac{DF_i}{DF_{CM}}$$

This represents a pro-rata allocation based on the ratio of the default fund of the clearing member to the total clearing member default fund DF_i/DF_{CM} with an additional granularity adjustment coming from the total number of clearing members (N) and through a CCP concentration factor (β), which depends on the exposure to the largest two clearing members compared to the average exposure.

Final rules

Under the final rules, effective from 1 January 2017, the hypothetical capital is defined by the following sum:

$$K_{CCP} = \sum_i EAD_i.RW.Capital\ Ratio$$

where EAD_i is the exposure of the CCP to clearing member i including client transactions guaranteed by the clearing member and accounting for margin held by the CCP (including the prefunded default fund contribution) against the transactions. The sum is over all clearing member accounts and client sub-accounts (which should enter the sum separately). For derivatives, EAD_i is calculated using the SA-CCR method with a MPR of 10 days. For SFT transactions, it is defined by:

$$EAD_i = \max(EBRM_i - IM_i - DF_i, 0)$$

where $EBRM_i$ is the exposure before risk mitigation according to the regulatory formulas including haircuts and IM_i and DF_i are the initial margin and default fund contributions respectively. The capital requirement for each clearing member is then given by:

$$K_{CM_i} = max\left(K_{CCP}.\left(\frac{DF_i^{pref}}{DF_{CCP} + DF_{CM}^{pref}}\right), 8\% \times 2\% \times DF_i^{pref}\right)$$

where DF_i^{pref} is the clearing member's prefunded default fund contribution, DF^{pref} the total prefunded default fund contribution from clearing members and DF_{CCP} is the CCP's own contribution to the default fund (which may be pari passu or junior to the member's contribution).

11
Client Clearing, Segregation and Portability

Never say no when a client asks for something, even if it is the moon. You can always try, and anyhow there is plenty of time afterwards to explain that it was not possible.

Richard Nixon (1913–1994)

11.1 OPERATIONAL ASPECTS

This chapter describes the clearing for institutions that are not members of a CCP. Such entities need to clear as clients (customers) of a general clearing member or GCM (known as a futures commission merchant or FCM in the US). Such clients may be traditional clients of banks, but may also be other banks and financial institutions that cannot, or find it inefficient to, become CCP members. This raises a number of issues in relation to the interaction between the client and their clearing member such as the impact of defaults and the treatment of margin passed between them.

11.1.1 General setup

A non-CCP member (referred to as 'client') wishing to clear an OTC contract must do so through a counterparty that is a GCM (referred to as 'clearing member') of the CCP in question. The general client-clearing setup is illustrated in Figure 11.1 where the relationship between clients and clearing members is essentially bilateral and the CCP does not bear the risk of the client. Note that clients can have a clearing relationship with more than one clearing member as shown.

Clearing members are most likely to be the large top-tier investment banks that have the economies of scale to be members of multiple CCPs. Indeed, the clients of such banks will naturally expect them to offer clearing services across different markets and provide a choice of CCPs where such choice exists. Smaller banks and other financial institutions are unlikely to find it possible and viable to become clearing members. Medium-sized 'second tier' banks may be on the threshold of this choice and may have to weigh up carefully the pros and cons of being clearing members at a given CCP.

The treatment of clients is different to that of clearing members. For example, whilst they still usually pay initial margins, they do not typically have to contribute to CCP default funds (for example, the SwapClear default fund is not based on client positions). The clearing member will charge clients fees and potentially earn returns on excess margins received (above those required by the CCP) to compensate them for the clearing service they provide and the additional risk they take in doing this.

The precise implementation of the above setup is done in two different ways, so-called principal-to-principal and agency.

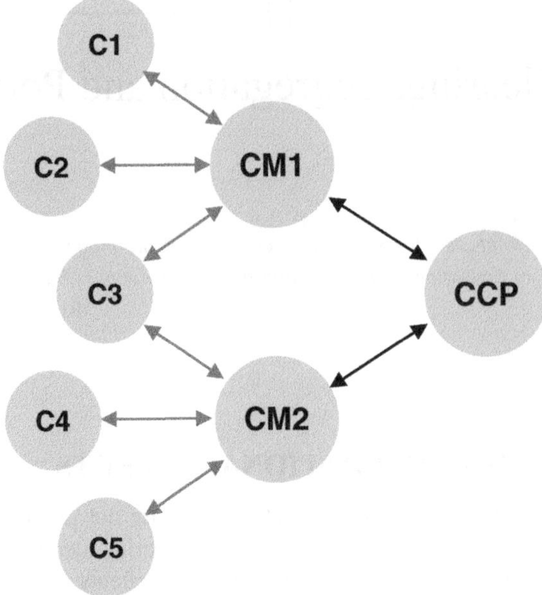

Figure 11.1 Illustration of the relationship between non-clearing members or clients (C1 to C5), clearing members (CM1 and CM2) and a CCP.

11.1.2 Principal-to-principal model

In this approach (used in Europe), as shown in Figure 11.2, there is a bilateral relationship between:

- CCP and clearing member
- Clearing member and client

The clearing member and client will typically negotiate and sign an ISDA Master Agreement (section 5.1.4), including a Credit Support Annex (or will have another agreement), to margin positions. Usual aspects such as the perception of credit risk may drive the nature of the bilateral agreement between the clearing member and client. However, another and potentially more important aspect in this relationship will be the attempt by the clearing member to mirror their own contractual relationship to the CCP in their relationship with the client. This will imply that, albeit implicitly, the client will be largely subject to the rules of the CCP in question although the CCP has no direct contractual relationship with, or obligations to the clients of clearing members.

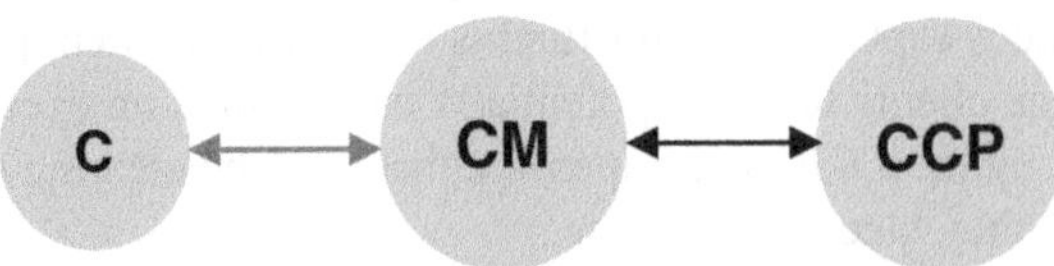

Figure 11.2 Illustration of the principal-to-principal model.

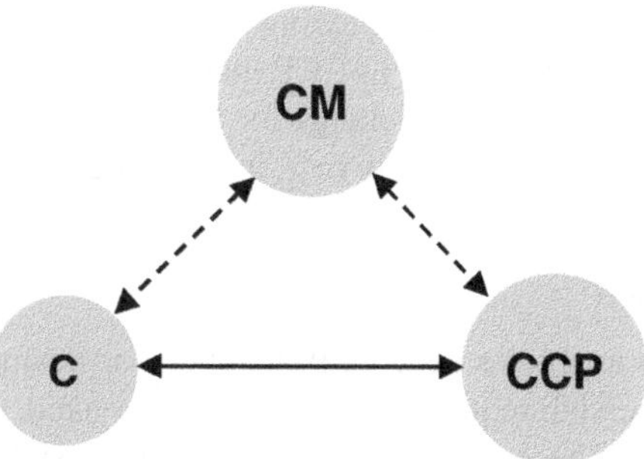

Figure 11.3 Illustration of the agency model.

11.1.3 Agency model

In the agency model, the client faces the CCP directly but their contractual requirements are guaranteed by the clearing member as shown in Figure 11.3. This is the historical approach that has been used in the US futures market and is the structure used for US OTC CCPs. In this arrangement, the client may be required to enter into an agreement directly with the CCP in relation to aspects such as margin posting. One clear difference between this approach and the principal-to-principal model is that the client will be more directly exposed to the CCPs contractual and operational requirements. However, the clearing member may still provide the client with some flexibility in its role as guarantor.

Since the clearing member guarantees the client's transactions, like the principal-to-principal approach, the clearing member is exposed to the default of the client. If a client defaults, the CCP will transfer positions and margin to the clearing member to manage the risk and unwind trades.

11.1.4 Margin requirements between client and CCP

Clearing members will impose CCP margin requirements on their clients, either directly in the agency model, or indirectly in the principal-to-principal model. However, they may offer some flexibility to ease the resulting liquidity requirements. These include:

- *Margin upgrading:* This allows clients to post margin that is not admissible by a CCP, perhaps because it is too illiquid or credit-risky. The clearing member will then provide a margin transformation service to upgrade the margin when posting to the CCP. Such liquidity services are likely to be extremely important to many clients due to the liquidity restrictions attached to CCP margin. Furthermore, since variation margin requirements must typically be made in cash, even the upgrading of liquid margin securities (e.g. US treasuries) may be required.
- *Margin posting frequency:* The clearing member may only require a certain periodicity of margin posting (e.g. daily), but will potentially be required to post more frequently to the CCP (e.g. intradaily). The clearing member may therefore effectively fund the margin temporarily on behalf of the client, thereby extending credit to them albeit for a short period of perhaps a few hours. Rennison (2013) reports that around a quarter of clients will benefit from this service (although more than half will post excess margin themselves to avoid intraday posting).

There may be other benefits provided by a clearing member to a client. For example, a clearing member may not pass on an increase in CCP margin requirements for a period of time (Rennison 2013). A clearing member will charge for the above services explicitly via fees or implicitly via requiring extra margin directly (e.g. initial margin buffers) and/or via haircuts.

11.1.5 Client point of view

A so-called client may be unable to be a CCP member, for example, because they do not conform to the CCP membership requirements. On the other hand, they may consider it inefficient or even dangerous to become a member due to the resulting requirements such as contributing to the CCP's default fund, adhering to strict margin posting rules and participating in fire-drills and auctions. By being a non-clearing member, it is not necessary to conform to certain CCP rules such as participation in an auction.

The client bears risk to the clearing member defaulting, which could be made worse if other clients of the clearing member are defaulting also. More generally, depending on the segregation model (section 11.3), the client will be exposed to:

- Their clearing member
- Jointly to their clearing member and their clearing member's other clients
- The CCP
- All of the above

This means that the client will not be indifferent to either the clearing member they use or the CCP they clear through, and must consider their choices carefully.

Note that a client will potentially execute a trade through an 'executing broker' and then clear it though a clearing member (or 'clearing broker'). These two entities do not have to be the same although there may be price benefits if they are. In terms of choosing a clearing member, the following factors are important:

- *Existing relationships:* Clearing members with whom a client already has a trading relationship and the related legal and operational agreements in place.
- *CCP access:* The range of CCPs to which a clearing member can provide access.
- *Product coverage:* Clearly, it is important to understand if a clearing member can offer to clear the full range of products required.
- *Credit quality:* The perceived default probability of the clearing member. This may be more important than that of the executing broker.
- *Cost:* Cost may be experienced by per trade fees (Rennison 2013 reports per-ticket fees of between US$200 and US$500). Some clearing members may also offer a discount for trades both executed and clearing through them. The cost structure needs to be transparent.
- *Margin requirements:* Although margin requirements and haircuts will generally be defined by the CCP in question, a clearing member's ability to fund margin requirement, offer upgrading services and give cross-margining benefits will be important considerations.
- *Expertise:* Advice on market practices, regulatory requirements and legal aspects.
- *Operational support:* A client will need help to adapt processes to the requirements of central clearing. In particular, the clearing member's ability to offer assistance with margining may be useful.

- *Reporting, systems integration and analytics:* Trade reporting with the appropriate information in the right format to the relevant authorities can be a significant problem. Integrated reporting and other analytics provided by the clearing member are other important considerations.

Depending on the clearing member and product in question, a client may have a choice of different CCPs. In terms of identifying which CCPs they may wish to use, clients may further consider:

- *Regulatory environment:* The legal and regulatory framework under which the CCP operates.
- *Relationship:* It is important to establish the form of the relationship, such as principal-to-principal or agency, and any other more subtle aspects.
- *Margin rules:* The margin rules of the CCP, which will largely determine how much margin the client will need to post. This will include any cross-margining benefits that are available.
- *Segregation:* The possible structures available for segregation of margins and the protection these offer (section 11.3).
- *Default management process:* The process and rules for managing a clearing member default, especially in relation to the porting of positions. The loss allocation rules of the CCP aside from default fund contributions (for example, variation margin gains haircutting – section 10.3.1) will also be of interest.

On a given CCP, a client will probably need a 'backup' clearing member to whom they could transfer trades in the event of the insolvency of their main clearing member, or for other reasons. Indeed, some clients consider the need to have at least three clearing members on a given CCP with whom they have a contractual relationship. This avoids having only one option in the event of a default, and therefore potentially being offered non-competitive terms by the surviving clearing member. Whether client relationships are split relatively evenly, or concentrated through a single clearing member with the others as fallback options is a balance of cost and risk. Whilst small clients may utilise a single CCP and clear predominantly through one, with perhaps another backup clearing member, larger clients may have a number of clearing member relationships across multiple CCPs. Rennison (2013) reports that most clients currently have two or more clearing members and in the future many plan to have four or more.

A client may also consider the need to clear through more than one CCP to provide the necessary product coverage and avoid a concentration of risk at their CCP of choice. It should also be noted that some clients (e.g. pension funds) may have very directional portfolios and may experience less benefit from concentrating clearing at a given clearing member and/or CCP. Indeed, such large and directional portfolios may expose clients to multipliers imposed by CCPs to protect against concentration risks. Cross-product margining (section 9.5), where a client gains a reduction in margin requirements for different products, can be an important aspect to reduce costs.

Clearing members may offer various services with respect to margin requirements. In particular, a clearing member may not require a client to post intraday margin even when they are required to post it to the CCP, and may give a margin upgrade service by allowing a client to post securities not eligible as margin by the CCP. Some clearing members may also offer 'single currency margining', where all margin requirements in different currencies required by the CCP are netted into a single payment in a pre-specified currency for the client. However, in order to use a CCP, a non-clearing member will inevitably have to commit to frequent posting of margin.

Whilst in some regions some end users such as pension funds,[1] corporates and smaller financial institutions are exempt from CCP clearing, they may still need to consider whether it will provide an advantage to them. Exempt parties who already commit to relatively strong bilateral margin posting may well see a move to clearing as beneficial, as long as the additional initial margin requirements are not prohibitive. However, some details should be carefully considered here. In a bilateral CSA (section 6.3.2), it is likely to be possible to post variation margin in securities (e.g. treasury bonds) as well as cash, whereas a CCP will probably require cash only. A client moving to clearing therefore potentially creates the liquidity risk that they cannot repo securities to post the necessary cash (noting that the repo market can function poorly in a severe crisis). This may be mitigated by their clearing member or third party via a margin transformation service, but this may increase liquidity and systemic risk generally (see next chapter).

Other exempt parties, such as governments, government agencies and multinational development banks, with only limited margin arrangements benefit from not posting margin (one-way CSA) or posting only limited margin (CSAs with high thresholds or rating triggers). Such entities are unlikely to see a move to clearing as beneficial. However, if bilateral counterparties push such entities to post more margin bilaterally (as is currently the case) then this may change.

11.1.6 Clearing member point of view

From the clearing member perspective, compared to bilateral trades, they face an additional risk as they (implicitly or explicitly) guarantee the client's performance to the CCP. They also bear a similar risk to what they would face in a bilateral relationship with the client, although this will be reduced due to the imposition of tighter conditions on contractual terms by virtue of mirroring the terms of the CCP. Clearing members can impose stricter margin conditions but beyond this, they bear the risk that a client does not perform in relation to the CCP. This risk could be worse than in bilateral markets: for example, a CCP may close out a client's portfolio at a price the clearing member believes to be extreme.

Fundamentally, clearing members offer a service for clients that has some underlying costs and risks, some of which are quantifiable and some that are not. Clearing members offering client clearing may see these extra costs and risks (above those expected in bilateral trades) via:

- *CCP membership requirements:* In order to offer client clearing, a clearing member may have tighter membership requirements such as having a larger net capital base. Some CCPs may charge more initial margin for client trades (although this is likely to be passed directly to clients).
- *Margin multipliers:* As described in section 9.4.2, CCPs may impose margin multipliers, for example in the event of excessive amounts of liquidity, credit or concentration risk. To the extent that client positions contribute to hitting such multipliers then clearing costs may be higher.

[1] In the case of pension funds, the exemption is a temporary one in Europe as described in section 4.2.3.

- *Default fund contributions:* Client clearing may impose greater default fund contributions on clearing members (although this is not always the case).
- *Asymmetry costs:* The clearing member takes additional risks to the extent that their obligations to the CCP are not perfectly matched by the client's obligations to them, for example, if a member allows their clients to post margin less frequently than required, or in securities not allowed, by the CCP. There is also a risk of not being able to pass on various methods of loss allocation (section 10.3.5) such as variation margin gains haircutting to clients.

In order to compensate for the above costs, the clearing member will obviously charge their clients in various ways for the service they provide. Ways in which this can be achieved include:

- *Periodic fees:* A fixed fee (such as monthly).
- *Per transaction fees:* A fee for clearing each transaction, probably proportional to the size of that transaction.
- *Haircuts:* Haircuts applied to margins (including initial margin) will potentially provide additional assets above those required to be posted to the CCP.
- *Segregation benefits:* Depending on the level of segregation, the clearing member may be able to hold onto margins (even in the absence of haircuts) and gain an economic advantage from this.

Clearing members can potentially terminate a client's positions, for example if they are no longer comfortable with the credit risk they are taking. This normally requires a notice period such as 30 days.

11.1.7 Portability

In the event of a clearing member default, a client has a number of potential options as to the treatment of their portfolio:

- *Porting to a backup clearing member:* The ideal solution is for the underlying portfolio to be ported (transferred) with the associated margin to another surviving clearing member, with whom the client already has a relationship. This is why clients will often make sure they have at least one backup clearing member with whom they have an established contractual relationship.
- *Transfer by CCP to another clearing member:* In the absence of a backup clearing member, the porting could be facilitated by the CCP directly who may auction the portfolio amongst other clearing members. This option is less attractive because the client may not have any bilateral agreement with the new clearing member and may think it likely that the price terms and associated margin requirements will be uncompetitive.
- *Termination by the CCP:* In the event that some kind of portability is not possible, the CCP may terminate the portfolio via the auction. From the client's point of view, this is a scenario that they would probably wish to avoid.

Portability is illustrated in Figure 11.4. The aim is that, in the event of default of their clearing member, clients 'port' their positions to a surviving clearing member who also assumes

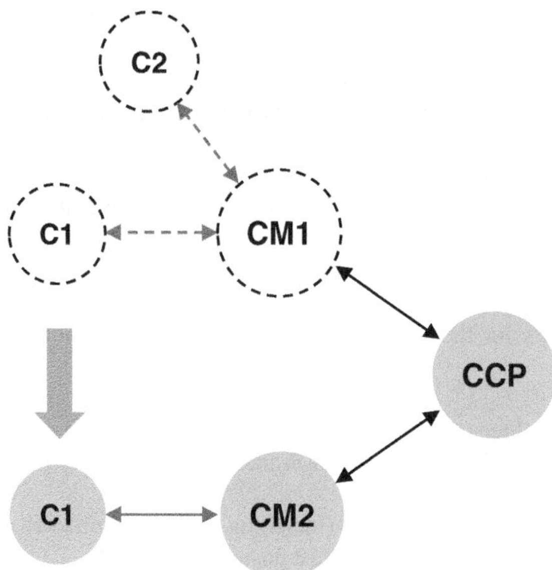

Figure 11.4 Illustration of a non-clearing member (C1) 'porting' from one clearing member (CM1) to another (CM2). Note that CM1 will have other clients (e.g. C2) that may not port trades to CM2 at the same time.

the margin in relation to the positions. This implies that the client faces limited disruption from the default event and this is clearly highly preferable to having all positions terminated, which will require the positions to be re-established at a time of potentially significant market stress. Furthermore, it is preferable that positions can be ported to a clearing member with whom the client already has a relationship rather than being distributed to multiple clearing members via an auction, which as mentioned above, could lead to adverse prices and extra margin requirements. Having a portfolio split up amongst clearing members may also lose some of the underlying netting benefits (although this depends on the level of segregation used as discussed in section 11.3).

To maximise the possibility to port cleanly following a default, a client needs to ensure that the processes and rules of the CCP are sound with respect to the following aspects:

- *Identification of positions and margins:* It must be possible for the CCP to identify immediately, the margin and positions associated with a given client.
- *Transferability:* Margin and positions must be immediately transferable and margin must be unencumbered. Preferably, the actual assets, and not their value (adjusted for margin), would be available.
- *Segregation:* Margin must be legally protected from the margin of the clearing member and that of their other clients.

The steps taken in porting could be that the client nominates an alternative clearing member to the CCP within a pre-specified time frame, and then the CCP asks that clearing member to assess the underlying portfolio. There is clearly a risk at this stage that the new clearing member refuses the request or requires additional margin. The latter could be the case either because the new clearing member disagrees with the price (variation margin) or the risk of the underlying portfolio (initial margin). Whilst the CCP rules on valuation and initial margin calculations should minimise such problems, they are likely to be more difficult in the aftermath of a clearing member default. The following factors determine a clearing member's likelihood in accepting such positions:

- *Relationship with client:* If the client has a strong relationship with the new clearing member and has cleared trades through them already.
- *Information on client account:* The relevant information on the client's portfolio and margin would need to be available in a timely fashion and in an easy to use format.
- *Market conditions:* Clearly volatile and illiquid market conditions will make it less likely that a clearing member would be inclined to accept new positions.
- *Size of portfolio:* A large portfolio will be more difficult to accept, especially in turbulent markets.
- *Directional position of clearing member:* The relative positions the clearing member already has, including those through other clients, will be important in establishing the degree of offset from the new portfolio. If this is good then there is a greater likelihood that they will be willing to facilitate porting.

Porting is a key advantage of central clearing (although we note that it could function in bilateral markets if margin were posted to a third party). However, it is also prone to a number of risks, which may lead to failure at the precise time when portability is key. These risks mainly relate to the way in which margin is segregated in the client clearing relationship. Portability may also be important in non-default scenarios. For example, Rennison (2013) reports that most clearing members can terminate a clearing agreement (although generally at least 30 days' notice is required) or reduce a client's clearing limit.

11.2 SEGREGATION, REHYPOTHECATION AND MARGIN OFFSET

11.2.1 The need for segregation

The issues that arise over segregation of margin are another important consideration. Segregation means the legal separation of margin, but also implies that there should be restrictions over investment of client margin. Segregation also effectively determines who pays for a CCP member default. Broadly speaking, commingling margins expose clients to the risk of default of the other parties involved (their clearing member, clients of the clearing member and the CCP itself). Segregation of margin reduces the risk that a client will lose some or their entire margin in the event of such a default. There is no free lunch however, as greater segregation is more costly, both operationally and in terms of the requirement for default funds and initial margins to be larger (to cover the losses that would otherwise be taken from margins in non-segregated accounts).

There is also the question of the legal enforcement of segregation across jurisdictions. If a segregation arrangement is found to be unenforceable upon the party holding margin defaulting, then the party who has posted the margin is at risk of having those funds commingled with the bankrupt party's estate, and becoming an unsecured creditor. Moreover, since the enforceability of segregation is most likely to be only tested in extreme scenarios, and is subject to judicial interpretations that likely depend on the facts in particular cases, identifying solid principles that will hold in all instances is effectively impossible.

There are also a number of historical cases that illustrate the perils and potential failures of segregation:

- *Barings Bank:* The collapse of Barings in 1995 created some problems in relation to segregation, as under Japanese law there were no rules to segregate Barings' client accounts from the bank's own positions on the Singapore International Monetary Exchange (SIMEX). US accounts were, however, transferred without major problems.
- *Lehman Brothers:* The Lehman failure in 2008 saw bilateral initial margins (known typically as independent amounts) posted by buy side clients such as hedge funds, being commingled or reused (rehypothecated) by Lehman in their role as a prime broker. After the bankruptcy, these clients had only a general unsecured claim for the amounts of initial margin posted. Such trades were under bilaterally negotiated documentation and clients did not enjoy any segregation protection. This was partly due to a lack of appreciation of the legal aspects, and partly because the default of Lehman was considered highly unlikely.
- *MF Global:* MF Global was a major derivatives broker that filed for bankruptcy in October 2011. It became clear that it had illegally transferred segregated client funds (of over US$1 billion) to third parties. Segregation was therefore in place but not effective due to fraud, and MF Global's clients lost significant amounts as a result (see section 6.1.5).
- *Peregrine Financial:* In 2012, Peregrine Financial Group collapsed after proprietor Russell Wasendorf admitted to a US$215.5 million gap between the client's assets he claimed he held and those he actually did hold on their behalf. Wasendorf was sentenced to 50 years in jail for misappropriating the funds.

It seems clear from experience that any form of segregation is prone to operational and legal risks in both bilateral and centrally cleared markets. Hence the definition and viability of segregation is critical to the success of client clearing.

11.2.2 The difference between variation and initial margins

Segregation should be considered differently for variation and initial margin. By definition, variation margin represents losses that have already been incurred and hence do not need to be afforded special protection. There is a possibility that the operational delays inherent in the variation margin posting process may create risks.[2] However, since such delays are typically no more than a day under central clearing, the embedded risks should be relatively small. Furthermore, variation margin could be become excessively costly unless it can be netted and rehypothecated, as illustrated in Figure 11.5. Here the clearing member receives net total variation margin of 20 (15+10–5), which is posted to the CCP. This is consistent with the view that variation margin has no net cost because it simply equates to gains and losses across the market (section 9.1.4).

[2] For example, consider a client posts variation margin against losses on positions, and these positions then gain value such that the client should receive back some of that variation margin. This part of the variation margin is subject to default risk until it is returned.

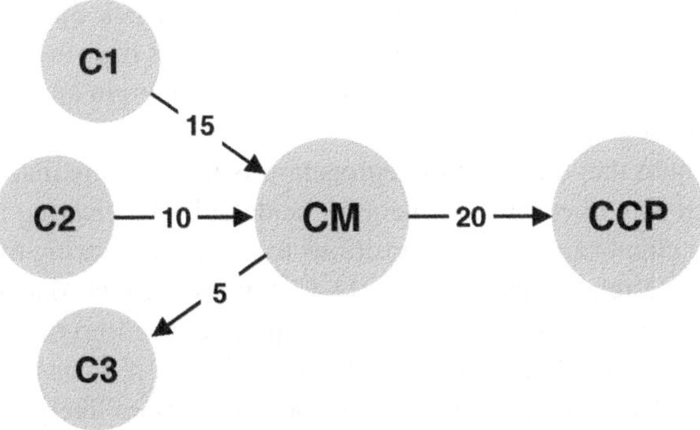

Figure 11.5 Illustration of the effective rehypothecation of variation margin by a clearing member. The payments are assumed netted which would not be possible under segregation.

As noted above, there will be some risk when variation margin is rehypothecated. If variation margin is posted by the client against losses, and positions then move back in the favour of the client, then this amount could be lost. However, this is a secondary issue when compared to the treatment of initial margins.

Initial margin is distinct from variation margin as it does not reflect current losses and as such, it may be relevant to apply additional protection. Consider the situation in Figure 11.6 where a clearing member collects a total amount of initial margin of 30 from three clients for their respective portfolios. However, due to the diversification of client positions, the CCP only requires 18 of initial margin. From the overall client point of view, they face risk over both the amount of 12 (held by the clearing member) and 18 (held by the CCP). They also face the risk that their own contribution to these amounts is not allocated. The clients could also claim that they do not need to post the full margin due to the diversification benefit from which the clearing member benefits. Therefore, many questions need to be answered.

The forthcoming discussion on segregation is therefore in relation to initial margin and not variation margin. However, there is also the question of 'excess margin' which clearing members may charge clients. This represents a buffer required by the clearing member above

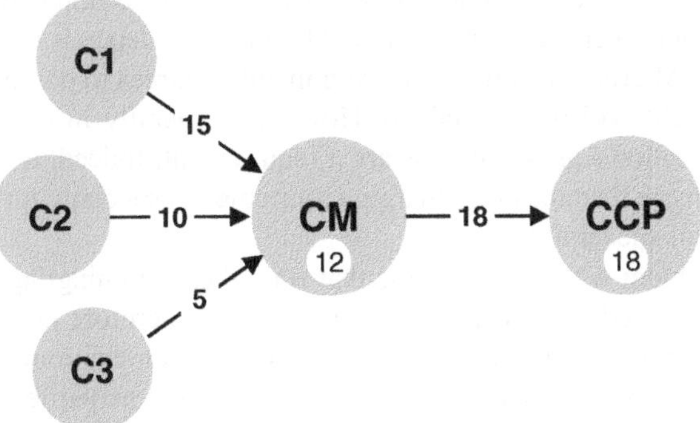

Figure 11.6 Illustration of the rehypothecation of initial margin by a clearing member. The client margins shown are calculated by the CM on a gross basis but required by the CCP on a net basis.

the initial margin amount required by a CCP, and covers the risk the clearing member has in meeting obligations of the CCP before being able to collect margins from the client. This excess margin will be considered as a component of initial margin and as such should (ideally) also benefit from segregation.

It is important to note that the issue of segregation is more subtle than simply the risk of initial margins posted by a client. In the event of the default of a clearing member, a client is most protected if the client can port their positions to a backup clearing member with whom they may already have a relationship (section 11.1.7). If the CCP is concerned that the client portfolio may not ported successfully, then it may liquidate (auction) the positions as soon as possible to avoid further risk. The CCP is less likely to do this if it has adequate margin held securely against the risks of that portfolio. Hence porting is more likely if significant margin is associated with the account and held safely at the CCP.

As described above, variation margin is naturally paid on a net basis without segregation. However, there needs to be more thought regarding the treatment of initial margins. The first fundamental point to consider is whether initial margins should be collected on a net or gross basis.

11.2.3 Net and gross margin

Broadly speaking, there are two possible setups for the way in which a CCP calculates client margin. The first is as shown in Figure 11.6 where the CCP requires initial margin on a net basis ('net margining'). Alternatively with 'gross margining', the CCP requires client initial margin on a gross basis. These situations are illustrated in Figure 11.7.

Net margining is clearly a cheaper solution since the benefit of diversification between client positions is accounted for. As shown in Figure 11.7, in practice this is a source of benefit for the clearing member who can derive profit from investing the excess margin held. This should in turn reduce costs imposed on clients. Net margining therefore does not reduce the margin charged to clients but it does change where it is held. However, it causes two obvious problems that need further consideration.

11.2.4 Net margin and portability

The most obvious problem with net margin relates to portability, since the margin held for each client at the CCP may be insufficient to port. Consider the example in Figure 11.7: client 1 may be unable to port because the margin held by the CCP depends on the portfolio effect with clients 2 and 3. Alternatively, if the clearing member agrees to port all clients' positions then the netting benefit will be maintained. However, generally in order to maximise the possibility to port positions, gross margins are a requirement. Indeed, it may be relevant for clients to post even more than the gross margin requirement, especially for large portfolios, to increase the chance of successful porting.

A more subtle problem with net margin is that it implies commingling. Margin posted on a net basis to a CCP is reduced by a portfolio effect. It is therefore not obvious to allocate the contribution of each client to the total margin. Whilst such commingled margin is more cost-effective, the downside is that it creates additional risk, as parties would be exposed to each other's losses. For example, a client is exposed to the losses from other clients of the clearing member.[3] In the situation represented in Figure 11.7, consider a default of the

[3] Although only if the clearing member also defaults, as described below.

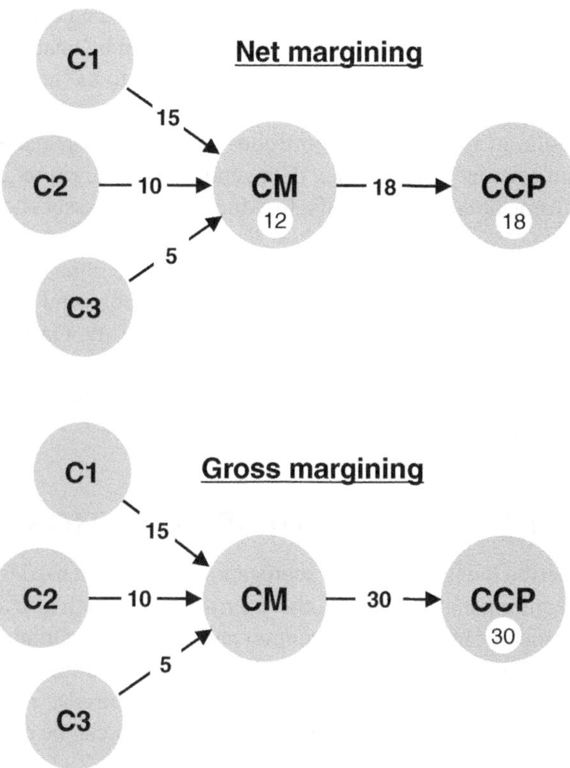

Figure 11.7 Illustration of net and gross initial margin requirements for clients. it is assumed that the clearing member charges client margin gross and holds the excess.

clearing member and client C1, with an associated loss of 15 on C1's portfolios. This loss is equal to the stand-alone margin requirement for C1's portfolio (i.e. it is not a completely improbable scenario). Yet, under net margining, this would have wiped out two thirds of the margin from the surviving clients C2 and C3 held at the CCP.[4]

Since gross margin is *additive* across clients, identification by a CCP of how much of a clearing member's margin is attributable to a particular client (for example) is more straightforward since this will represent the initial margin requirement for that portfolio on a stand-alone basis. Additionally, such margin could more obviously be legally and operationally segregated. On the other hand, since net margin would be reduced by a portfolio effect, it is not clear how much margin to allocate to each client.

Net margining does not prevent segregation. However, to facilitate segregation of client margins held by a CCP, some calculation would need to be made by the clearing member and provided to the CCP on a frequent basis. This would then define dynamically which component of the total initial margin posted by the clearing member should be allocated to a given client. It could be argued that gross margining is more consistent with the idea of segregation.

However, using gross margins does not imply trivial segregation. There are still legal and operational hurdles to overcome to ensure efficient segregation. However, the amounts to

[4] C2 and C3 contribute initial margins of 6 and 3 respectively. The total margin from all clients is 18, of which 15 is lost on C1's default. Therefore, only a third of the client margin (3/9) remains.

segregate are more clearly defined by the initial margins required on each client subportfolio. There is the question of any excess margin that the CCP would be unable to identify without direction from a clearing member (this is sometimes referred to as 'unallocated excess', see discussion in section 11.3.3). For example, in Figure 11.7 (bottom) the CCP would expect margin of 30 as the sum of the individual portfolios of the three clients. Suppose it actually had 33 in the relevant account (for example, the overall initial margin requirement may have decreased), it would not be able to identify to which client to associate the extra 10% of margin.

In summary, net margin is cheaper but misaligned with the concept of segregation, and exposes clients to risks from defaults of their clearing member and other clients of their clearing member, as well as potentially compromising portability. On the other hand, gross margin is less risky and more consistent with segregation and can, in theory, guarantee there is sufficient margin for porting. However, this is a clearly more costly setup both in terms of loss allocation and operational aspects associated to segregation.

11.3 METHODS OF SEGREGATION

This section will describe the initial margin segregation approaches used in practice that conform to regulatory requirements. In general, these terms refer to both *operational* segregation (i.e. margin held physically in different accounts) and *legal* segregation (margin with legal protection as belonging to a single participant). We will also see that operational and legal segregation can differ in certain circumstances and that either assets or their value may be subject to segregation rules. In general, methods of segregation can be characterised as:

- *No segregation:* The case of no segregation would give no protection on initial margin posted, and a client would potentially be fully at risk by the failure of their clearing member, clients of the clearing member and the CCP itself. This is not used in practice.
- *Omnibus segregation:* This refers to segregation between the account of the clearing member (the 'house account') and those of their clients (the 'omnibus account'). Typically, margin in a house account can be used to cover losses of a client of that member, but not vice versa. However, *all* assets in an omnibus account can be used to meet the obligations of a given client.
- *Legal segregation:* This corresponds to commingled accounts where the contribution of each client is tracked and legally (but not operationally) segregated.
- *Full physical segregation:* This is full physical segregation on an operational basis.

Net margining would more naturally apply to no segregation and gross margining would be more obviously suited to legal or full physical segregation. As shown in section 11.2.3, omnibus segregation could use either net or gross margining. The case of no segregation is not covered since this does not occur in practice (and is generally not allowed by regulation) as all account structures used in practice involve some degree of segregation.

The general trend seems to be that fully physically segregated gross margin is viewed as an ideal solution but potentially also rather costly, and hence some form of commingling of margins is a reasonable additional option. Segregation considerations may also be driven by the nature of the clearing member's client portfolios, for example, whether they are likely to be ported individually or collectively.

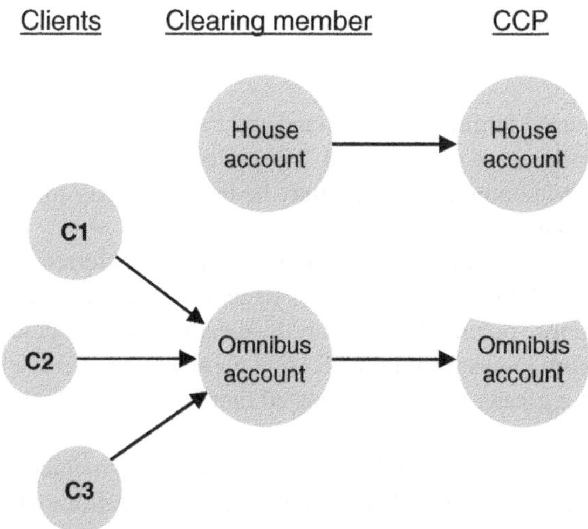

Figure 11.8 Illustration of omnibus segregation. As shown, the clearing member does not post the margin to the CCP in entirety, which could be the case if margin were required on a gross basis by the clearing member but passed to the CCP on a net basis.

11.3.1 Omnibus segregation

Omnibus segregation, sometimes referred to as the US futures style approach, refers to the commingling of client margin in a consolidated or omnibus account, which means that client margins are effectively mixed by the CCP. The omnibus account is segregated from the account of the clearing member themselves (the house account) and other omnibus accounts (if they exist), as shown in Figure 11.8. Positions in the omnibus account can be netted, and the CCP may require margin for client positions on either a net (historically used in US futures markets) or gross basis. In the former case (as shown), not all the margin may need to be passed to the CCP and some may still be held by the clearing member.

Margin held in an omnibus account is not exposed to losses on other accounts, but is at risk of losses within that account. This method of segregation therefore puts a client's margin at risk in the event of a default by their clearing member, together with default(s) of other clients of that clearing member[5] (known as 'fellow customer risk'). In such a case, the loss waterfall to allocate losses on the client account would proceed as follows:

- Initial margin of the client.
- Any remaining initial margin (in the house account) of the clearing member.
- Any remaining default fund of the clearing member.

The latter two components would also be impacted by the clearing member's own default and (if relevant) the default of any other clients. If the above resources are not sufficient, the remaining margin in the omnibus account (from non-defaulting clients) would be used before the mutualised default fund.

[5] Note that a given client is only exposed to other clients in the event of the default of the clearing member, as otherwise the clearing member will remain contractually responsible over the client margin.

Whether margin is taken by the CCP on a net or gross basis, also influences the loss dynamics:

- *Net omnibus structure:* Margins are calculated and transferred on a net basis. Mutual client risk exists since margins are commingled. Margin of other non-defaulting clients held in that clearing member's omnibus account may be used to satisfy the overall margin shortfall in the client account.
- *Gross omnibus structure:* Margins are calculated and transferred on a gross basis and suffer the same mutual client risk as above. Excess margin may be held by the clearing member and is therefore potentially at risk if the clearing member defaults.[6] Whilst there is more margin to absorb losses from joint clearing member and client defaults, an individual client is exposed to a greater risk having posted more margin.

Omnibus segregation clearly offers efficiencies: the clearing member may either call for less margin on a net basis or (more likely) hold excess margin from which they may derive returns, thereby potentially reducing charges levied on clients. It is also operationally less intensive as individual accounts do not need to be set up. However, the cost of this segregation is that clients are exposed to losses arising from the default of other clients. This effect can also be seen as a form of moral hazard since strong credit quality clients of a clearing member are exposed to the risk of weaker clients. Omnibus accounts also hinder portability since margins are commingling and may be insufficient for porting to be successful (unless all client positions can be ported together).

It is also important to note that omnibus segregation would not fulfil the requirements for a bank to benefit from relatively small capital charges to qualifying CCPs when clearing through another clearing member (see section 10.4.9).

11.3.2 Individually segregated accounts

The mutual client risk in an omnibus account can be avoided through a greater level of segregation (Figure 11.9). If client margin is held in individual accounts at the CCP level, then margin in a client account can only be used to cover losses related to the default of that client. In such as setup, margin would clearly need to be required on a gross basis and, additionally, any margin in excess of that called by the CCP should ideally be passed on to the CCP, also to gain protection. Individual account segregation aims to ensure that a client's assets are not available to be used to satisfy the obligations of other clients of the clearing member. A client is then protected from the failure of their clearing member and other clients of their clearing member. This also maximises the possibility of porting since the gross initial margin should be available and protected in any default scenario.

Individual accounts will clearly be more expensive since CCPs cannot mutualise losses across omnibus accounts and must increase loss absorbency elsewhere (e.g. by having a larger default fund). Such increased costs are likely to be passed on via clearing members to clients. The maintenance of separate accounts is also more operationally costly.

Even in a fully segregated case, the client is still at risk to CCP loss allocation. This is because clearing members generally make their obligations to clients conditional on the CCP performing on its obligations. To avoid this risk, there is the possibility of a 'full asset

[6] In the 'gross omnibus with excess' structure described later, this margin is also passed to the CCP.

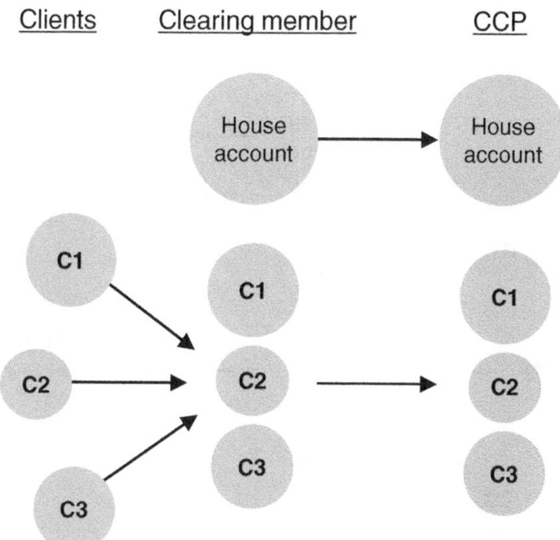

Figure 11.9 Illustration of individually segregated accounts. Margin would be required on a gross basis. In the case of non-cash margin, segregation may be of the assets themselves or their (post-haircut) value.

segregation' solution where the client deals directly with a CCP and their initial margin is protected by the loss waterfall in a similar way to that of members (the client would then only be exposed to the default of the CCP). The client also faces the risk from the failure of their clearing member and costs relating to the porting of positions (e.g. higher initial margins required) or the inability to port positions (e.g. losses due to the price achieved in an auction). If segregation is based on the value of assets (after haircuts have been applied) then liquidation risk also exists. Finally, the client is also exposed to any legal or operational problems associated with the segregation.

11.3.3 LSOC

The legally segregated operationally commingled (LSOC) protection model aims to balance the benefits of omnibus and individual segregation, and has been driven by regulatory requirements in the US,[7] although as yet is not a requirement under any other regulations and does not appear in the CPSS-IOSCO guidelines. (Note that whilst LSOC is currently a US requirement, we will still use general terms below such as 'clearing member' and not the US-specific terms such as 'FCM'.)

The main goal of LSOC is to protect against fellow customer risk (described in section 11.3.1) for omnibus segregation, without losing the operational benefits of combining client accounts. The LSOC model is illustrated in Figure 11.10. A CCP must separate client and house accounts, and the former can be held together but must be allocated to each client with such allocation updated at least daily. The aim of this is to eliminate fellow customer risk where a clearing member and their client(s) default simultaneously. In such a case, the initial

[7] LSOC was suggested by the CFTC in 2010.

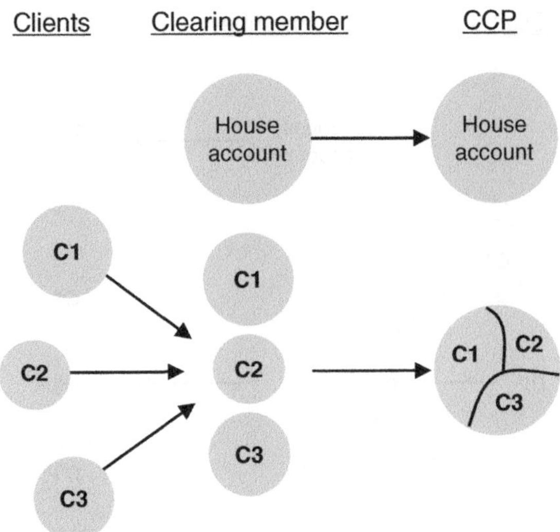

Figure 11.10 Illustration of the LSOC account structure. At the CCP level, the client margin is legally segregated although from an operational point of view it is commingled.

margin of other surviving clients is legally segregated at the CCP and cannot be used to cover any resulting losses (even when such losses have exhausted any initial margin and default funds held directly against them). LSOC would most obviously be used in conjunction with gross margining to enhance portability, although in theory net margins could be used.[8]

To achieve the LSOC model, whilst client margins are still pooled, the clearing member makes a segregation calculation and may (depending on the precise method used) report to the CCP the margin attributable to a given client in relation to the initial margin required by the CCP. The clearing member assures the CCP that it has not used any client margin to meet the obligations of other clients. In order for this to be possible, the following operational requirements must be met:

- Clients are identified to the CCP (in the case of new clients this must occur as soon as a trade is cleared).
- The CCP must have full information on the portfolio of each client.
- Margin attribution is either obvious to the CCP (which would be the case for gross margins with no excesses), or is reported by the clearing member to the CCP daily.

If one or more clients default and then the clearing member in turn defaults, the CCP can use margins attributed only to a particular client to offset losses arising from their own default, and not the default of other clients. In some setups, a CCP may be able to use the margin of non-defaulted clients at the bottom of the waterfall (e.g. after the mutualised default fund and

[8] However, regulators may mandate the use of gross (initial) margins. For example, CFTC regulation 39.13(g)(8) states '[a] derivatives clearing organization shall require its clearing members to collect customer initial margin, as defined in Sec. 1.3 of this chapter, from their customers, for nonhedge positions, at a level that is greater than 100% of the derivatives clearing organization's initial margin requirements with respect to each product and swap portfolio.' See http://www.cftc.gov/LawRegulation/FederalRegister/FinalRules/2012-1033.

potentially the CCP's own capital). Due to the likely provision of aggressive loss allocation methods at this point, this may make only a small difference in practice. Regulation may give protection to a client for any margin posted via the clearing member to the CCP in this way.[9]

One complexity of LSOC is the treatment of excess margin, which is an amount required by the clearing member in excess of the initial margin required by the CCP (see Figure 8.4 in section 8.2.2). As mentioned above, this represents a buffer above the initial margin for new trades and/or due to the risk the clearing member has in meeting obligations of the CCP before being able to collect margins from the client. In the 'LSOC without excess' model,[10] the CCP accepts only the initial margin required and the clearing member holds the excess amount. Such an approach is more straightforward, assuming gross margining is used, as it does not require the clearing member to report to the CCP the breakdown of initial margins since the CCP will expect to receive the sum of stand-alone requirements for all clients. However, the CCP will be left holding excess margin when initial margin requirements drop and before this margin is requested by the clearing member to be returned. Additionally, sometimes clearing members may, temporarily at least, fund incremental client initial margin by posting to the CCP before they have received the relevant amount from the client. In such a case, the initial margin would (incorrectly) be assumed by the CCP to be client margin. Such discrepancies may only exist for short periods.

In the 'LSOC with excess' model, the situation becomes more complex as the extra excess margin needs to be pledged to the CCP. This is operationally more difficult as there must be daily reporting of the excess margin by the clearing member to the CCP to inform them which part of the excess belongs to which client. In certain situations, such as a clearing member allocating more margin than actually exists (post-haircuts), such a report may be rejected. Without any further information, the CCP will define any additional margin as 'unallocated excess', which would be returned to the clearing member in the event of their default but not attributed to any of their clients. In the event that a client's initial margin requirement reduces, the CCP would also categorise the reduction as unallocated excess. Such excess would not be automatically allocated by the CCP to, for example, the increased initial margin requirements of another client. Such a re-allocation, if possible, would only be made after further instruction from the clearing member. Whilst more complex, 'LSOC with excess' offers more protection and seems to be the standard method emerging. Regulation has again moved to provide protection to excess margin posted in this way.[11]

In the event of clients posting assets and not cash, legal segregation in the LSOC model is based on the post-haircut value. If haircuts are conservative then the CCP may use the additional value across all client positions (i.e. it is not segregated vis-à-vis a particular client). If haircuts are too small then the total client margins will need to be reduced on a pro rata basis (and a given client account may therefore be under-margined).

As mentioned above, gross margining applies only to initial margins. It follows that variation margin can still be posted on a net basis and correspondingly represents certain risks for clients. Typically, a CCP is responsible only for the *net* variation margin of all clients of a defaulted clearing member. This means that a client with a variation margin gain at the time

[9] For example, CFTC regulation 22.15, http://www.cftc.gov/ucm/groups/public/@lrfederalregister/documents/file/2012-1033a.pdf.

[10] There is also the 'LSOC with unallocated excess' model where excess margin will be passed to the CCP but the CCP does not know the client-specific nature of this excess margin. In the event of the default of the clearing member, the CCP cannot use this unallocated excess margin and must return it to the estate of the defaulted member.

[11] For example, CFTC regulation 22.13.

of default of their clearing member does not have recourse to the CCP for this amount, and will instead only have a claim on the estate of their defaulted clearing member (which may include gains made after this default and prior to the porting or close out of their trades). Variation margins will typically be separated from initial margins so, for example, a CCP requiring additional initial margin but needing to pay back variation margin will only do the latter when the former has been received (i.e. it will not offset initial and variation margins in opposite directions).

The LSOC with excess method seems a likely contender to be the market standard account structure for OTC client clearing in the future (as least as far as regulation is concerned). However, whilst having all excess margin held by the CCP protects a client against the default of the clearing member and other clients, some potential risks and problems do exist:

- Clients may not be guaranteed to receive the actual assets posted. This is a potential problem for pension funds and asset managers, as margins would correspond to actual investments made. Furthermore, only the post-haircut value of assets may be protected.
- The margin posted is potentially subject to investment risk.
- LSOC rules do not typically apply to variation margin. Hence, any variation margin posted by a client that contributes to a net variation margin loss across other clients is not protected by the CCP.
- The client is at risk of fraud or operational errors by the clearing member, which they would not be as exposed to in a full segregation model

11.3.4 Example

As an example of the above segregation concepts, the following is a description of the account structures available at LCH.Clearnet (for OTC and other products) under EMIR regulation.[12] As shown in Figure 11.11, the following accounts are available for clients (note that under EMIR it is not a requirement to offer an LSOC account):

- *OSA Net:*[13] In this case, margins from clients are collected on a net basis and held in a single omnibus account. Typically, this is used for exchange-traded products.
- *OSA Gross:* This is as above but with gross margins collected. In the event of default, each client has shared claims over the assets in the account for the purpose of porting or liquidation.
- *ISA (individually segregated account):* Margin is not commingled with any other client or house margins and therefore can be subject to independent porting procedures. An 'asset tagging' model can be used to protect assets which can be ported physically (rather than just the post-haircut value).

The growth of OTC clearing is prompting CCPs to continue to develop a range of account structures for client clearing based on a series of options such as:

- Margin segregated from that of other clients (to prevent fellow customer risk).

[12] http://www.lchclearnet.com/about_us/corporate_governance/ltd_account_structures_under_emir.asp.

[13] OSA stands for Omnibus Segregated Account.

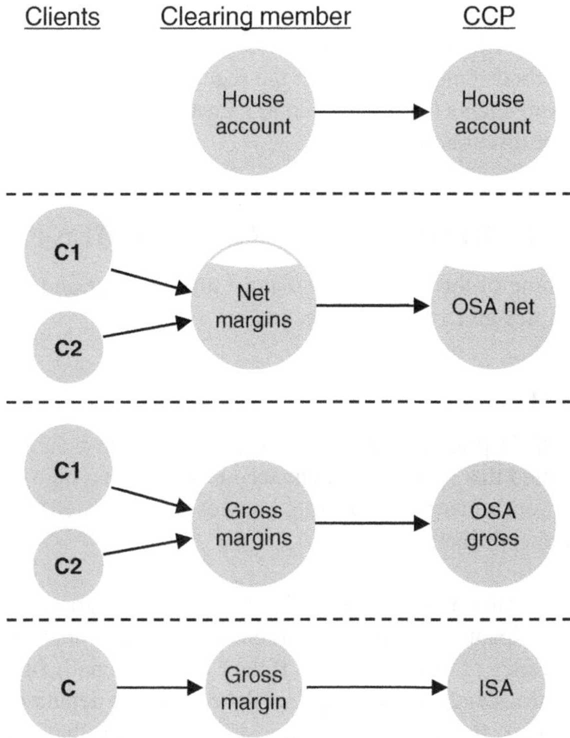

Figure 11.11 Illustration of different account structures offered by LCH.Clearnet under EMIR.

- Are the actual assets or just their value segregated? (in the former case to mitigate against liquidation risk.)
- Segregate with third party custodian or not? (SwapClear 'Premium Segregated Account Offering'.)

For example, SwapClear[14] has further recently disclosed segregation plans based on segregation method (omnibus or individual) and the type of protection (asset or value). The latter case determines whether the actual securities are posted (which can be ported directly) as opposed to only their value. This leads to four account structures named AssetOmni, AssetSeg, ValueOmni and ValueSeg. In AssetOmni and ValueOmni clients are exposed to fellow customer risk but in the former case not to the decline in value of other clients' margin securities. There is also a fifth 'premium segregated' account structure where assets are held by a custodian of the client's choosing.

11.3.5 The liquidity impact of segregation

Segregation clearly offers greater protection to clients. However, legal and operational segregation limits rehypothecation or reuse of assets and will clearly have a negative liquidity

[14] http://www.swapclear.com/service/customer_protection_under_emir.html.

effect. Given that CCPs already require high-quality liquid assets, segregation approaches could amplify any negative liquidity impacts of clearing. This in turn is likely to lead to margin transformation methods emerging to meet the requirements from CCPs for high-quality assets and the need from clients for segregation as a means to protect their margin assets (see next chapter for further discussion).

11.4 REGULATORY REQUIREMENTS

This section details some of the different regulatory rules in relation to client margins with reference to the principles given in the last section.

11.4.1 CPSS-IOSCO

The CPSS-IOSCO (2012) principles provide some guidance on behaviour with respect to client clearing. It is noted that individual client accounts provide a high degree of protection by restricting use of client's margin to covering only losses associated with that client. CPSS IOSCO (2012) recommends that:

> A CCP should, at a minimum, have segregation and portability arrangements that effectively protect a participant's customers' positions and related collateral [margin] from the default or insolvency of that participant. If the CCP additionally offers protection of such customer positions and collateral against the concurrent default of the participant and a fellow customer, the CCP should take steps to ensure that such protection is effective.[15]

This requires omnibus segregation as a minimum but does not require further segregation. CPSS-IOSCO (2012) also requires the CCP to disclose whether client margin is protected on an individual or omnibus basis.

11.4.2 Dodd–Frank/CFTC

The following discussion corresponds to requirements around products designated as swaps under Dodd–Frank (this is not precisely defined but seems to apply generally to OTC derivatives as opposed to, for example futures, and is therefore relevant from the point of view of OTC clearing). In the US, the *Dodd–Frank Act* requires that any person holding assets from a client to margin or guarantee swaps cleared through a CCP must register as a futures commission merchant ('FCM'). FCMs must segregate client margin from their own funds, separately account for these assets, and furthermore not use such margin to guarantee transactions of their own proprietary clients or those of other clients.

Further to the above, in 2012 the CFTC[16] required the LSOC model to be implemented together with gross margining (variation margin can still be settled on a net basis). This represented a balance between the full legal protection offered by full segregation and the greater efficiencies of other approaches. LSOC is intended to facilitate porting of client positions and

---

[15] CPSS-IOSCO (2012) principle 14.

[16] 'Protection of Cleared Swaps Customer Contracts and Collateral; Conforming Amendments to the Commodity Broker Bankruptcy Provisions', http://www.cftc.gov/PressRoom/Events/ssLINK/federalregister011112d.

margin in the event of a failure of an FCM. The LSOC rule does not address the investment risks faced by clients.

11.4.3 EMIR

The European Market Infrastructure Regulation (EMIR), which makes the clearing of standardised swaps in Europe mandatory, essentially specifies that CCPs must offer a minimum of two account structures:

- An Omnibus Segregated Account model (OSA), which segregates clearing member positions and assets from those of their clients. It is not specified whether such an account should be margined on a net or gross basis.
- An Individually Segregated Account model (ISA), where excess margin is posted to the CCP and distinguished from the margin of other clients.

EMIR also specifies that CCPs must offer portability in each account structure. Gross omnibus accounts can be extended to be legally segregated but operationally commingled to mimic the LSOC structure matching the regulations issued by the CFTC under Dodd Frank. EMIR differs from Dodd Frank in requiring the offering of 'individual client segregation'. Such clients will obviously gain a higher degree of protection at greater cost.

11.4.4 Basel III and capital implications

Basel III capital requirements for CCPs (discussed in detail in section 10.4) propose favourable capital treatment for OTC derivatives exposures that are centrally cleared if, among other things, the CCP and/or clearing member effectively segregate client positions and assets, and assure portability in the event of a clearing member insolvency.

Part IV

Analysis of the Impact and Risks of Central Clearing

12

Analysis of the Impact of Clearing and Margining

Without reflection, we go blindly on our way, creating more unintended consequences, and failing to achieve anything useful.

Margaret J. Wheatley (1941–)

12.1 THE CLEARING LANDSCAPE

Based on estimates from the Financial Stability Board (FSB 2013) as of the start of 2013, around US$158 trillion and US$2.6 trillion of OTC interest rate derivatives and credit derivatives respectively were cleared. This represents 41% and 12% of the total outstanding notional amounts in these products respectively. This total OTC notional already represents more than double the exchange-traded derivative market size (e.g. see Figure 2.4).

A question that should be asked is what difficulties will exist in increasing clearing across the bilateral OTC derivative market. This chapter aims to assess the impact of clearing, and highlight the advantages and disadvantages that may influence the rate of increase of cleared OTC notional amounts. We will also discuss the liquidity impact of the mandatory clearing requirements and bilateral margining rules.

12.1.1 Bilateral vs. central clearing

We begin in Table 12.1 by contrasting at a high level some of the differences between bilateral and central clearing. Bilateral clearing follows a 'survivor pays' approach where parties hold capital against possible losses when their counterparties default. Such capital is typically calculated based on a one-year time horizon and is sensitive to credit quality (e.g. a bank would need to hold more capital against a weaker rated counterparty). As a result, the risk sensitivity and potential procyclicality of this capital is small. In theory, incentives are strong as losses are borne in general by those taking the risks, although the process in the event of default is uncoordinated, with each party closing out transactions individually. In a bilateral market, variation margin may be used, but typically not initial margins (historically).

Central clearing (and in terms of many characteristics bilateral initial margining) is very different and follows a 'defaulter pays' approach. The main loss absorbency is provided by initial margins. These are based on a short time horizon (e.g. five days for OTC clearing or 10 days for bilateral margining requirements) and are usually relatively insensitive to credit quality (section 9.2.3). This can potentially make initial margins much more sensitive to market factors, which in the extreme can lead to procyclicality (which in turn can be mitigated by aspects such as using long time horizons and stressed data periods). Loss mutualisation via

Table 12.1 Comparison of bilateral vs. central clearing. Note that bilateral initial margins correspond more closely to the central clearing characteristics.

	Bilateral clearing (no initial margin)	**Central clearing (bilateral clearing with initial margin)***
Model	Survivor pays	Defaulter pays
Loss absorbency	Capital	Initial margin (and default funds and capital)
Risk horizon	~1 year	~5 days
View	Long-term (e.g. based on fundamental credit analysis and ratings)	Short-term (e.g. dependent on short-term market volatility)
Credit quality sensitivity	Strong	Weak
Market risk sensitivity/ procyclicality	Small	Potentially large (although reduced by using stressed data, for example)
Incentive	Losses aligned to risks	Loss mutualisation and potential moral hazard
Default close out	Uncoordinated bilateral close out	Coordinated auctions
Margining	Variation margin or none	Variation and initial margin
Segregation	None	Initial margin segregation

* This shares many of the characteristics of central clearing but does not involve loss mutualisation or coordinated auctions.

default funds (and capital for default funds) is used to absorb large losses but potentially creates adverse incentives. There are centralised auctions for closing out a defaulter's portfolio which may be more efficient than close outs in bilateral markets. Both variation and initial margin are posted and the latter will normally require segregation, which is complex and costly to achieve.

Table 12.1 should illustrate that central clearing and initial margining has both advantages and disadvantages which may be difficult to define precisely (for example, risk sensitivity is probably a good thing but in the extreme can lead to procyclicality which is clearly not). What is also clear is that central clearing changes many aspects of OTC derivatives trading and the underlying risks. For example, looking only at loss absorbency in more detail, in a bilateral market with no margining this is based only on capital held by each party (Figure 12.1, top left), whereas in a bilateral market with margins[1] (Figure 12.1, top right) loss absorbency is provided jointly between capital and margins. However, in a centrally cleared market, a single capital amount is replaced by margins, mutualised default funds and the associated capital requirements for both these components[2] (Figure 12.1, bottom). Whether clearing is preferable is not obvious but it is certainly *different* and potentially more complicated.

It is also relevant to note that hedging introduces more complexity to the above. Consider the case of a bank providing a typical end user trade and executing the corresponding hedge

[1] Variation and potentially also initial margin.

[2] There are two distinct types of capital covering trade exposure and default fund exposures as described in section 10.4.2.

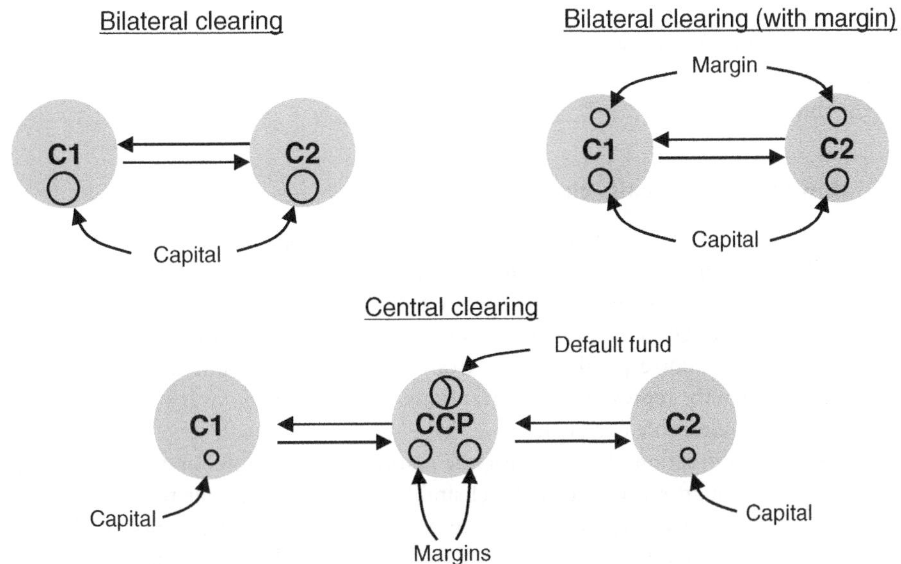

Figure 12.1 Comparison of loss allocation in bilateral (no margins), bilateral with margin and centrally cleared markets.

in bilateral and centrally cleared markets as shown in Table 12.2. In a bilateral market, there are two exposures that arise from the original trade and its hedge. The latter would typically be with another bank or financial institution under a margin agreement. In a centrally cleared market, we assume the institution in question is acting as a clearing member and the original trade therefore has bilateral exposure and an exposure to the relevant CCP. The hedge trade will now have an exposure to (potentially a different) CCP. This means that two exposures in a bilateral market become three[3] exposures in a centrally cleared one. There is also a potential proliferation of costs via initial margin and default fund requirements.

Table 12.2 Comparison of bilateral and centrally cleared markets showing the exposures created in a typical scenario when hedging an end user trade.

	Trade	**Hedge**
Bilateral market	Exposure to end user • CVA* • Capital*	Exposure to hedge counterparty • CVA* • Capital*
Centrally cleared market	Exposure to end user • CVA* • Capital* Exposure to CCP • Initial margin • Default fund • Default fund capital	Exposure to CCP • Initial margin • Default fund • Default fund capital

*Potentially reduced by any margin agreement.

[3] Note that if the institution executed a hedge with a non-clearing member then this would become four exposures, as they would act as clearing member for both the hedge and original transaction.

An issue also exists due to the bifurcation of bilateral trades especially for hedged positions. Given not all transactions can be cleared this can create inefficiencies as offsetting trades may fall into CCP and bilateral regimes. Such inefficiencies will be seen by increased costs (e.g. initial margins).

12.1.2 How much is currently cleared?

The only OTC market with a significant amount centrally cleared is that of interest rate products. FSB (2013) reports[4] that 41% of the current OTC interest rate market between G15 dealers is centrally cleared whilst an analysis by ISDA (2014) indicates a higher fraction of 56%.[5] The FSB data suggests that this figure could increase to 75% if all eligible transactions were cleared whilst the corresponding value from ISDA is 80%.[6] The non-clearable interest rate products are mainly represented by swaptions, cross-currency swaps and transactions denominated in non-clearable currencies.

Hence a significant fraction of the interest rate market that is eligible for clearing is already cleared but around a quarter is not currently clearable. In order to clear the remaining fraction two developments are necessary: the expansion of product coverage from global CCPs (e.g. interest rate swaptions) and the growth of local CCPs to clear other currencies (e.g. Mexican peso). There is obviously a question of to what extent such expansion should be pushed. The same question applies to the clearing of other products.

12.1.3 What should be cleared?

Historically, CCPs have been affiliated with exchanges and have therefore been responsible for the clearing of standard exchange-traded products. Such products are generally simple, liquid, short-dated and can readily be cleared. Furthermore, the initial margin requirements for exchange-traded products are relatively straightforward to quantify since these usually depend on characterising a single liquid risk factor (e.g. equity index) over a short time horizon (e.g. one-day).

Central clearing of OTC products presents a number of problems due to their relative complexity, illiquidity and long-dated characteristics compared to exchange-traded products. The considerations as to whether or not a given product is suitable for central clearing were discussed previously in section 8.2.4. It seems likely that only a relatively small number of OTC derivatives products are actually suitable. However, a large part of the OTC market can be cleared via a relatively small number of product types (for example, even the current level of cleared interest rate swaps is around a quarter of the total OTC derivatives market).[7]

There does seem, however, to be a general view that many OTC derivatives will not be centrally cleared. For example, Duffie et al. (2010) state 'There will remain a population of customized derivatives that are more suitably negotiated or risk-managed bilaterally. Whether or not derivatives contracts are traded or cleared centrally, there must be high standards

[4] See footnote 1.

[5] ISDA estimates that \$202 trillion of interest rate products are centrally cleared. This makes up 56% of the total market size of \$561 (reported earlier in Figure 2.5) when corrected for the double counting of CCP notionals.

[6] Note that ISDA (2014) reports the non-clearable fraction as 13% as they use the total size of the market including double counting of CCP positions as a reference.

[7] For example, using the value of US\$158 trillion quoted at the start of this chapter and the total size of the OTC derivatives market shown in Figure 2.4.

for collateral [margin] arrangements, operational infrastructure, and transparency.' A similar view is expressed by the Canadian Securities Administrators Derivatives Committee who state: 'For example, there may be a derivative contract for which a CCP cannot manage the risk and is therefore not suitable for a mandatory clearing obligation.'[8] CCPs themselves agree with this point, for example: 'Certain products don't lend themselves to going to the security of a clearing house. They are difficult to price and difficult to margin. It could actually damage the security of a clearing house to force things in there that shouldn't really be in there.'[9] Such comments are potentially problematic since they raise the issue that the most dangerous OTC derivatives, which are the ones more likely to cause the next financial crisis, may be too complex to be cleared.

It is hard to envisage exotic, illiquid or highly structured OTC derivatives being centrally cleared in the near future, or ever. Furthermore, the costs attributed to clearing even non-standard derivatives may prove to be prohibitive. However, a danger here is that the most important products to be cleared through CCPs are probably the most risky, from the point of view of the stability of the CCP, and vice versa. As noted by Heller and Vaus (2012), 'Derivatives that are hard to value and which may consequently experience jumps in valuations and poor market liquidity could represent intolerable risks for CCPs.' This leads to the question of why, if an OTC derivative represents an 'intolerable' risk for a CCP, it would it be left in a (supposedly more dangerous) bilateral market.

Standardisation of products to aid central clearing is a major hurdle but a necessary one so that CCPs can offer broad product coverage. We noted in section 8.2.4 that a contract could be standardised but still complex. This is a particularly important point to note for credit derivatives products. A single-name CDS is standard and has a payoff that appears quite simple: it is a swap where one party pays a premium in return for receiving a contingent payment if a pre-specified credit event occurs. However, we could also describe this product as being an out-of-the-money digital barrier option (see discussion in section 8.2.4). A CDS index would then be a portfolio of out-of-the-money barrier options. Furthermore, CDS contracts are relatively illiquid (compared to interest rate swaps for example) and become even more so in a crisis. The standardisation of a product does not make it less complex or more liquid and may simply hide the complexity. Complexity of products can increase adverse selection problems where clearing members have better knowledge of the inherent risk of a trade than the CCP through which they clear.

A related question is whether simple and relatively low-risk OTC products should be cleared (on the basis that this should be reasonably easy) or exempt (since they do not represent a danger to financial markets). An example of these opposing views has been illustrated with respect to FX products. Market participants have resisted the idea of central clearing for FX products on the basis that the exposures are generally much smaller and settlement risk is the most significant risk (see section 4.2.6). However, Duffie (2011) argues against this, pointing out that whilst many contracts are short-dated, some FX trades have significant credit exposure because FX rates can be volatile, have fat tails and be linked strongly to sovereign risk.

[8] Canadian Securities Administrators, CSA Consultation Paper 91-406, 'Derivatives: OTC Central Counterparty Clearing', http://www.osc.gov.on.ca/documents/en/Securities-Category9/csa_20120620_91-406_counterparty-clearing.pdf.

[9] Speech by Mark Ibbotson COO of NYSE Liffe, 3 June 2009, Mondo Visione Exchange Forum and referenced in Norman (2011).

The problem with the acceptance that many products cannot be cleared is that it seems to go against some of the fundamental aims of clearing in relation to the global financial crisis (GFC). With possible hindsight bias, the failure and bailout of AIG is often cited as a reason for mandatory clearing. Large banks had purchased large amounts of default protection in the form of credit default swaps on subprime mortgages from AIG's financial products subsidiary (AIGFP). Following the ratings downgrade of AIG, AIGFP was unable to post the massive amounts of margin that it was contractually obliged to do. Due to a potentially severe systemic contagion effect, US authorities decided to essentially bail out AIG for an amount in excess of US$100 billion. An example of the view that mandatory clearing would have prevented the AIG situation is (IMF 2010) 'If these contracts had been novated to central counterparties, the collateral [margin] calls still would have been problematic for AIG, but they would have come sooner and more frequently. Hence, uncollateralized exposures would not have been given the chance to build to levels that became systemically critical.' Such arguments seem to ignore the fact that the trades that AIGFP engaged in were non-clearable due to their complexity and AIGFP did not even post full variation margin, let alone initial margin.

With the above comments in mind, there are two schools of thought with respect to centrally cleared products. The first is that by clearing products that are relatively easy to deal with, such as interest rate swaps, a large fraction of OTC derivatives notional can be centrally cleared with the residual remaining forever bilateral. An alternative view could be that the products that are difficult to clear are precisely the biggest danger in terms of potential future financial crises. The latter view would imply that a long-term aim should be to clear as many OTC derivatives as possible. However, OTC market products tend to be customised, and relatively illiquid, which limits the ability to clear them through a CCP. As a minimum, a certain amount of standardisation of contractual terms is required before a product can be cleared by a CCP. Moreover, CCPs may not see it as beneficial to clear certain low-volume products where the cost of product development dominates the potential profits from clearing.

12.1.4 The number of CCPs

The quantitative study by Duffie and Zhu (2010) finds, not surprisingly, that it is inefficient to have more than one CCP in the market due to the loss of netting benefits. The multilateral netting advantages and efficiency gains from other economies of scale (e.g. of operational costs) suggest a relatively small number of CCPs is preferable to a larger CCP population. For example, if the same product is cleared by two CCPs, the loss of netting efficiencies will increase capital requirements for CCP members (and their clients), and potentially increase the costs in the event of a close out where CCPs may need to replace offsetting positions that could otherwise be netted.

However, there are number of factors that will push the total number of CCPs upwards. Jurisdictional fragmentation is the first obvious hurdle to CCP consolidation as regulators in several major jurisdictions have made it clear that products traded (or firms located) within their region must be cleared there. Indeed, clearing across jurisdictions gives rise to complicated legal problems such as differences in bankruptcy law. Jurisdictional fragmentation will reduce the benefit of economies of scale and potentially complicate coordination in a crisis where multiple CCPs may be closing out portfolios of the same defaulting clearing member.

CCPs clearing two or more different types of products are also problematic. The more liquid product would likely be closed out more quickly and have access to the defaulter's initial margin and default fund before claims for the more illiquid product were met. This could create an effective priority where members predominantly trading in the more liquid products (for example, interest rate swaps compared to credit default swaps) would benefit by having an effective first claim on initial margins and default funds. The possibility of unequal treatment can be avoided by product separation within a CCP which will clearly be more expensive. It is also avoided by having OTC CCPs where only one asset class (or several asset classes of similar liquidity) is cleared. This is one reason why some OTC CCPs have been focused around a single asset class and even product type.

The number of CCPs also depends on competition. In one sense, competition may be preferable, as market forces will determine that the CCP landscape and costs (via margins) may be competitive. There is likely to be a degree of consolidation of CCPs to reflect competitive forces. An OTC CCP may start with a single goal and therefore be focused in terms of region and asset classes. Growth will naturally involve expanding the geographical base, markets and products covered. The move to central clearing is naturally limited in the early stages due to the lack of benefit until a critical mass of products is cleared. Too much competition may be counterproductive for the overall risks that CCPs represent. Competition between CCPs can be dangerous and perhaps a preferable solution would be a single monopolistic CCP that concentrates on strong and conservative risk management and not on providing attractive costs to potential members.

In reality, many competing forces will define the number of CCPs that exist globally and policymakers, regulators and market participants will face difficult trade-offs when determining the best legal and jurisdictional arrangements. The balance of forces described above means that it seems likely that some sort of equilibrium may be established with the total number of CCPs. Jurisdictional considerations are likely to result in multiple CCPs for a given product, preventing economies of scale. It seems reasonable that the financial markets would be best served via a reasonable number of CCPs, which are large enough to offer good product coverage but not so large that they creates monopolistic issues, severe systemic risk or geopolitical problems.

12.1.5 Choosing a CCP

Given there will be a significant number of CCPs, a question will arise in terms of the choice of which CCP to use. For a clearing member, such a decision may depend upon:

- *Regulatory recognition:* Whether or not a CCP is recognised by a national regulator (potentially as a recognised third country CCP) will be a primary consideration since it will fundamentally influence capital requirements.
- *CCP rules and requirements:* The membership requirements of the CCP with respect to minimum capital, operational aspects (e.g. frequency of margin posting, fire drills and auctions) and default fund contributions.
- *Product coverage:* The range of products offered by the CCP that can lead to netting and margining benefits.
- *Margining:* The eligibility of various forms of securities as margin, and the initial margin calculation methodology, are key aspects in determining the quality and quantity of (initial) margin that would need to be posted. The possibility of cross-margining across different products or even with other CCPs would also be relevant considerations.

- *Client clearing:* The offering of the CCP in terms of client clearing (e.g. segregation methods) and the potential number of clients who may be interested in accessing the CCP through the clearing member.
- *Diversification:* A large clearing member would likely have a substantial exposure to a CCP due to the large volume of trades they may clear. A key decision is to what extent this exposure may be deemed too large and the clearing member may therefore diversify by clearing the same products with another CCP with the loss of diversification benefits.[10] Aspects such as the potential systemic importance of the CCP and their support in a financial crisis would also play a role in this decision.

With respect to clients, additional considerations when choosing a CCP would be the methods of segregation that they are offering and also the likelihood of being able to port their portfolio in the event of default of a clearing member (see also the discussion in section 11.1.5).

12.2 BENEFITS AND DRAWBACKS OF OTC CLEARING

In this section, we consider the advantages and disadvantages of clearing (and initial margining) and describe some of the important differences between bilateral and centrally cleared markets. The aim is not (and should not be) to define whether (OTC) clearing is beneficial or not overall. Clearing has strengths and weaknesses and will therefore be beneficial in certain products and less so in others.

12.2.1 Advantages

A CCP performs many functions and therefore offers a number of distinct advantages compared to bilateral OTC markets. Some of the potential advantages of central clearing are:

- *Multilateral netting:* Contracts traded between different counterparties but cleared through a CCP can be netted. This increases the flexibility to enter new transactions and terminate existing ones and may reduce margin costs. In bilateral markets, there is a strong incentive to return to original counterparties to unwind positions creating a bargaining position for banks with respect to their clients. Netting efficiencies created by clearing can balance this effect.
- *Credit risk mitigation:* A CCP reduces the need for credit risk assessment of multiple counterparties and provides a separation of market risk and credit risk. This is essentially achieved via loss mutualisation so that when a default creates losses that exceed the financial commitments from the defaulting member, these losses are distributed, reducing their impact on any one member. Thus a counterparty's losses are dispersed partially throughout the market, making their impact less dramatic and lessening the possibility of systemic problems.
- *Price transparency and fungibility:* CCPs create price transparency since cleared products are subject to variation margin requirements based on mark-to-market prices determined by the CCP. Such price transparency reduces disputes about margin requirements.

[10] These netting benefits could be restored via interoperability and cross-margining between CCPs but this then would create more concentration risk.

Fungibility makes trading out of positions through a CCP easy and due to netting benefits, unlike bilateral markets, can be done with any other counterparty.

- *Legal and operational efficiency:* The margining, netting and settlement functions undertaken by a CCP potentially increase operational efficiency and reduce costs. CCPs may also reduce legal risks in providing a centralisation of rules and mechanisms.
- *Liquidity:* A CCP will improve market liquidity by allowing market participants to trade easily and benefit from multilateral netting. Market entry is enhanced through the ability to trade anonymously and the mitigation of counterparty risk. Derivatives traded through a CCP need to be valued on a daily basis due to daily margining and cashflow payments, leading to a more transparent pricing of products.
- *Transparency:* A CCP can monitor clearing members' aggregate activity across products and therefore evaluate the risks faced by individual market participants. This may disperse panic that might otherwise be present in bilateral markets due to a lack of knowledge of the exposure faced by certain institutions. On the other hand, a particularly large exposure will be discouraged via aspects such as margin multipliers (section 9.4.2) and a CCP is potentially in a position to identify and prevent such exposures becoming excessive. Central clearing can play an important role in supporting standardisation and competition in derivative markets.
- *Portability:* Clients can be protected from clearing member failure and are potentially able to port trades to another clearing member in a default (or other) situation. The netting benefits of porting all of a defaulted client's trades (and indeed sometimes multiple clients) may create stability as these trades will not need to be closed out.
- *Default management:* A well-managed central auction means that transactions are more easily hedged, offset and replaced following a clearing member default. This may result in smaller price disruptions than uncoordinated replacement of positions during a crisis period. Netting also reduces the total number of positions and notional amount that needs to be replaced in the event of a default, which may reduce price impact from terminating a large portfolio. A CCP may also be in a better position to 'war game' and resolve potential problems in OTC derivative markets.

Of course, not all of the above can be seen as unambiguous advantages of CCPs compared to bilateral markets. In some cases it could be questioned whether a true overall advantage exists as, for example, loss mutualisation to manage credit risk may create moral hazard problems (section 10.1.1). Furthermore, it could be argued that some of the functions are potentially redundant, for example, bilateral trade compression (section 5.2.3) can be used to facilitate multilateral netting.

12.2.2 Disadvantages

As with the benefits of clearing, it is not possible to list definitive and completely objective drawbacks, but some of the obvious disadvantages of central clearing for OTC derivatives are:

- *Cost:* CCPs impose potentially large charges via initial margins and fees. Clearing members face further charges through default fund contributions and capital requirements. The significant increase in overall margin, together with the liquidity, credit quality and no rehypothecation requirements, will add up to a significant overall cost. Additional safety such as segregation and portability arrangements increase such costs further.

- *Netting bifurcation:* Multiple CCPs reduce netting benefits. A significant amount of bilateral OTC derivative positions will also exist due to non-standard contracts together with end user and foreign exchange exemptions. This 'unbundling' of cleared and non-cleared trades causes problems and may lead to multilateral netting benefits not dominating over the loss of bilateral benefits (section 5.2.6).
- *Margin procyclicality:* Whilst a moderate increase in margins during more volatile periods may not be unreasonable, a significant increase in margins close to a crisis period could have a destabilising impact on prices and create contagion effects (margin procyclicality can be obviously reduced by conservative assumptions, such as the use of stress periods, but this will then in turn increase costs).
- *Duplication:* CCPs will have to duplicate many functions that already exist in large banks such as settlement functionality, risk management, margining procedures and legal support. Regulators will have to supervise more systemically important financial institutions (SIFIs). There may be a significant barrier to entry into certain markets due to the inherent costs of clearing. Regulatory arbitrage will potentially increase, driven by exemptions and different clearing requirements across regions and asset classes.
- *Operational risk:* CCPs through their rules, such as margin requirements, potentially create a more tightly coupled system where operational problems may be amplified.

12.2.3 Homogenisation

A key feature of central clearing is homogenisation. In bilateral market, differences in prices are driven largely by credit quality, margin terms and funding costs. CCPs remove such differences and potentially create a more homogeneous market where counterparties are interchangeable. This enhances fungibility but creates other pricing dependencies such as through CCP-specific rules (for example, initial margin requirements).

If a major OTC derivatives player defaults in a bilateral market, it may not be clear how big the associated counterparty risk losses will be, nor which institutions will be most exposed. This uncertainty is mitigated through a CCP allocating extreme losses across all members. The neutrality and ability of a CCP to disperse losses mitigates information asymmetry that can propagate stress events in bilateral markets, which should reduce systemic risk.

In a centrally cleared market using a CCP, all parties are more or less equal and the CCP acts as guarantor for all obligations. An institution has no need to assess the creditworthiness of counterparties they trade with through the CCP and may therefore reduce resources spent on monitoring individual members. An institution with better than average risk management (credit quality assessment, margin management, hedging) may lose out in this situation. In a bilateral market, the pricing of CVA (section 7.3.1) will naturally cause institutions with a worsening credit quality to have higher costs and therefore provide an incentive to improve their financial health. However, when clearing through a CCP, as long as a member is posting the relevant margin, the issue of their declining credit quality may be ignored, at least up to a point (for example, see the discussion on the removal of rating triggers on initial margin requirements in section 9.2.3). This may allow poor-quality institutions to build up bigger positions than they would normally be able to do in bilateral markets. Heterogeneity of CCP members will cause problems as member interests diverge. The problems that the Euro currency has suffered from 2010 gives a sense of the potential difficulties with heterogeneity in a membership organisation.

12.2.4 Moral hazard and informational asymmetry

CCPs face an asymmetric information problem since their members (generally large banks) may have better information about the valuation and risk of the relatively complex OTC derivatives being cleared (Pirrong 2012b). This could be particularly acute if CCPs try to provide clearing services for more complex and/or illiquid OTC derivatives, where CCP risk managers are likely to be at a serious informational disadvantage to clearing members and exposed to potential adverse selection. Of course, CCPs can try to mitigate informational asymmetries, but this will potentially lead to excessive costs through, for example, CCP rules and margin requirements. This could making clearing too expensive for certain institutions and products.

CCPs also face moral hazard problems through the loss mutualisation process. Due to loss sharing, each clearing member (on behalf of themselves and their clients) has an incentive to trade excessively because they may not bear the associated costs in their entirety. Of course, this moral hazard can be partially mitigated by CCPs setting initial margins, default fund contributions and rules to reflect the true risk being introduced by a given clearing member (e.g. multipliers for large exposures). However, there will always be a danger that a member can shift risk from their own balance sheet to that of the CCP where, due to loss mutualisation, it is borne by the other clearing members.

Pirrong (2010) notes that, whilst clearing creates fungible instruments, fungibility is not free due to moral hazard and adverse selection. To mitigate these effects is costly, especially in more heterogeneous situations. Pirrong argues that in some circumstances, it can be more efficient to forego risk sharing in order to control moral hazard and adverse selection costs.

12.3 SIDE EFFECTS

This section reviews some of the likely side effects of mandatory OTC clearing (of standardised contracts) and their potential impact as OTC CCPs develop.

12.3.1 Futurisation

'Futurisation' refers to designing futures contracts to closely mimic OTC derivatives. Futures are highly standardised but come in a narrow range of contract types. An obvious advantage of futurisation would be enhanced liquidity and reduced costs and margin requirements (recall that futures generally have initial margins based on a one-day time horizon as opposed to the five days typically used for OTC derivatives – see section 9.2.1). It will also be possible to offset margins for 'futurised' OTC products with those for more traditional futures and other exchange-traded products. The obvious disadvantage is that a futurised version cannot by definition match the original OTC product precisely, which leads to some mismatch and possible residual risk for hedging purposes.

There is some evidence that futurisation can work. For example, the CME deliverable swap future[11] seems to have attracted interest from both clearing members and clients. This is a three-month contract that delivers a CME-cleared OTC swap at maturity (although given the rationale of the product, users will more likely choose to roll or close out the contract). This product is margined with a two-day liquidation period as opposed to the OTC underly-

[11] http://www.cmegroup.com/trading/interest-rates/deliverable-interest-rate-swap-futures.html.

ing swap, for which the period is (at least) five days. On the other hand, the ICE credit index future has to date not been successful[12] due to significantly different economic terms compared to its OTC counterparty (the index future does not provide default protection and references a new index that would be unknown at the trade date).[13]

There have also been claims that futurisation could be simply a means of CCPs becoming more competitive on pricing without a commensurate reduction in risk. As discussed in section 9.4.3, SwapClear accused a rival CCP, International Derivatives Clearing Group (IDCG), of having initial margin requirements that were too small. IDCG actually cleared interest rate futures, which were argued to be structured so as to be economically identical to the interest rate swaps that members wanted to clear. This allowed various advantages of futures markets to be utilised such as segregation of margin and portability, which (at the time) were not available for OTC-cleared trades. It also meant that IDCG used a close out assumption of only one day compared to the five days generally used for cleared OTC derivatives. This alone would be expected to make initial margins smaller by more than a factor of two.[14]

It could be questioned whether converting an OTC derivative contract into a futures contract really makes it less risky or just a regulatory arbitrage or marketing gimmick. A clue may come from the fact that the investment bank Jefferies is suing IDCG alleging that they lost tens of millions of US dollars due to differences between the futures and swaps.[15] The alleged differences arise in part from a convexity effect stemming from the different margin requirements in OTC and cleared markets (see section 9.1.3). The impact of margining practices on pricing has been a key area since the GFC and it is not therefore surprising that attempting to make OTC derivatives more liquid and/or fungible is not without its perils.

The point about OTC derivatives is that they can be designed to perfectly reproduce the required economic characteristics, such as the cashflows an end user requires to hedge. Even if a futures contract can be created that is economically very similar, this will not necessarily translate into an exact match in terms of price movements and cashflows. Any reduction in costs from futurisation have to be balanced against potential mismatches created by the more standard contractual terms. Hedgers may prefer to have lower cashflow mismatch and accounting volatility, even if this is achieved through less fungible and more expensive OTC products. End users will have to decide how accurately they want to hedge given the balance of factors reflected by futures and OTC contracts.

12.3.2 Regulatory arbitrage

Rules such as mandatory clearing and bilateral margin requirements can lead to regulatory arbitrage. In an environment where CCPs will compete with one another, a clear incentive for regulatory arbitrage will exist. The obvious route will be to make use of various differences

[12] 'After three months, Ice CDS index future has less than 70 open contracts', 2 October 2013, http://www.risk.net/risk-magazine/feature/2295480/after-three-months-ice-cds-index-future-has-less-than-70-open-contracts.

[13] Credit indices 'roll' every six months, which can involve names being replaced in the index (although most names remain the same).

[14] Based on the square root of time rule giving $\sqrt{5}=2.24$. Also used was a relatively short 'look-back' period of only 125 days meaning that an event such as the Lehman bankruptcy would cease to impact initial margins within half a year.

[15] See, for example, 'Jefferies Sues International Derivatives Clearing on Rate Swaps Contracts', Bloomberg, 19 September 2013, http://www.bloomberg.com/news/2011-09-19/jefferies-group-sues-international-derivatives-clearing-group-on-rate-swap.html.

in global regulatory regimes and exemptions to mandates. Indeed, the futurisation above could be argued to represent some sort of regulatory arbitrage, at least if it is done with the sole aim of reducing costs and not creating a new and economically relevant contract.

The obvious rules and exemptions that may be subject to optimisations, misuse and regulatory arbitrage are:

- *Definition of 'standardised' transactions:* The most obvious problem would be that an OTC transaction could be made non-standard to circumvent the mandatory clearing requirement. Indeed, this is the fundamental reason for margin requirements for non-cleared bilateral trades.
- *End user or non-financial exemptions:* Clearing and initial margining rules exempt certain parties. An obvious arbitrage would be for an institution to gain an advantage from such an exemption from claiming that the entity undertaking a given transaction is exempt (for example, being a subsidiary of a parent company).
- *Hedging transactions:* Where exemptions are given for hedging transactions[16] (e.g. the non-financial end user hedging exemption under Dodd–Frank, discussed in section 4.2.6) there is the question of precise definition. For end users, such as an airline hedging exposure to fuel costs, the definition of what constitutes a hedge is partly subjective since it depends on choices such as the time horizon for hedging and contract type (e.g. future, swap or option). The Ashanti case discussed later (section 13.2.3) illustrates that end users with every incentive to hedge may in fact be speculating. Rules exempting genuine hedging transactions are difficult to enforce and require regulators to be highly knowledgeable about the activities of end users.
- *Geographic differences:* There seems to be general agreement on regulatory rules regarding clearing and margining in the major regions. However, any differences can potentially lead to problems as an institution may clear through a particular geographical entity or domicile them there so as to obtain the most favourable regulatory treatment.
- *FX exemptions:* A flat exemption from clearing and margin requirements for an entire asset class in the form of foreign exchange transactions, could be subject to abuse if a product classified as such contains material risks that are not intended to be exempted themselves.
- *Thresholds:* Some clearing requirements are subject to thresholds such as the EMIR threshold where non-financial counterparties would need to clear (section 4.2.6), or the threshold below which bilateral initial margins do not apply (section 6.5.3). Such thresholds can lead to potential optimisations where institutions may aim to remain just below a given threshold or even attempt to count a threshold more than once.

We note that regulatory requirements have already identified the possibility of creating the wrong incentives or creating regulatory arbitrage opportunities. For example, as mentioned above, the bilateral margining requirements neutralise any benefit from avoiding the mandatory clearing requirement (for example by structuring a transaction to be deliberately non-standard). Other obvious requirements to avoid regulatory arbitrage are that the margining threshold must be shared between a consolidated group of entities (preventing an entity having additional threshold by virtue of having a number of separate legal entities), and that only the FX cashflows of a cross-currency swap are exempt from bilateral margin rules (section

[16] There is also the related aspect of allowing of one-time rehypothecation of initial margin for a hedge discussed in section 6.2.3.

6.5.2). Despite attempts to prevent obvious 'holes' in regulation creating regulatory arbitrage opportunities, problems will likely persist. Indeed, history suggests that financial institutions are always likely to be at least one step ahead of regulators in 'optimising' against regulatory requirements.

It is also interesting to note that many exemptions are focused more on large banks, who pose the greater systemic risk, whilst simultaneously avoiding imposing unfair costs on other OTC market participants (e.g. a corporate hedging their economic risk).[17] On the other hand, a clearing mandate may favour large banks that can access clearing in all major OTC CCPs and benefit from the client clearing services they provide.

12.3.3 Netting optimisation

With mandatory clearing reducing certain netting efficiencies by bifurcating cleared and bilateral trades, there is an increased need to look at methods such as trade compression to win back such benefits where possible. Additionally, with initial margin costs via clearing and bilateral margin requirements, any third party solution that aims to optimise netting efficiencies and reduce margin and capital requirements is of interest. At the time of writing, one up-and-running initiative is TriOptima's triBalance service[18] that aims to reduce bilateral and CCP exposures simultaneously, subject to various counterparty risk and funding tolerances. Other third parties planning broadly similar offerings include NetOTC[19] and LMRMKTS,[20] but precise details are not yet available (at the time of writing). What is clear is that the goal will be to optimise both bilateral and cleared trades across the entire market with the reduction in counterparty risk, funding and capital costs in mind. The implementation of such optimisations can be actioned via unwinds, novations and overlay trades.

Another way to achieve additional netting benefits is though CCP linkage via interoperability (section 8.5.1). This is a likely development that will attempt to balance the netting benefits lost due to the proliferation of CCPs for regional and product reasons. Interoperability causes two opposing effects: a reduction in exposure arising from inter-CCP netting and an additional exposure between CCPs. If the former dominates the latter (for example, as suggested by Cox et al. 2013) then interoperability can further enhance netting benefits. However, this potentially creates greater systemic risk arising from CCPs being more (closely) interconnected.

12.3.4 Re-leveraging

As shown in section 6.4.1, margining mitigates credit risk and leverage in a derivative transaction but only by reducing the claims of other creditors. Hence margin may make derivatives positions look safer but this will not necessarily apply to the entire balance sheet of an institution. The idea of re-leveraging is in a similar vein to this argument, by implying that mandatory clearing and margining will potentially incentivise market participants to adjust their capital structures.

[17] Although they will still have greater indirect costs due to the hedging needs of the banks.

[18] http://www.trioptima.co.uk/services/triBalance.html.

[19] http://netotc.com/.

[20] http://www.lmrkts.com/.

One clear impact of mandatory clearing and margining requirements is that they will reduce the leverage in the OTC derivatives market. However, Pirrong (2011) points out that this is not equivalent to reducing the leverage in the financial system as a whole. In being forced to reduce leverage in one set of transactions, market participants can simply increase leverage in others. If an institution has a given target leverage, it will probably respond to clearing and margin mandates by utilising a lower derivative exposure to increase leverage elsewhere on their balance sheets and potentially counteract the overall risk reduction intention of these mandates.

12.3.5 Pricing behaviour

The bilateral OTC market has always priced components such as CVA into trades which are by their nature counterparty-specific. Recent years have also seen components such as funding and margin terms impact pricing of trades (especially those involving end users). Whilst cleared trades reduce some of these components, they also create additional charges such as through initial margin requirements. Clients clearing trades will experience different costs depending on the requirements of the CCP in question, and potentially also the relationship between their clearing member and the CCP.

Even institutions such as end users *not* clearing trades will experience the pricing effects of clearing. Whilst a trade itself may not be subject to clearing (and margining) requirements, the trade(s) executed as a hedge will. This may mean that end users will see the costs of components such as initial margin, even if their actual trades are exempt from the requirements. These effects are already being observed with, for example, clients being told by a bank that a price is high due to 'being the wrong way round at the CCP'.[21]

Finally, it should be noted that pricing in costs of clearing is not easy since they depend on many complex and subjective aspects. For example, pricing in the economic cost of initial margin posting against a given position over its entire maturity is complex since the initial margin is typically a value-at-risk (VAR) calculation that would need to be projected through the lifetime of the transaction. Furthermore, the initial margin calculation (and other related aspects such as haircuts) can change through time at the discretion of the CCP in question. Banks will likely have to make difficult decisions in relation to initial margin pricing, such as whether to price in the entire lifetime cost against a long-dated trade when a transaction is likely to be unwound early. It therefore seems that initial margins will create a greater need to consider behavioural aspects in pricing. It may not even be clear when executing a trade if it may one day be covered by a clearing mandate (see discussion on 'frontloading' in section 4.2.6).

The increase in client clearing will also create new dynamics. *Many* clients will require margin services from clearing members or other third parties, which could fall into two categories:

- Short-term funding of margin posting (e.g. intraday).
- Transformation of assets for cash (for example, to be able to make a variation margin payment).

[21] Meaning that the CCP used for clearing the hedge will charge more initial margin since the hedge will not be offsetting with respect to the rest of the portfolio of the client and/or clearing member. This may be even more significant due to the use of margin multipliers to penalise large portfolios.

It is also important to note that clearing transfers default risk from clients such as end users to CCP members, who are more likely to be systemically important financial institutions.

12.4 IS THERE A BETTER IDEA?

During the financial crisis, taxpayers bailed out failing financial institutions to quite staggering levels. The only attempt to avoid the inherent unfairness and moral hazard from such bailouts, the Lehman bankruptcy, illustrated the problems associated with the failure of a large OTC derivative counterparty. Clearly, aspects within financial markets and OTC derivatives markets in particular need to change. In this light, the criticism of aspects of OTC clearing is not very helpful unless there are other better and/or less costly ways of making these markets safer.

A useful starting point is to examine the different functions that a CCP offers with respect to clearing of OTC derivatives:

- *Netting:* CCPs provide multilateral netting benefits which can reduce the exposure across different cleared products.
- *Margining:* A CCP sets certain margin requirements and handles the operational processing of the associated margin. It is also responsible for the associated valuation and settlement of margin and cashflows.
- *Transparency:* CCPs can increase transparency since they have full knowledge of all positions executed through them.
- *Loss sharing:* A key component of central clearing is insurance via a loss mutualisation process whereby any excess loss that is caused by the default of a CCP member is absorbed collectively by the other CCP members.
- *Default management:* In the event of default of a member, a CCP will invoke a default management process to hedge and close out (probably via an auction involving the CCP members as bidders) the defaulter's portfolio. This can reduce the disruptive effect of a large default.

One fair point is that bilateral markets can perform the first three components on the above list, for example:

- Trade compression services can facilitate multilateral netting (section 5.2.3).
- Margining can be achieved via CSAs (section 6.3.1) and mandatory margin requirements.
- Trade repositories[22] can improve transparency.

Hence one valid argument is that CCPs *may* perform tasks that are redundant, although it might be that CCPs may perform them better and/or more efficiently. This is not completely clear as it depends on the eventual CCP landscape (for example, the number of CCPs and their product coverage) and the economies of scale that can be achieved through clearing. Furthermore, *if* CCPs can perform the first three functions better than bilateral markets then there would be no need for mandatory clearing, as market participants would naturally seek CCP benefits.

[22] For example, the DTCC Global Trade Repository.

Loss sharing is a feature of cleared markets that is not present in bilateral ones. Whilst mutualisation of losses has some potential advantages in terms of preventing a contagion effect resulting from a default, it also raises moral hazard problems as the risks brought to the CCP by a given member are shared. Furthermore, it is not clear what overall benefit (if any) the insurance represented by loss mutualisation will create in an OTC derivative market where the major counterparties tend to be large and systemic. Indeed, in such a case an insurance mechanism is likely to be flawed because there is no natural diversification of risks (this could be compared to the monoline example in section 2.3.4). The way in which this may play out in practice is that a CCP may suffer multiple joint defaults of OTC derivative clearing members and the losses this imposes on surviving members (e.g. default funds, rights of assessment, variation margin gains haircutting or tear-ups) could precipitate further failures.

This leaves default management as a function provided by a CCP which is neither redundant (i.e. achievable in a bilateral OTC market) or not obviously beneficial. The centralised auction process used by CCPs for replacing/hedging defaulted positions is likely more efficient than the equivalent uncoordinated version that occurs in a bilateral OTC market. Hence any criticism of mandatory clearing requirements should provide an alternative to the CCP default management process for dealing with the unwinding and/or replacement of positions resulting from a bankruptcy of a large financial institution. For example, such an alternative is put forward by Pirrong (2012b), who proposes that this function might be unbundled from the other functions performed by CCPs (which may not reduce systemic risk, and may in fact in certain situations increase it). Bilateral markets have shown their ability to design such initiatives when the credit derivative market achieved something broadly similar via the 'big bang protocol' in 2009, which paved the way for auction settlement for credit events.

13
The Cost and Impact of Clearing and Margining

Any change, even a change for the better, is always accompanied by drawbacks and discomforts.
Arnold Bennett (1867–1931)

13.1 OVERVIEW

Mandatory clearing and bilateral margining requirements will have one stark impact on the OTC derivatives market: a significant increase in margin requirements. Whilst it is not surprising that post-GFC regulation was focused around the reduction of counterparty risk, a concern is that the related funding and liquidity impacts of such regulation are in danger of being overlooked. This chapter considers the cost implications of the clearing and margining mandates and their potential liquidity effects. Assessing this is difficult because it will be driven by subtle aspects such as the quality of margin required, segregation and the functioning of repo markets. Nevertheless, it is important to characterise the impact of the increase in margin as a balance between reducing counterparty risk but increasing funding liquidity risk.

13.1.1 Strengths and weaknesses of margin

During the global financial crisis (GFC), the reliance of financial institutions on short-term debt made them particularly vulnerable to the outbreak of problems in longer-dated markets (such as subprime mortgages). Excessive reliance on short-term funding markets has been cited by many as an important contributor to the severity of the GFC.

In one sense it is not a surprise that mandatory clearing and initial margin requirements have been a regulatory response to the crisis. On the other hand, these regulations aim to outlaw the right of parties to take bilateral counterparty risk in an OTC transaction. The problem is that the initial and variation margin requirements faced by market participants because of mandatory clearing and margining requirements will create significant funding needs. It is then important to examine the likely sources of such funding, especially those involving short-term instruments, and their potential to create liquidity risks.

Figure 13.1 illustrates the interplay between margining, counterparty risk and funding. By taking more margin and other resources, it is possible to reduce counterparty risk. Variation margin taken on a frequent basis (e.g. daily) reduces counterparty risk quite significantly, as illustrated in section 7.3.2. This can be reduced even more by bilateral initial margins or central clearing (in the latter case it is reduced further by the presence of the default fund). However, an increase in margining is surely not free, and most obviously it creates funding

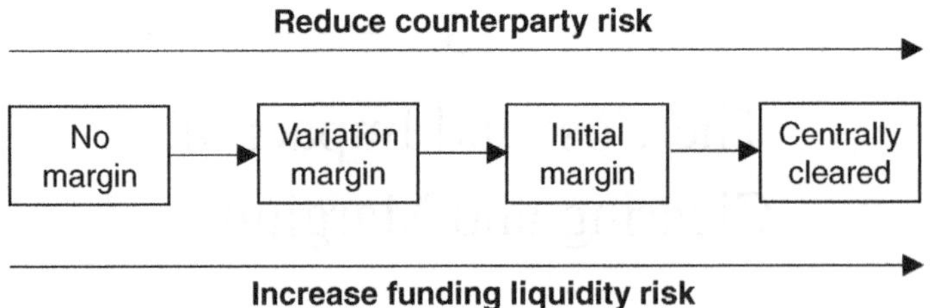

Figure 13.1 Illustration of the reduction of counterparty risk and creation of funding liquidity risk due to increased margining.

liquidity risk due to the difficulty for some market participants to post liquid margin, especially during turbulent periods. In section 7.3.5, this was characterised as the conversion of CVA (counterparty risk) to FVA (funding risk).

It is therefore important to consider the funding liquidity risk created by clearing and margin requirements. Generally, it is relevant to consider two broad effects that arise from both clearing and bilateral margining requirements:

- Increases in *variation margin* requirements due to the tighter requirements compared to bilateral markets.
- The impact of the additional *initial margin* requirements

Both of the effects are important but they create rather different liquidity strains. We will therefore discuss variation and initial margins and their relationship to funding liquidity risk in more detail below.

13.1.2 Variation margin

It can be argued that variation margin is not expensive since it only represents a settlement of running profit and loss and as such is a zero-sum game (one party's loss of variation margin is another's gain). This zero-cost variation margin idea has been expressed in various quantitative and qualitative ways, for example:

- The Hull and White (2012) argument that funding value adjustment (FVA), which can be seen to represent the cost of variation margin, need not be considered in valuation and financial statements as discussed in section 7.3.3.
- The fact that OTC derivatives markets have converged on CSAs with low thresholds (but typically no initial margins) as the standard margining terms, at least for sophisticated participants (e.g. the interbank market). This corresponds closely to full variation margining.
- The fact that a standard pricing method emerging since the crisis is that of 'OIS discounting' (section 9.1.1), which is relevant in the case of perfect variation margin exchange.

However, it can be argued that variation margin is not completely free and without additional liquidity risk for two reasons.

First, variation margin must be paid in relatively liquid securities or cash (indeed, CCPs typically allow only the latter) whilst some market participants will have access only to illiquid non-eligible assets. For example, consider an airline hedging its exposure to the price of aviation fuel via an oil swap or forward contract. The airline will make (lose) money on those hedges in the event of high (low) fuel prices, which will be balanced economically by higher (lower) fuel costs over the period of the hedge. However, when margin is brought in to this picture then cash margin against losses on a derivative cannot be funded by cheap fuel price benefits, which accrue over time. The result of this is that the airline may have liquidity problems in relation to using derivatives with associated variation margins. This could be a good example why, for an end user carrying out hedging trades, these trades should be exempt from clearing and margin requirements (as they likely will be). However, this raises other issues such as how to clearly define that the trades are actually hedges. History suggests that this may create problems, as discussed in section 13.2.3.

A second problem with variation margin is the inherent delay caused by non-immediate posting (which can be days or at least hours). This interrupts the flow of variation margin through the system and causes funding liquidity risk. This effect will be particularly strong in volatile markets and even more so when there is a large asset price shock. Furthermore, central counterparties have a privileged position with respect to margin exchange and may therefore interrupt margin flow significantly for their own benefit (if not that of the market in general). The 1987 stock market crash provides some important illustrations of this effect (see the discussion in section 14.2.5).

13.1.3 Initial margin

Even if variation margin is zero-cost and should therefore be a natural consequence of OTC derivatives trading, the same is definitely not true of initial margin. Initial margin is expensive because it represents over-margining and moves far away from a zero-sum-game market. This is especially true since initial margin requires segregation so as to not to create counterparty risk of its own. Furthermore, initial margins are likely to create further risks such as operational and legal.

It is interesting to compare variation and initial margin properties, as shown in Table 13.1. Some clear disadvantages of initial (compared to variation) margin are that it cannot be (generally) rehypothecated and must be segregated. These aspects create additional liquidity costs and operational and legal risk (see, for example, the MF Global example described in section 11.2.1). Additionally, initial margin calculations are subjective and complex due to their need

Table 13.1 Comparison of variation and initial margin properties.

	Variation margin	**Initial margin**
Expensive	Moderately*	Very*
Rehypothecation allowed	Yes	No
Segregation required	No	Yes
Procyclical	No	Yes
Subjective calculation	No	Yes
Methodology for calculation	Relatively easy	Complex

* This depends on the flow of variation margin through the financial system and the liquidity of initial margin required.

to assess the future (rather than current) exposure at some arbitrarily defined confidence level and time horizon. On the other hand, variation margins can be defined objectively since they relate directly to mark-to-market adjustments and require only relatively straightforward pricing approaches.[1]

13.2 EXAMPLES

The operation of margining mechanisms relies heavily on the extension of credit (Bernanke 1990). This could imply that in certain cases margining may be irrelevant or even lead to problems that would not exist in a non-margined world. There are some historical examples that shed light on these aspects.

13.2.1 American International Group (AIG)

As discussed already in section 2.3.4, the example of AIG is probably the best example of the funding liquidity problems that can be induced by margin posting. In September 2008, AIG was essentially insolvent due to the margin requirements arising from credit default swap trades executed by their financial products subsidiary AIGFP. Due to the systemic importance of AIG, the Federal Reserve Bank created a secured credit facility of up to US$85 billion to allow AIGFP to post the margin they owed and avoid the collapse of AIG. This implies that the liquidity risk AIGFP took via margin agreements was converted (back) into credit risk, leading to the question of whether or not AIGFP posting margin had any actual value.

In this example, one of the key aspects was that AIGFP posted margin as a function of their credit rating. This created a 'cliff-edge' effect as a downgrade of AIG led to a very large margin requirement. As noted previously, linkages of margin requirements to ratings have generally been removed or diluted in recent years in both bilateral and centrally cleared markets (e.g. see section 9.2.3).

13.2.2 The BP Deepwater Horizon oil spill

In 2010, British Petroleum (BP) experienced the largest accidental marine oil spill in the history of the petroleum industry. This caused loss of life, severe environmental problems and, of course, (projected) financial losses for BP themselves. Not surprisingly, in the aftermath of these problems some of BP's trading partners (including banks trading OTC derivatives) had credit risk concerns. These concerns were compounded after their credit rating was downgraded by the major rating agencies (Moody's, Standard & Poor's and Fitch) and its credit spreads widened significantly. This example, like the AIG one, illustrates that dramatic deterioration in perceived creditworthiness can create a vicious and unpredictable 'death spiral'.

The BP situation played out as follows. First, there is some anecdotal evidence of banks giving some flexibility in terms of margin posting. An obvious way to interpret this is that banks believed that, whilst BP was certainly experiencing significant idiosyncratic credit problems, it was unlikely to fail. On the other hand, forcing the contractual posting of margin

[1] Admittedly, mark-to-market prices will not be without disagreements but no product is likely to be centrally cleared if its valuations cannot be reasonably well defined in terms of the relevant price data and/or valuation models. Variation margin calculations for bilateral derivatives are more of an issue since these products will typically be more non-standard and exotic.

(which may have been triggered by the resulting credit rating downgrades of the company) may have caused BP liquidity problems that would have possibly induced a death spiral and made their failure more likely. BP then borrowed a total of US$5 billion from banks to ease their liquidity problems as a result of additional margin demands arising from the aforementioned credit rating downgrades.[2]

One interpretation of this is that banks were re-absorbing the credit risk of BP that had been previously transferred to BP as funding liquidity risk via margin requirements. Furthermore, this was being done at the very time when the margin arrangements were most important. It therefore implies that the margin arrangements were at least partially irrelevant since they failed at the time they were most needed. The above is a good example of the dangers of funding liquidity risk. Collectively banks were essentially converting BP's funding liquidity back into counterparty risk or credit risk (either by waiving margin requirements temporarily or by lending to BP).[3] Presumably, this may be done in the view that long-term credit risk is better than shorter-term funding liquidity risk. However, the mitigation of counterparty risk via margin seems counterproductive in such a case.

This example, like AIGFP, shows also the danger of rating triggers that require additional margin posting at the point where credit quality is declining. It could also be argued that the above case is a strong justification for initial margins (which may have given better security to BP's counterparties). On the other hand, future regulation would likely exempt a company such as BP undertaking 'hedging activities'. The following example provides some additional insight into this problem.

13.2.3 Ashanti

Ashanti (now part of AngloGold Ashanti Limited) was a Ghanaian gold producer. When gold prices rose in September 1999, Ashanti experienced very large losses of US$450 million on OTC derivatives contracts (gold forward contracts and options) used to hedge their exposure to a falling gold price. If the price of gold had indeed fallen then Ashanti would have made a profit on the derivatives contracts to offset losses on their gold reserves. However, they now found themselves in the opposite situation. Market participants commented that Ashanti had hedged an unusually high proportion of its total reserves.

The negative value of Ashantis' hedge book meant that its OTC derivatives counterparties (17 banks in total) were due further variation margin payments totalling around US$280 million in cash. Such margin terms had been agreed prior to the derivative contracts being traded. Any further increases in the price of gold would increase the margin requirements even further. Ashanti had a funding liquidity problem: it had the physical gold to satisfy contracts but not the cash to make the interim variation margin payments (margin calls are due immediately whereas most of their gold was underground). Note also that this problem was related to the large price movement and not rating triggers on margin posting, as in the previous two examples.

---

[2] For example, see 'Collateral Demands Growing for BP', Kate Kelly, CNBC, 28 June 2012, http://www.cnbc.com/id/37979759.

[3] It could be argued that the credit risk could at least be appropriately priced with respect to the creditworthiness of BP at the time. However, this illustrates that a margin agreement can expose an institution to volatility arising from their own credit risk, which is a risk that may be more effectively managed by banks.

To solve its liquidity crisis, Ashanti then struck an agreement making it exempt from posting margin for just over three years.[4] In exchange, Ashanti issued counterparties with warrants convertible into their own shares. This is then another example of liquidity risk being converted into credit risk as margin agreements are deemed impractical, which in turn is at the time that they are most important.

Again, it could be argued that this is a good argument for exemptions for end users hedging with derivatives (as exist for both central clearing and initial margining mandates). Indeed, under clearing and initial margin rules, a counterparty such as Ashanti would likely be exempt due to being a commercial end user executing trades for hedging purposes.[5] However, it seems to be generally believed that Ashanti had gone too far in using derivatives as a risk management tool and had hedged excessively (around 10 times its then annual gold production). Another term for hedging excessively is speculating, a view which even the chief executive of Ashanti seemed to share:

> I am prepared to concede that we were reckless. We took a bet on the price of gold. We thought that it would go down and we took a position.[6]

13.3 THE COST OF MARGINING

13.3.1 Margin and funding

There is no question that margin reduces counterparty risk and initial margin can, if large enough, eradicate it completely (for example, Figure 7.8). It is therefore not surprising that regulators have imposed high margin requirements on OTC derivatives both directly via bilateral margin requirements, and indirectly via the central clearing mandate. Whilst it can be unanimously agreed that margin reduces counterparty risk, there is significant disagreement about the potential costs and side effects of the higher margin requirements.

When margin is posted in cash, interest is typically paid based on a short-term rate such as the overnight indexed swap (OIS) rate, as discussed in sections 6.2.2 and 9.1.1 for bilateral and centrally cleared trades respectively. This is not surprising for variation margin since it may only be held for a day (due to the variation of exposure) and therefore only a short-term interest rate can be paid. Conversely, initial margins may be held for much longer. However, due to the need to segregate, plus potential restrictions on rehypothecation of initial margin, it will be hard for initial margin holders to generate higher returns in order to pay significantly higher rates. Furthermore, the need for CCPs to be able to liquidate initial margin rapidly in stressed market conditions prevents them following investment strategies to generate additional returns. Therefore, whilst a short-term rate is not necessarily the most appropriate 'fair' margin rate, especially for long-dated exposures where margin may be held in substantial amounts for a long period, it is the only rate that is practical. Put another way, margin requirements are expensive due to margin providers providing longer-term funding at shorter-term rates.

The above may lead to a negative carry problem due to an institution funding the margin posted at a rate significantly above LIBOR but receiving only the OIS rate (less than LIBOR)

---

[4] 'Ashanti wins three-year gold margin reprieve', GhanaWeb, 2 November 1999, http://www.ghanaweb.com/GhanaHomePage/economy/artikel.php?ID=8923.

[5] Unless it would be possible to identify that the sum of all positions, both centrally cleared and bilateral, was excessive in terms of the economic hedging requirements.

[6] Mr. Sam Jonah, the chief executive of Ashanti, referring to their financial problems (see footnote 4 for citation).

for the margin posted. This is the origin of FVA discussed in section 7.3.3. Furthermore, if (initial) margin is posted in forms other than cash then these will likely attract conservative haircuts. These haircuts are all costly as they reduce the value of the margin from its current price to the price in a worst-case scenario.

When posting and receiving margin, institutions are becoming increasingly aware of the need to optimise their margin management as, during the GFC, funding efficiencies have emerged as an important driver of margin usage. Margin management is no longer a back-office cost centre but can be an important asset optimisation tool, delivering the most cost-effective margin. An institution must consider the 'cheapest-to-deliver' cash margin and account for the impact of haircuts and the ability to rehypothecate non-cash margin. For example, different currencies of cash will pay different OIS rates and non-cash margin, if rehypothecated, will earn different rates on repo. The optimisation of margins posted across both bilateral and centrally cleared trades (where there is optionality) will also become increasingly important (for example, increasing bilateral margin usage of non-CCP eligible securities).

13.3.2 How expensive?

As mentioned previously, it is hard to assess the additional margin requirements from mandatory clearing and bilateral margining rules. However, it seems reasonable that figures into the trillions of dollars will be required by the regulatory reforms. Relevant estimates of various types can be found in Singh (2010), Sidanius and Zikes (2012) and Heller and Vause (2012).

There seems to be a significant question as to the actual costs of margin in terms of the liquidity needs of market participants. The objections to central clearing and bilateral margin requirements, discussed in section 4.1.7, are predominantly based on the perceived costs of margin needs across both mandates. For example, Singh (2010) estimates US$2 trillion of additional margin requirements globally to support the central clearing mandate. Increased netting benefits are unlikely to counteract this effect due to the inefficiencies of clearing (the number of CCPs and inability to clear all OTC derivatives).

Regarding the sensitivity of margin requirements to market structure, Heller and Vause (2012) estimate that a single CCP clearing all CDS positions would require approximately 25% less margin than three regionally-focused CDS CCPs. They further estimate the benefits of clearing both single-name and index CDS to be 50%, and clearing both IRS and CDS to be 25%. Hence it seems likely that the degree of fragmentation of clearing between different CCPs will have a significant impact on the total cost.

Duffie et al. (2014) study the CDS market and show that the demand for margin will increase due to either bilateral margin rules or mandatory clearing. They also show that in this situation, clearing (compared to bilateral margin rules) will lead to lower margins as long as there is not a significant proliferation of CCPs.

There are arguments that increased margin requirements will not actually be as costly as some argue. For example, as mentioned in section 9.1.4 regarding variation margin, BCBS-IOSCO (2013b)[7] state (emphasis added):

[7] Interestingly, the wording here is even stronger than the original consultative document (BCBS-IOSCO 2012), which states (emphasis added): 'In this respect, the BCBS and IOSCO have focused solely on features associated with the collection of initial margin, as the exchange of *variation margin* represents a net transfer between derivative counterparties, the net liquidity impact associated with its exchange is not likely to be material in the ordinary course of business.'

> In the case of variation margin, the BCBS and IOSCO recognise that the regular and timely *exchange of variation margin* represents the settlement of the running profit/loss of a derivative and *has no net liquidity costs* given that variation margin represents a transfer of resources from one party to another.

Another example is CGFS (2013):

> The variation margin payments, on the contrary, should not have a first-order effect on the demand for collateral, as variation margin is a one-way payment and hence does not affect the net demand for collateral [margin] assets.

These statements suggest that margin costs and benefits are symmetric and/or that the 'velocity of margin' is infinite.[8] In reality, this is not true (as discussed in section 13.1.2) due to a frictional drag on margin from operational delays between margin posting and settlement and also since institutions may have to hold excess funds to fulfil potential variation margin calls. Large derivatives players have hundreds of margin calls per day in both directions, representing potentially hundreds of millions of US dollars of cash and securities.[9] Margin velocity is also subject to resistance as margin flow (especially high-grade liquid margin) within the financial system has fallen significantly and adversely influenced global liquidity in recent years. Singh and Aitken (2009b) show that counterparty risk during and in the aftermath of the recent crisis resulted in a decrease of up to US$5 trillion in high-quality margin due to reduced rehypothecation, decreased securities lending activities and the hoarding of unencumbered margin.

Initial margin requirements are also suggested to be of insignificant cost, even if their amounts seem large. For example, Milne (2011) argues that the overall private cost of margin is low due to Modigliani–Miller type arguments (entities required to post extra margin will simply borrow more). Mello and Parsons (2012) show that a non-margined derivative is equivalent to a margined derivative and a line of contingent credit to fund the margin. This implies that the cost of initial margin requirements and mandatory central clearing is actually zero (although the authors accept that different treatments – for example, regulatory or accounting of non-margined and margined derivatives – may create second-order differences). Albanese et al. (2011) have proposed that a solution to initial margin requirements is margin lending, where a third party essentially funds the required margin posting. Such a liquidity provision creates potentially dangerous problems because the fee for margin lending will increase as the credit quality of the borrower increases. The examples in section 13.2 all illustrate these problems. Furthermore, the failure of entities such as conduits and SIV (structured investment vehicles)[10] during the crisis suggests that, in extreme markets, margin-lending mechanisms could simply freeze completely.

Despite the complaints around margin rules, there is anecdotal evidence from the industry suggesting that margin may not be 'expensive'. Some large banks have begun to post 'lazy

[8] Margin clearly does not circulate around the financial system completely smoothly. Furthermore, the cost an institution incurs due to not yet receiving margin owed is not offset by an equal and opposite benefit from their counterparty who still holds the margin due to inefficiencies such as operational delays and settlement.

[9] For example, see ISDA margin survey (2013b, Table 4.5).

[10] Essentially such vehicles made use of short-term funding to make long-term investments. They failed because it was simply impossible to 'roll' the short-term funding.

Table 13.2 Comparison of haircuts (in %) applied by prime brokers before and after the start of the credit crisis. Adapted from Milne (2009); original source International Monetary Fund Financial Stability Report.

	April 2007	August 2008
US Treasury bonds	0.25	3
Investment-grade corporate bonds	0–3	8–12
High-yield corporate bonds	10–15	25–40
Equities	15	20
Investment grade credit default swaps	1	5
Senior leveraged loans	10–12	15–20
Mezzanine leveraged loans	18–25	35+
Collateralised loan obligations (AAA)	4	10–20
Prime mortgage-backed securities	2–4	10–20
Consumer asset-backed securities	3–5	50–60
Collateralised debt obligation (AAA)	2–4	n/a
Collateralised debt obligation (AA)	4–7	n/a
Collateralised debt obligation (A)	8–15	n/a
Collateralised debt obligation (BBB)	10–20	n/a
Collateralised debt obligation (Equity)	50	n/a

assets' as initial margin bilaterally in advance of mandatory margin requirements. This seems to have been a more useful way to utilise less-liquid assets (compared, for example, to attempting to repo them) and results in a reduction in RWAs (risk-weighted assets) associated with capital charges for counterparty risk. The two obvious problems with this are that this type of margin will be illiquid and/or have significant credit risk and, even with significant haircuts, may not absorb risk in stressed market conditions. This is illustrated by the values in Table 13.2, which show that more complex, illiquid, and credit risky assets such as structured finance securities had massively increasing haircuts at the start of the financial crisis.

Counterparty risk reduction can be only achieved by high-quality liquid assets, which are expensive to use whereas cheaper assets will have risk reduction that is massively overstated due to being highly illiquid and potentially even useless in crises. Due to the quality of margin required by CCPs and under the mandatory margin requirements (section 6.5.2), it is therefore likely that margin, unlike the posting of lazy assets, will indeed be expensive.

13.3.3 Variation margin

A key risk of clearing is the increased need for margin, the funding of which can lead to various dynamics that can be destabilising, especially during periods of stress. The most obvious problems would be expected to relate to initial margins as variation margin does not represent extra margin. However, despite the statements quoted in the last section, it is important to understand that variation margin is costly and creates significantly liquidity risk. A good starting point (in reference to the 1987 stock market crash) is:

> The following discussion of CME cash flows emphasizes variation margin payments because, as will be discussed, these payments placed the greatest stress on the financial system during the week of October 19.
>
> Brady (1988)

Heller and Vause (2012) quantify the potential impact of variation margin calls in stressed markets. One of their conclusions is: 'Variation margin calls on G14 dealers from CCPs that cleared all of their IRS or CDS positions could cumulate over a few weeks to a substantial proportion of their current cash holdings, especially under high market volatility.'

Variation margin has the potential to contribute to financial stress as argued by Pirrong (2013). The mechanism of mark-to-market and (sometimes very large) variation margin posting on a daily and sometimes intradaily basis leads to a very tight coupling between CCPs, clearing members and their clients. During stressed periods, rigid variation margin requirements can lead to substantial spikes in short-term liquidity needs. The size and timescale of these requirements could be billions of dollars during a period of hours. This arises from the non-perfect velocity of variation margining in the financial system. Furthermore, this velocity may slow in a crisis period as institutions may attempt to hold on to margins for longer due to liquidity needs, and worries about credit quality. At the same time, the ability to obtain short-term credit is likely to be at its most difficult (in normal conditions, banks routinely finance margin calls, but during exceptional conditions, they may be less willing to do so). The near-collapse of CME, OCC and CBOT in the 1987 crisis (section 14.2.5) were as a result of these dynamics.

Variation margin requirements can also lead to feedback effects. Large price moves and their associated variation margin requirements may lead to fire sales that in turn may lead to further price moves in other markets. These effects exist in bilateral OTC markets too, but the process here is generally less rigid and concentrated in nature. Hence, the very mechanism that is intended to reduce counterparty risk can potentially create systemic risk.

In the event of a clearing member default, the short-term liquidity requirements of variation margin on a CCP could be severe, as CCPs will need to pay out variation margin against losses incurred by the defaulter. Heller and Vause (2012) note that this would require a CCP to have access to short-notice liquidity backstops worth several billion dollars. Without this, a CCP may struggle to meet the variation margin requirements given the time horizons (hours) involved. Again, this conforms to the experience from the 1987 crash which are discussed later in section 14.2.5.

A further issue is that variation margin is made more expensive by a CCP as it has to typically be in cash. This could lead to a large liquidity squeeze in the event of a large market movement catalysing large variation margin requirements. This might be especially difficult if standard methods for transforming assets into cash, such as the repo market, become more strained in such situations. Indeed, repo markets have already been shown to be potentially fragile in crisis periods.

One important feature of variation margin is that it exposes market participants to mark-to-market volatility, which in turn may increase their likelihood of default (as in the case of monolines and AIG, section 2.3.4). This is also shown by Kenyon and Green (2013), who refer to a 'virtual default' as one which is created by the forced mark-to-market effect of margining which otherwise would be avoided. Whether virtual defaults are correct or not is another matter. However, the likelihood is that tighter coupling to mark-to-market via methods such as variation margining would create more, not fewer, defaults.[11]

[11] As an example of this see 'Here's What That Deutsche Bank Trade Was Really All About', CNBC, 7 December 2012, http://www.cnbc.com/id/100290894. This example is of an *alleged* avoidance of mark-to-market losses that may have otherwise led to a default or government bailout.

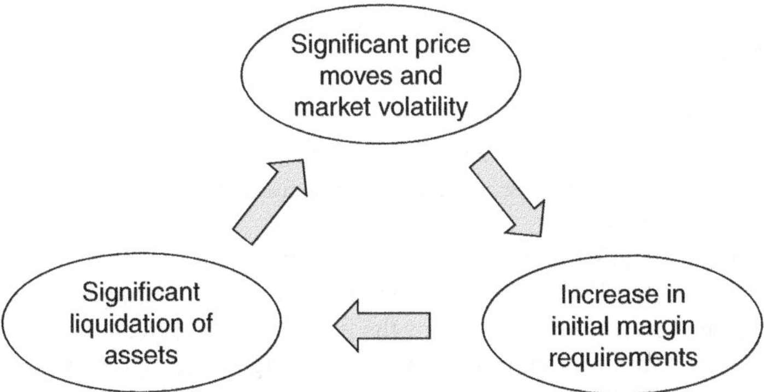

Figure 13.2 Illustration of potential feedback loop involving initial margins.

13.3.4 Initial margin

Like variation margin, initial margin has the potential to cause perverse feedback effects in volatile markets as illustrated in Figure 13.2. This could be driven by the risk sensitivity (and in the extreme procyclicality) of initial margins leading to larger requirements in volatile markets, in turn creating liquidations and large price moves. Such problems may spill over into other markets as if CCP members have to meet unexpected margin calls in one market, they may sell assets in another and therefore drive prices down. Of course, methodologies for initial margin calculation that produce stable results can reduce these problems.

Unlike variation margin, initial margin can at least be posted in non-cash securities. However, the admissibility of such securities represents a difficult balance. On the one hand, if a CCP allows a wide range of securities to be posted then this relieves the liquidity strain of posting. On the other hand, having liquid and high credit quality margin that retains its value even in a crisis period implies a more narrow range of eligible securities. Competition between CCPs may also lead to more relaxed margin restrictions, which ultimately increases the risk of failure.

The lack of rehypothecation of initial margins, although providing greater safety, potentially also exacerbates liquidity problems as margin is essentially stuck in the system. Increases in initial margin also affect all market participants simultaneously.

Related to the above dynamic is the difficulty a CCP has in balancing prudency and competitiveness when setting initial margin requirements. Knott and Milne (2002) provide a discussion with respect to the risk of margin requirements being too low.

13.3.5 Converting counterparty risk to liquidity risk

There are a number of real problems with posting margin and clearing relating to the fact that counterparty risk has been transformed into funding liquidity risk. An interesting example is to consider an institution that is exempt from the bilateral margining and clearing mandates and is deciding on the optimal way in which to transact. With respect to margin posting, the following problems may exist:

- The institution may struggle to find suitable liquid margin to post and margin requirements may be procyclical.
- If the institution relies on third party liquidity providers to provide margin or margin upgrading services then the fees for these services will increase in a crisis period and/or as the credit quality of the client worsens. These mechanisms expose the client directly to the variability of their own credit risk, which they may not be able to manage as effectively as other parties such as banks.
- The institution could mitigate the above problem by agreeing contractually to post less liquid margin. This could be either in a bilateral CSA or via a clearing member providing a margin upgrading service. This transforms the liquidity risk again and concentrates it with systemically important financial institutions such as large clearing members.
- In the event banks themselves provide contingent lines of credit to fund the margin posting (to banks), this represents a regulatory arbitrage as banks may achieve lower capital charges even though their credit risk position overall is unchanged.[12]
- Any margining or clearing agreement may reduce credit risk for the institution's OTC derivatives counterparties, but will increase credit risk to other creditors (section 6.4.1).

Another way to look at this problem is via the valuation adjustment components that are faced by banks (and priced into trades), as discussed in 7.3. The relevant costs to consider are those relating to credit value adjustment (CVA), representing counterparty risk together with funding value adjustment (FVA) and associated capital charges. Table 13.3 compares these costs under different margin terms, which has the impact of reducing counterparty risk as more margin is taken (including default funds for cleared trades). Regarding funding, with no margin agreement the situation is defined as moderate as no margin is received but nor does any have to be posted. Bilateral margin (full variation margin) is the most beneficial funding situation since in such a case there is no FVA cost (according to the Hull and White argument mentioned in section 13.1.2). Bilateral initial margins and clearing increase funding costs due to initial margin and default fund requirements.[13] Capital requirements generally reduce in line with more margins being posted, although the situation with cleared trades may not be as beneficial due to the additional capital requirements on the default fund exposure.

The above qualitative assessment shows a balance between counterparty risk and funding costs. Indeed, Gregory (2012) makes a quantification of CVA and FVA as a function of the margining and shows that a bilateral margin agreement (no initial margin) is most optimal

Table 13.3 Comparison of counterparty risk, funding and capital costs under different margin terms.

	Bilateral (no margin)	**Bilateral (variation margin)**	**Bilateral (initial margin)**	**Cleared**
Counterparty risk (CVA)	High	Medium	Low	Low
Funding (FVA)	Medium	Low	Very high	Very high
Capital	High	Medium	Low	Medium

[12] For example, the bank would not have the equivalent of a CVA capital charge for the loan they (or another bank) effectively provide.

[13] These are both listed as very bad. Cleared trades have the additional cost of default fund contributions whereas bilateral initial margins may be more conservative (for example, a 10-day time horizon is used rather than the five days normally used for CCP initial margin calculations).

from a price perspective. The bottom line is that margin redistributes counterparty risk and converts it into other financial risks. It is not completely clear that this redistribution and conversion is beneficial to financial markets generally. This is highlighted by the following quote,[14] which states:

> The economic effect of the requirement to provide cash collateral [margin] is to convert the primary risk for companies from that associated with counterparty exposure into liquidity risk. Non-financial companies are highly experienced in managing their counterparty risk with financial institutions; managing liquidity risk in collateral requirements is substantially more difficult for them and is less efficient.

Another illustration of the cost of margin can be seen in the behaviour of multilateral development banks (MDBs) such as the World Bank or European Bank for Reconstruction and Development (EBRD). Thanks to their strong credit quality, such entities have typically enjoyed the benefits of one-way CSAs (section 6.3.2) when trading with investment banks. However, this leads to charges for CVA, FVA and capital[15] that in recent years have increased substantially due to the tighter funding and regulatory environments in which such investment banks are operating. An obvious way to reduce these large charges would be for MDBs to post variation margin via entering two-way CSAs. The actual situation is that MDBs are only considering margin posting because investment banks may increase charges prohibitively or even cease trading with them. They are not doing it because they assess that the charges for counterparty risk, funding and capital exceed the inherent costs of funding liquidity risk they would then face when posting margin.

13.3.6 Manifestation of funding liquidity risks

It is useful to ask how the increased funding liquidity risk resulting from larger margin requirements may manifest itself in reality. Here, it is useful to consider several components separately:

- *Variation margin:* In one sense, variation margin is natural as it represents what one party owes to another. However, as illustrated above, variation margin can cause liquidity problems especially for certain users of OTC derivatives. A particular issue in this respect is a large variation margin requirement that may arise in volatile markets or from a large price movement.
- *Initial margin:* In addition to creating additional 'deadweight' costs due to segregation and non-rehypothecation, initial margin can potentially create procyclicality problems as margin requirements increase during a period of financial stress.
- *Default funds:* Default fund contributions and rights of assessment are potentially subject to wrong-way risks as losses and calls to a default fund create funding stresses and will likely occur in highly stressed periods (following at least one clearing member default) where funding is difficult.

[14] European Association of Corporate Treasurers, Open Letter to the Commissioners of the European Union, 7th November 2011, http://www.eactnew.org.uk/docs/EACT-letter-to-EU-Commissioners_07-11-11.pdf.

[15] Including charges for any initial margins the MDB may also hold.

13.4 IMPLICATIONS

Margining reduces counterparty risk and ensures that 'defaulters pay'. In the aftermath of the Lehman default, CCPs (e.g. CME and LCH.Clearnet) were rightly vociferous about the fact that they had avoided losses, as their initial margins were enough. Central clearing and initial margins therefore seem to be a sensible idea for making OTC derivatives markets safer and reducing the likelihood of future financial crises. However, the efficiency with which margining really reduces counterparty risk is questionable as the examples above illustrate.

The impact of central clearing and initial margins will be discussed in more detail in the next chapter but for now, there are some important observations to be made about the potential weaknesses of increases in margin requirements such as:

- In a financial crisis, large negative asset shock will lead to large variation margin requirements which may be difficult to fund.[16]
- Procyclicality of initial margin requirements or haircuts can exasperate liquidity problems in a crisis, for example as observed by increases in haircuts in the recent European sovereign crisis.[17]
- Margin requirements (initial or variation) could be funded by increased borrowing or the sale of assets leads to liquidity strains and downward price pressure.

Certain authors have argued quite strongly against OTC derivatives central clearing for reasons such as feedback effects in liquidity requirements (increased margin volatility leading to higher margins leading to strains on liquidity and so on). For example, see Pirrong (2013).

[16] For example, an obvious place to do this is via the repo market, which represented a particular point of systemic failure in the crisis.

[17] For example, see 'LCH Raises Margin Costs for Trading Spanish Government Bonds', http://www.bloomberg.com/news/2012-06-19/lch-lifts-margin-costs-for-trading-most-spanish-government-bonds.html.

14
Risks Caused by CCPs

> *When Black Friday comes I'll collect everything I'm owed and before my friends find out I'll be on the road.*
>
> Steely Dan ('Black Friday')

14.1 OVERVIEW

This chapter discusses the risk created by the *mandatory* clearing of OTC derivatives. We will cover the risks that CCPs themselves face and the corresponding risks to which clearing members (and their clients) are exposed. It is important to keep in mind that the risks of central clearing should be balanced against those of not; after all, bilateral OTC derivatives markets have been proven to contribute to significant instability in financial markets. Central clearing of OTC derivatives is not a panacea but may be a safer alternative to the previous bilateral setup.

14.1.1 General risks created by CCPs

By taking initial margin, a CCP transforms counterparty risk into other forms of risk. Most obviously, funding liquidity risk arises due to the nature of margining, as discussed at length in the previous chapter. However, operational and legal risks also exist, which we will consider later in this chapter.

Regarding the general risk posed by CCPs (especially those clearing significant volumes of OTC derivatives), two obvious concerns arise:

- *Central nodes of failure:* Mandatory clearing will increase the importance of CCPs as key central nodes within financial markets. As such their failure or even distress could initiate a major disturbance. This also creates a too big-to-fail dilemma: if a CCP would be saved from failure then this would likely be at the expense of the taxpayer and would therefore create moral hazard.
- *Shock amplifiers and propagators:* Given their size and interconnections, CCPs could amplify systemic shocks and allow a financial disturbance to propagate through the market as a result of their actions (for example, in relation to margin requirements).

Although CCPs are presumably viewed as very unlikely to default and therefore fail to return initial margins (which are not generally part of a loss allocation process), the sheer size of initial margin that a large clearing member may have committed to a CCP is a concern. Given that a CCP failure is possible, clearing members should assess their exposure in order to avoid significant losses that could threaten their own solvency. It is not clear whether and how such exposures will be covered by the large exposure requirements applied to banks (BCBS 2013a). Since some CCPs may be perceived as 'too big to fail' then applying exposure limits would also reduce the associated moral hazard problems and force clearing members to seek diversification across CCPs.

14.1.2 Risks for clearing members

Clearing members directly face the risk of CCP failure through their initial margins. However, probably more importantly, they face the risk of the distress of a CCP which may result in the loss of default fund contributions, potential additional exposure arising from rights of assessment and other loss allocation methods such as variation margin gains haircutting (VMGH) and tear-up. As described below (section 14.3.4), this exposure is particularly complex and is similar to a second loss position in a collateralised debt obligation (CDO). It is important to understand that CCP default is not an easily characterised event as it is with the default of most institutions. In general, a clearing member can experience CCP-related losses via a number of mechanisms:

- Auction costs (for example, by taking on a portfolio that cannot be hedged easily, which eventually leads to losses due to market volatility)
- Default fund utilisation
- Rights of assessment
- VMGH
- Tear-up
- Forced allocation
- Other loss allocation methods
- CCP failure

In order to assess the risks faced by being a member of a CCP, a clearing member would naturally attempt to make a detailed evaluation of the risk management framework of the CCP, covering aspects such as:

- Membership criteria
- The number of other clearing members and their creditworthiness
- Initial margin and default fund requirements and their expected coverage
- Capital requirements (depending on regulatory recognition of the CCP)
- External liquidity access
- Investment policies
- Flexibility of the CCP to listen to policy changes suggested by clearing members
- Operational capacity (especially in default scenarios)
- Default management process
- Loss waterfall and recovery and resolution mechanisms

14.1.3 Risks for non-clearing members

Non-clearing members ('clients') who clear indirectly through a clearing member face different risks but may also have additional protection. In the event of the failure of the CCP, clients may be protected as long as their clearing member is solvent. Conversely, in the event of default of their clearing member, the CCP may provide protection and ensure continuity through margin segregation and portability. Finally, since clients do not contribute to default funds, they do not have this direct exposure to CCPs that exists for clearing members.

However, the above are dependent on certain important operational and legal aspects. Protection from clearing member and CCP failure depends on segregation and protection of initial margins. As noted in section 11.1.5, clients can potentially be exposed to CCPs, clearing members and even other clients of clearing members. Clients also bear the risk of not being able to port their portfolio of trades in the event of their clearing member defaulting, leading to a possible close out of these positions at unfavourable prices.

The exposure of clients to CCP rules is also very important. If clearing members contractually pass on the effects of loss allocation methods, such as VMGH, then clients may face unfair and arbitrary reduction of gains. Clearing members may prefer loss allocation methods such as VMGH and tear-up (if they can pass losses onto their clients directly) rather than experiencing losses via default funds, rights of assessment or forced allocation, which they must bear directly. However, clients may be at risk from VMGH and tear-up if they are contractually exposed to these methods of loss allocation.

14.2 HISTORICAL CCP FAILURES AND NEAR MISSES

We will now look at what can be learned from past CCP failures (and near-failures), which provides some enlightening evidence as to the potential weaknesses of central clearing. However, it is probably fair to put this in context and emphasise that CCP distress and failure is historically less common and severe than that of banks.

14.2.1 New York Gold Exchange Bank (1869)

The first relevant failure to consider is that of the New York Gold Exchange Bank on Black Friday in 1869. This did not involve a CCP as such, but the bank did operate a clearing division and had a role insuring against default losses. Black Friday was caused by two speculators attempting to corner the gold market on the Gold Exchange.[1] The bank owed money to those who profited from the ensuing price collapse but had not received funds from those who had lost. This causes a major problem for the bank and ensuing panic in the market.

14.2.2 Caisse de Liquidation (1974)

The Caisse de Liquidation was a French CCP. In the period leading up to the failure, prices in the Paris White Sugar Market were extremely volatile, partly caused by speculation. Prices had quadrupled and then suffered a very large downwards correction, which hit speculators. Many participants defaulted on margin calls and created losses for the CCP (one member in particular, the Nataf Trading House, had a very large position).

As a result of the losses of the Nataf Trading House, the Ministry of Commerce closed the sugar market and invoked a regulation that deemed that on re-opening, contracts would be settled at the average price of the last 20 days (far higher than the price when trading was suspended). This can be seen as a form of variation margin haircutting or partial tear-up

[1] For more information see the Blog of Craig Pirrong at http://streetwiseprofessor.com/?p=4023.

(sections 10.3.1 and 10.3.2). However, this judgement was reversed in the courts and two of the Nataf Trading House's guarantors refused to cover sums they owed, resulting in the Caisse de Liquidation becoming insolvent. The sugar market remained closed for another 18 months.

Hills et al. (1999) outline some reasons for the failure of the Caisse de Liquidation:

- *Initial margins:* The Caisse de Liquidation did not increase initial margins despite the increase in gold prices and correspondingly large increase in volatility, even though clearing members themselves had requested they do so. Initial margins were set based on absolute moves which (as described in section 9.3.4), is a problem in a rising market.
- *Large position monitoring:* They did not act on the relatively large speculatory position (in comparison to the entire market) in sugar futures held by the Nataf Trading House.
- *Transparency:* The loss allocation process in the event of the default of a clearing member was not transparent (and as described above there were legal problems in trying to enforce loss allocation).

14.2.3 COMEX (1980)

The Commodity Exchange Inc. (COMEX) was the leading gold and options exchange which also traded silver contracts. Leading up to the problems, a consortium led by the Hunt Brothers[2] had been attempting to corner the silver market, creating an order of magnitude increase in prices. Eventually, in response to the accumulation of a massive position, the COMEX changed their rules regarding leverage. The so-called 'Silver Rule 7' placed heavy restrictions on the purchase of commodities and significantly reduced the ability of any large contract holder to use leverage to buy silver. Since the Hunt brothers had borrowed heavily to finance their purchases this left them in a very constrained position.

On 'Silver Thursday' (27 March 1980), silver prices dropped significantly by about 50%. As a result of this and the COMEX rule change, the Hunt Brothers were unable to meet their obligations, which caused panic in the markets. Their obligations were so large that the US government forced banks to issue lines of credit totaling around US$1 billion to prevent a crisis. These credit lines were backed by most of the assets of the Hunt brothers, who eventually, following civil charges, were declared bankrupt.

Although this exchange is not related to a CCP failure, it illustrates the danger of allowing such a large position to accumulate and then taking retrospective action much too late.

14.2.4 Commodity Clearing House (1983)

The Kuala Lumpur Commodity Clearing House in Malaysia had only been operating for three years when it was brought down as a result of a crash in palm oil futures. Six clearing members then defaulted on a total of US$70 million, leading to trading being suspended. A report from the Malaysian government blamed the CCP for inactivity between a severe squeeze on market prices and the default of the first clearing member. Officials at the CCP were also criticised for lack of experience (Hills et al. 1999). Interestingly there has recently been an increase in centrally cleared OTC palm oil swap contracts as hedges for long-dated exposures. Limited liquidity on long-dated CPO listed derivatives means users are looking to use centrally cleared swaps.

---

[2] Nelson Bunker Hunt and William Herbert Hunt, sons of a Texas oil billionaire.

14.2.5 Hong Kong Futures Exchange and 1987 crash

The 1987 stock market crash was another example of an unprecedented price collapse, in this case involving the equity markets. The only CCP that actually failed was the Hong Kong Futures Exchange Clearing Corporation, but other CCPs had extreme problems. Both of these aspects are worthy of discussion.

In 1987, three separate entities were involved with the central clearing of the Hong Kong futures market:

- *Hong Kong Futures Exchange (HKFE):* The exchange essentially running the futures market.
- *International Commodities Clearing House Hong Kong Limited (ICCH (HK)):* The CCP providing a clearing service.
- *Hong Kong Futures Guarantee Corporation (HKFGC):* The default fund (guarantee fund) essentially guaranteeing trades.

After a period of significant growth, on so-called Black Monday (19 October 1987) the Hong Kong stock market (Hang Seng Index) dropped by almost 50%. The market was subsequently closed for the rest of the week and was expected to fall again on opening. This led to fears that margin calls would not be met and that the total losses would exceed the financial resources of the CCP. This prompted a rescue package for the CCP to be put together by the government and private institutions (Hills et al. 1999). The default fund (HKFGC) contained capital of HK$15 million and reserves of HK$7.5 million, and yet the HKFE needed to borrow almost HK$2 billion. After contributions from shareholders, large brokers and members of the HKFE, the bailout cost the government (taxpayer) in the region of HK$1 billion.

One of the causes of the HKFE failure was the lack of strict margin practices together with the fact that initial margin requirements for futures had not been increased even though the underlying market had risen significantly in the preceding period (again, this is the problem of absolute and relative returns discussed in section 9.3.4). Furthermore, the strange setup of exchange, CCP and default fund had led to moral hazard issues which created the wrong incentives, for example:

- Exchange members could not participate in the management of the default fund.
- The CCP was responsible for monitoring positions, but was not exposed to losses in the event of default.
- The default fund was exposed to losses but the HKFGC had no say in risk monitoring or setting standards for clearing members (which was the job of the CCP).

Whilst the HKFE represented the only CCP failure as a result of the 1987 crash, there are other examples of CCP distress in this period, including losses to default funds, that are worth discussing. In the US, although there were no failures, uncertainties and fears about the viability of CCPs intensified the already significant market disruption. It is probably fair to say that the CCPs of the Chicago Mercantile Exchange (CME), Options Clearing Corporation (OCC) and the Chicago Board of Trade (CBOT) were very close to failure and only prompt action from the Federal Reserve prevented a catastrophe (Pirrong 2013).

Due to the very large price moves on and around Black Monday, the magnitude of margin calls was extremely large. This created a number of interrelated problems:

- Difficulties in receiving variation margin payments due from those with losing positions, despite in some cases multiple intraday margin calls being made.
- CCPs 'absorbing' significant amounts of liquidity by collecting some variation margin payments but not always paying out on the winning positions in a timely manner.
- Large increases in volumes of trades and unprecedented price volatility creating operational problems, such as errors and delays in confirming trades, which was made worse by a lack of automated payment systems in some cases. Since some trades were reconciled only at the end of the day, many leveraged positions had losses well in excess of their posted margins.
- A lack of linked clearing arrangements (cross-margining, section 9.5) so that, for example, members hedging options (OCC) with futures contracts (CME) did not have gains and losses offset and were therefore caught in a variation margin trap. The OCC had asked CME to agree to cross-margining prior to the 1987 crash (Norman 2011).

The net result of the very heavy liquidity problems caused by the above was that the CME came close to having insufficient margin to start trading on 20 October. Failure of the CME was only averted due to its bank advancing the CCP US$400 million just minutes prior to the market opening so that it could make variation margin payments totalling US$2.5 billion (IMF 2010).

At the OCC, a large clearing member had difficulties in paying margin (and only did so after an emergency loan from its bank) and the OCC itself was late in making payments to clearing members and suffered a significant loss due to a clearing member default. Around three quarters of this loss (after using retained earnings) caused a hit to the default fund with rights of assessment used to bring the default fund to its previous level (although the default fund hit was only a fraction of the total default fund size).

Without the strong support from the Federal Reserve (both explicit and implicit in terms of liquidity injections and public statements respectively), a large CCP failure in 1987 was a significant possibility. An interesting review of this crisis in given in Bernanke (1990).

14.2.6 BM&FBOVESPA (1999)

The most recent CCP distress scenario was that of the Bolsa de Valores, Mercadorias & Futuros de Sao Paulo (BM&FBOVESPA) stock exchange located in Brazil. A sudden FX move of the Brazilian Real by around 50% with respect to the US dollar occurred in 1999 when the new President of the Central Bank decided to release control over the exchange rate, triggering a massive currency devaluation. This led to the default of two banks that were clearing members, with losses that exceeded the margins and default funds held by the BM&FBOVESPA CCP. The central bank intervened and bailed out the two banks in question, thus preventing the collapse of the CCP.

14.2.7 Lessons from past CCP failures

In the last 40 years, three CCPs have failed (Caisse de Liquidation, Kuala Lumpur Commodity Clearing House and Hong Kong Futures Exchange) and another three have come close to failure (the Chicago Mercantile Exchange, the Options Clearing Corporation and BM&FBOVESPA). The common sources of the failures can be identified as:

- Large underlying price moves (e.g. commodities, stocks, FX).
- Defaults stemming from losses in relation to the above market moves.
- Initial margins and default funds being insufficient to absorb losses.
- Liquidity strains arising from delays (for operational reasons as well as solvency problems) in the flow of variation margin in and out of CCPs caused by CCPs and/or clearing members. The lack of cross-margining applied to variation margin payments between CCPs in the 1987 crisis caused a further problem in this respect.
- Initial margin calculations not being updated according to changes in market conditions (e.g. after a large asset price and associated volatility increase).
- Operational problems arising from excessive volumes and large price moves.

In summary, failures are a result of a combination of large market volatility, failure of members and large asset price shocks coupled with inadequate margins and default funds. There are several overall lessons to be gleaned from these CCP failures and near-failures.

- Operational risk must be controlled as much as possible (for example, after the 1987 crash, electronic reporting of trades was introduced so that the system would not be exposed to these weaknesses again).
- Variation margins should be recalculated frequently and collected promptly (intradaily in volatile markets). More automated payment systems can help to avoid liquidity shortfalls and cross-margining linkage arrangements between CCPs can relieve liquidity problems caused by hedging activity across different CCPs. CCPs must not interrupt the velocity of margin, especially in volatile periods.
- Initial margin and default funds should be resilient to large negative asset shocks or gaps in market variables and to extreme dependency (for example, the concept of correlation increasing in a crisis).
- A CCP should carefully monitor positions, penalise concentration and act quickly in the case of excessively large positions.
- A CCP should have availability to external liquidity sources since it could otherwise default due to being illiquid but not insolvent.

14.3 IMPORTANT CONSIDERATIONS

14.3.1 Hindsight bias

One problem in assessing the safety and need for central clearing is hindsight bias, which is the natural tendency to see past events as more predictable than they in fact were. One obvious example is the use of the AIG failure as a rationale for mandatory clearing (section 12.1.3). Obviously, mandatory clearing would have forced AIG to post much more margin than they actually did, which in turn would have prevented AIG from having such a large exposure. However, institutions and regulators did not require AIG to post initial margin because they perceived, based on the evidence available at the time, that the default probability of AIG was negligible (a view supported by rating agencies). It should perhaps not be assumed that a CCP in the same environment would have taken a different view. Furthermore, the impact on a CCP of an AIG-like clearing member failing could have been significant and led to heavy losses for the clearing members, who in turn may have been exposed already via bilateral markets.

Another problem of hindsight bias is the case of the Lehman failure and the success in LCH.Clearnet and CME in managing the risk they faced. The CCPs were not having to deal with the type of transactions that had caused Lehman to fail in the first place. It will never be known what the impact would have been if (for example) a large fraction of the credit derivatives market had been centrally cleared in 2008. The CCP framework for clearing CDS has not yet been tested by any major problems in this market.

The point is that analysis over the last crisis and the potential impact CCPs might (or might not) have had is rather futile. Regulation should be intended to prevent the next crisis, not the last one. Furthermore, regulation must avoid preventing the last crisis occurring again and in doing so creating an environment that leads to the next crisis.

14.3.2 Race to the bottom?

The potential danger of competition for risk assessment was provided by rating agencies. Up to 2007, a plethora of ever-more complex products were given good quality ratings driven by the fact that rating agencies were essentially paid for giving such ratings and competing with one another in doing so. Kenyon and Green (2012) have argued that CCPs could become the 'new rating agencies', drawing analogies to the way in which the rating agencies played a role in the GFC by providing extremely optimistic ratings to protection-providing firms such as AIG and monoline insurers, and giving even more spurious ratings to structured products.

Kenyon and Green also take issue with the privileged positions CCPs will have with respect to valuation. They argue that valuation risk will be concentrated within the CCP as they have discretion over the pricing models to be used and the associated market data. The privileged position could lead to CCPs becoming an oligopoly and creating high barriers to entry. On the other hand, CCPs may compete on product coverage and margins, which could dangerously lead to a race to the bottom.

14.3.3 Distributive effects and the big picture

As noted by Pirrong (2013), it is also important to look beyond the impact of clearing on OTC derivatives markets only. OTC derivatives make up only a subset of an institution's balance sheet. Crucially, as shown in sections 5.1.6 and 6.4.1, netting and margining (the effects of which clearing aims to increase) do not eliminate risk. What they actually achieve is to redistribute risk by changing the seniority of various creditors: OTC derivatives become more senior whilst other creditors are effectively demoted.

The redistribution effects of clearing do not seem to always be properly considered. For example the MAGD (2013) consider the economic impact of mandatory clearing, margin requirements for non-centrally cleared derivatives and capital requirements for derivatives exposures and state:

> In its preferred scenario, the group found economic benefits worth 0.16% of GDP per year from avoiding financial crises. It also found economic costs of 0.04% of GDP per year from institutions passing on the expense of holding more capital and collateral to the broader economy. This results in net benefits of 0.12% of GDP per year.

This argument seems to ignore the big picture in term of the redistributive effects of clearing and a potential negative growth effect from changes in financial markets brought about by the reduction in seniority of other creditors.[3]

CCPs are often touted as reducing systemic risk. Yet the clearing mandate covers OTC derivatives and so CCPs can therefore at best reduce systemic risk in OTC derivatives markets. Of course, based on past experience, reducing systemic risk in derivatives (aka weapons of financial destruction) will be rather close to reducing systemic risk in financial markets on the whole. However, this assumes that markets will not adapt in response to mandatory clearing.

It may be realistic to make OTC derivatives more senior and demote others since these other creditors may be less systemically important. However, it is important to foresee the potential changes brought about by clearing. Faced with a deleveraging in derivatives markets, market participants will likely find other ways to create leverage and obtain alternative forms of credit to support the increase in required margin (financial engineering has regularly proved to be particularly useful at achieving such goals). These changes in capital structures in turn may create risks in areas of financial markets that have previously been viewed as relatively benign. It could be that regulation is too focused on OTC derivatives and is therefore blinkered to other possible dangers.

14.3.4 Mutualisation and CCPs as CDOs

Mutualisation of losses is an efficient insurance mechanism for risk sharing. It works well when risks are relatively idiosyncratic and independent (e.g. car insurance). However, it works less well as risks become more correlated and systemic as illustrated by monoline insurers (see section 2.3.4). Therefore, if the failure of a clearing member is an idiosyncratic event then the loss mutualisation via the default fund of the CCP may enhance stability. However, in the case of a more systematic failure then this process will be less helpful.

Related to the above is the concept that a CCP waterfall may behave rather like a CDO, which has been noted by a number of authors including Murphy (2013) and Pirrong (2013). The comparison, illustrated in Figure 14.1, is that the 'first loss' of the CDO is covered by 'defaulter pays' initial margins and default funds together with CCP equity. Clearing members, through their default fund contributions and other loss allocation exposures such as rights of assessment, have a second loss position on the hypothetical CDO. Of course, the precise terms of the CDO are unknown and ever-changing as they are based on aspects such as the CCP membership, portfolio of each member and initial margins held. However, what is clear is that the second loss exposure should correspond to a relatively unlikely event since otherwise it would imply that initial margin coverage was too thin.

The second loss position that a CCP member implicitly is exposed to is therefore rather senior in CDO terms. Such senior tranches are well known to be heavily concentrated in terms of their systemic risk exposure (see, for example, Gibson 2004, Coval et al. 2009 and Brennan et al. 2009) and perform very badly during large, market-wide shocks. Furthermore, a consequence of such structures is that they concentrate wrong-way risk (Gregory 2012, Chapter 15).

The implication of the systemic and wrong-way risk concentration via the senior tranche exposure created by a CCP, by analogy to CDOs, would be:

[3] This point is made by Craig Pirrong in his blog – http://streetwiseprofessor.com/?p=7672.

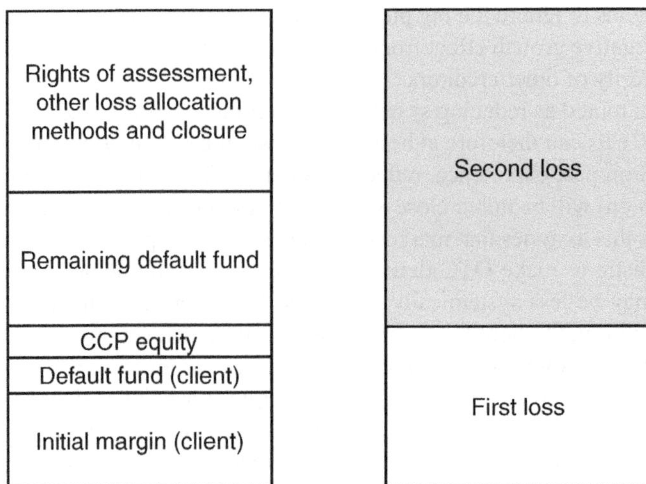

Figure 14.1 Comparison between a CCP loss waterfall (inverted) and a CDO structure.

- The risk concentrated within a CCP will be systemic in nature.
- Correlation between losses from different clearing member defaults is likely to be high.
- Losses will hit the mutualised default fund precisely when clearing members are under financial stress (wrong-way risk). For surviving clearing members, the impact of losses to their default funds, rights of assessments, variation margin gains haircutting and other loss allocation methods could cause them also to fail.
- Loss allocation methods increase interconnections between CCP participants during periods of stress.
- Default funds and associated capital charges should therefore be very large and expensive.

Of course, bilateral markets can also be heavily exposed to all of the above and may be even more vulnerable. However, it is important to see that CCPs are not magic in that they potentially create exactly the same systemic risks and interconnections that exist in non-cleared markets.

14.3.5 The need for margin

Mandatory clearing and margin rules will bring about a sharp increase in the amount and quality of margin required to back OTC derivatives positions. This will likely create pressure in the financial system in order to obtain the relevant assets that can be posted. Methods involving gross margining and segregation to give clients better protection and enhance the possibility for portability (section 11.1.7) will create further strains in this respect.

CCPs are likely to be under pressure to expand the set of eligible securities for initial margin purposes. Accepting more risky and illiquid assets creates additional risks and puts more emphasis on the calculation of haircuts that can also increase risk if underestimated. CCPs admitting a wide range of securities can become exposed to greater adverse selection as clearing members (and clients) will naturally choose to post margin that has the greatest risk (relative to its haircut) and may also present the greatest wrong-way risk to a CCP (e.g. a European bank would most likely choose to post European sovereign debt where possible).

Financial engineering has proved very efficient at designing methods such as securitisation for creating assets that have the appearance of being liquid and of strong credit quality. However, such assets can generally become very illiquid in crisis periods and are vulnerable to extreme tail risk. Hence they are likely to be less useful in the very cases where they are most needed, such as the default of one or more clearing members.

Since margin transfer can create operational risk, the precise way in which margin is transferred is also important. Margin may be transferred via title transfer (common in Europe) where the receiver has the authority to invest the securities. Clearing members and other third parties may offer 'margin transformation' services for institutions to obtain the securities they need for margin purposes. Such structures are risky for two potential reasons. First, they are most likely to become extremely fragile in stressed periods (for example, repo markets in the last crisis), and second, they disguise wrong-way risk as the wrong-way securities are essentially passed through a third party.

14.3.6 The impact of mandatory clearing

There should be no question mark over central clearing in general, nor over clearing of OTC derivatives. Like many forms of risk mitigation, market participants could determine their costs and benefits and use them (or not) accordingly. The question that arises is over mandatory clearing and whether the regulatory requirements represent the optimal scenario for risk control.

A problem with mandatory clearing is it may create more systemic risk as large banks are forced to clear only certain standardised transactions. This may have a detrimental effect on net exposure due to the 'unbundling' of netting between standard and non-standard contracts (section 5.2.6). Exemptions for end users and FX transactions may also create sub-optimal outcomes and the possibility for regulatory arbitrage. Any differences between regulations globally may also be arbitraged. Portability requirements for client clearing also splits netting sets, either at the time of porting or prior to this due to the need for gross margining (section 11.2.4).

14.3.7 Transparency

CCPs can improve transparency (although there are other ways of doing this such as via trade repositories). However, the greater transparency within exchange-traded markets has has not prevented them from being the scene for financial problems due to extraordinarily large positions that suitable transparency should prevent. In 1995, Barings Bank was brought down by a rogue trader, Nick Leeson. The underlying positions were not private as they were exchange-traded futures on the Singapore International Monetary Exchange (SIMEX). According to the strategy Leeson was supposed to be executing, Nikkei futures contracts traded on the SIMEX would be hedged with positions executed on the Osaka Securities Exchange (OSE) in Japan.

The transparency supposedly associated with exchange-traded derivatives did not prevent the collapse of Barings Bank. Nor did the margin requirements that were required to support the large speculator positions carried by Leeson which eventually led to the collapse of Barings. More recent rogue trader incidents such as Société Générale (2008) and UBS (2011) also involved exchange-traded products. The benefits of greater transparency in these markets should not be overstated.

14.3.8 Interconnectedness

Central clearing changes the OTC derivatives network to a hub-and-spoke type system (for example see Figure 3.2). Whilst this may create greater stability and transparency, it has obvious drawbacks. A CCP at the central hub constitutes a single point of failure. It reduces the possibility for diversification of errors and a single mistake or failure at the CCP (as opposed to at one of its members) has the potential to be catastrophic.

Importantly, it is not clear to what extent mandatory clearing will reduce the interconnectedness within the OTC derivatives market. Since a significant number of bilateral transactions will still exist, the financial topology will be made up of the less interconnected centrally cleared system overlaid with a more connected bilateral network (e.g. see Figure 3.5). It is not clear that mandatory clearing of some (i.e. standardised) OTC derivatives will create a less interconnected system overall. Large banks appear to be less interconnected via clearing, however, such banks will likely be clearing members at most or all significant OTC CCPs. These banks will also be a significant source of credit to their clients, other clearing members and even CCPs themselves. Margin transfers also generally require the transfer of bank deposits and therefore require the stability of clearing and settlement systems at these large banks.

Furthermore, it is not even clear that connectivity can be linked straightforwardly to reduced systemic risk. For example, Gai and Kapadia (2010) show theoretically that increased connectivity and risk sharing can actually lower the probability of a contagious default.

Heterogeneity is also an important concept in a centrally cleared market since mechanisms such as loss sharing via default funds create uniformity. In a bilateral market, counterparties can charge each other for the credit risk they take (for example, via credit value adjustment, see section 7.3.1) and such charges will be higher for weaker credit quality institutions. In a centrally cleared market, there is homogeneity since initial margins depend primarily on the portfolio being cleared and not the credit quality of the clearing member (or client) clearing it. Such homogeneity can allow weaker credit quality counterparts to benefit at the expense of those with better credit quality.

If the credit quality of market participants is relatively uniform and counterparty exposure is an inherent but unwanted consequence of trading in a market then it seems central clearing may be worthwhile. However, significant heterogeneity would be expected to create problems. Central clearing could, for example, redistribute the burden of default losses from smaller counterparties (e.g. end users and smaller banks) to larger counterparties (e.g. clearing members such as large dealers). This would shift the burden of default losses to more systemically important financial institutions.

The above intuition is backed by some theoretical studies. Borovkova and El-Mouttalibi (2013), for example, find that in a relatively homogeneous CCP system, the presence of the CCP enhances the systems stability. However, their results also suggest that in a heterogeneous system, the presence of a CCP creates greater instability and contagion with the probability of CCP failure being substantially higher.

14.4 RISKS FACED BY CCPS

14.4.1 Default risk

The key risk for a CCP is the default of a clearing member and, more importantly, the possible associated or knock-on effects that this could cause. In particular, the fear factor in the aftermath of a default event could create further problems such as:

- *Default or distress of other clearing members:* Given the nature of participants in the OTC derivatives market, default correlation would be expected to be high and defaults unlikely to be idiosyncratic events.
- *Failed auctions:* If the CCP does not receive reasonable economic bids in an auction, then it faces imposing significant losses of its member via rights of assessment and/or alternative loss allocation methods (e.g. VMGH, tear-up or forced allocation). Imposing losses on other clearing members will potentially catalyse financial distress of these members, even possibly leading to further defaults.
- *Resignations:* It is possible for clearing members to leave a CCP, which they would be most likely to do in the aftermath of a default, although this cannot be immediate (typically a member would need to flatten their cleared portfolio and give a pre-defined notice period such as one month). However, since initial margins and default funds would need to be returned to a resigning clearing member,[4] their loss could be felt in real terms as well as the potential negative reputational impact it may cause with respect to other members.
- *Reputational:* Remedying a clearing member default may involve relatively extreme loss allocation methods. Even if this ensures the viability and continuation of the CCP, the methodology for assigning losses may be considered unfair by certain clearing members and their clients. Methods such as VMGH and tear-ups may be viewed as imposing losses on them simply because they have winning positions. These positions may not of course be winning overall as they may be balanced by other transactions (bilateral or at a different CCP). They may also be client trades that are executed as hedges for commercial risk. The negative views in relation to such loss allocation could cause problems and may have consequences such as resignations.

14.4.2 Non-default loss events

CCPs could potentially suffer losses from other non-default events, which is important since they handle large amounts of cash and other securities. Examples of potentially significant loss events could be:

- *Fraud:* Internal or external fraud.
- *Operational:* Operational losses could arise due to business disruption linked to aspects such as systems failures.
- *Legal:* Losses due to litigation or legal claims including the risk that the law in a given jurisdiction does not support the rules of the CCP. For example, if netting and margining terms are not protected by regional laws.
- *Investment:* Losses from investments of cash and securities held as margin and other financial resources within the investment policy, or due to a deviation from this policy (e.g. a rogue trader).

It is also likely that non-default losses and default losses may be correlated and therefore potentially hit the CCP concurrently. One reason for this is that a default scenario is likely to cause a significant market disturbance and increase the likelihood of operational and

[4] At the time of leaving a CCP, despite having a flat book a clearing member may still have to be returned excess initial margin deposited. Furthermore, they would likely still have some default fund contribution to be returned as this may not be driven entirely by the risk of their portfolio at the time (e.g. it may be related to trading volumes over a previous period).

investment problems. Furthermore, the large spread of potential winners and losers in a default scenario increases the risk of legal challenges and fraudulent activity.

14.4.3 Model risk

CCPs have significant exposure to model risk through margining approaches. Unlike exchange-traded products, OTC derivatives prices often cannot be observed directly via market sources. This means that valuation models are required to mark-to-market products for variation margin purposes. The approaches for marking-to-market must be standard and robust across all possible market scenarios. If this is not the case then timely variation margin calls may be compromised.

CCPs are probably most exposed to model risk via their initial margin approaches. Particular modelling problems could arise from misspecification with respect to volatility, tail risk, complex dependencies and wrong-way risk. For example, an adverse correlation across market and credit risks could mean that a CCP could be faced with liquidating positions in a situation where there are significant market moves. A lesson from previous CCP failures (section 14.2.7) is that initial margin methodologies need to be updated as a market regime shifts significantly. On the other hand, such updates should not be excessive as they can lead to problems such as procyclicality (section 9.3.5).

Another important feature of models is that they generally impose linearity. For example, model-based initial margins will increase in proportion to the size of a position. It is important in this situation to use additional components such as margin multipliers (section 9.4.2) to ensure that large and concentrated positions are penalised and their risk is adequately covered. This is an example of qualitative adjustments to quantitative models being important.

14.4.4 Liquidity risk

A CCP faces liquidity risk due to the large quantities of cash that flow through them due to variation margin payments and other cashflows. CCPs must try to optimise investment of some of the financial resources they hold, without taking excessive credit and liquidity risk (e.g. by using short-term investments such as deposits, repos and reverse repos). However, in the event of a default, the CCP must continue to fulfil its obligations to surviving members in a timely manner.

Although CCPs will clearly invest cautiously over the short term, with liquidity and credit risk very much in mind, there is also the danger that the underlying investments they hold must be readily available and convertible into cash. In attempting to secure prearranged and highly reliable funding arrangements, the sheer size of CCP initial margin holdings may be difficult. For example, a typical credit facility may extend at most to billions of dollars whilst some large CCPs will easily hold tens of billions in initial margins. If a CCP does not have liquidity support from, for example, a central bank then this could be problematic.

Such potential liquidity problems seem to already be in the mind of regulators. The CPSS-IOSCO (2012) principals require a CCP to have enough liquid resources to meet obligations should one or two of its largest clearing members collapse. Under this guidance, bonds (including government securities) may only be counted towards a CCP's liquidity resources if they are backed with committed funding arrangements, so that they can be converted into cash immediately. For example, in the US, the Commodity Futures Trading Commission (CFTC) has further defined this as 'readily available and convertible into cash pursuant to prearranged and highly reliable funding arrangements, even in extreme but plausible market conditions'.[5] This would require CCPs to have committed facilities rather than blindly assuming that they could readily repo securities and would imply, for example, that US treasury securities are not considered to be as good as cash. These rules are controversial, not least since they may not be required by all regulators, and may lead to competitive pressures.[6]

Another liquidity pressure for clearing could come from the Basel III leverage ratio requirements. The leverage ratio is defined as a bank's tier one capital (at least 3%) divided by its exposure and aims to reduce excessive risk taking. The definition of exposure includes the gross notional of centrally cleared OTC derivative transactions. Under the principal-to-principal clearing model used, for example in Europe (section 11.1.2), a client transaction would be classed as two separate trades (clearing member with client and clearing member with CCP). Potentially, both trades would count towards the leverage ratio further increasing capital requirements (see also section 10.4.9 on capital for such trades).

Whilst the above requirements can be seen as regulators being very aware of the potential liquidity risks that CCPs face, they also run the risk of reducing clearing services offered.[7]

14.4.5 Operational and legal risk

The centralisation of various functions within a CCP can increase efficiency but also expose market participants to additional risks, which become concentrated at the CCP. Like all market participants, CCPs are exposed to operational risks, such as systems failures and fraud. A breakdown of any aspect of a CCP's infrastructure would be catastrophic since it would affect a relatively sizeable number of large counterparties within the market. Aspects such as segregation and the movement of margin and positions through a CCP, can be subject to legal risk from laws in different jurisdictions.

14.4.6 Other risks

Other risks faced by CCPs are:

- *Settlement and payment:* A CCP faces settlement risk if a bank providing an account for cash settlement between the CCP and its members is no longer willing or able to provide it with those services.
- *FX risk:* Due to a potential mismatch between margin payments and cashflows in various currencies (although CCPs typically require variation margin in cash in the transaction currency).
- *Custody risk:* In case of the failure of a custodian.
- *Concentration risk:* Due to having clearing members and/or margins exposed to a single region.
- *Sovereign risk:* Having direct exposure to the knock-on effects of a sovereign failure in terms of the failure of members and devaluation of sovereign bonds held as margin.
- *Wrong-way risk:* Due to unfavourable dependencies, such as between the value of margin held and creditworthiness of clearing members.

[5] CFTC Regulation 39.33 (c)(3)(i), http://www.cftc.gov/LawRegulation/FederalRegister/ProposedRules/2013-19845.

[6] For example, see 'CME threatens to flee US as regulators challenge liquidity of US Treasury collateral', Risk, 5 November 2013, http://www.risk.net/risk-magazine/news/2305083/cme-threatens-to-flee-us-as-regulators-challenge-liquidity-of-us-treasury-collateral.

[7] For example, see 'BNY to shut down clearing service', International Financing Review, 7 December 2013.

14.5 KEEPING CCPS SAFE

Funnelling market activity through one institution leads to a concentration of risk. A key problem for regulators is to ensure that, especially in buoyant markets, CCPs do not become more competitive and therefore increase the likelihood of failing during volatile markets and crashes. However, despite the best efforts of CCPs, their members and regulators, one must still contemplate the possibility that, at some point, a CCP will fail.

14.5.1 Will they be allowed to fail?

The failure of a CCP has the potential to cause a major disruption and temporary breakdown in a cleared market. This could also have cross-border dimensions due to the global nature of the OTC derivatives market and CCP membership. Given the mandate that has been given to CCPs to clear more OTC derivatives, such a failure could be expected to be far worse than even the failure of a large bank. Whilst the *probability* of CCP failure might be smaller than that of another financial institution (thanks to tight regulation and mutualisation of losses), it represents a far more extreme and systemic event.

A critical point is that, as noted by Pirrong (2011), an institution such as a CCP could be *solvent* but *illiquid* due to major funding problems in the financial markets. Hence, even though solvent, the CCP would struggle to meet the immediate requirements to pay margin. In such a situation, a CCP would require access to external liquidity due to a short-term liquidity gap. Ideally, this would be provided by commercial providers of liquidity although such facilities are likely to be expensive due to the Basel III requirements for capital to be held against the provision of these facilities. Furthermore, relying on banks or other market participants to provide liquidity to a stricken CCP may be naïve, as the market conditions that have caused the CCP default may mean that such institutions are also severely financially constrained. This implies that a liquidity injection from a central bank is the only way to avoid a potentially catastrophic liquidity-induced CCP failure. Not surprisingly, regulators view this liquidity support as a last resort[8] and may require them to have facilities such as committed lines of credit and repo in place to attempt to avoid this necessity. Some CCPs may enjoy overnight liquidity from central banks such as LCH.Clearnet and Eurex, which (via having full banking licenses) can benefit from such support although must also (as a bank) comply with Basel III legislation.

In an ideal world, liquidity support for CCPs would not extend to an unlimited bailout (although the difference between the two may be subtle). However, in the GFC, regulators believed that the default of a highly interconnected financial institution such as Bear Stearns or AIG would drag down the entire economy. If the failure of a single large participant in the OTC derivatives market is capable of endangering the entire financial system then so is the failure of a CCP that clears OTC derivatives. Therefore, governments are likely to have little choice as to whether or not to support a failing OTC CCP. This realisation is problematic since taxpayers bailing out a CCP is no better than bailing out other financial institutions such as banks. Indeed, a CCP bailout represents a bank bailout of sorts since it protects the banks that are CCP members (that may be viewed as having taken an excessively large exposure to the CCP).

[8] For example, see 'BoE's Carney: liquidity support for CCPs is a 'last-resort' option', Risk, November 2013, http://www.risk.net/risk-magazine/news/2309908/boes-carney-liquidity-support-for-ccps-is-a-last-resort-option.

Due to the concentration of risk they are exposed to, OTC CCPs will therefore be too-big-too-fail. This has clear problems as even the thought that a CCP may be saved from failure creates systemic risk, as market participants treat them as risk-free (to be compared with the situation with monoline insurers and banks discussed in section 2.3.4). If a CCP is too big to fail then clearing members have the incentive to channel risk into centrally cleared markets. It is also important to note that a central bank supporting a global CCP would advantage those clearing members that are not even under the central bank's jurisdiction.

Ultimately, the public faces the possibility of a costly CCP bailout, even though central clearing of OTC derivatives market was meant to prevent this type of problem. If the costs of financial crises are ultimately borne by the taxpayer then CCPs may not actually make the financial markets any safer. The answer to this problem is to make sure the possibility of a CCP failure is extremely small. CCPs must therefore be subject to close prudential regulation to a degree that parallels that of other systemically important financial institutions. CCPs should also have very clear loss allocation methods (section 10.3) and make other provisions to mitigate the fear that could develop in case they suffer financial distress, such as writing living wills.[9] This makes CCP failure less likely, whilst accepting it can never be impossibility.

14.5.2 Governance

CCP governance is becoming increasingly important as more of the OTC derivatives market moves to mandatory clearing. Governance arises from global regulators, such as IOSCO, and local regulators in each relevant region. Clearing members, with their expertise in issues such as valuation and margining approaches, should also be key stakeholders. Some general areas of importance are:

- *Operational:* The CCPs ability to cope with all operational aspects, including the processing of high trade volumes in volatile markets and the segregation of margins.
- *Default management:* The management of a default scenario, maximising the chance of a successful close out of the underlying portfolio.
- *Loss absorbance:* Ensuring adequate loss absorbance from initial margins and default funds, despite competitive forces. Margin methodologies and stress tests are important aspects here. CCPs should also be forced to take significant equity losses before imposing losses on clearing members to ensure they have 'skin in the game'.
- *Recovery and resolution:* There should be clear and pre-defined loss allocations rules for dealing with losses, and resolution mechanisms in case CCPs have liquidity problems or become insolvent.
- *Cross-border co-operation:* In the case of a single CCP operating across jurisdictions, then the relevant authorities in such regions must be key stakeholders in the regulation of the CCP. Additionally, regulatory rules across regions should be harmonised to prevent arbitrages.
- *Interoperability:* Interoperability can be beneficial and allow efficiencies such as cross-margining to be realised. However, it also makes CCPs more dependent on one another and increases cross-border dependencies.

[9] For example, see http://www.efinancialnews.com/story/2011-08-01/dealers-demand-clearers-living-wills?ea9c8a2de0ee111045601ab04d673622.

14.5.3 Disclosure

Given their growing importance as central nodes in financial markets, together with the fact that clearing members may have very large exposures to certain CCPs, disclosure is very important. Some noteworthy aspects are:

- *Membership requirements:* The conditions for an institution to become a clearing member, expulsion rules and the current clearing members using the CCP.
- *Margin and default fund methodologies:* The model, data set and stress tests used to define initial margin and default fund requirements. If relevant, assumptions for cross-margining, including the mechanics if this operates across more than one CCP.
- *Default management:* The process and methodology for managing a defaulted clearing member's portfolio.
- *Waterfall and loss allocation methods:* The loss allocation mechanism in case the initial margin and default funds of a defaulted clearing member are insufficient to cover losses.
- *Segregation:* The different segregation choices and their operational and legal implementation, including the enforceability of the rules in various justifications.

14.5.4 Insurance schemes

Another idea to enhance the safety of central clearing is some form of systemic risk insurance. For example, Koeppl and Monnet (2012) propose including a systemic risk insurance programme to complement other CCP functions. This would be achieved by a CCP charging members an additional fee for taking on net derivatives positions. These additional fees would build up an additional fund. Alternatively, such a fund could be administered across multiple CCPs by a 'Meta-CCP', as suggested by Maegerle and Nellen (2011). The financial resources built up to cover systemic risk pre-crisis could then be used after other resources to support the CCP.

Of course, even with an additional systemic risk fund then CCP failure cannot be prevented with certainty. An idea that fits with the systemic risk insurance concept is that a CCP requiring central bank support could be given this by way of a temporary loan. Then going forward, the CCP would charge additional fees to cover the cost of this loan. Conceptually, these provide a means for a CCP to price in the cost of a bailout both pre- and post-crisis.

15
The Future Impact on Financial Markets

You should never make predictions, especially about the future.
Samuel Goldwyn (1879–1974)

15.1 REGULATORY CHANGE

The global financial crisis (GFC) that started in 2007 has had a major negative impact on financial markets and the economy in general. The GFC was blamed partly on OTC derivatives and their counterparty risks and opacity, neither of which was well controlled due to the historic light regulation of this market. A clear example of this is the bankruptcy of Lehman Brothers and the close out of the millions of OTC derivatives contracts traded by Lehman (many of which are still subject to legal wrangling several years later). It was therefore not surprising that much of the post-GFC regulatory reform has focused on OTC derivatives and, in particular, the mitigation of counterpary risk.

The most obvious way to make OTC derivative markets safer is to force banks to hold much larger amounts of capital against the counterparty risks they face. Indeed, Basel III capital rules first published in 2009 have done this via changes to the existing requirements, and the introduction of a new capital charge for credit value adjustment (CVA). This alone should make OTC derivatives safer and prevent banks from taking the kind of risks they did leading up to the GFC where many OTC derivative risks were backed by only very thin capital holdings. Higher capital charges may have been the only major change to OTC derivatives were it not for another interesting feature of the GFC that had not gone unnoticed.

In the aftermath of the Lehman bankruptcy in 2008, central counterparties (CCPs) had functioned well, especially in comparison to the bilateral OTC markets, which struggled to deal with such a significant default scenario. CCPs essentially stand between parties and guarantee trade performance. They have strict rules such as the posting of initial margins to which members must comply. They also have a centralised auction process for dealing with a member default, and it was this mechanism, together with the security offered by initial margins, that seemed to be relatively effective in the aftermath of the Lehman default. This led to the obvious conclusion that CCPs could tame the OTC derivatives market by reducing counterparty risk and increasing transparency.

The recognition that CCPs could reduce risk in the OTC derivative market led to the clearing mandate. Policymakers and regulators agreed that all standardised OTC derivatives should be cleared by CCPs with a progressive timescale. The treatment of only standardised products was necessary because the model of a CCP requires standardisation for a product to be cleared. The clearing mandate would be significant because previously CCPs had mainly[1]

[1] With the exception of LCH.Clearnet's SwapClear service, which had already cleared a significant portion of the (interbank) interest rate swap market.

cleared trades only in the smaller and simpler exchange-traded derivative market. OTC clearing would represent a major step into the unknown.

A primary impact of the clearing mandate would be the requirement of OTC counterparties to post initial margin. Although margin agreements in bilateral OTC markets between sophisticated counterparties were common, they only usually required variation margin that covered the current value of a position. Initial margin is an extra amount to cover additional costs that may occur in a default scenario. These initial margins required by CCPs would likely represent a significant cost for the OTC derivatives market. Given the hurdles to clearing, most notably the cost of initial margin, counterparties may prefer traditional bilateral markets. Since the clearing mandate could only apply to standardised OTC products, this would lead to an obvious regulatory arbitrage involving trading non-standard products to avoid the clearing mandate. In order to counter this, mandatory bilateral margin requirements were also introduced. Since variation margin was already relatively common in bilateral markets, the most significant impact of this would be initial margin requirements. This meant that cleared or bilateral OTC derivatives would be subject to initial margins as a defence against counterparty risk.

15.2 THE IMPACT

Regulatory reform has led to three major mandates to reduce counterparty risk in OTC derivative markets: increased capital requirements, clearing of standardised products and bilateral margins for non-standardised products. This has occurred so quickly that there has been little time to contemplate whether these measures will actually make financial markets safer and minimise the prospect of future financial crises. There is also the question as to the cost of regulation on the economy in general.

A major impact of the clearing and margining mandates is cost. Moving OTC derivatives to a CCP creates costs via initial margin, the need for liquid margin securities, segregation requirements and a reduction in rehypothecation. Bilateral margining rules have a similar effect. Due to the existence of multiple CCPs, clearing also potentially leads to a loss of netting benefits, although these may be recovered if the CCP market reaches a critical size and efficiency. The bifurcation between bilateral and centrally cleared markets for non-standard and standard products will create further inefficiencies. This means that aspects such as interoperability will become increasingly important in reducing costs. However, interoperability creates linkages between CCPs similar to the ones that are commonly viewed as being dangerous in bilateral markets. Another important development will be the optimisation of bilateral and cleared positions as an extension of methods such as trade compression, already used independently in both markets.

The global regulatory requirement for high-quality initial margin for (cleared and non-cleared) OTC products is increasing the demand for high-quality margin assets. To manage margin requirements better, institutions will have to take an enterprise-wide view of margin. Asset optimisation of OTC derivatives portfolios will be essential in reducing risk and capital charges. Margin transformation methods for participants to exchange non-eligible securities for assets that can be used bilaterally or posted to a CCP will be important. There may well be additional risks as the dynamics created by margin requirements can lead to excessive and potentially destabilising price movements.

Another impact is the extension of risk mitigation methods such as margin calculations to OTC products. Due to their long-dated nature and relative complexity, this is a challenge. Furthermore, the products that members may be most keen to clear through a CCP could be more toxic, for example due to wrong-way risk that cannot be readily managed in a bilateral market. CCP risk management will become a key topic.

15.3 GOOD OR BAD?

CCPs have been proven historically to be beneficial in reducing risk in derivative products. However, they are no panacea and the question of whether they really make OTC markets safer will not be known, at least until there is another major disturbance within these markets. CCPs also create risks such as moral hazard that need to be controlled to avoid an increase in systemic risk.

Another important consideration is the privileged position of CCPs with respect to aspects such as margin calculations and bankruptcy rules that aid the default management process. It remains to be seen what detrimental effect this privileged position could have on market prices and the availability of cash and assets for margin purposes. CCPs have the right to set and change the rules for valuations, margin requirements and the treatment of a default. This may not provide the best treatment for clearing members, their clients and other creditors in a large default scenario. A CCP could survive a large default but by doing so may induce a negative impact on other market participants that otherwise would not have been the case.

Perhaps the question of whether CCPs are beneficial for OTC derivatives loses sight of the main problem. Financial risk does not disappear, it is merely converted into different forms. CCPs may make OTC markets safer through mechanisms such as netting and margining. This will, however, increase risk in other parts of the market due to the privileged position of CCPs and the reaction of market participants to aspects such as stricter margin requirements. There is then the question of whether regulation is focusing on the OTC derivatives market too much. Since it has been the source of previous financial disturbances, this is hardly surprising.

Thanks to clearing and margining rules, a financial crisis catalysed by OTC derivatives is hopefully less likely. Unfortunately, a financial crisis catalysed by something else may be even more likely than it was prior to the regulatory reaction to the GFC.

Glossary

Backloading	The process of clearing old legacy trades that are not subject to mandatory clearing. This may be done so as to preserve netting benefits with newer cleared trades.
Basel III	The third regulatory standard on bank capital requirements with implementation from 2013. A significant amount of Basel III relates to additional capital requirements for the counterparty risk of OTC derivatives.
BCBS	Basel Committee on Banking Supervision.
Bilateral netting	Netting between two counterparties.
BIS	Bank for International Settlements.
CBOT	Chicago Board of Trade.
CCP	Central Counterparty (an entity that interposes itself between counterparties to contracts traded in financial markets as the buyer to every seller and seller to every buyer).
CCP12	A global not-for-profit organisation with the aim of developing clearing and risk management practices.
CCR	Counterparty Credit Risk.
CDO	Collateralised Debt Obligation.
CDPC	Credit Derivative Product Company.
CDS	Credit default swap (a credit derivative contract covering the risk that a specified credit(s) will default).
CEM	Current exposure method.
CFTC	Commodity and Futures Trading Commission.
Clearing member	A member of a CCP (sometimes referred to as just a member).
Client clearing	The process of clearing via a clearing member by a party not a member of the CCP.
Close out	The process of terminating trades with a defaulted counterparty.
Close out netting	The settlement of more than one obligation through a single net payment in the event of default.

Clearinghouse	*see* CCP.
CLS	Continuously Linked Settlement (a multi-currency cash settlement system, eliminating settlement risk for FX payments).
CME	Chicago Mercantile Exchange.
Collateral	*see* margin.
Counterparty credit risk (counterparty risk)	The risk that a counterparty will not perform on a financial contract (usually refers to a derivative).
CPSS	Committee on Payment and Settlement Systems.
CRD IV	Capital Requirements Directive IV (the implementation of the Basel III capital requirements in the European Union).
Credit exposures	The amount owed to a party based on the current value of their contracts after taking account of netting and margining arrangements.
Cross-currency basis	The spread paid in a cross-currency swap which represents aspects such as the funding costs in the two different currencies.
Cross-currency swap	An agreement between two parties to exchange interest rate and principal payments in two different currencies.
Cross-margining	A methodology for reducing margin requirement by offsetting positions in different portfolio (for example portfolios cleared at different CCPs).
CSA	ISDA Credit Support Annex defining the rules for the posting of margin in bilateral transactions.
Customer clearing	*see* client clearing.
CVA	Credit Valuation Adjustment.
DCO	Derivatives Clearing Organisation (another term for a CCP that is used in the US).
Default fund	A mutualised fund held by a CCP to absorb losses that cannot be covered by financial resources contributed by defaulted members.
Dependence	A statistical relationship between two or more random variable (note: correlation as it is usually defined in finance is just one way to represent dependency).
Dodd–Frank	Dodd–Frank Financial Regulatory Reform Bill.
DPC	Derivative Product Company.
DTCC	Depository Trust and Clearing Corporation.
DVA	Debt Valuation Adjustment.
EC	European Commission.
EMIR	European Market Infrastructure Regulation.
End user	An entity such as a corporate or pension fund using derivatives contracts for managing their economic risk.
EP	Expected positive exposure.

EU	European Union.
Exchange	A centralised marketplace where participants can trade standardised financial contracts.
Fair value	An accounting term for the unbiased estimate of the market value of a an asset.
FAS	Financial Accounting Standards.
Fat tails	A fat-tailed probability distribution has larger probabilities of extreme values (compared to a normal distribution).
FCM	Futures Commission Merchant (the term for a clearing member used in the US).
Forced allocation	A process of loss allocation where a CCP forces a clearing member to accept a trade at a defined price.
Forward	Similar to a future but not standardised and traded bilaterally rather than on an exchange.
Funded default fund (or pre-funded default fund)	The default fund already committed by a clearing member to a CCP.
Funding liquidity risk	The risk of being able to fund required contractual financial payments at some time in the future.
Future	A standardised contract between two parties to buy or sell a specified asset at a specific price at a specified time in the future.
FVA	Funding Valuation Adjustment.
FX	Foreign exchange.
GCM	General clearing member.
GFC	Global Financial Crisis (a general term used to refer to the credit crisis from 2007 and the financial problems that followed over the next several years).
Guarantee fund	*see* default fund.
Haircut	A discount applied to a security held as margin to account for its price variability.
IASB	International Accounting Standards Board
ICE	IntercontinentalExchange (a CCP clearing products including CDS).
ICM	Individual clearing member.
IDCG	International Derivatives Clearing Group.
IFRS	International Financial Reporting Standards (a set of global financial reporting standards).
IFRS 13	IASB guidance for how to perform fair value measurement under IFRS taking effect from 1 January 2013.
IM	Initial Margin.

IMM	Internal Model Method (a regulatory approved model used by a bank for defining their capital requirements).
Interbank	Between two banks (typically refers to the major derivatives dealers).
Interest rate swap	An agreement between two parties in which one stream of future interest payments is exchanged for another based on a specified notional amount.
Interoperability	A linkage arrangement between two or more CCPs that may facilitate benefits such as mutual offset and cross-margining.
IOSCO	International Organization of Securities Commissions (an association of organisations that regulate the world's securities and futures markets).
ISDA	International Swaps and Derivatives Association (a trade organisation of OTC derivatives market participants).
LIBOR	London Interbank Offered Rate (an estimated average interest rate for banks lending to one another).
LCH	London Clearing House.
LCH.Clearnet	A CCP that services exchange-trades and OTC derivative products which was formed by a merger between the London Clearing House and Clearnet.
Margin	An amount of cash or other financial assets in order to secure a credit exposure in a legally enforceable way.
Mark to market	The value of a financial transaction according to current market prices
MiFID	Markets in Financial Instruments Directive (a European Union law that provides harmonised regulation for investment services with the main objective of increasing competition and consumer protection).
MiFIR	Markets in Financial Instruments Regulation.
MPR	Margin Period of Risk.
MTA	Minimum Transfer Amount.
Multilateral netting	Netting between more than two counterparties such as provided by a CCP and/or trade compression services.
Mutual offset	The ability to offset trades executed across different CCPs resulting from an interoperability arrangement between the CCPs.
NCM	Non-clearing member.
Netting	The offsetting of cashflows or values between different counterparties.
NIMM	Non-IMM (*see* IMM) – a simple but risk-sensitive capital approach proposed for banks.
OIS	Overnight Index Spread.
OIS discounting	The process of valuation that uses the OIS rate (rather than LIBOR) for discounting.
OTC	Over-the-counter.
OTC CCP	A CCP that clears OTC derivatives.
Pari passu	Of equal seniority (as applied to different bankruptcy claims).

PFE	Potential Future Exposure.
Pledge	A means of providing margin where in the event of default of the party providing the margin the ownership is transferred to the surviving party (*see* also title transfer).
Porting	The process by which a client of a clearing member transfers their positions to another clearing member.
QIS	Quantitative Impact Study.
Qualifying CCP or QCCP	A CCP licensed by a regulator and deemed to comply with global standards.
Rehypothecation	The reuse of pledged margin.
Repo (repurchase agreement)	A sale of securities with the agreement to buy them back at a pre-specified time and price. As such, it is a way to convert securities into cash for a pre-defined period.
Reserve fund	*see* default fund.
Rights of assessment	Additional contribution required to a CCP default fund.
SCSA	Standard CSA (a CSA with more standard terms aimed to reduce counter-party risk and funding costs).
SEC	Securities and Exchange Commission.
SIFI	Systemically Important Financial Institution.
SIMM	Standardised Initial Margin Model.
SPAN	Standard portfolio analysis of risk.
SPV	Special Purpose Vehicle.
Title Transfer	A means of providing margin where assets are transferred outright (*see* also pledge).
Unfunded default fund	The default fund contribution not yet made by a clearing member that may be required due to rights of assessment.
VAR	Value-at-Risk.
VM	Variation margin.
WWR	Wrong-way risk.

References

Albanese, C., F. D'Ippoliti and G. Pietroniero, 2011, 'Margin lending and securitization: regulators, modelling and technology', working paper.

Artzner, P., F. Delbaen., J.-M. Eber., D. Heath, 1999, 'Coherent measures of risk', Mathematical Finance 9 (July), pp 203–228.

Bank for International Settlements (BIS), 2010, 'Standards for payment, clearing and settlement systems: review by CPSS-IOSCO.' Press Release, 2 February, http://www.bis.org/press/p100202.htm.

Bank for International Settlements (BIS), 2013a, Statistical release: OTC derivatives statistics at end-December 2012', May, http://www.bis.org/publ/otc_hy1305.pdf.

Bank for International Settlements (BIS), 2013b, 'Macroeconomic Impact Assessment of OTC derivatives regulatory reforms', August, http://www.bis.org/publ/othp20.htm.

Basel Committee on Banking Supervision (BCBS), 2004, 'Basel II: International Convergence of Capital Measurement and Capital Standards: a Revised Framework', June, http://www.bis.org/publ/bcbs107.htm.

Basel Committee on Banking Supervision (BCBS), 2009, 'Revisions to the Basel II market risk framework', July, http://www.bis.org/publ/bcbs158.pdf.

Basel Committee on Banking Supervision (BCBS), 2010, 'Capitalisation of bank exposures to central counterparties – initial consultative document', December, http://www.bis.org/publ/bcbs190.htm.

Basel Committee on Banking Supervision (BCBS), 2011a, 'Basel III: a global regulatory framework for more resilient banks and banking systems – revised version', June, http://www.bis.org/publ/bcbs189.htm.

Basel Committee on Banking Supervision (BCBS), 2011b, 'Capitalisation of bank exposures to central counterparties – second consultative document', November, http://www.bis.org/publ/bcbs206.htm.

Basel Committee on Banking Supervision (BCBS), 2012a, 'Fundamental review of the trading book', May, http://www.bis.org/publ/bcbs219.pdf.

Basel Committee on Banking Supervision (BCBS), 2012b, 'Capital requirements for bank exposures to central counterparties', July, http://www.bis.org/publ/bcbs227.pdf.

Basel Committee on Banking Supervision (BCBS), 2013a, 'Supervisory framework for measuring and controlling large exposures', June, http://www.bis.org/publ/bcbs246.pdf.

Basel Committee on Banking Supervision (BCBS), 2013b, 'The non-internal model method for capitalising counterparty credit risk exposures – consultative document', July, http://www.bis.org/publ/bcbs254.pdf.

Basel Committee on Banking Supervision (BCBS), 2013c, 'Capital treatment of bank exposures to central counterparties – consultative document', July, http://www.bis.org/publ/bcbs253.pdf.

Basel Committee on Banking Supervision and Board of the International Organization of Securities Commissions (BCBS-IOSCO), 2012, 'Margin requirements for non-centrally-cleared derivatives', Consultative Document, July, http://www.bis.org/publ/bcbs226.pdf.

Basel Committee on Banking Supervision and Board of the International Organization of Securities Commissions (BCBS-IOSCO), 2013a, 'Margin requirements for non-centrally cleared derivatives – second consultative document', February, http://www.bis.org/publ/bcbs242.pdf.

Basel Committee on Banking Supervision and Board of the International Organization of Securities Commissions (BCBS-IOSCO), 2013b, 'Margin requirements for non-centrally cleared derivatives – final report issued by the Basel Committee and IOSCO', September, http://www.bis.org/publ/bcbs261.htm.

Basel Committee on Banking Supervision (BCBS), 2014a, 'The standardised approach for measuring counterparty credit risk exposures', April, http://www.bis.org/publ/bcbs279.pdf.

Basel Committee on Banking Supervision (BCBS), 2014b, 'Capital treatment of bank exposures to central counterparties', April, http://www.bis.org/publ/bcbs282.pdf.

Bates, D. and R. Craine, 1999, 'Valuing the futures market clearinghouse's default exposure during the 1987 crash', Journal of Money, Credit & Banking, 31(2), (May), pp 248–272.

Bernanke, B., 1990, 'Clearing and settlement in the Crash', Review of Financial Studies, pp 133–151.

Bliss, R. and R.S. Steigerwald. 2006. 'Derivatives clearing and settlement: a comparison of central counterparties and alternative structures', Federal Reserve Bank of Chicago Economic Perspectives (Fourth Quarter), pp 22–29.

Borovkova, S. and H.-L. El-Mouttalibi, 2013, 'Systemic risk and centralized clearing of OTC derivatives: a network approach', http://ssrn.com/abstract=2334251 or http://dx.doi.org/10.2139/ssrn.2334251.

Brady, N., 1988, 'Report of the Presidential Task Force on Market Mechanisms', US Government Printing Office, Washington DC.

Brennan, M.J., J. Hein and S-H. Poon, 2009, 'Tranching and rating', European Financial Management, 15(5), pp 891–922.

Brouwer, D.P., 'System and method of implementing massive early terminations of long term financial contracts', 6 November 2012, US Patent 8,306,905 B2.

Burgard, C. and M. Kjaer, 2011, 'In the balance,' *Risk*, November, pp 72–75.

Committee on the Global Financial System (CGFS), 2010, 'The role of margin requirements and haircuts in procyclicality', CGFS Paper No. 36, http://www.bis.org/publ/cgfs36.pdf.

Committee on the Global Financial System (CGFS), 2013, 'Asset encumbrance, financial reform and the demand for collateral assets', May 2013, http://www.bis.org/publ/cgfs49.pdf.

Committee on Payment and Settlement Systems and the Technical Committee of the International Organization of Securities Commissions (CPSS-IOSCO), 2004, 'Recommendations for central counterparties', November, http://www.bis.org/publ/cpss64.pdf.

Committee on Payment and Settlement Systems and the Technical Committee of the International Organization of Securities Commissions (CPSS-IOSCO), 2010. 'Guidance on the Application of the 2004 CPSS-IOSCO Recommendations for Central Counterparties to OTC Derivatives CCPs: Consultative Report', May, http://www.bis.org/publ/cpss89.pdf.

Committee on Payment and Settlement Systems and the Technical Committee of the International Organization of Securities Commissions (CPSS-IOSCO), 2012, 'Principles for financial market infrastructures', April, http://www.bis.org/publ/cpss101.htm.

Cont, R., R.P. Mondescu and Y. Yuhua, 2011, 'Central clearing of interest rate swaps: a comparison of offerings', available at SSRN: http://ssrn.com/abstract=1783798.

Coval, J., J. Jurek and E. Stafford, 2009, 'Economic catastrophe bonds,' American Economic Review, 99(3), 628—66.

Cox, N., N. Garvin and G. Kelly, 2013, 'Central counterparty links and clearing system exposures', Research Discussion Paper, Reserve Bank of Australia, October, http://www.rba.gov.au/publications/rdp/2013/pdf/rdp2013-12.pdf.

Deloitte and Solum Financial LLP (Deloitte-Solum), 2013, 'Counterparty risk and CVA Survey', February, available at www.solum-financial.com.

Douady, R., 2013, 'The Volatility of Low Rates', Riskdata, https://www.riskdata.com/files/resources/white_papers/The%20Volatility%20of%20Low%20Rates3%20final.pdf.

Duffie, D., 2011, 'On the clearing of foreign exchange derivatives', Graduate School of Business, Stanford University, http://www.darrellduffie.com/uploads/policy/DuffieClearingFXDerivatives2011.pdf.

Duffie, D. and H. Zhu, 2011, 'Does a central clearing counterparty reduce counterparty risk?', Review of Asset Pricing Studies, 1(1), pp 74–95.

Duffie, D., Li., A. and T. Lubke, 2010, 'Policy perspectives on OTC derivatives market infrastructure' (March), FRB of New York Staff Report No. 424, http://ssrn.com/abstract=1534729.

Duffie, D., M. Scheicher and G. Vuillemey, 2014, 'Central clearing and collateral demand', ECB working paper no 1638.

Elliott, D., 2013, 'Central counterparty loss-allocation rules', Financial Stability Paper No. 20 – April, Bank of England, http://www.bankofengland.co.uk/research/Documents/fspapers/fs_paper20.pdf.

European Commission, 2010, 'Commission proposal for a regulation on OTC derivatives, central counterparties and trade repositories – 15.09.2010', http://ec.europa.eu/internal_market/financial-markets/docs/derivatives/20100915_impact_assessment_en.pdf

European Securities and Markets Authority (ESMA), 2012, 'Draft technical standards under the Regulation (EU) No 648/2012 of the European Parliament and of the Council of 4 July 2012 on OTC Derivatives, CCPs and Trade Repositories', September, http://www.esma.europa.eu/system/files/2012-600_0.pdf.

Financial Stability Board, 2013, 'OTC derivatives market reforms: fifth progress report on implementation', April.

Gai, P. and S. Kapadia, 2010, 'Contagion in financial networks', Bank of England working paper no. 383, http://www.bankofengland.co.uk/research/Documents/workingpapers/2010/wp383.pdf.

Gemmill, G., 1994, 'Margins and the safety of clearing houses', Journal of Banking and Finance, 18(5), pp 979–996.

Gibson, M., 2004, 'Understanding the risk of synthetic CDOs', Finance and Economics Discussion Paper, 2004–36, Federal Reserve Board, Washington DC.

Gregory, J., 2008, 'A free lunch and the credit crunch', August, pp 74–77.

Gregory, J., 2009, 'Being two-faced over counterparty credit risk', Risk 22(2), pp 86–90.

Gregory, J., 2012, 'Counterparty credit risk and CVA: a continuing challenge for global financial markets', John Wiley and Sons.

Group of 20 (G20), 2009, 'Leaders' Statement: The Pittsburgh Summit', http://www.g20ys.org/upload/files/Pittsburgh_0.pdf.

Group of 20 (G20), 2010, 'The G-20 Toronto Summit Declaration', http://www.g20.utoronto.ca/2010/to-communique.html.

Hardouvelis, G. and D. Kim, 1995, 'Margin requirements: price fluctuations, and market participation in metal futures', Journal of Money, Credit and Banking, 27(3), pp 659–671.

Hartzmark, M., 1986, 'The effects of changing margin levels on futures market activity, the composition of traders in the market, and price performance', Journal of Business, 59(2), pp S147–S180.

Heller D. and N. Vause, 2012, 'Collateral requirements for mandatory clearing of over-the-counter derivatives', BIS Working Paper No 373.

Hills, B., D. Rule and S. Parkinson 1999, 'Central counterparty clearing houses and financial stability', Bank of England Financial Stability Review, June, pp 122–34.

Hull, J., 'OTC derivatives and central clearing: can all transactions be cleared?', 2010, Banque de France Financial Stability Review No. 14 'Derivatives – Financial innovation and stability', July.

Hull, J. and A. White, 2012, 'The FVA Debate' Risk, 25th anniversary edition, July, pp 83–85.

International Monetary Fund (IMF), 2010, 'Making over-the-counter derivatives safer: the role of central counterparties', Chapter 3, Global Financial Stability Report (GFSR) April, http://www.imf.org/External/Pubs/FT/GFSR/2010/01/pdf/chap3.pdf.

ISDA, 2012, 'Initial margin for non-centrally cleared swaps: understanding the systemic implications', November, http://www2.isda.org/attachment/NTA5Nw==/Margin%20for%20Uncleared%20Presentation%20FINAL.pdf.

ISDA, 2013a, 'Risk sensitive capital treatment for clearing member exposure to central counterparty default funds', March, http://www2.isda.org/attachment/NTQ1Ng==/Capital%20Treatment%20for%20Exposure%20to%20CCP%20Default%20Funds.pdf.

ISDA, 2013b, 'CCP Loss Allocation at the End of the Waterfall', August, www.isda.org.

ISDA, 2013c, 'ISDA Margin Survey 2013', www2.isda.org.

ISDA, 2013d, 'Standardised initial margin model for uncleared derivatives', December, http://www2.isda.org/attachment/NjE2Ng==/SIMM%20for%20Non-cleared%2020131210.pdf.

ISDA, 2014, 'Interest rate derivatives: a progress report on clearing and compression', www2.isda.org.

Jorion, P., 2007 'Value-at-risk: the new benchmark for managing financial risk', 3rd edition, McGraw-Hill.

Kenyon, C. and A. Green, 2012, 'Will central counterparties become the new rating agencies', working paper, http://ssrn.com/abstract=2181291.

Kenyon, C. and A. Green, 2013, 'Collateral-enhanced default risk', working paper, http://www.defaultrisk.com/pp_model253.htm.

Knott, R., and A. Mills, 2002, 'Modelling risk in central counterparty clearing houses: a review', Financial Stability Review, December, pp 162–174.

Koeppl, T.V. and C. Monnet, 2012, 'Central counterparty clearing and systemic risk insurance in OTC derivatives markets', December, http://www.econ.queensu.ca/files/other/CCP_RF_final.pdf.

Kroszner, R., 1999, 'Can the financial markets privately regulate risk? The development of derivatives clearing houses and recent over-the-counter innovations', Journal of Money, Credit, and Banking, August, 569–618.

Macroeconomic Assessment Group on Derivatives (MAGD), Macroeconomic impact assessment of OTC derivatives regulatory reforms, August 2013, http://www.bis.org/publ/othp20.pdf.

Maegerle, J. and T. Nellen, 2011, 'Interoperability between central counterparties', Swiss National Bank Working Papers 2011–5.

Mello, A., and J. Parsons, 2012, 'Margins, liquidity, and the cost of hedging', Working Paper, MIT Center for Energy and Policy Research.

Merton, R.C., 1974, 'On the pricing of corporate debt: the risk structure of interest rates', Journal of Finance, 29(2), pp 449–470.

Murphy, D., 2013, 'OTC derivatives: bilateral trading and central clearing: an introduction to regulatory policy, market impact and systemic risk', Palgrave Macmillan.

Milne, A., 2009, 'The fall of the house of credit', Cambridge University Press.

Milne, A., 2011, 'The economics and public policy of clearing and settlement networks', working paper, Loughborough University School of Business and Economics.

Milne, A., 2012, 'Central counterparty clearing and the management of systemic default risk', working paper, Loughborough University School of Business and Economics.

Norman, P., 2011, 'The risk controllers: central counterparty clearing in globalised financial markets', John Wiley and Sons.

O'Kane, D., 2013, 'Optimizing the compression cycle: algorithms for multilateral netting in OTC derivatives markets', working paper, http://ssrn.com/abstract=2273802.

Pirrong, C., 1998, 'A positive theory of financial exchange organization with normative implications for financial market regulation' (May), http://ssrn.com/abstract=10598.

Pirrong, C., 2010a, 'The economics of clearing in derivatives markets: netting, asymmetric information, and the sharing of default risks through a central counterparty', University of Houston Working Paper.

Pirrong, C., 2010b, 'The inefficiency of clearing mandates', Cato Institute Policy Analysis.

Pirrong, C., 2011, 'The economics of central clearing: theory and practice', ISDA Discussion Paper Series Number One, May, http://www2.isda.org/attachment/MzE0NA==/ISDAdiscussion_CCP_Pirrong.pdf.

Pirrong, C., 2013, 'A bill of goods: CCPs and systemic risk', working paper, Bauer College of Business, University of Houston, http://www.bauer.uh.edu/spirrong/pirrong_bdf_boe_ecb_clearing_130506_pdf.pdf.

Piterbarg, V., 2010, 'Funding beyond discounting: collateral agreements and derivatives pricing', Risk, 2, pp 97–102.

Pykhtin, M. and S. Zhu, 2007, 'A guide to modelling counterparty credit risk', GARP Risk Review, July/August, pp 16–22.

Pykhtin, M. and A. Sokol, 2013, 'Exposure under systematic impact', Risk, September, pp 100–105.

Rennison, J., 2013, 'Into the unknown: Risk OTC client clearing survey', 31 May, http://www.risk.net/risk-magazine/feature/2270671/into-the-unknown-risk-otc-client-clearing-survey.

Segoviano M.A., and M. Singh, 2008, 'Counterparty risk in the over-the-counter derivatives market' (November). IMF Working Papers.

Sidanius, C. and F. Zikes, 2012, 'OTC derivatives reform and collateral demand impact', Bank of England Financial Stability Paper No. 18 (October), http://www.bankofengland.co.uk/research/Documents/fspapers/fs_paper18.pdf.

Singh, M., 2010, 'Collateral, netting and systemic risk in the OTC derivatives market', November, IMF Working Papers.

Singh, M. and J. Aitken, 2009a, 'Deleveraging after Lehman – evidence from reduced rehypothecation', March, IMF Working Papers 09/42, pp 1–11, available at SSRN: http://ssrn.com/abstract=1366171

Singh, M. and J. Aitken, 2009b, 'Counterparty risk, impact on collateral flows and role for central counterparties', IMF Working Paper 09/173, Washington: International Monetary Fund.

Index